Lovesick Ellie

2

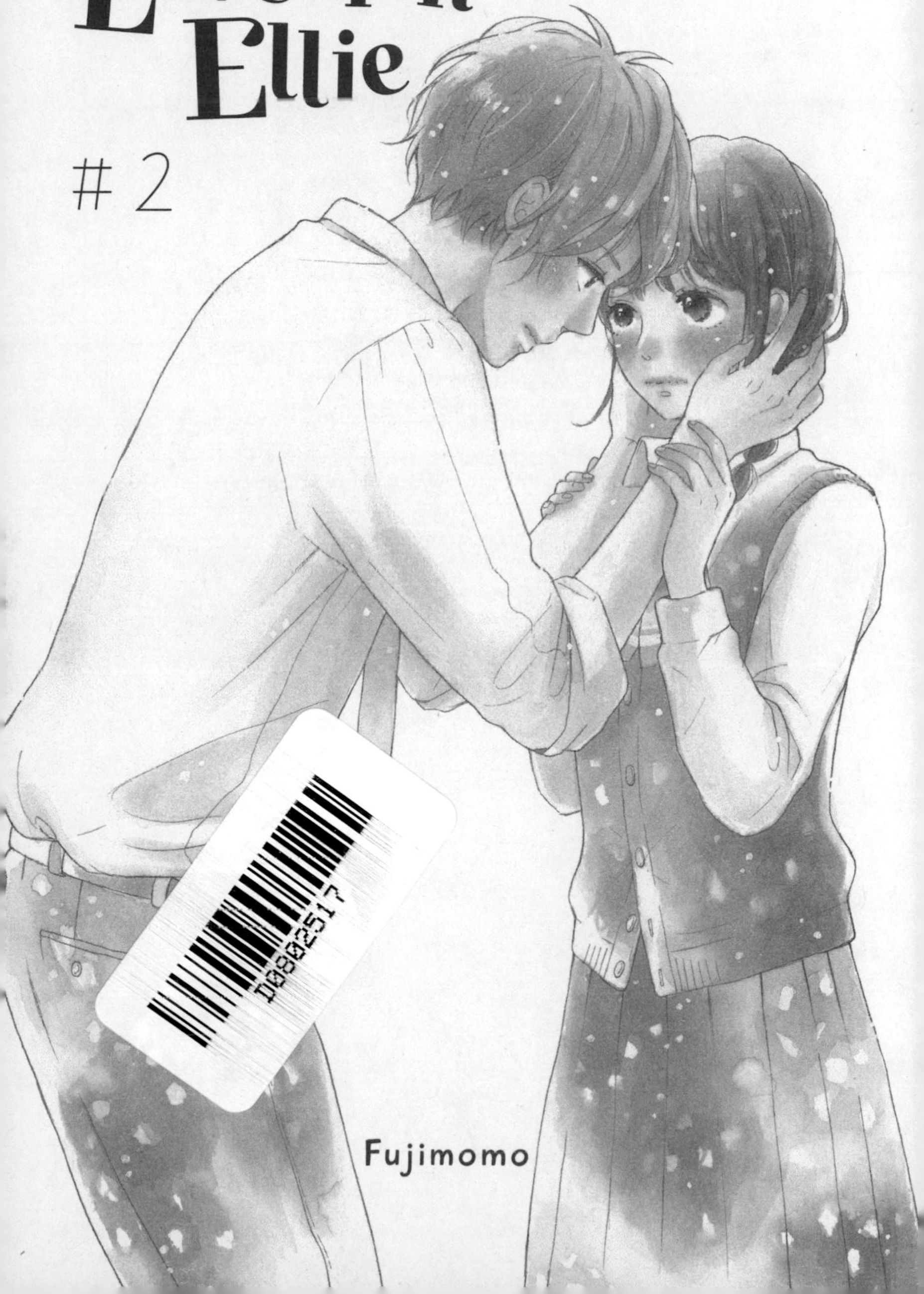

Fujimomo

characters

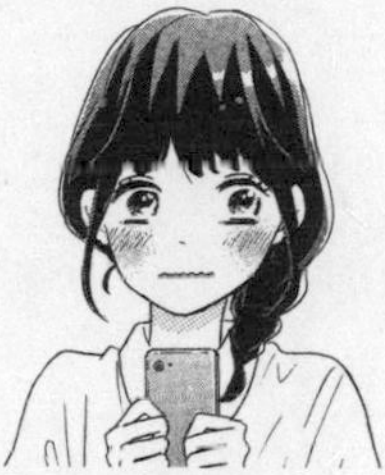

ERIKO ICHIMURA
Ellie
A plain high school girl. Spends her days tweeting Omie-kun-centric fantasies.

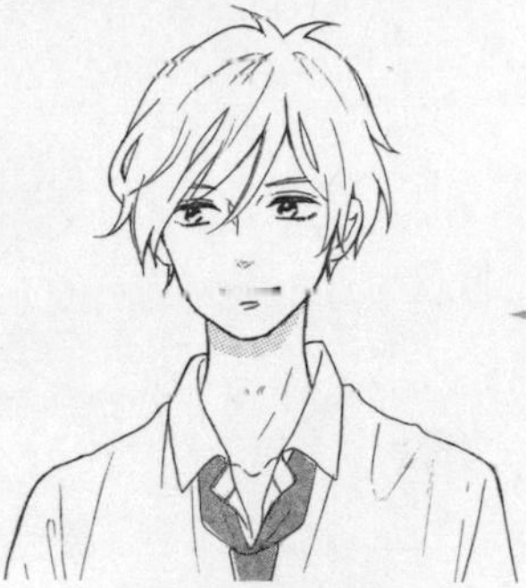

AKIRA OHMI
Omie-kun
Everyone's favorite popular boy on the outside. Irritable and childish on the inside.

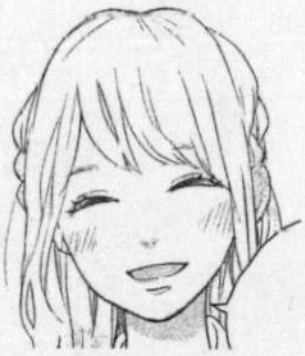

SARA-CHAN
Ellie's first friend.

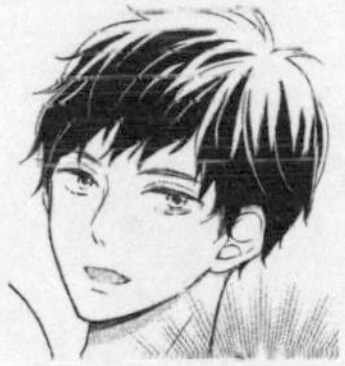

SHIOTA-SENSEI
Ellie's homeroom teacher and Omie-kun's uncle.

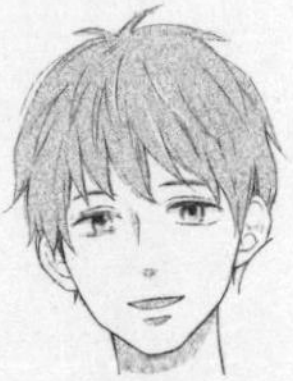

AOBA-KUN
Omie-kun's middle school classmate.

story

Ellie spends her high school days in complete obscurity, but she has a hobby: tweeting fantasies about handsome, smooth-spoken Omie-kun. One fateful day, Omie-kun discovers her tweets, and Ellie finds herself in hot water! However, not only does Omie-kun find her interesting, but they get closer and closer amidst her panicking... In fact, they end up going to the festival together! And as if the evening wasn't eventful enough, they miss the last bus! What will they do now?!

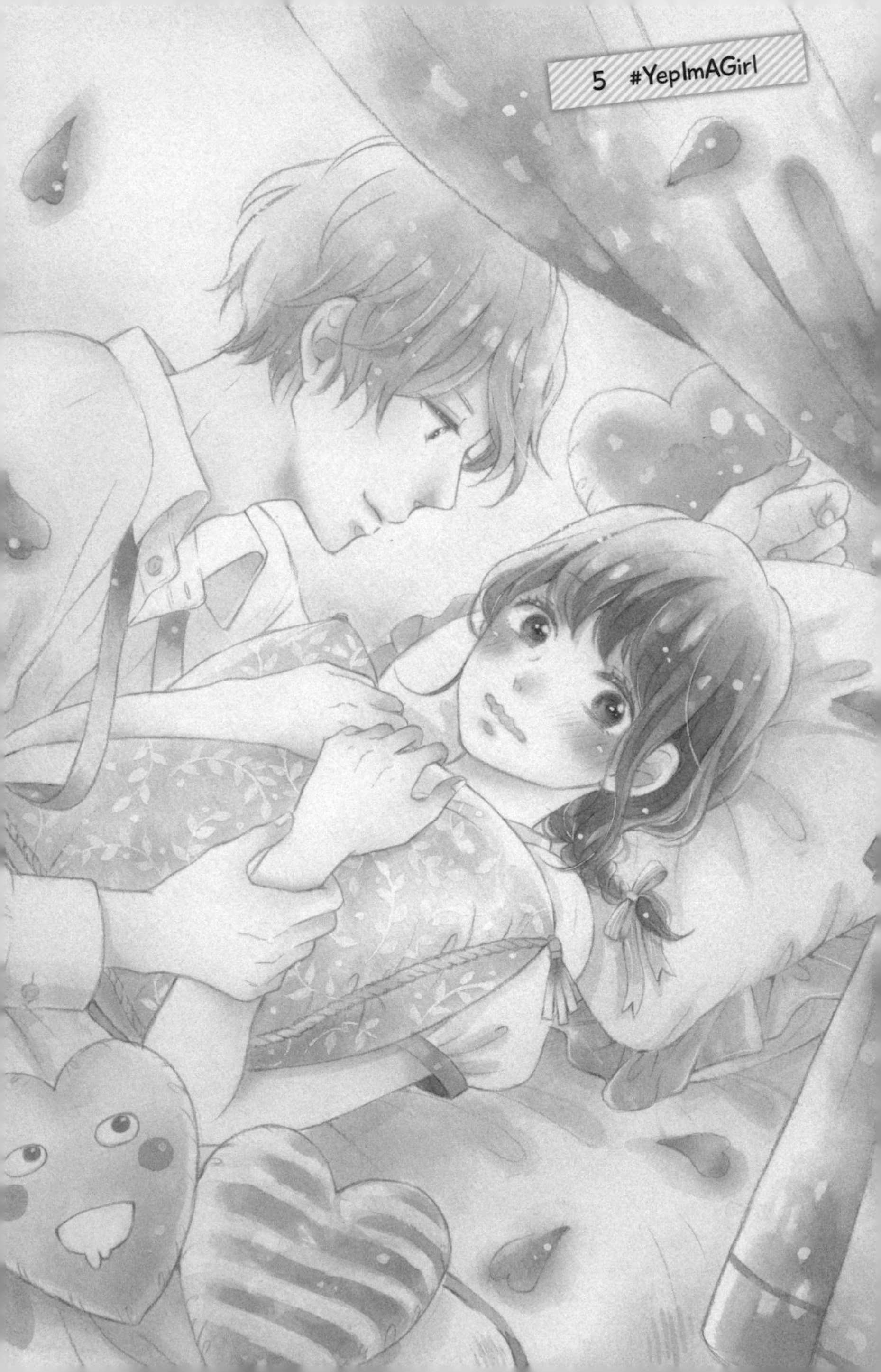
5 #YepImAGirl

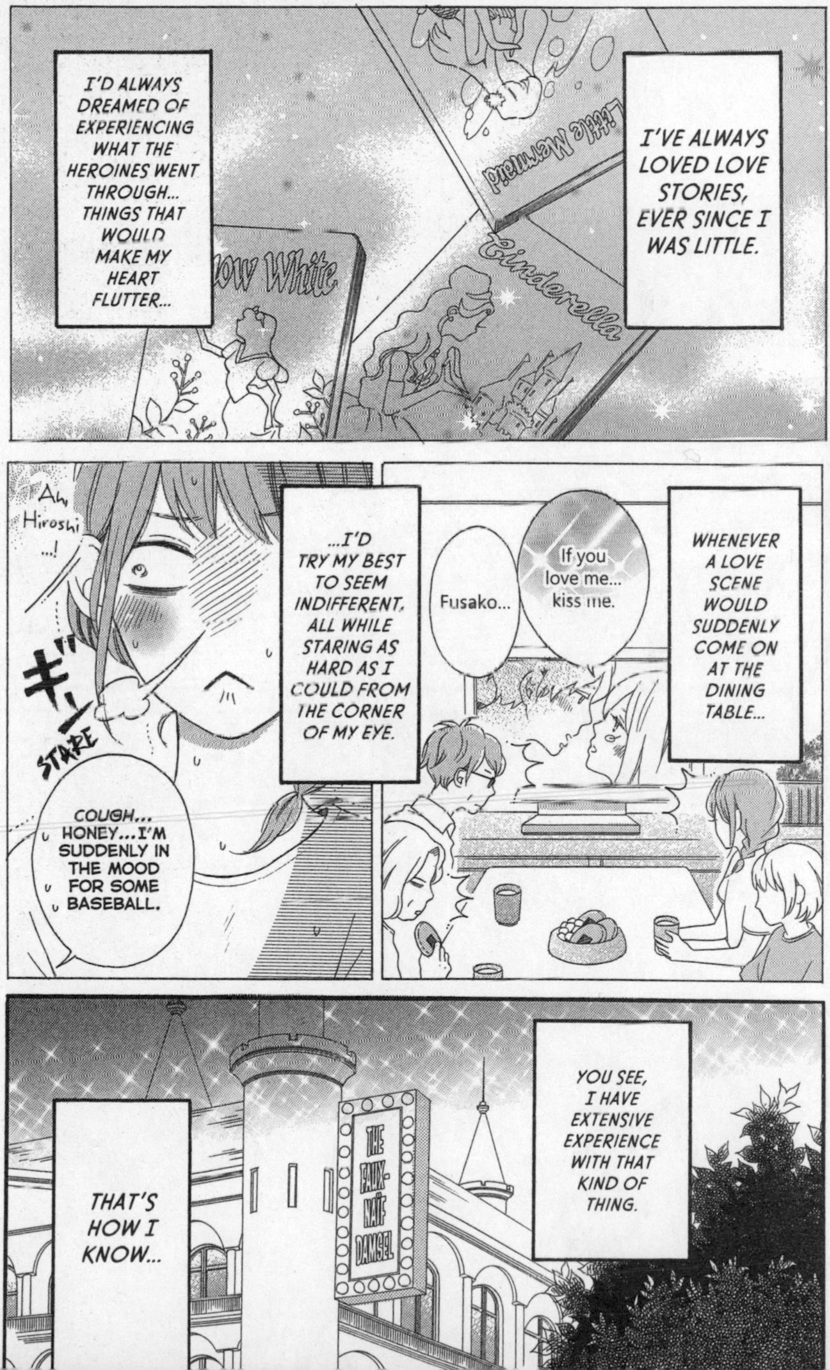
I'VE ALWAYS LOVED LOVE STORIES, EVER SINCE I WAS LITTLE.
Little Mermaid
Cinderella
I'D ALWAYS DREAMED OF EXPERIENCING WHAT THE HEROINES WENT THROUGH... THINGS THAT WOULD MAKE MY HEART FLUTTER...
WHENEVER A LOVE SCENE WOULD SUDDENLY COME ON AT THE DINING TABLE...
If you love me... kiss me.
Fusako...
...I'D TRY MY BEST TO SEEM INDIFFERENT, ALL WHILE STARING AS HARD AS I COULD FROM THE CORNER OF MY EYE.
Ah, Hiroshi ...!
ギン
STARE
COUGH... HONEY...I'M SUDDENLY IN THE MOOD FOR SOME BASEBALL.
YOU SEE, I HAVE EXTENSIVE EXPERIENCE WITH THAT KIND OF THING.
THE FAUX-NAÏF DAMSEL
THAT'S HOW I KNOW...

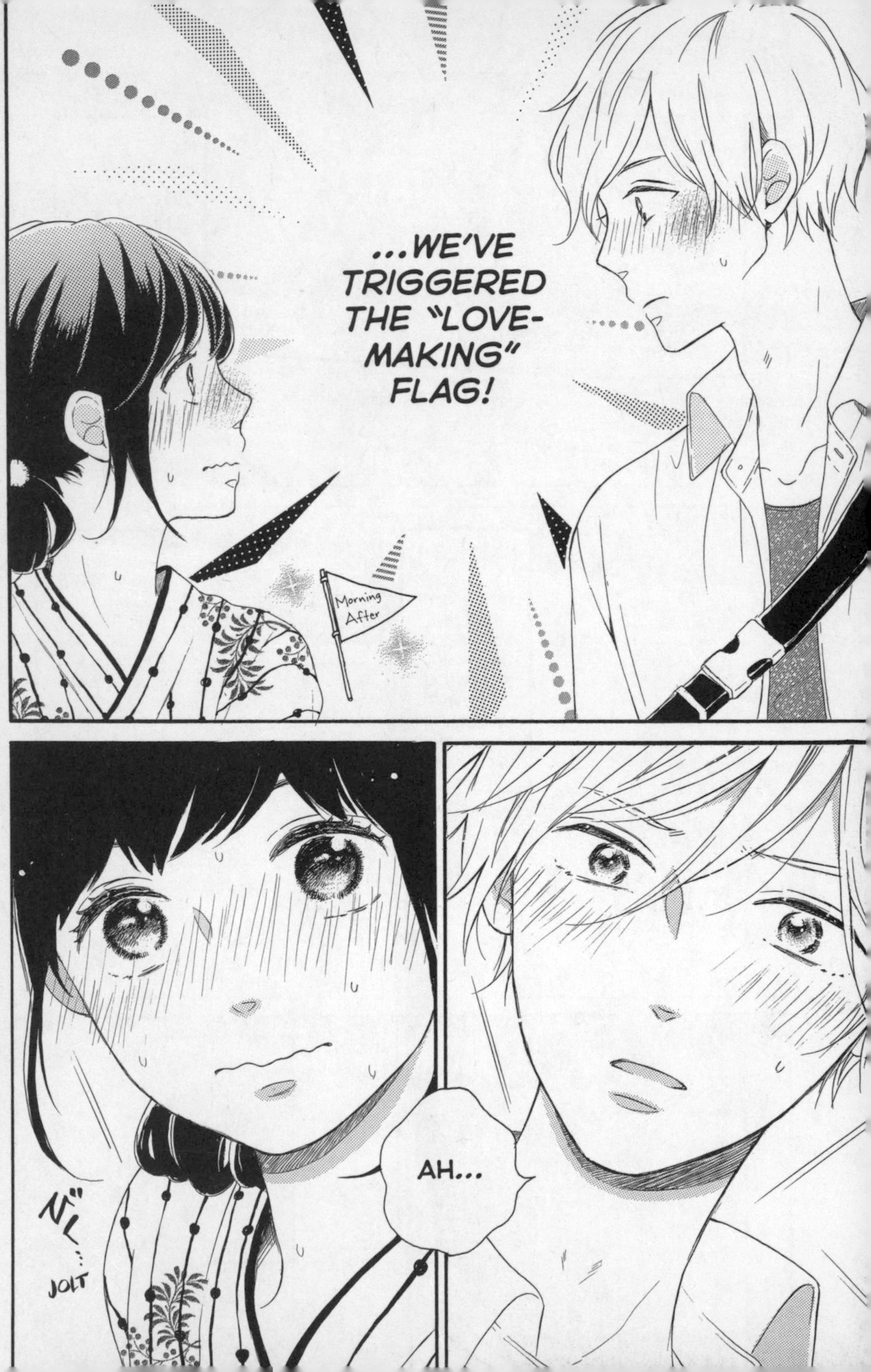
...WE'VE TRIGGERED THE "LOVE-MAKING" FLAG!
Morning After
AH...
ビル...
JOLT

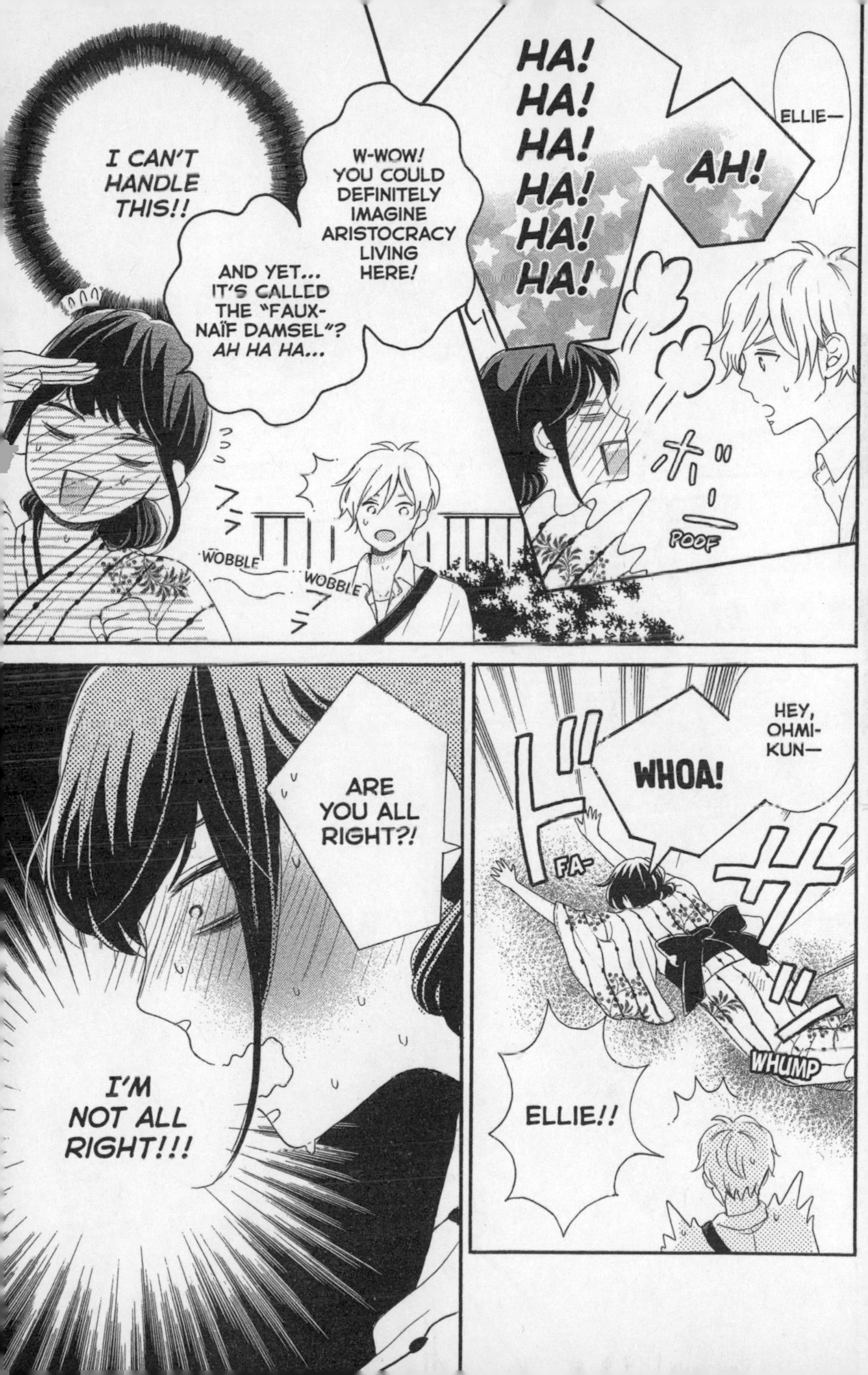
ELLIE—
AH!
HA! HA! HA! HA! HA! HA!
POOF
W-WOW! YOU COULD DEFINITELY IMAGINE ARISTOCRACY LIVING HERE!
AND YET... IT'S CALLED THE "FAUX-NAÏF DAMSEL"? AH HA HA...
I CAN'T HANDLE THIS!!
WOBBLE
WOBBLE
HEY, OHMI-KUN—
WHOA!
FA-
WHUMP
ELLIE!!
ARE YOU ALL RIGHT?!
I'M NOT ALL RIGHT!!!

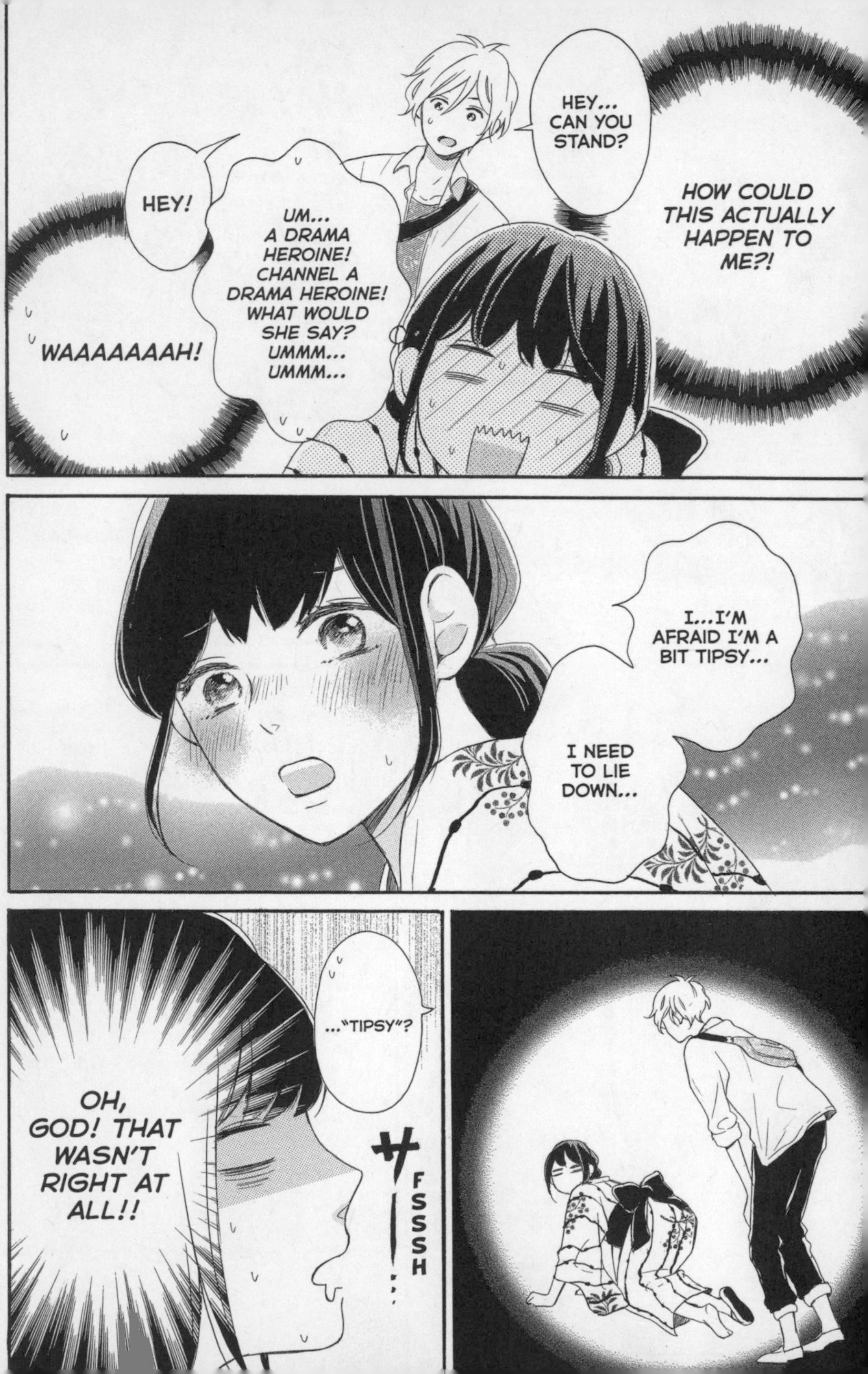
HEY... CAN YOU STAND?
HOW COULD THIS ACTUALLY HAPPEN TO ME?!
HEY!
UM... A DRAMA HEROINE! CHANNEL A DRAMA HEROINE! WHAT WOULD SHE SAY? UMMM... UMMM...
WAAAAAAAH!
I...I'M AFRAID I'M A BIT TIPSY...
I NEED TO LIE DOWN...
..."TIPSY"?
FSSSH
OH, GOD! THAT WASN'T RIGHT AT ALL!!

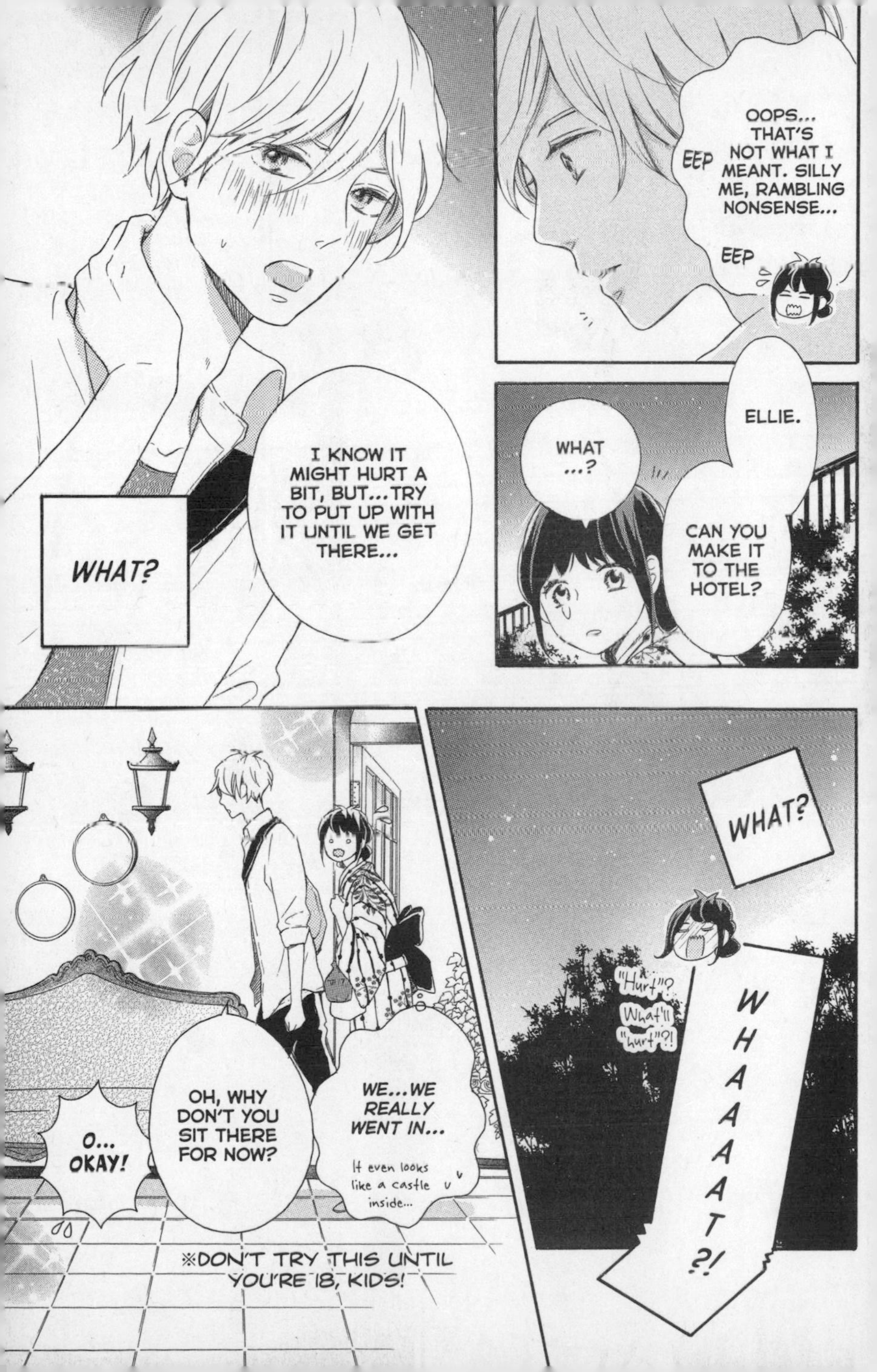
OOPS... THAT'S NOT WHAT I MEANT. SILLY ME, RAMBLING NONSENSE...
EEP
EEP
ELLIE.
CAN YOU MAKE IT TO THE HOTEL?
WHAT ...?
I KNOW IT MIGHT HURT A BIT, BUT...TRY TO PUT UP WITH IT UNTIL WE GET THERE...
WHAT?
WHAT?
WHAAAAAT?!
"Hurt"? What'll "hurt"?!
WE...WE REALLY WENT IN...
It even looks like a castle inside...
OH, WHY DON'T YOU SIT THERE FOR NOW?
O... OKAY!
※DON'T TRY THIS UNTIL YOU'RE 18, KIDS!

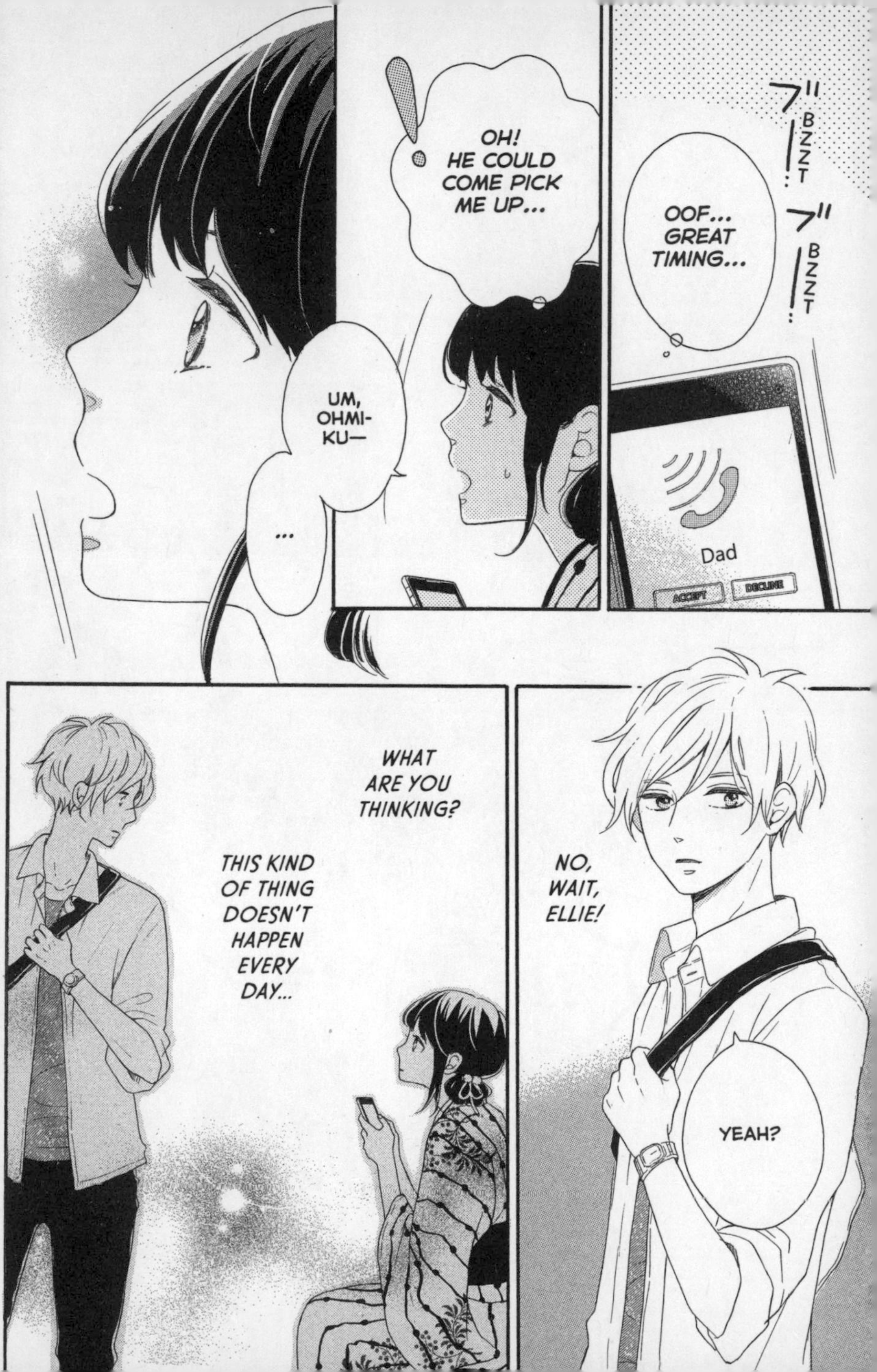

BZZT
BZZT
OOF... GREAT TIMING...
Dad
ACCEPT
DECLINE
OH! HE COULD COME PICK ME UP...
UM, OHMI-KU—
...
NO, WAIT, ELLIE!
YEAH?
WHAT ARE YOU THINKING?
THIS KIND OF THING DOESN'T HAPPEN EVERY DAY...

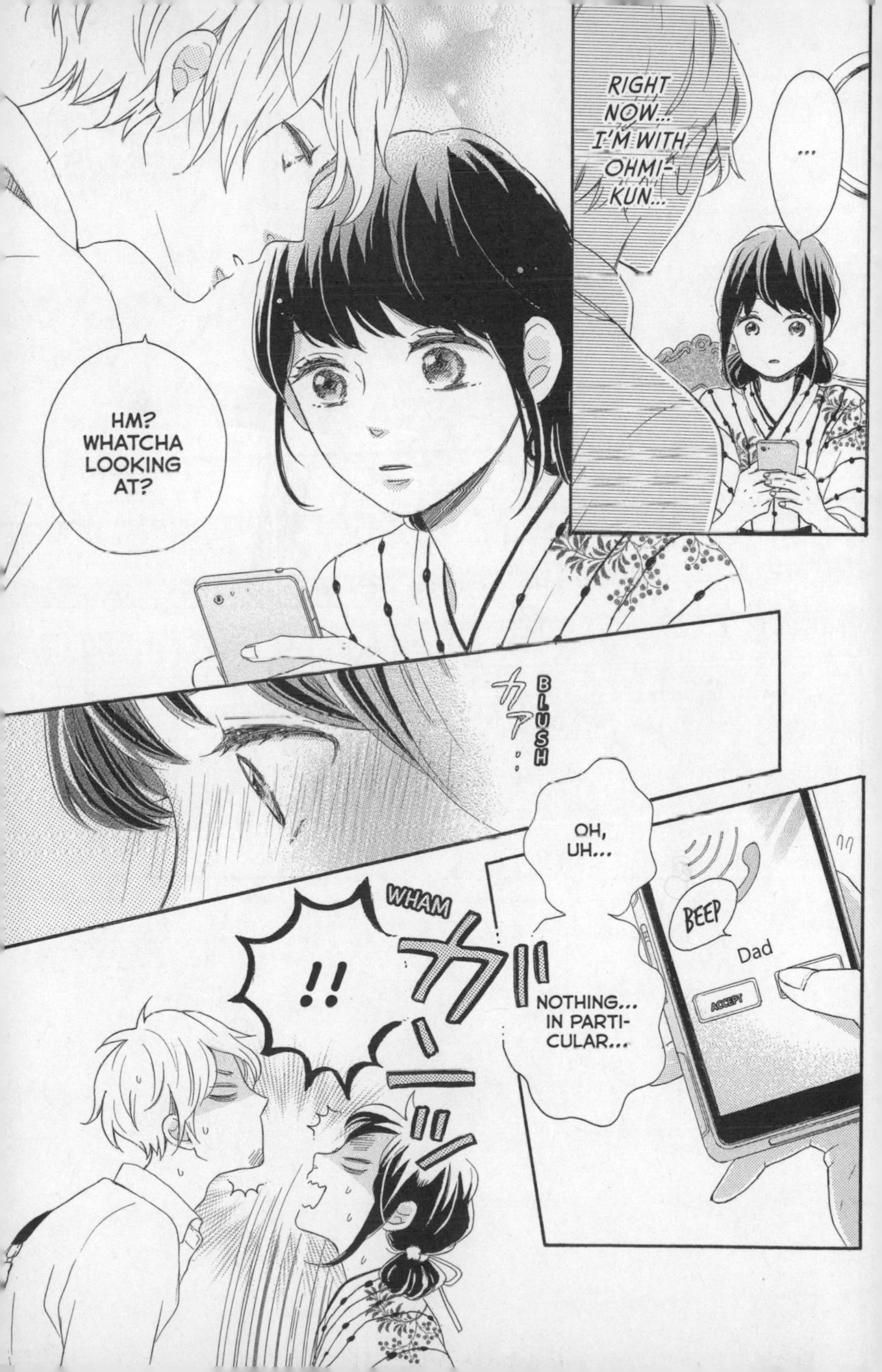
...
RIGHT NOW... I'M WITH OHMI-KUN...
HM? WHATCHA LOOKING AT?
BLUSH
OH, UH...
BEEP
Dad
ACCEPT
NOTHING... IN PARTICULAR...
WHAM
!!

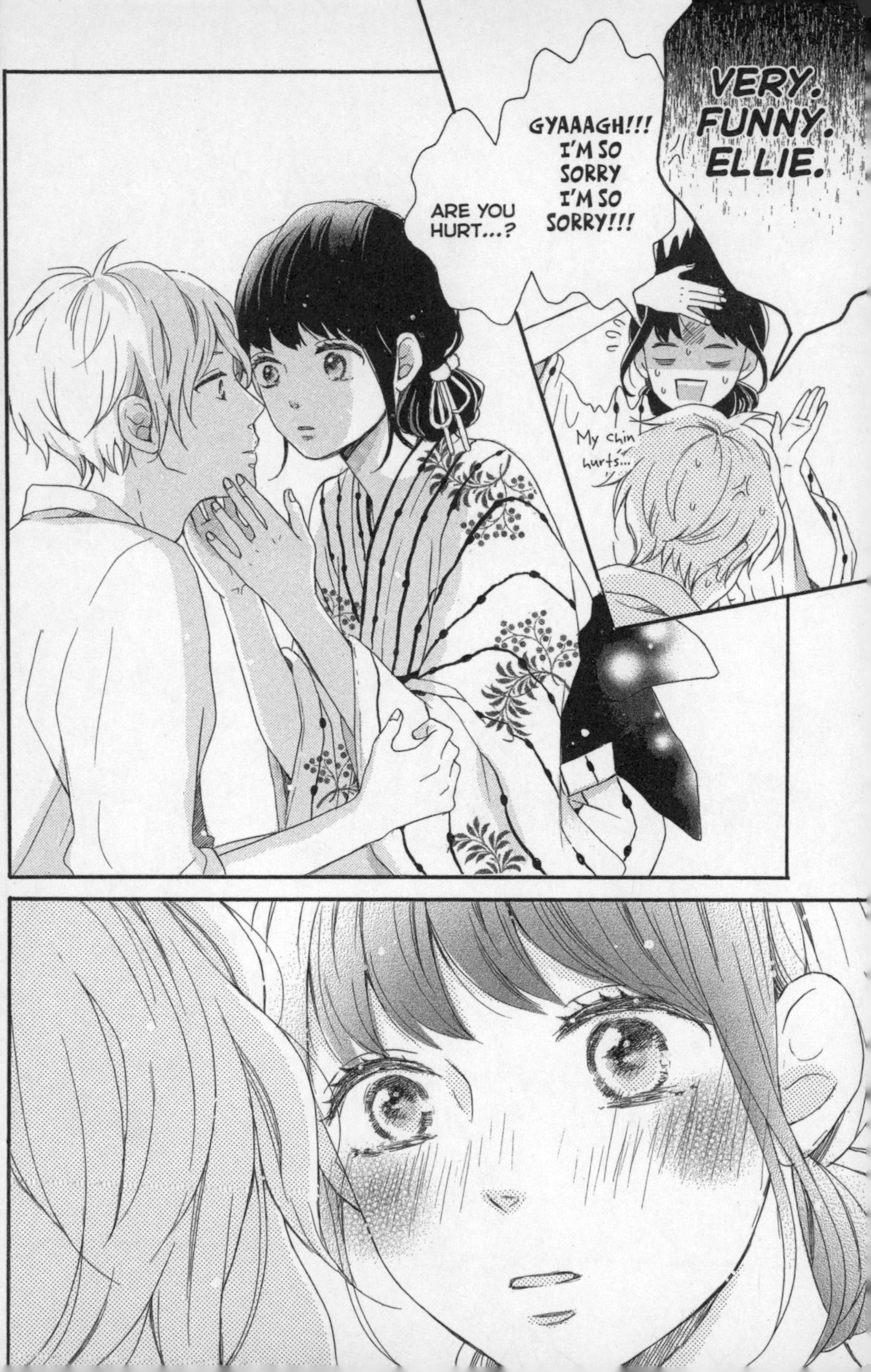
VERY. FUNNY. ELLIE.
GYAAAGH!!! I'M SO SORRY I'M SO SORRY!!!
My chin hurts...
ARE YOU HURT...?

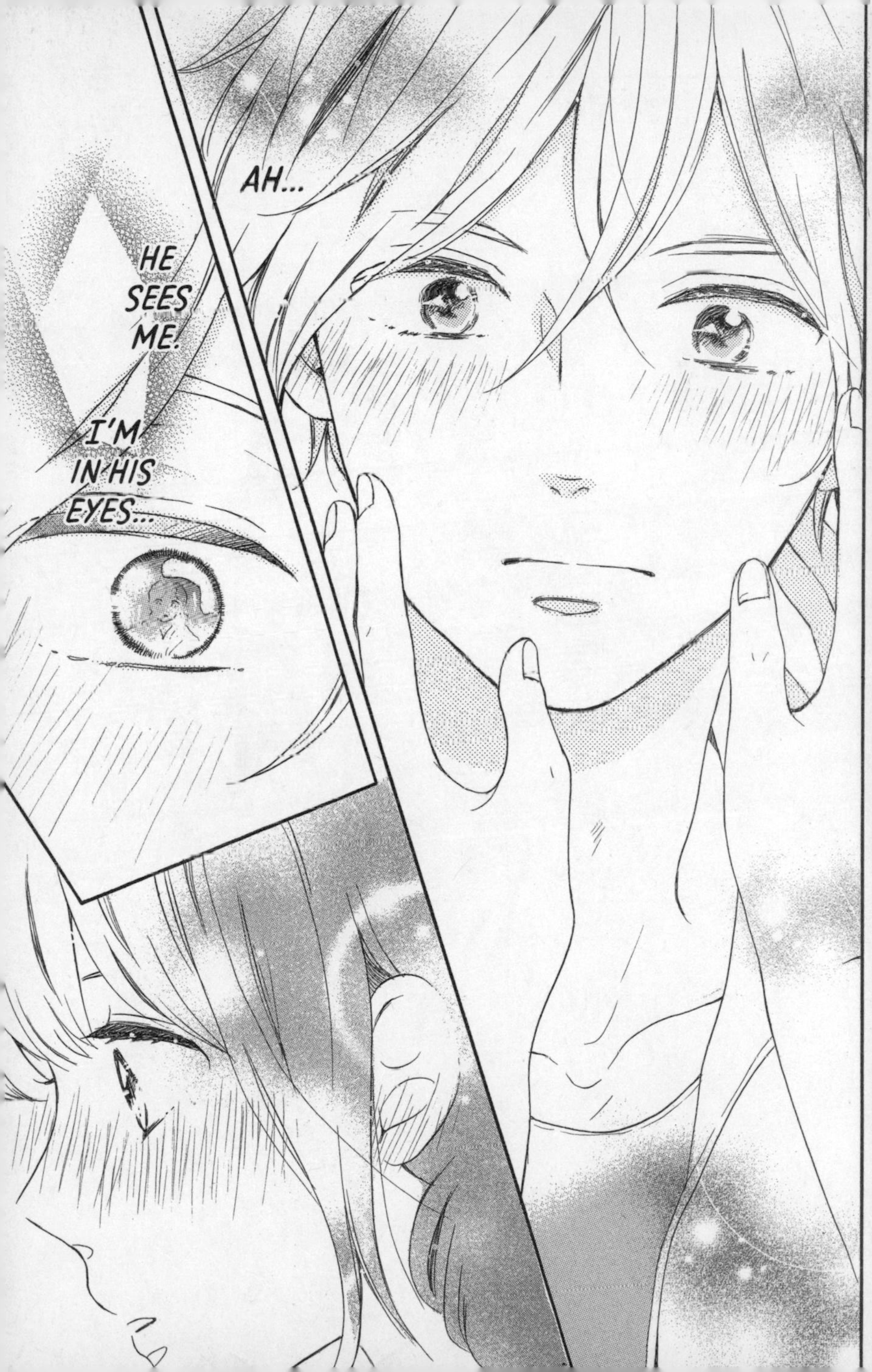
AH...
HE SEES ME.
I'M IN HIS EYES...

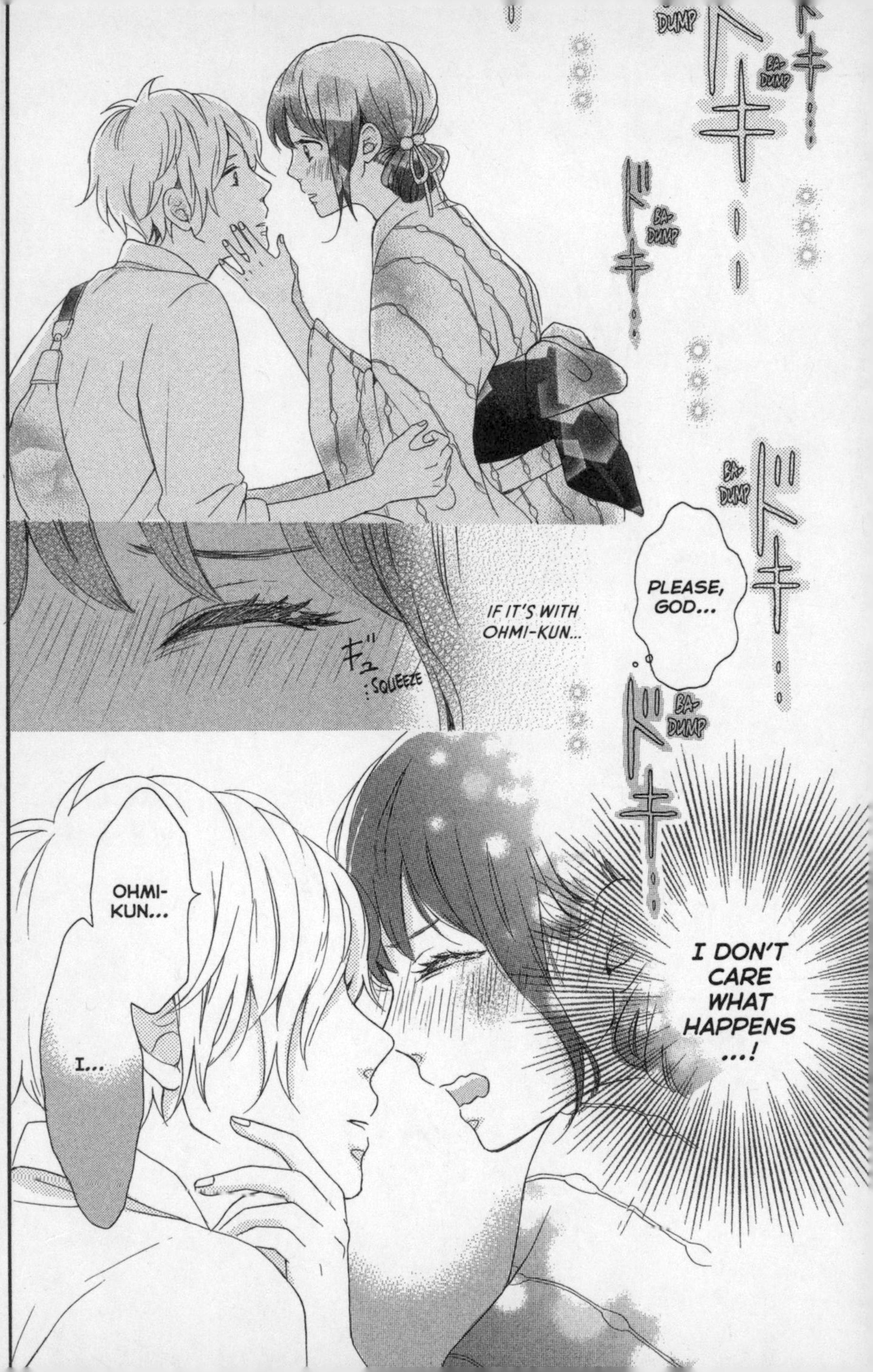
DUMP
BA-DUMP
BA-DUMP
BA-DUMP
PLEASE, GOD...
BA-DUMP
IF IT'S WITH OHMI-KUN...
SQUEEZE
I DON'T CARE WHAT HAPPENS...!
OHMI-KUN...
I...

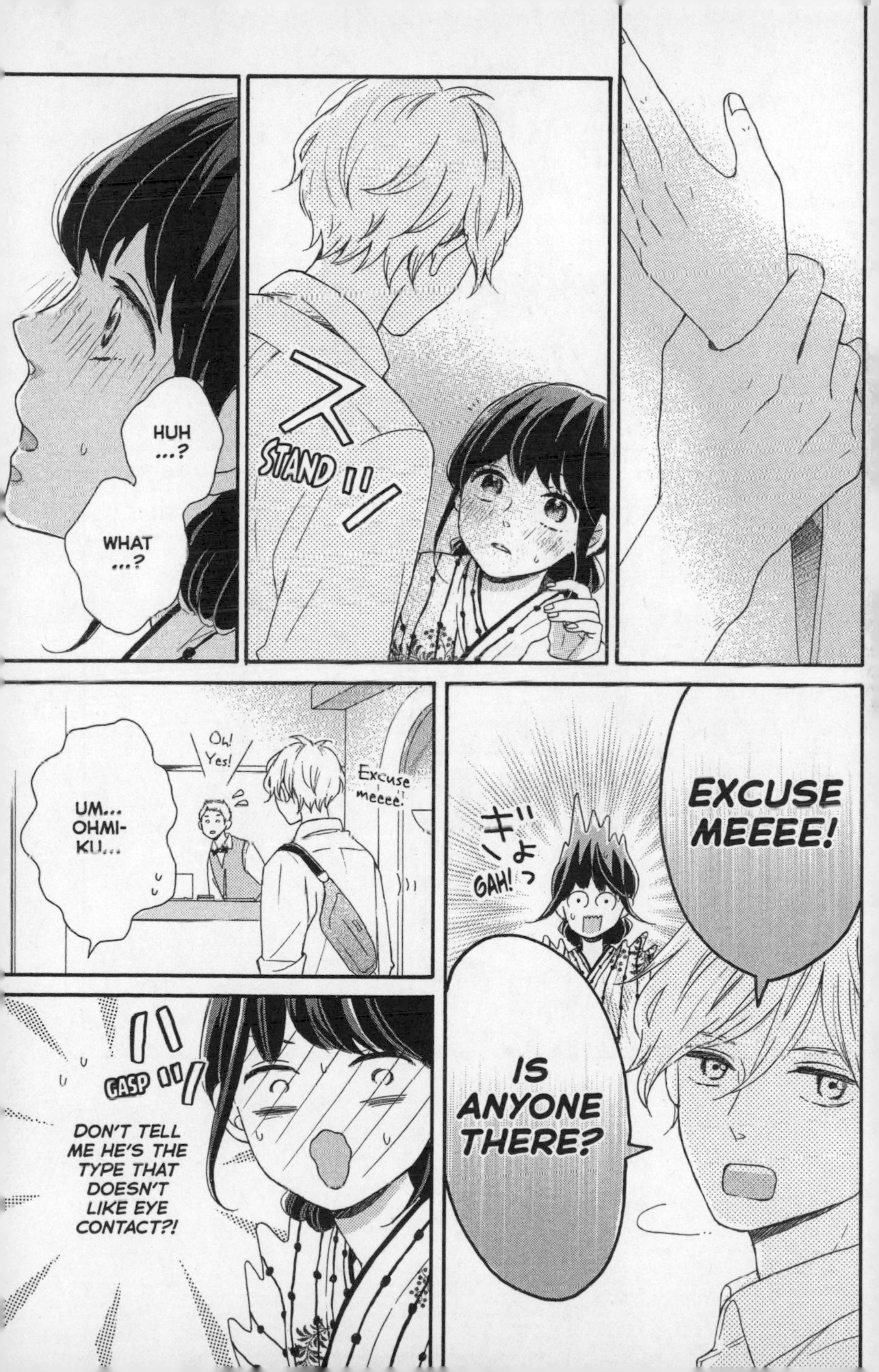
ス
STAND
HUH ...?
WHAT ...?
EXCUSE MEEEE!
ギょっ
GAH!
IS ANYONE THERE?
Excuse meeee!
Oh! Yes!
UM... OHMI-KU...
GASP
DON'T TELL ME HE'S THE TYPE THAT DOESN'T LIKE EYE CONTACT?!

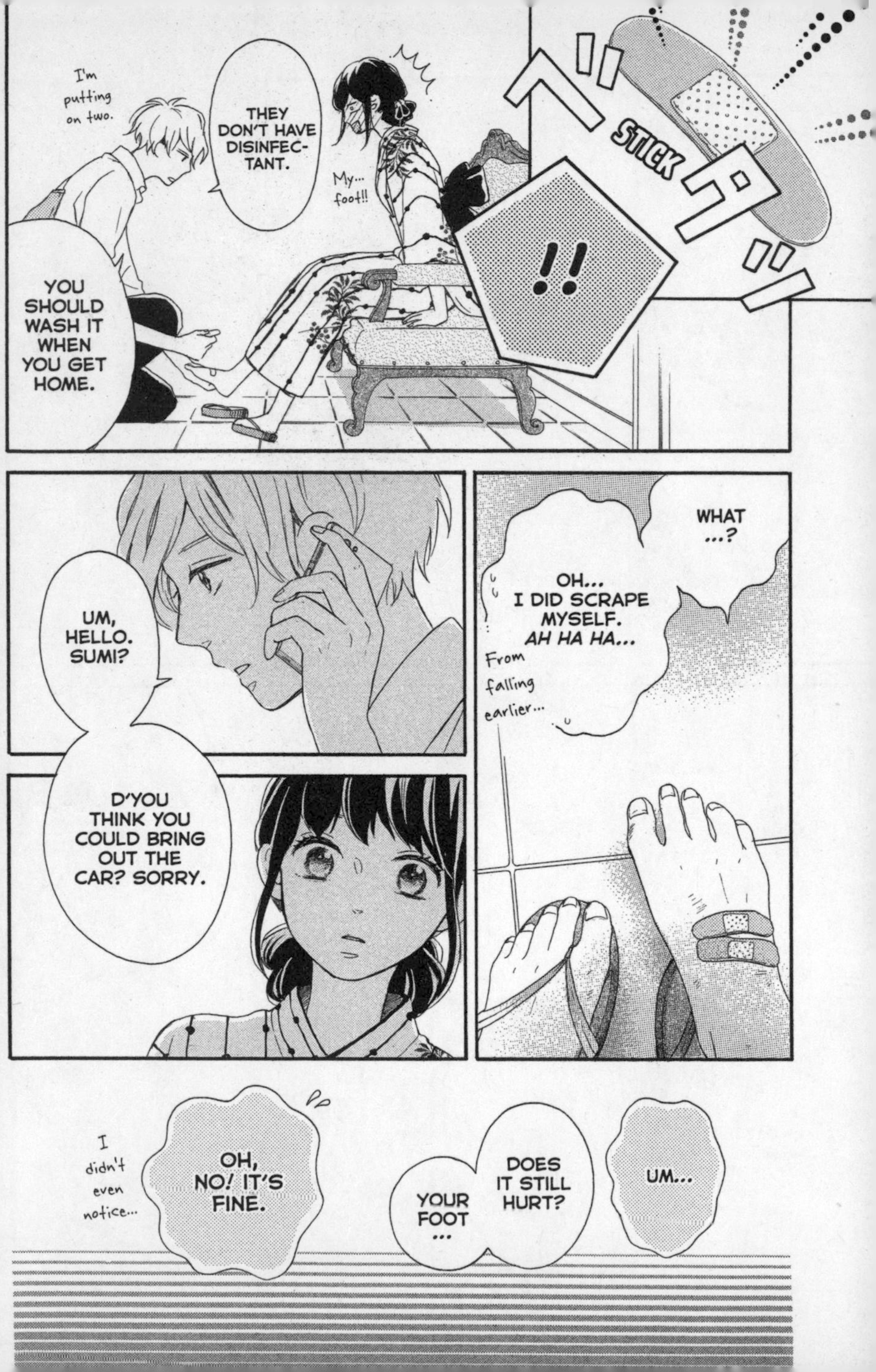
STICK
!!
THEY DON'T HAVE DISINFECTANT.
My... foot!!
I'm putting on two.
YOU SHOULD WASH IT WHEN YOU GET HOME.
WHAT ...?
OH... I DID SCRAPE MYSELF. AH HA HA...
From falling earlier...
UM, HELLO. SUMI?
D'YOU THINK YOU COULD BRING OUT THE CAR? SORRY.
UM...
DOES IT STILL HURT?
YOUR FOOT ...
OH, NO! IT'S FINE.
I didn't even notice...

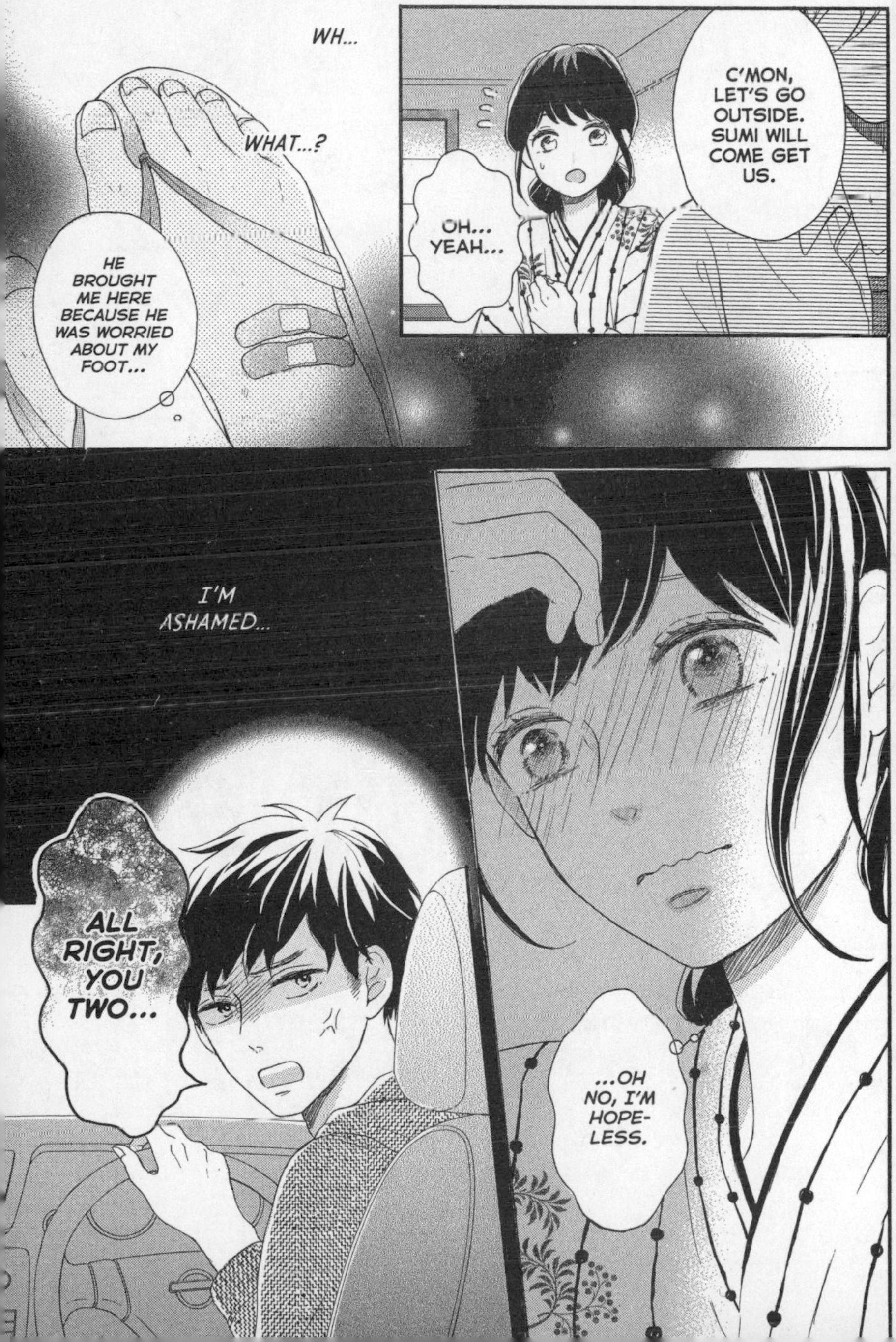
C'MON, LET'S GO OUTSIDE. SUMI WILL COME GET US.
OH... YEAH...
WH...
WHAT...?
HE BROUGHT ME HERE BECAUSE HE WAS WORRIED ABOUT MY FOOT...
I'M ASHAMED...
...OH NO, I'M HOPELESS.
ALL RIGHT, YOU TWO...

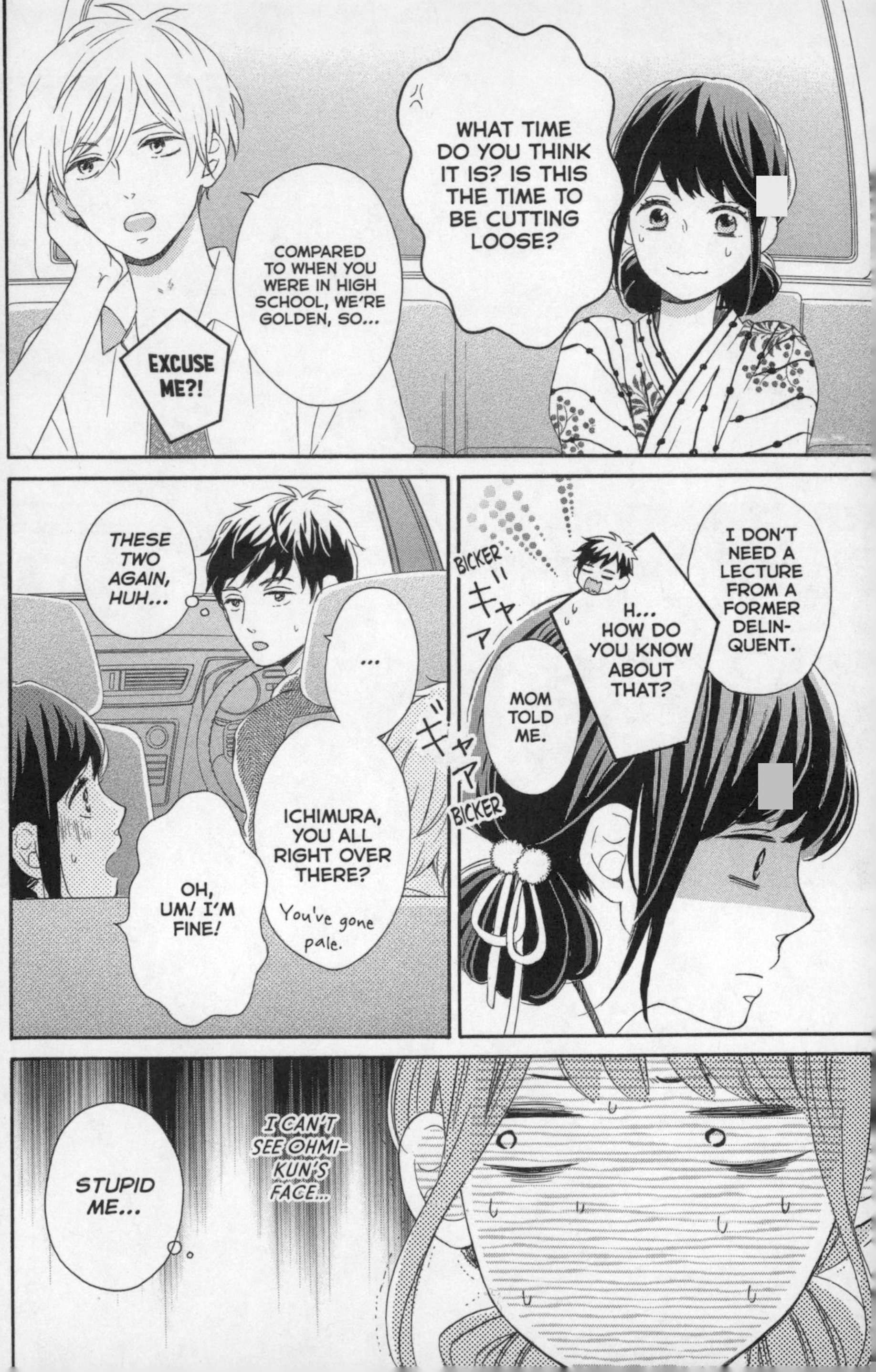
WHAT TIME DO YOU THINK IT IS? IS THIS THE TIME TO BE CUTTING LOOSE?
COMPARED TO WHEN YOU WERE IN HIGH SCHOOL, WE'RE GOLDEN, SO...
EXCUSE ME?!
I DON'T NEED A LECTURE FROM A FORMER DELIN-QUENT.
BICKER
H... HOW DO YOU KNOW ABOUT THAT?
MOM TOLD ME.
BICKER
...
THESE TWO AGAIN, HUH...
ICHIMURA, YOU ALL RIGHT OVER THERE?
You've gone pale.
OH, UM! I'M FINE!
I CAN'T SEE OHMI-KUN'S FACE...
STUPID ME...

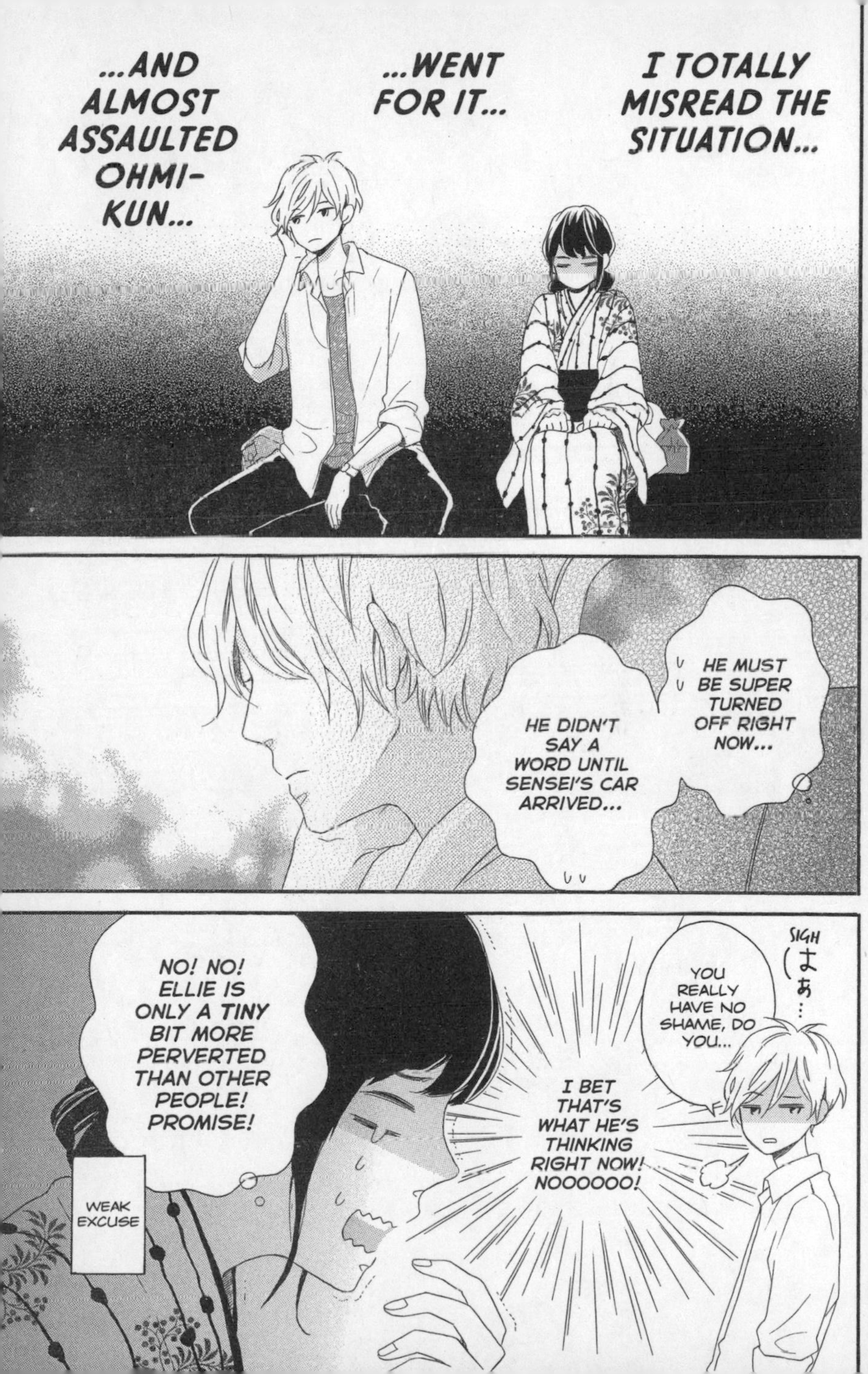
I TOTALLY MISREAD THE SITUATION...
...WENT FOR IT...
...AND ALMOST ASSAULTED OHMI-KUN...
HE MUST BE SUPER TURNED OFF RIGHT NOW...
HE DIDN'T SAY A WORD UNTIL SENSEI'S CAR ARRIVED...
SIGH
はぁ…
YOU REALLY HAVE NO SHAME, DO YOU...
I BET THAT'S WHAT HE'S THINKING RIGHT NOW! NOOOOOO!
NO! NO! ELLIE IS ONLY A TINY BIT MORE PERVERTED THAN OTHER PEOPLE! PROMISE!
WEAK EXCUSE

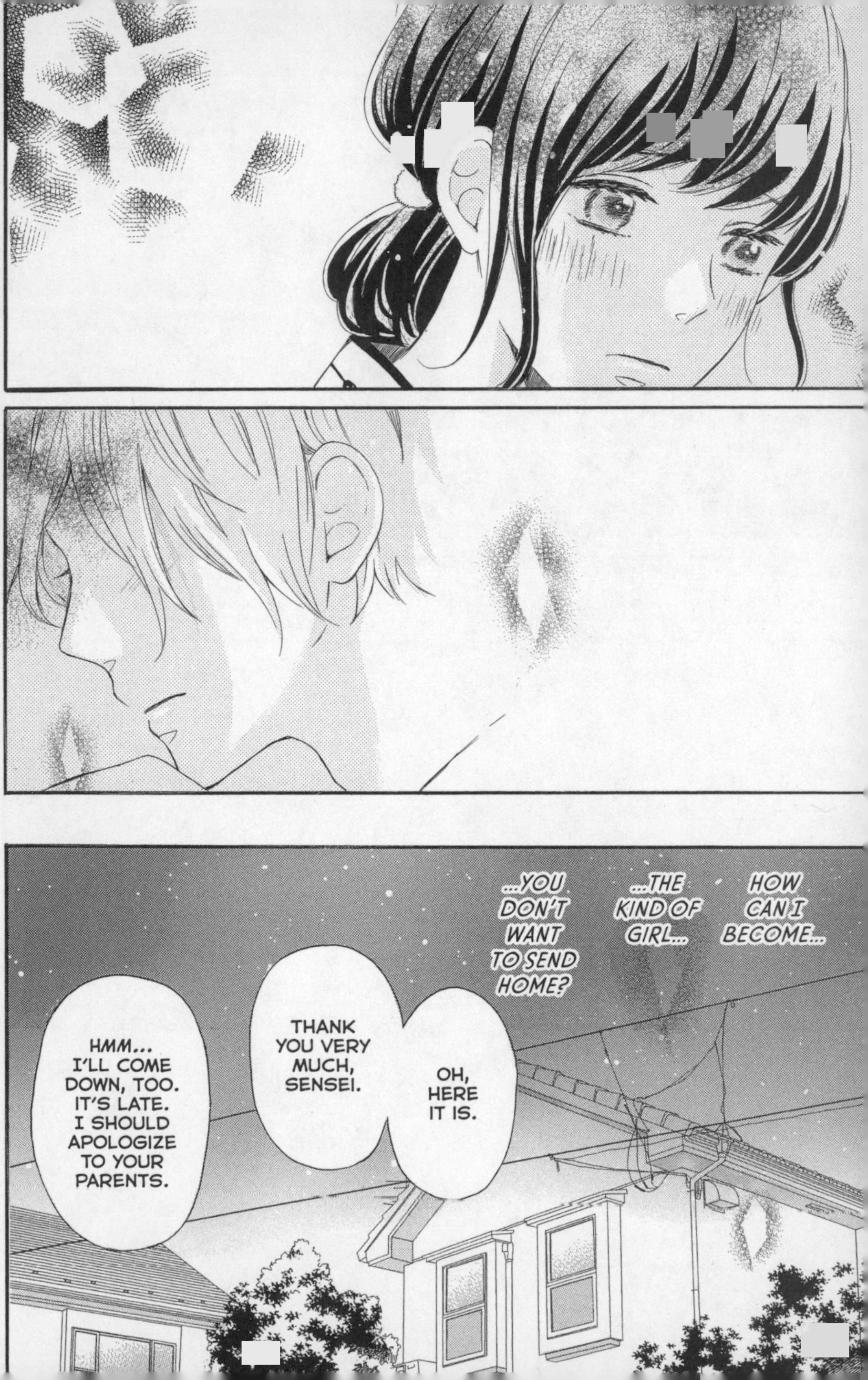
HOW CAN I BECOME...
...THE KIND OF GIRL...
...YOU DON'T WANT TO SEND HOME?
OH, HERE IT IS.
THANK YOU VERY MUCH, SENSEI.
HMM... I'LL COME DOWN, TOO. IT'S LATE. I SHOULD APOLOGIZE TO YOUR PARENTS.

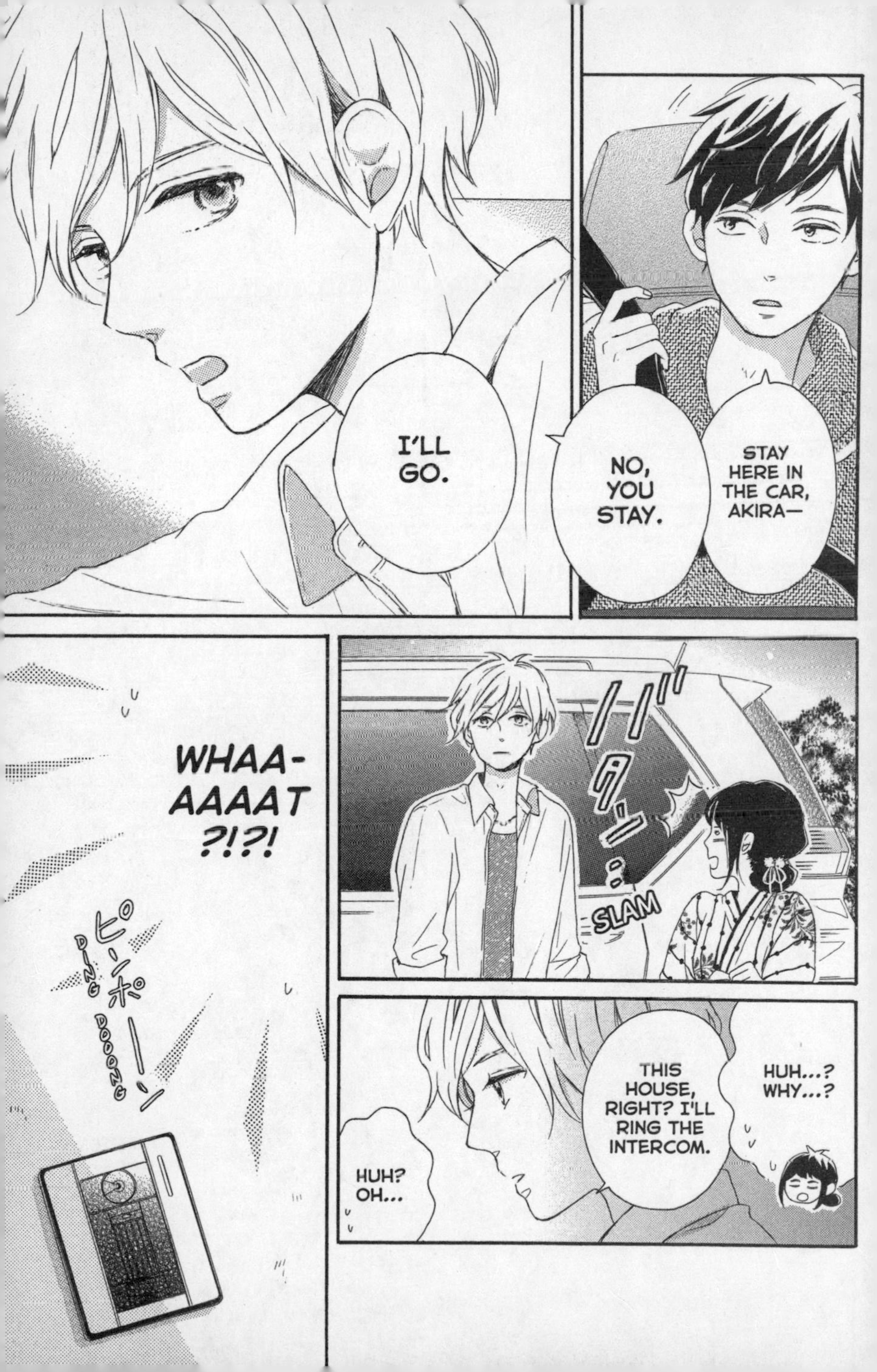
STAY HERE IN THE CAR, AKIRA—
NO, YOU STAY.
I'LL GO.
SLAM
HUH...? WHY...?
THIS HOUSE, RIGHT? I'LL RING THE INTERCOM.
HUH? OH...
WHAA-AAAAT ?!?!
ピンポーン
DING DOOONG

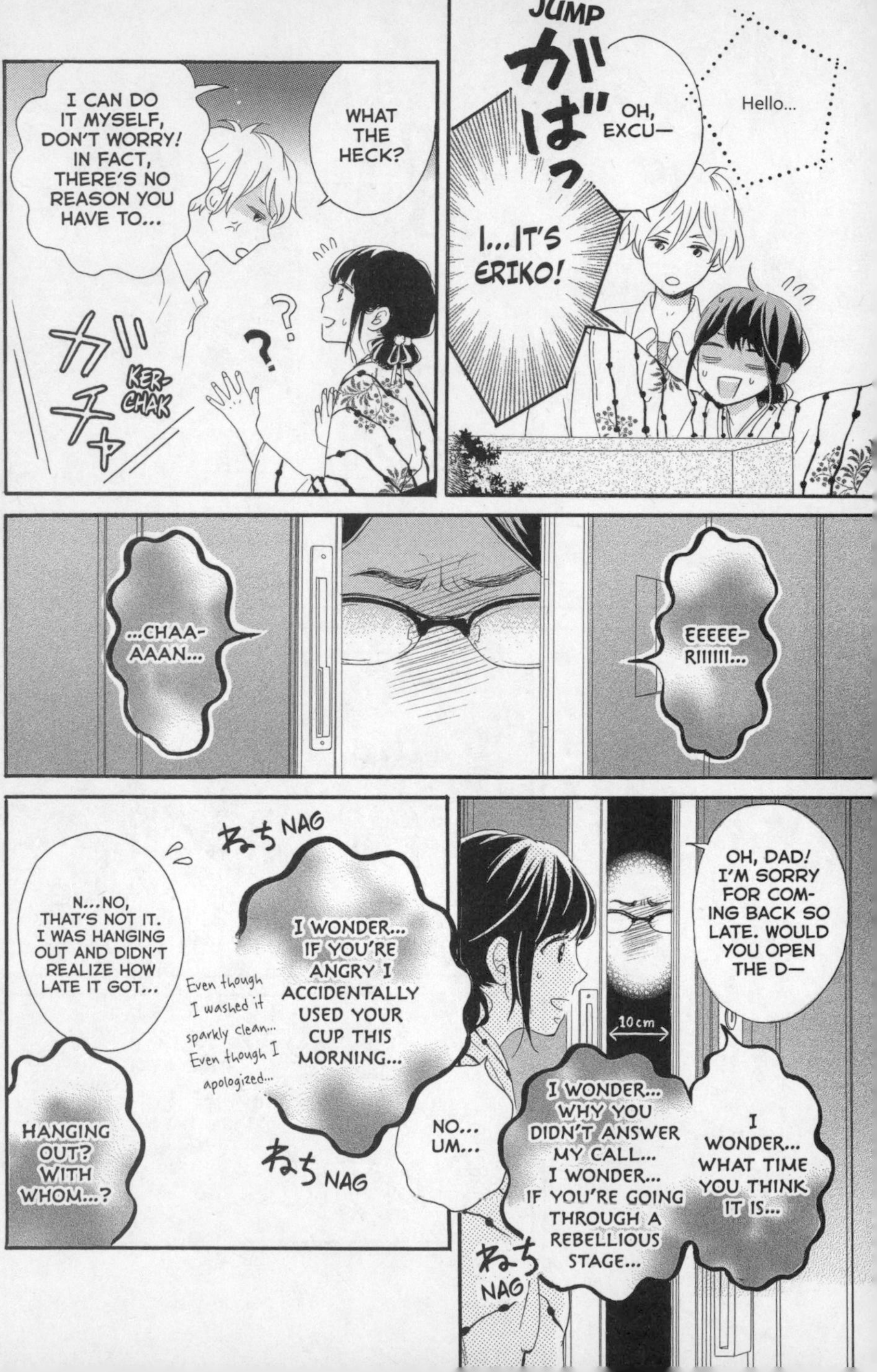
Hello...
OH, EXCU—
JUMP
がばっ
I...IT'S ERIKO!
WHAT THE HECK?
I CAN DO IT MYSELF, DON'T WORRY! IN FACT, THERE'S NO REASON YOU HAVE TO...
カチャ
KER-CHAK
EEEEE-RIIIIII...
...CHAA-AAAN...
OH, DAD! I'M SORRY FOR COMING BACK SO LATE. WOULD YOU OPEN THE D—
I WONDER... WHAT TIME YOU THINK IT IS...
10cm
I WONDER... WHY YOU DIDN'T ANSWER MY CALL... I WONDER... IF YOU'RE GOING THROUGH A REBELLIOUS STAGE...
NO... UM...
ねち NAG
ねち NAG
I WONDER... IF YOU'RE ANGRY I ACCIDENTALLY USED YOUR CUP THIS MORNING...
Even though I washed it sparkly clean... Even though I apologized...
ねち NAG
N...NO, THAT'S NOT IT. I WAS HANGING OUT AND DIDN'T REALIZE HOW LATE IT GOT...
HANGING OUT? WITH WHOM...?

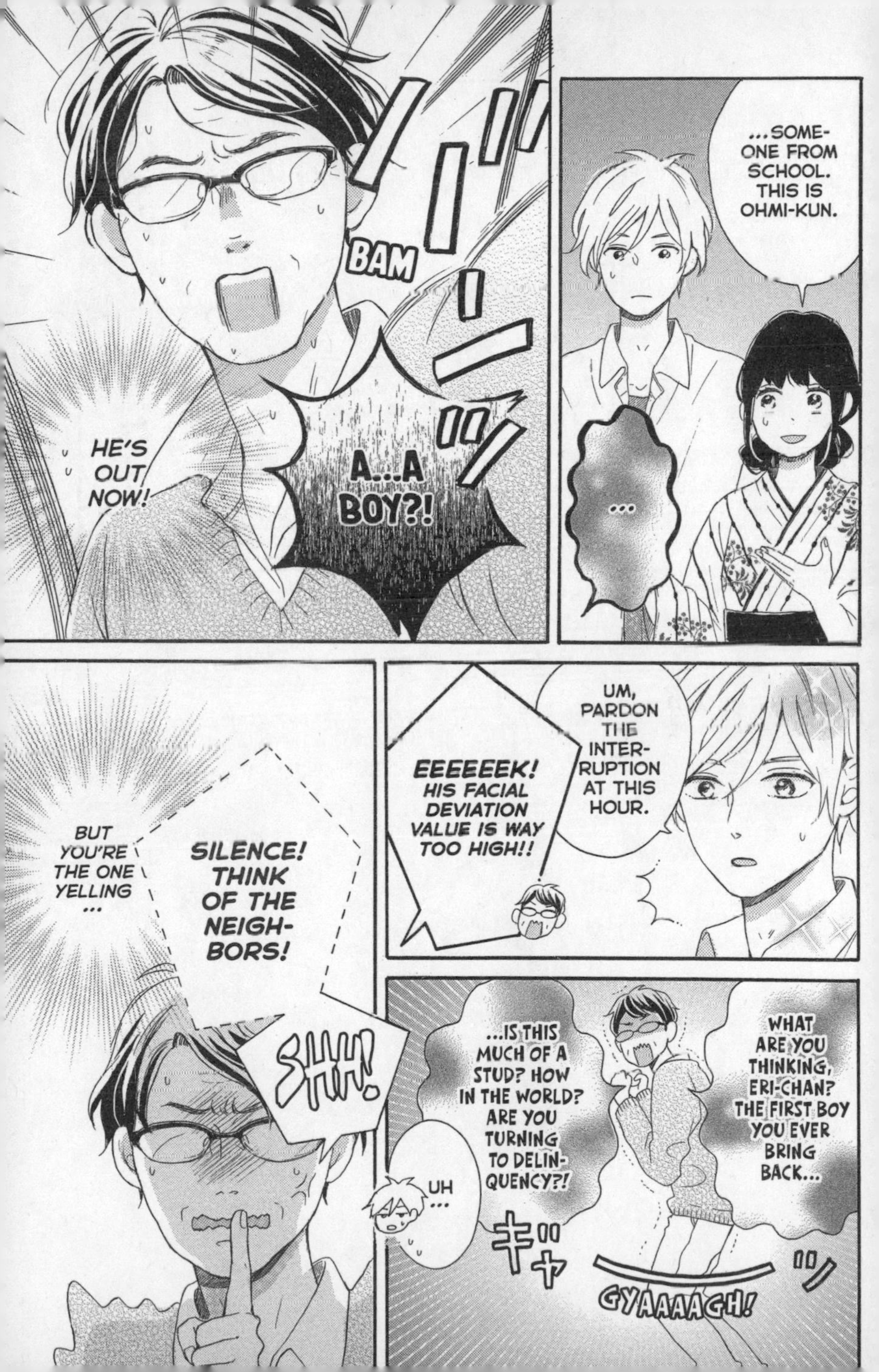
...SOME-ONE FROM SCHOOL. THIS IS OHMI-KUN.
...
BAM
A...A BOY?!
HE'S OUT NOW!
UM, PARDON THE INTER-RUPTION AT THIS HOUR.
EEEEEEK! HIS FACIAL DEVIATION VALUE IS WAY TOO HIGH!!
WHAT ARE YOU THINKING, ERI-CHAN? THE FIRST BOY YOU EVER BRING BACK...
...IS THIS MUCH OF A STUD? HOW IN THE WORLD? ARE YOU TURNING TO DELIN-QUENCY?!
UH...
GYAAAAGH!
SILENCE! THINK OF THE NEIGH-BORS!
BUT YOU'RE THE ONE YELLING...
SHH!

UM...I'M SORRY. MY DAD IS A LITTLE...YOU KNOW...
IT'S FINE... THIS IS THE MAN YOU GOT HALF YOUR GENES FROM... SO...YEAH.
Deeeaaaar! Did you know that Eri-chan is turning into a delinquent?!
WHAT?!
UM!
I APOLOGIZE FOR STOPPING BY SO LATE IN THE EVENING.
HUH...? HOLD ON... OHMI-KU—
IT WAS MY IDEA. ERIKO-SAN IS COMPLETELY BLAMELESS, SIR.

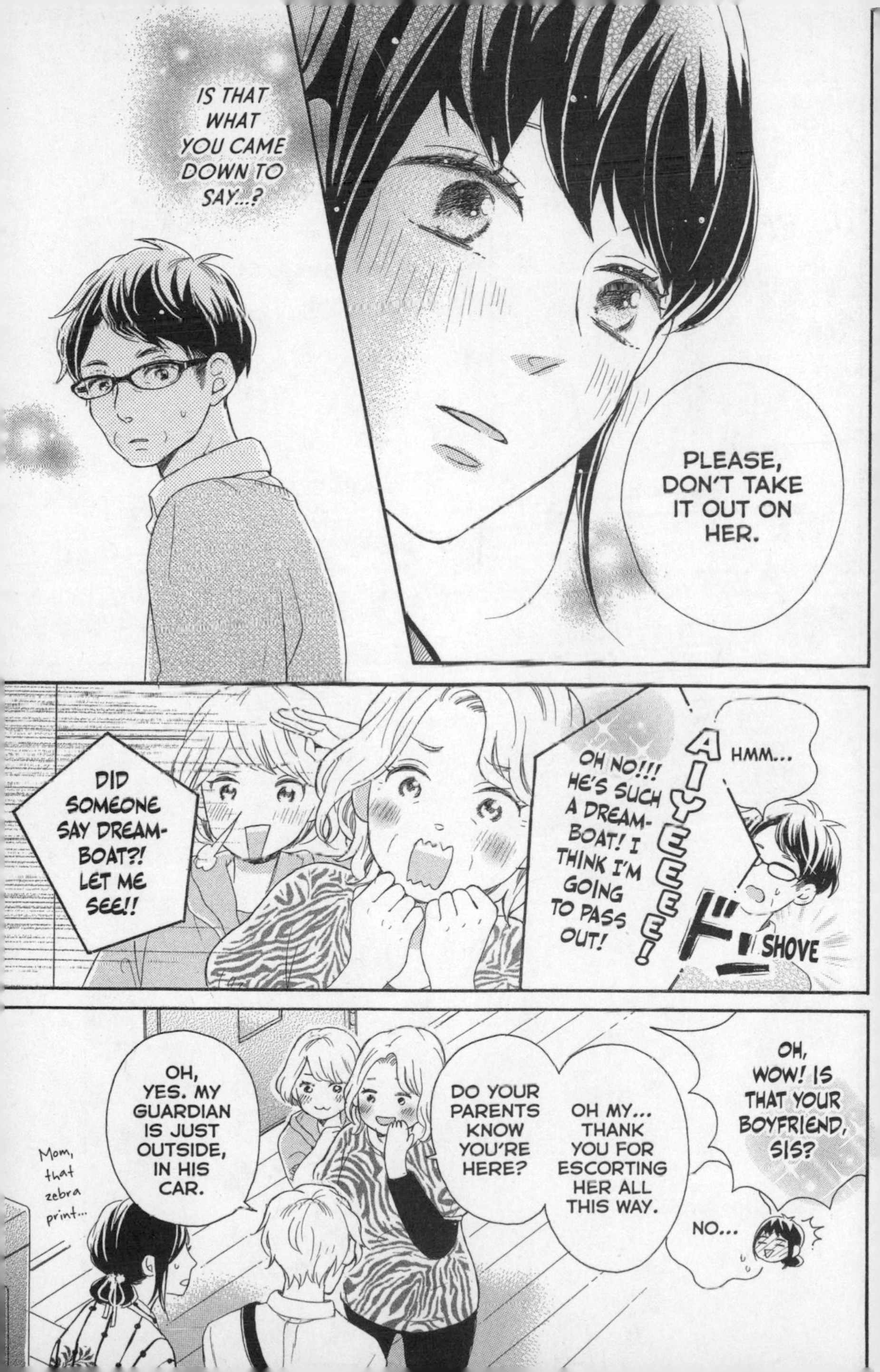
PLEASE, DON'T TAKE IT OUT ON HER.
IS THAT WHAT YOU CAME DOWN TO SAY...?
HMM...
AIYEEEEE!
OH NO!!! HE'S SUCH A DREAM-BOAT! I THINK I'M GOING TO PASS OUT!
SHOVE
DID SOMEONE SAY DREAM-BOAT?! LET ME SEE!!
OH, WOW! IS THAT YOUR BOYFRIEND, SIS?
NO...
OH MY... THANK YOU FOR ESCORTING HER ALL THIS WAY.
DO YOUR PARENTS KNOW YOU'RE HERE?
OH, YES. MY GUARDIAN IS JUST OUTSIDE, IN HIS CAR.
Mom, that zebra print...

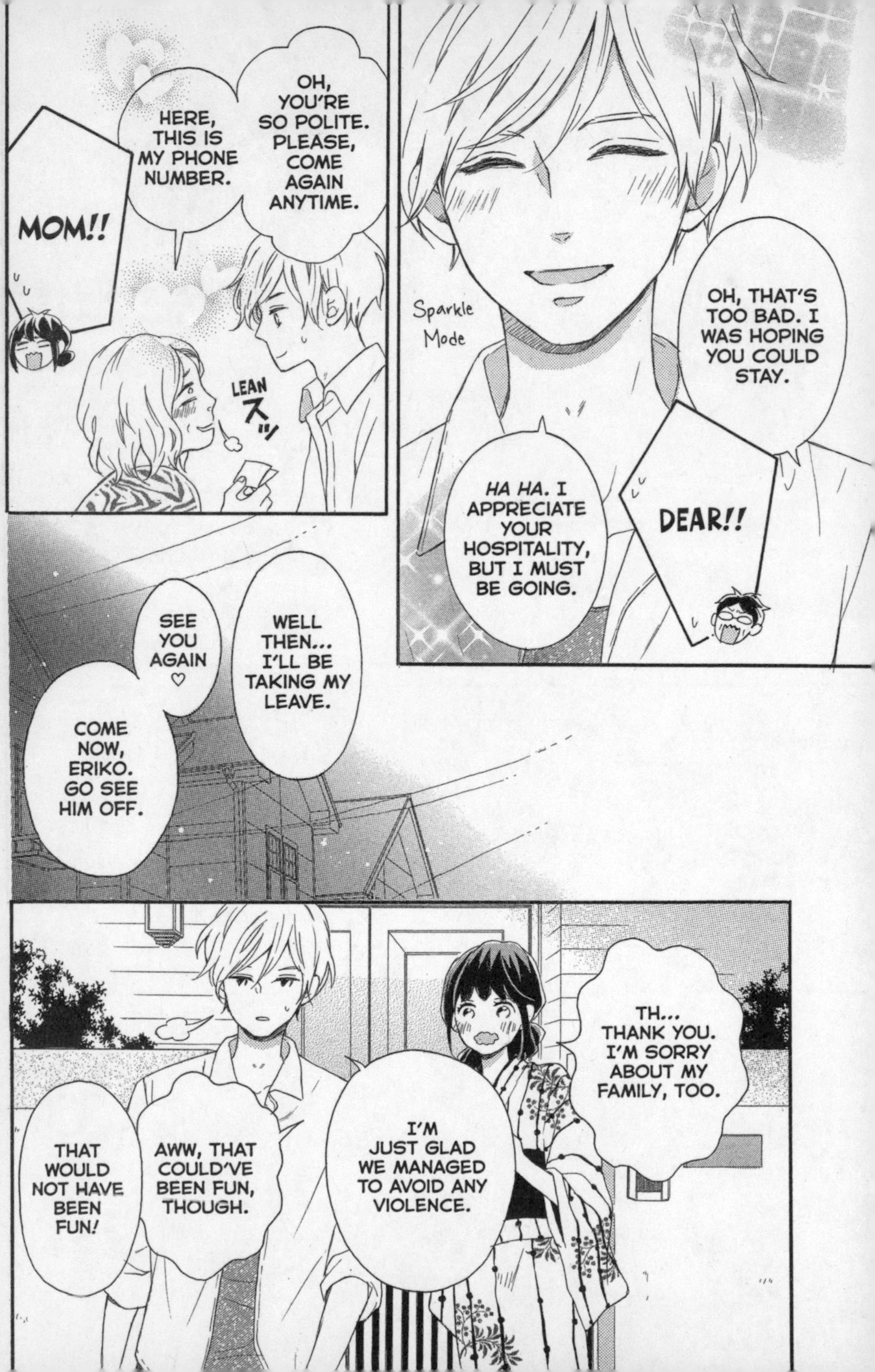
OH, THAT'S TOO BAD. I WAS HOPING YOU COULD STAY.
Sparkle Mode
DEAR!!
HA HA. I APPRECIATE YOUR HOSPITALITY, BUT I MUST BE GOING.
OH, YOU'RE SO POLITE. PLEASE, COME AGAIN ANYTIME.
HERE, THIS IS MY PHONE NUMBER.
MOM!!
LEAN
スッ
WELL THEN... I'LL BE TAKING MY LEAVE.
SEE YOU AGAIN ♡
COME NOW, ERIKO. GO SEE HIM OFF.
TH... THANK YOU. I'M SORRY ABOUT MY FAMILY, TOO.
I'M JUST GLAD WE MANAGED TO AVOID ANY VIOLENCE.
AWW, THAT COULD'VE BEEN FUN, THOUGH.
THAT WOULD NOT HAVE BEEN FUN!

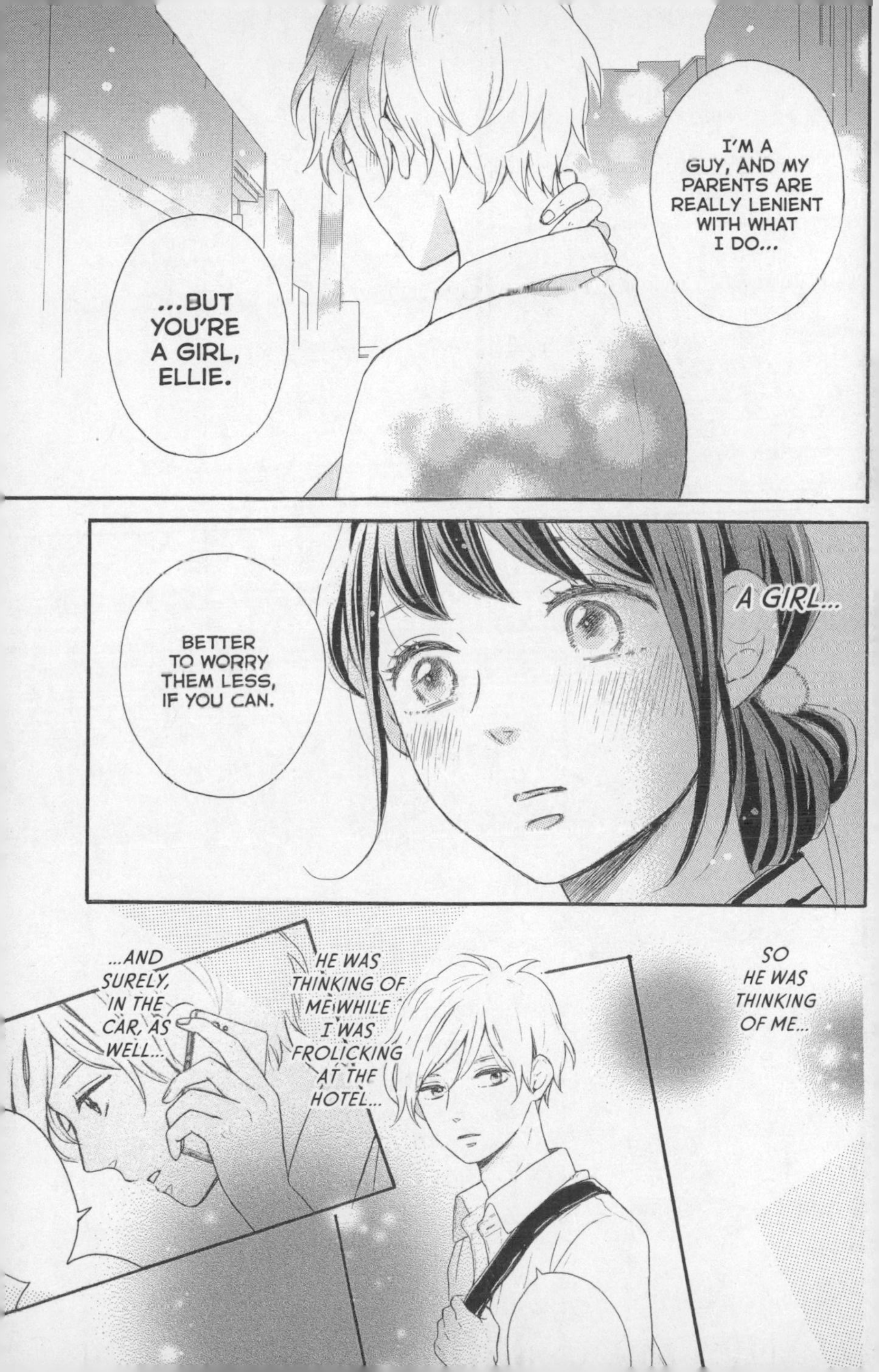
I'M A GUY, AND MY PARENTS ARE REALLY LENIENT WITH WHAT I DO...
...BUT YOU'RE A GIRL, ELLIE.
BETTER TO WORRY THEM LESS, IF YOU CAN.
A GIRL...
SO HE WAS THINKING OF ME...
HE WAS THINKING OF ME WHILE I WAS FROLICKING AT THE HOTEL...
...AND SURELY, IN THE CAR, AS WELL...

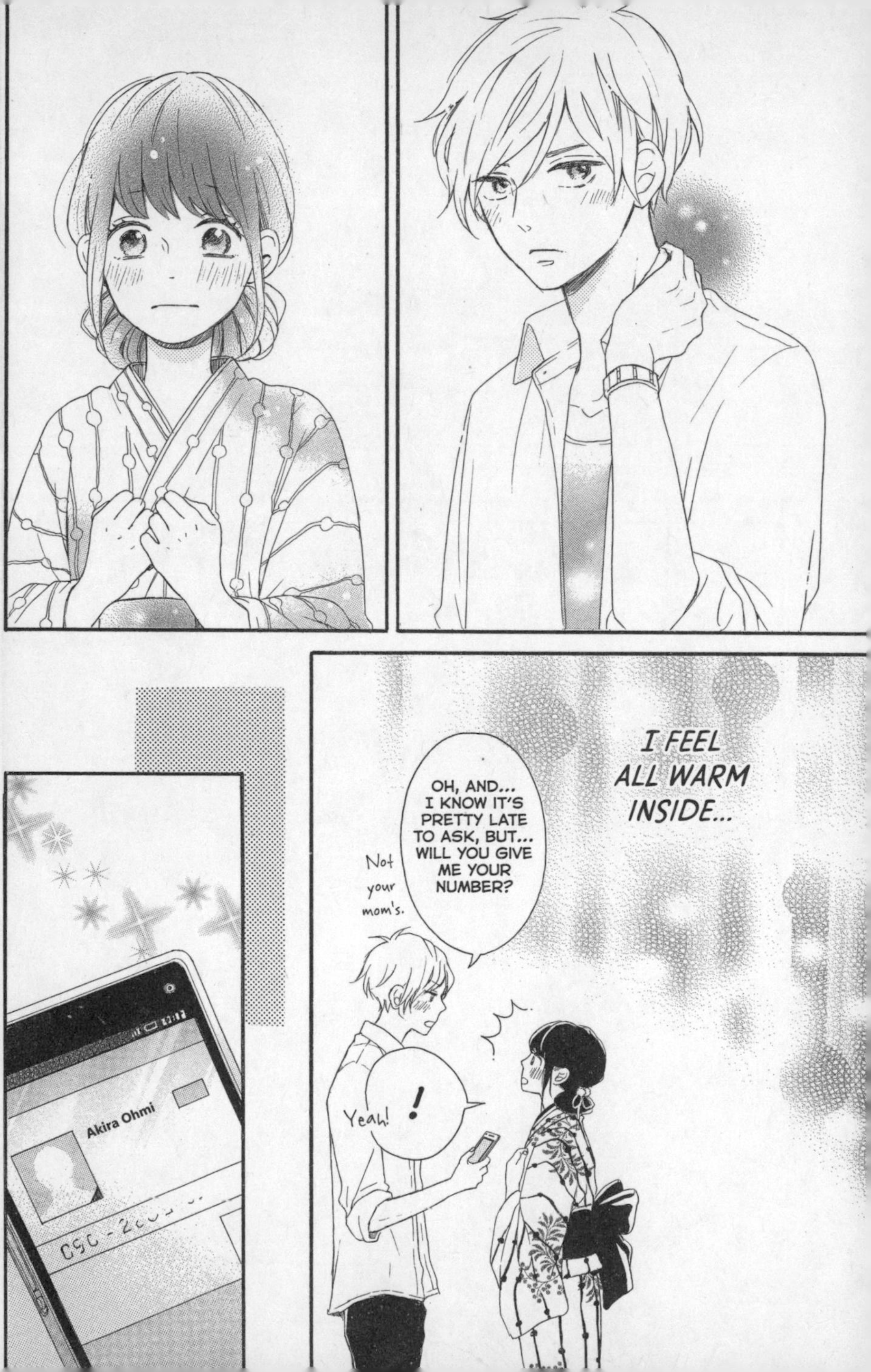
I FEEL ALL WARM INSIDE...
OH, AND... I KNOW IT'S PRETTY LATE TO ASK, BUT... WILL YOU GIVE ME YOUR NUMBER?
Not your mom's.
!
Yeah!
Akira Ohmi

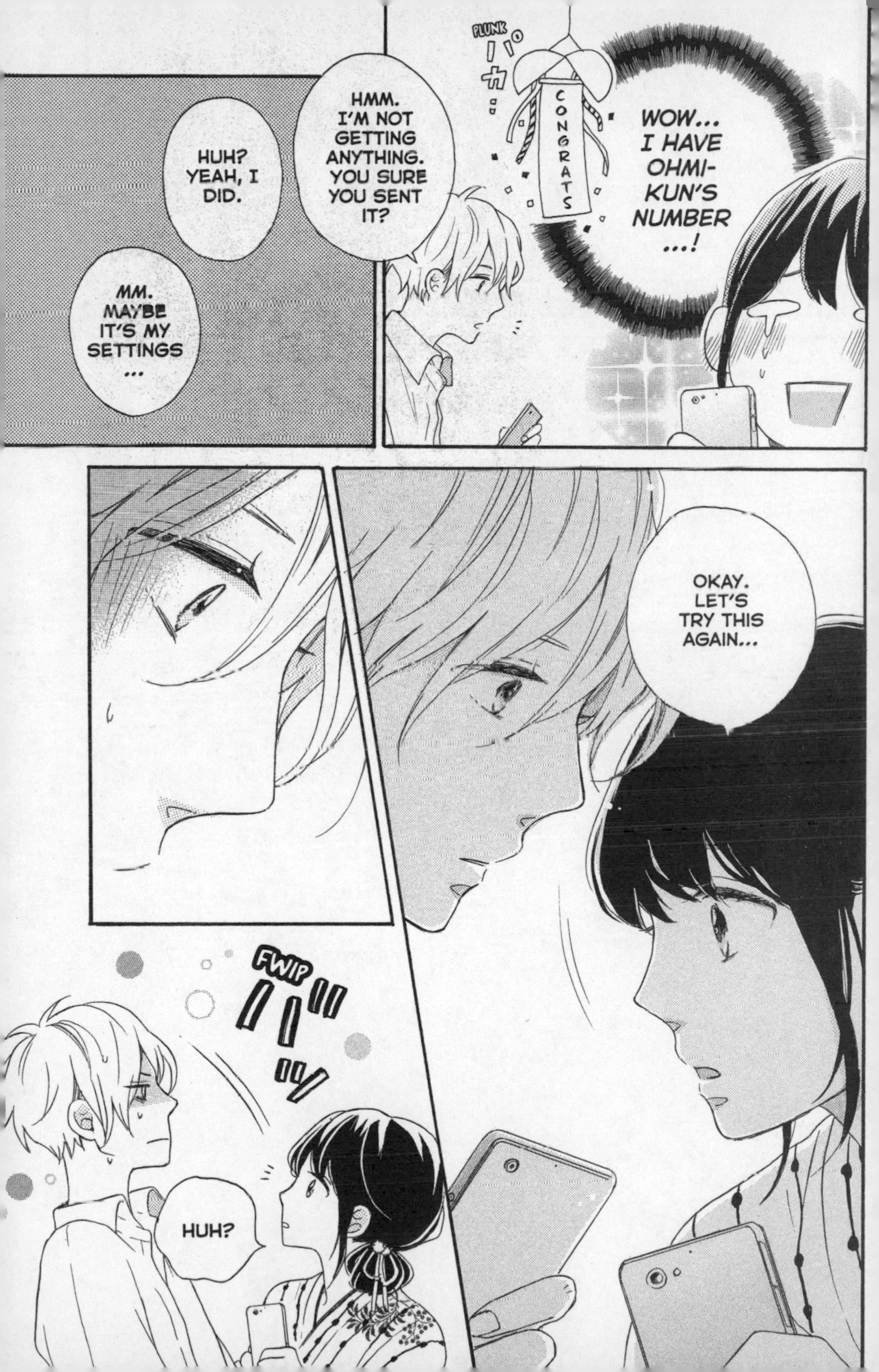
PLUNK
パカ
CONGRATS
WOW... I HAVE OHMI-KUN'S NUMBER ...!
HMM. I'M NOT GETTING ANYTHING. YOU SURE YOU SENT IT?
HUH? YEAH, I DID.
MM. MAYBE IT'S MY SETTINGS ...
OKAY. LET'S TRY THIS AGAIN...
FWIP
HUH?

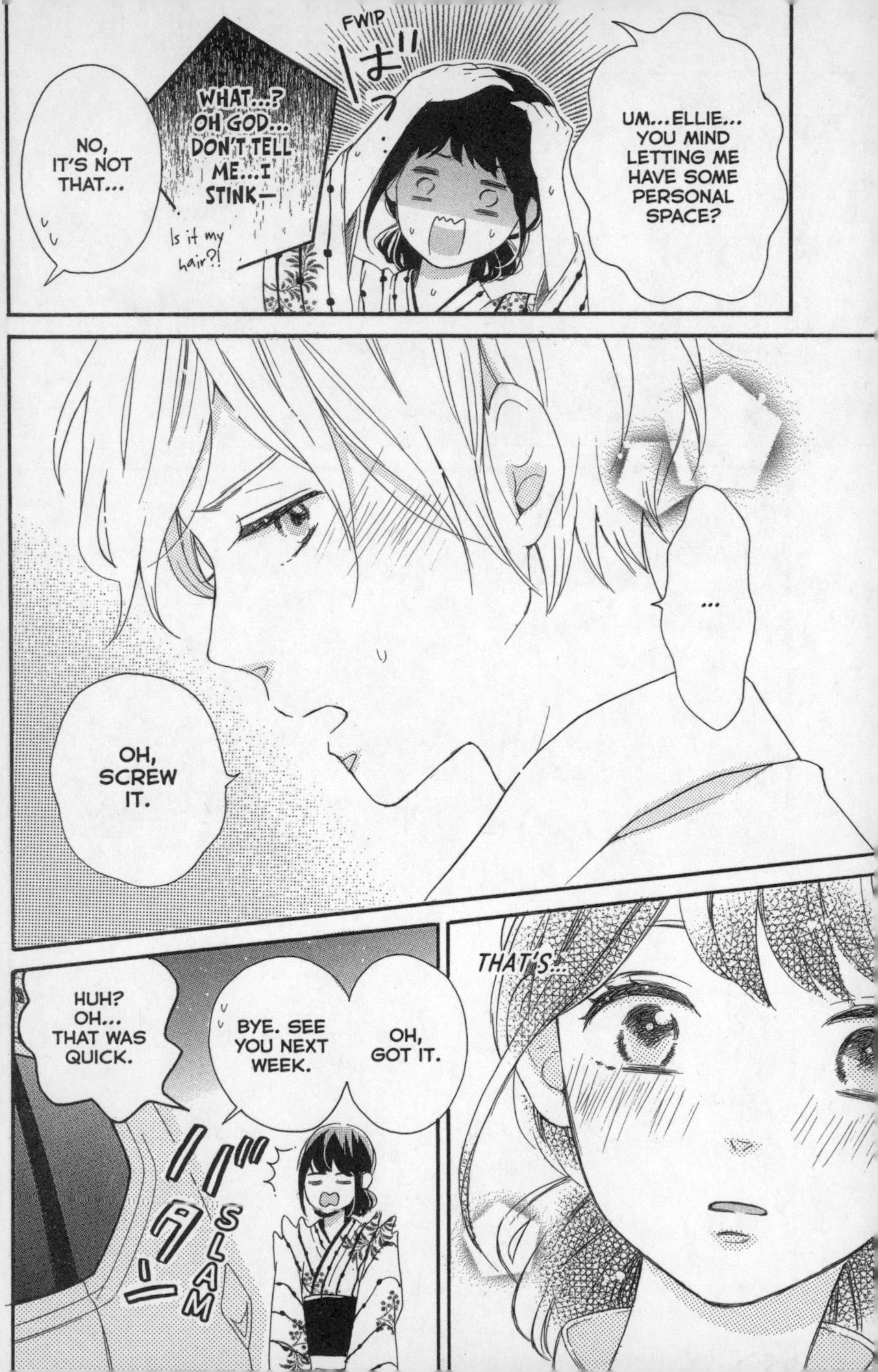
FWIP
UM...ELLIE... YOU MIND LETTING ME HAVE SOME PERSONAL SPACE?
WHAT...? OH GOD... DON'T TELL ME...I STINK—
Is it my hair?!
NO, IT'S NOT THAT...
...
OH, SCREW IT.
THAT'S...
OH, GOT IT.
BYE. SEE YOU NEXT WEEK.
HUH? OH... THAT WAS QUICK.
SLAM

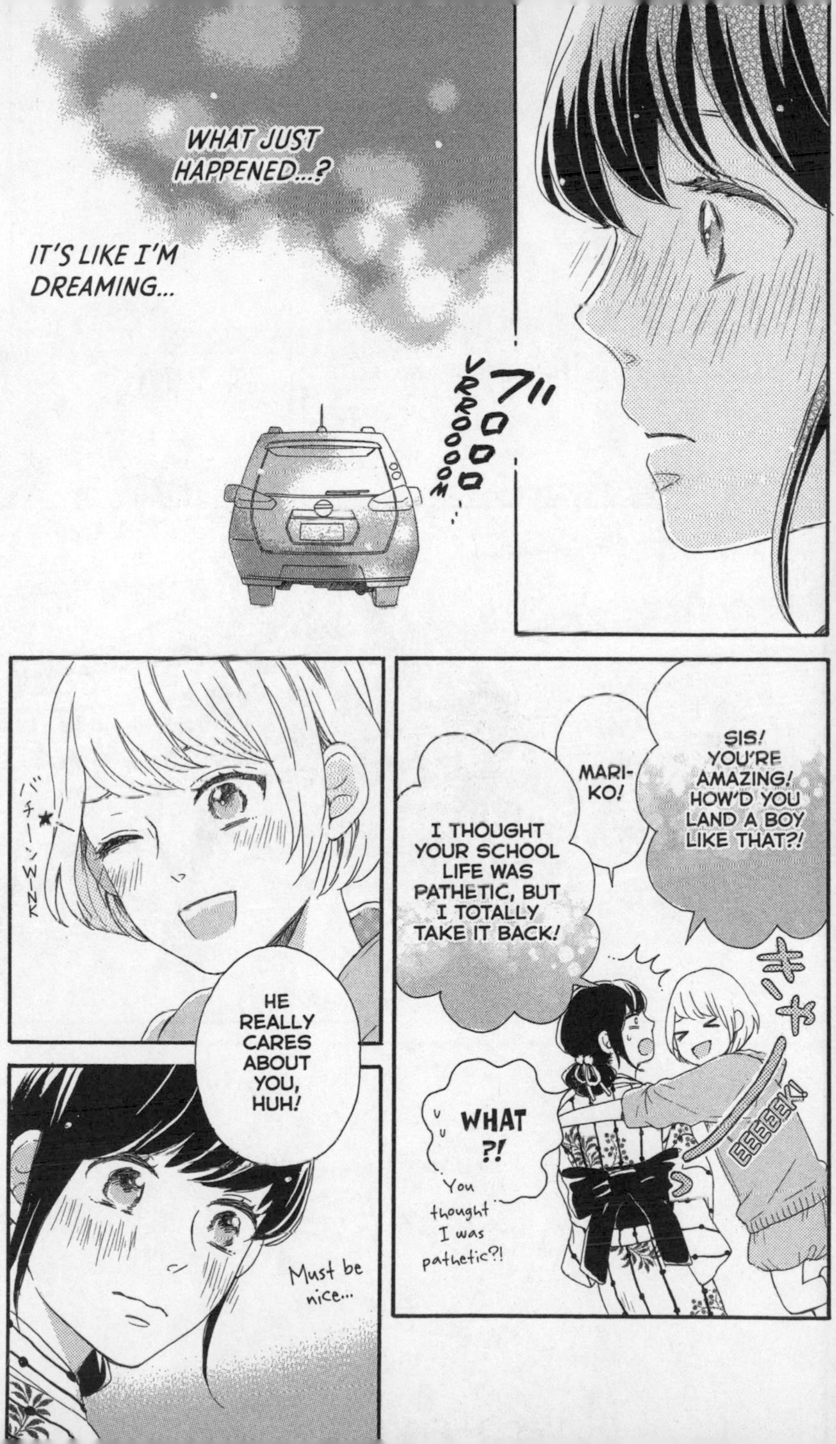

WHAT JUST HAPPENED...?
IT'S LIKE I'M DREAMING...
VRROOOOOM...
SIS! YOU'RE AMAZING! HOW'D YOU LAND A BOY LIKE THAT?!
MARI-KO!
I THOUGHT YOUR SCHOOL LIFE WAS PATHETIC, BUT I TOTALLY TAKE IT BACK!
EEEEEK!
WHAT?!
You thought I was pathetic?!
WINK
HE REALLY CARES ABOUT YOU, HUH!
Must be nice...

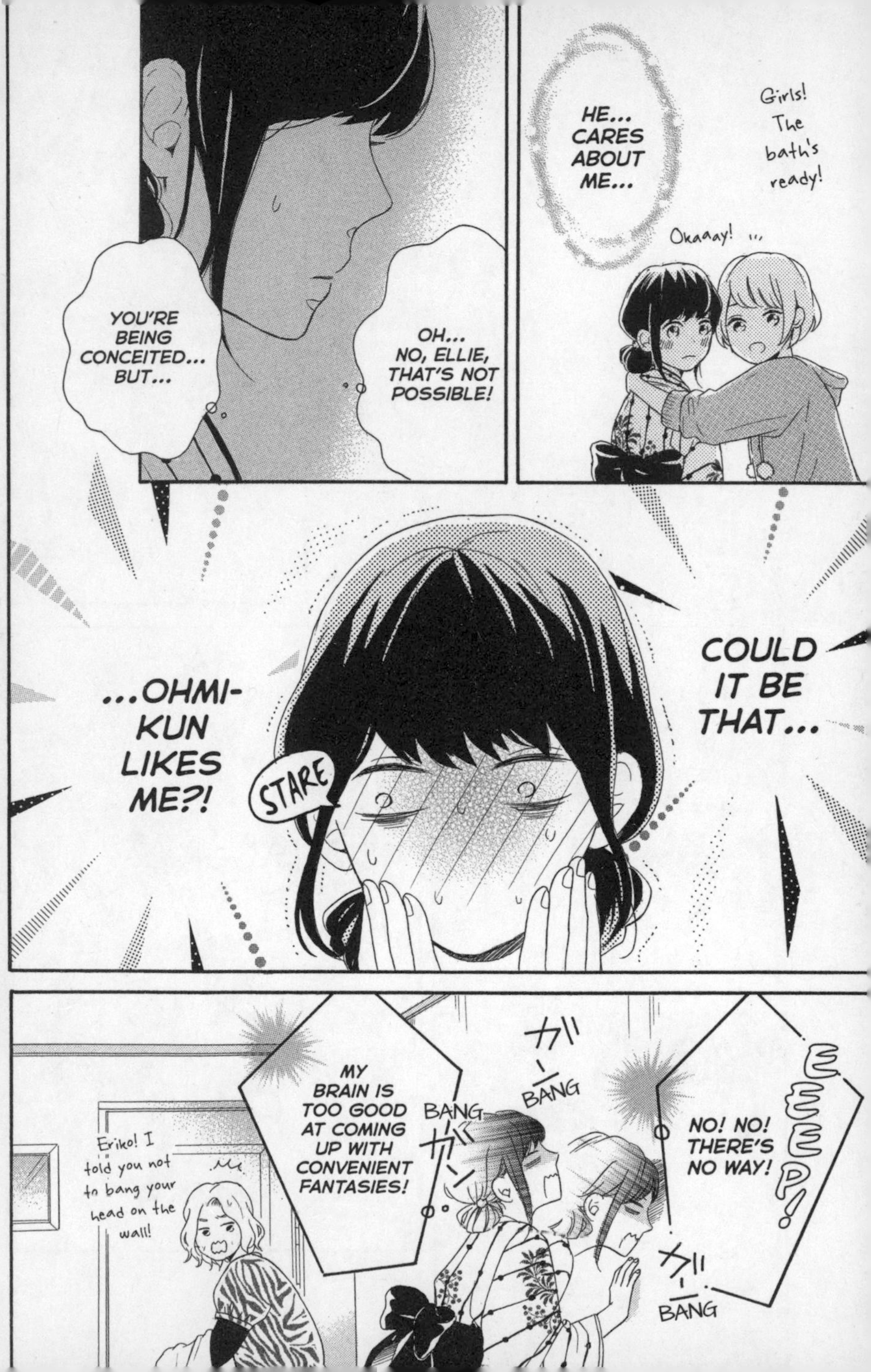
Girls! The bath's ready!
HE... CARES ABOUT ME...
Okaaay!
OH... NO, ELLIE, THAT'S NOT POSSIBLE!
YOU'RE BEING CONCEITED... BUT...
COULD IT BE THAT...
STARE
...OHMI-KUN LIKES ME?!
EEEP!
NO! NO! THERE'S NO WAY!
BANG
BANG
MY BRAIN IS TOO GOOD AT COMING UP WITH CONVENIENT FANTASIES!
Eriko! I told you not to bang your head on the wall!
BANG

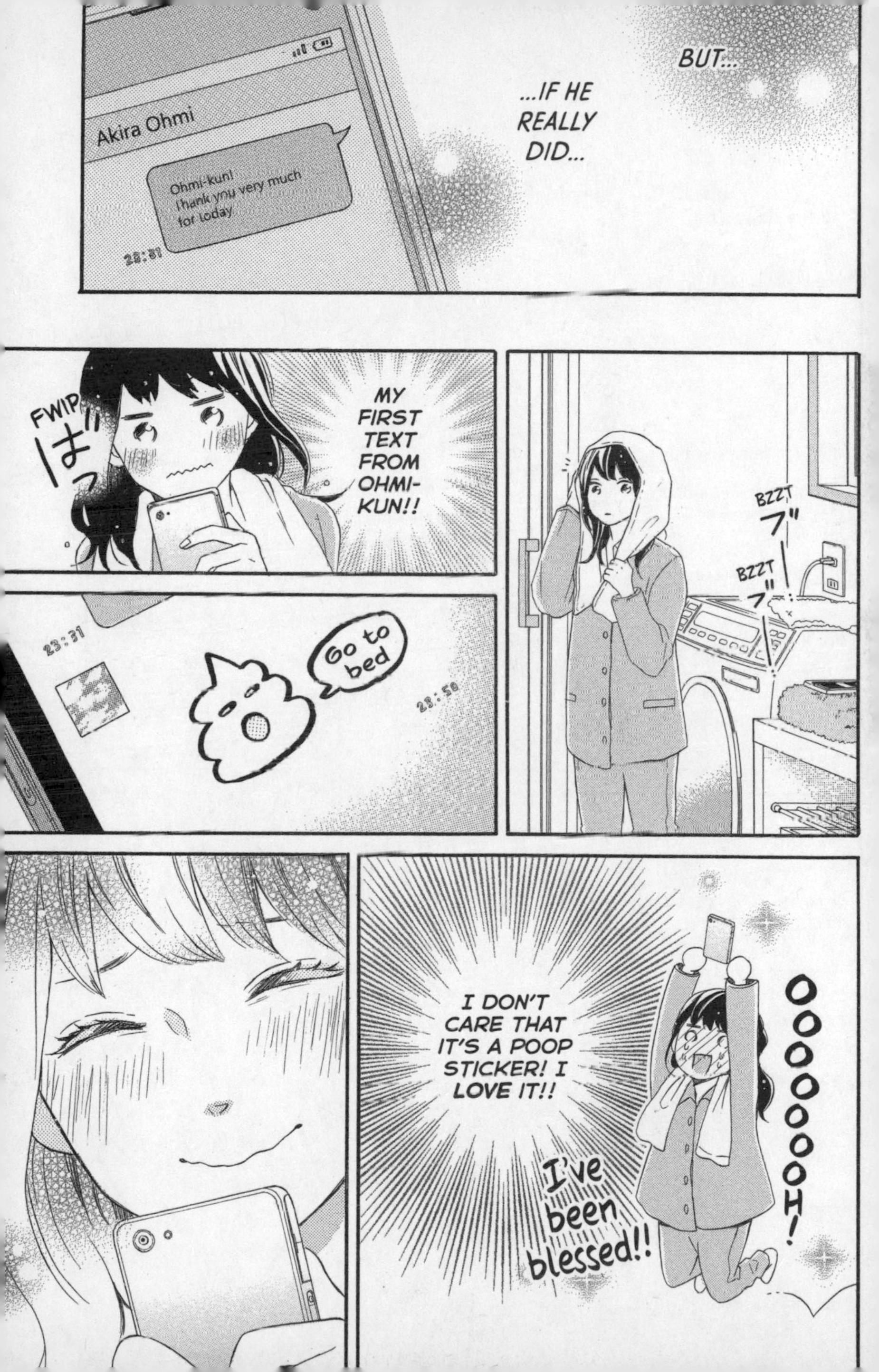
BUT...
...IF HE REALLY DID...
Akira Ohmi
Ohmi-kun! Thank you very much for today
23:31
BZZT
ブ
BZZT
ブ
MY FIRST TEXT FROM OHMI-KUN!!
FWIP
はっ
23:31
Go to bed
23:50
OOOOOOOOH!
I DON'T CARE THAT IT'S A POOP STICKER! I LOVE IT!!
I've been blessed!!

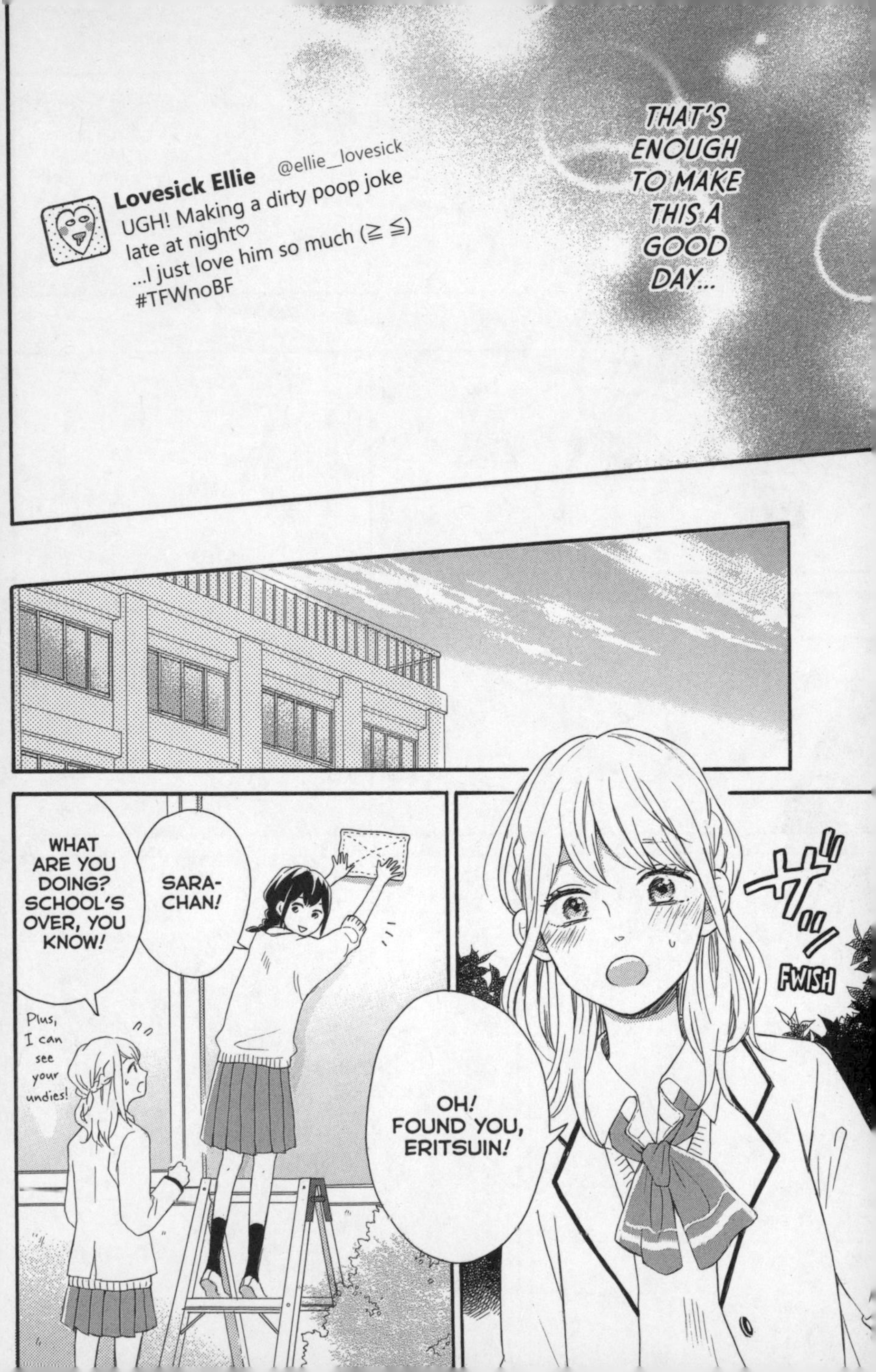
THAT'S ENOUGH TO MAKE THIS A GOOD DAY...
Lovesick Ellie @ellie_lovesick
UGH! Making a dirty poop joke late at night♡
...I just love him so much (≧≦)
#TFWnoBF
ザッ
FWISH
OH! FOUND YOU, ERITSUIN!
SARA-CHAN!
WHAT ARE YOU DOING? SCHOOL'S OVER, YOU KNOW!
Plus, I can see your undies!

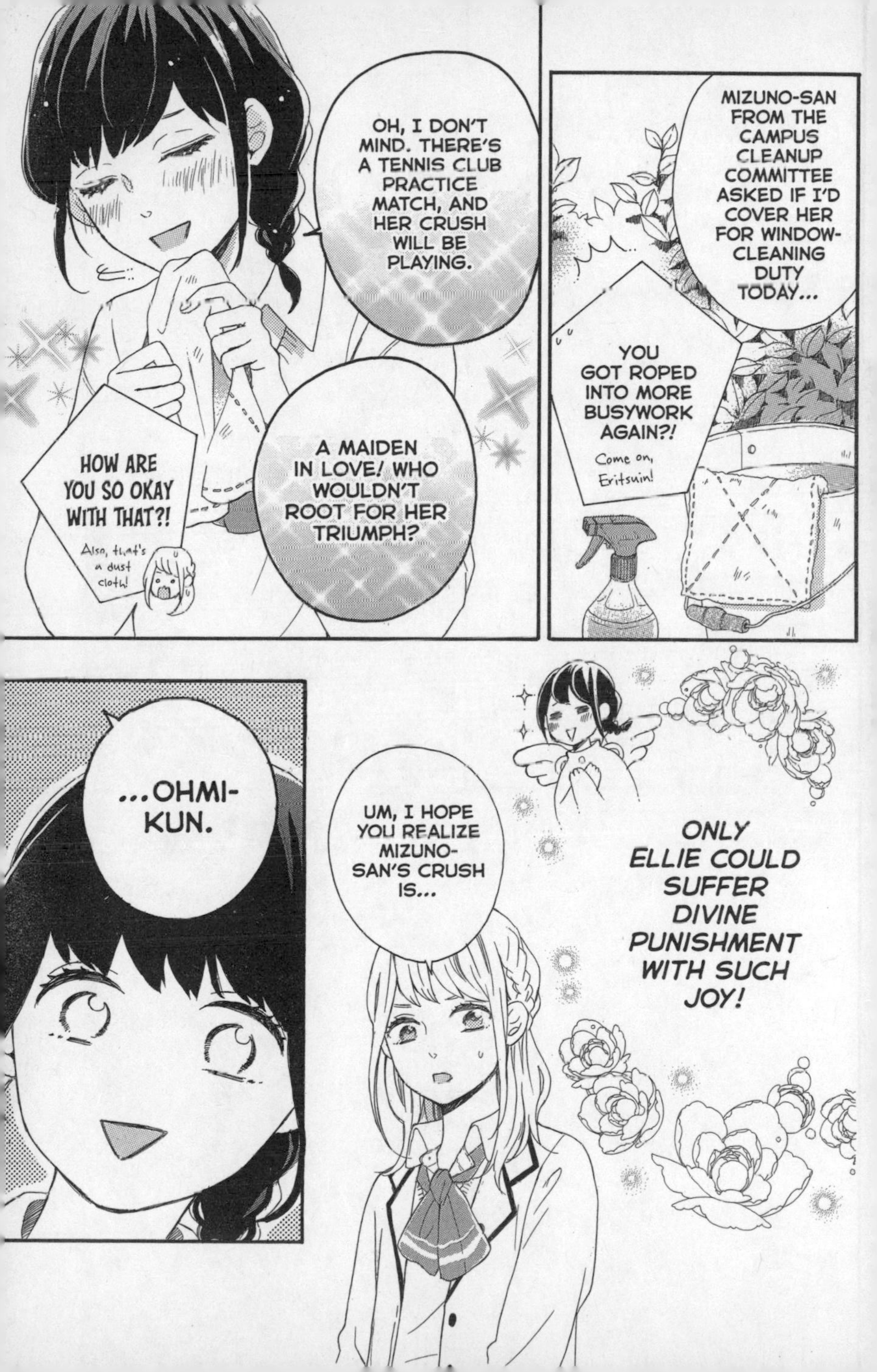

MIZUNO-SAN FROM THE CAMPUS CLEANUP COMMITTEE ASKED IF I'D COVER HER FOR WINDOW-CLEANING DUTY TODAY...
YOU GOT ROPED INTO MORE BUSYWORK AGAIN?!
Come on, Eritsuin!
OH, I DON'T MIND. THERE'S A TENNIS CLUB PRACTICE MATCH, AND HER CRUSH WILL BE PLAYING.
HOW ARE YOU SO OKAY WITH THAT?!
Also, that's a dust cloth!
A MAIDEN IN LOVE! WHO WOULDN'T ROOT FOR HER TRIUMPH?
ONLY ELLIE COULD SUFFER DIVINE PUNISHMENT WITH SUCH JOY!
UM, I HOPE YOU REALIZE MIZUNO-SAN'S CRUSH IS...
...OHMI-KUN.

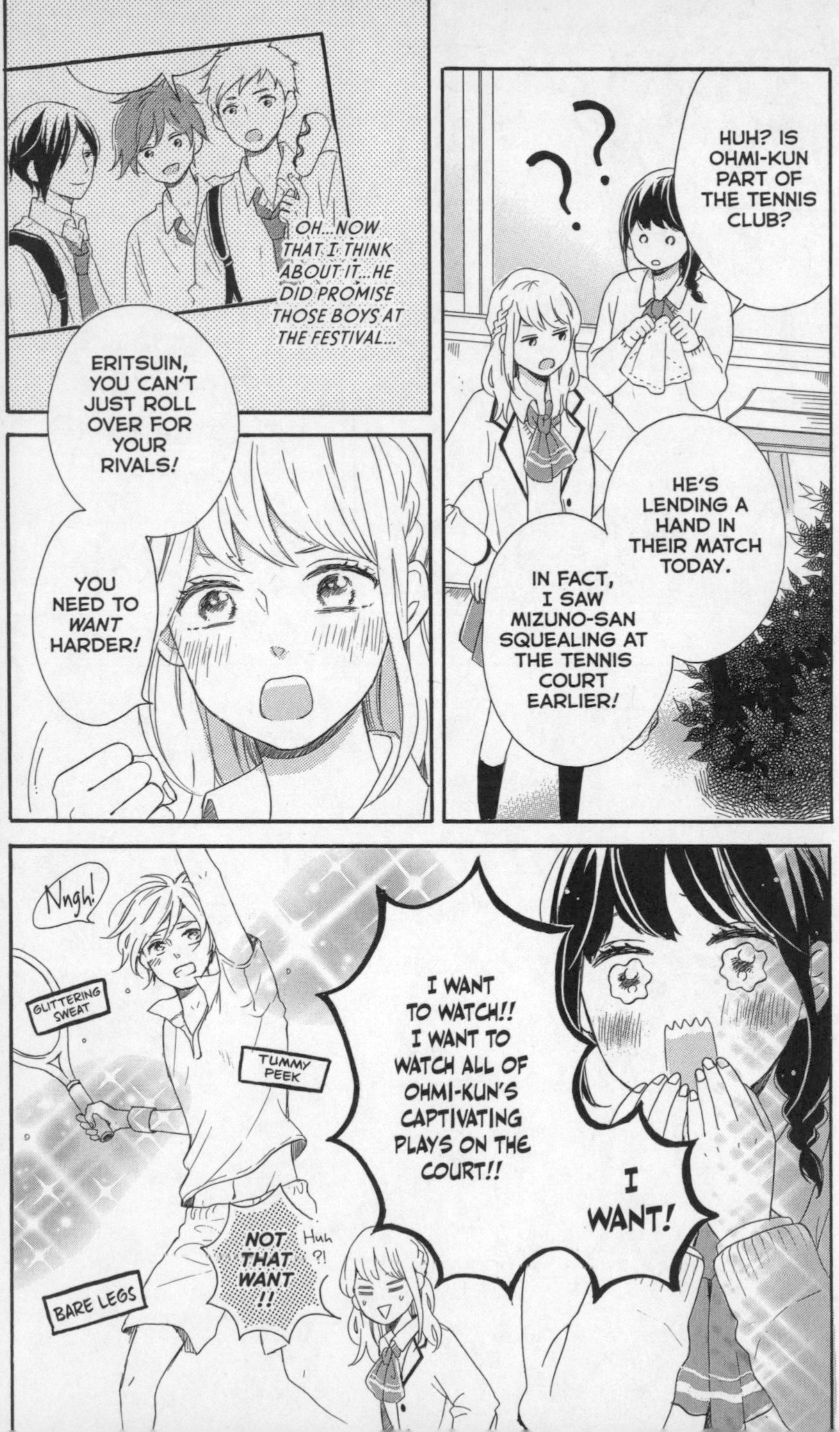
HUH? IS OHMI-KUN PART OF THE TENNIS CLUB?
HE'S LENDING A HAND IN THEIR MATCH TODAY.
IN FACT, I SAW MIZUNO-SAN SQUEALING AT THE TENNIS COURT EARLIER!
OH...NOW THAT I THINK ABOUT IT...HE DID PROMISE THOSE BOYS AT THE FESTIVAL...
ERITSUIN, YOU CAN'T JUST ROLL OVER FOR YOUR RIVALS!
YOU NEED TO *WANT* HARDER!
I WANT TO WATCH!! I WANT TO WATCH ALL OF OHMI-KUN'S CAPTIVATING PLAYS ON THE COURT!!
I WANT!
Nngh!
GLITTERING SWEAT
TUMMY PEEK
Huh ?!
NOT THAT WANT!!
BARE LEGS

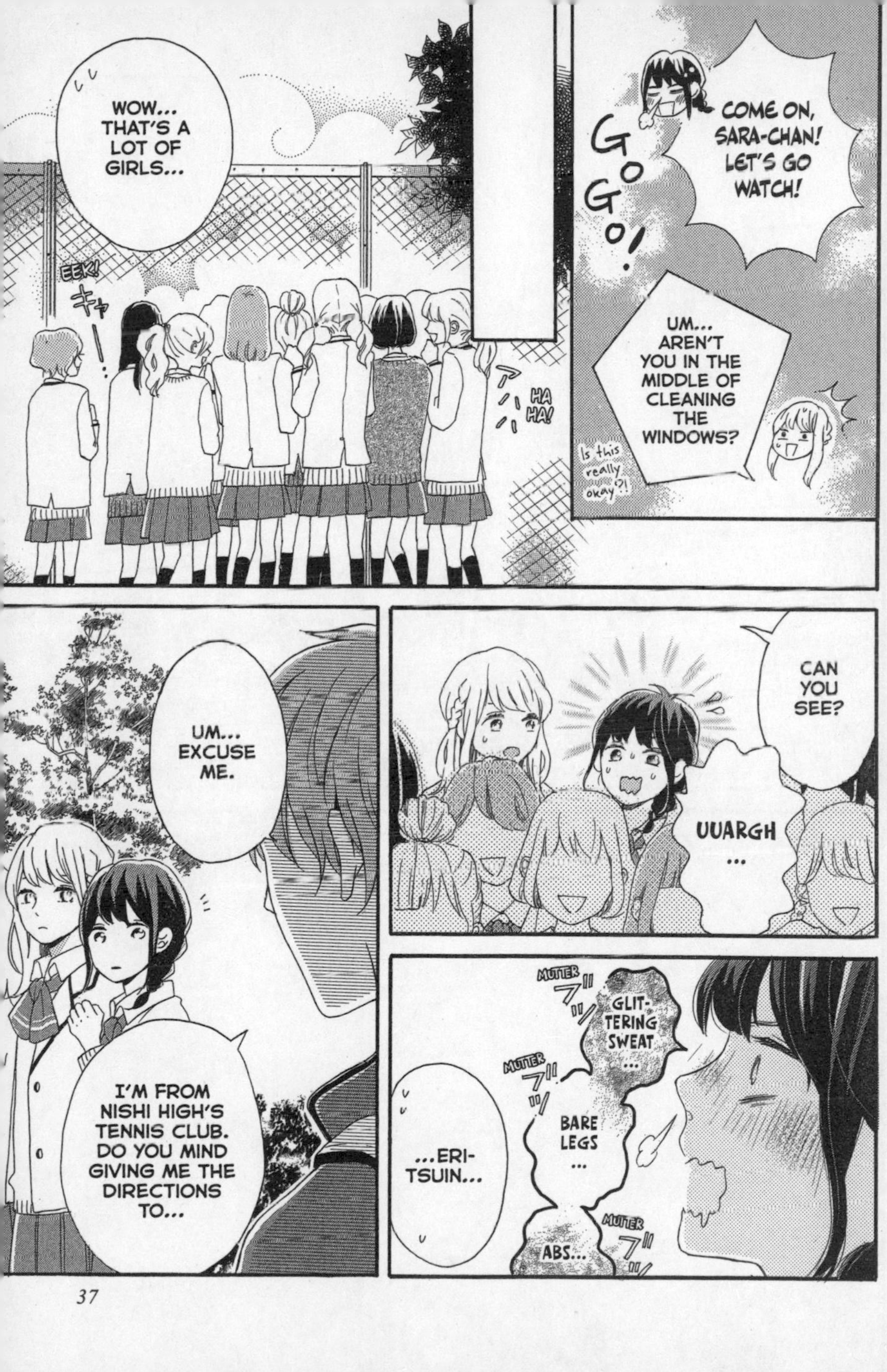
GO GO!
COME ON, SARA-CHAN! LET'S GO WATCH!
UM... AREN'T YOU IN THE MIDDLE OF CLEANING THE WINDOWS?
Is this really okay?!
WOW... THAT'S A LOT OF GIRLS...
EEK!
HA HA!
CAN YOU SEE?
UUARGH ...
MUTTER
GLITTERING SWEAT ...
MUTTER
BARE LEGS ...
MUTTER
ABS...
...ERI-TSUIN...
UM... EXCUSE ME.
I'M FROM NISHI HIGH'S TENNIS CLUB. DO YOU MIND GIVING ME THE DIRECTIONS TO...

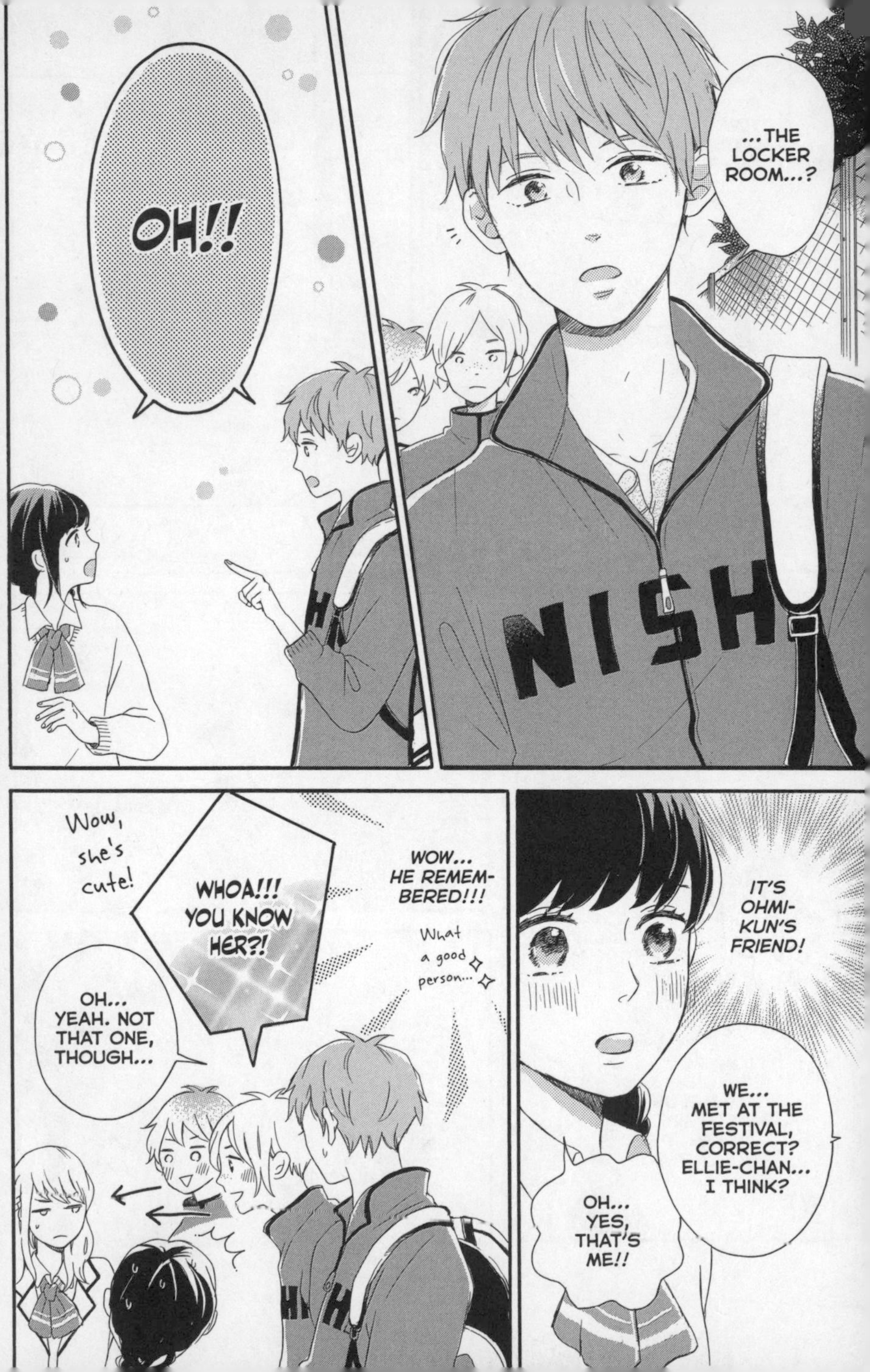
...THE LOCKER ROOM...?
OH!!
IT'S OHMI-KUN'S FRIEND!
WE... MET AT THE FESTIVAL, CORRECT? ELLIE-CHAN... I THINK?
OH... YES, THAT'S ME!!
WOW... HE REMEMBERED!!!
What a good person...
WHOA!!! YOU KNOW HER?!
Wow, she's cute!
OH... YEAH. NOT THAT ONE, THOUGH...

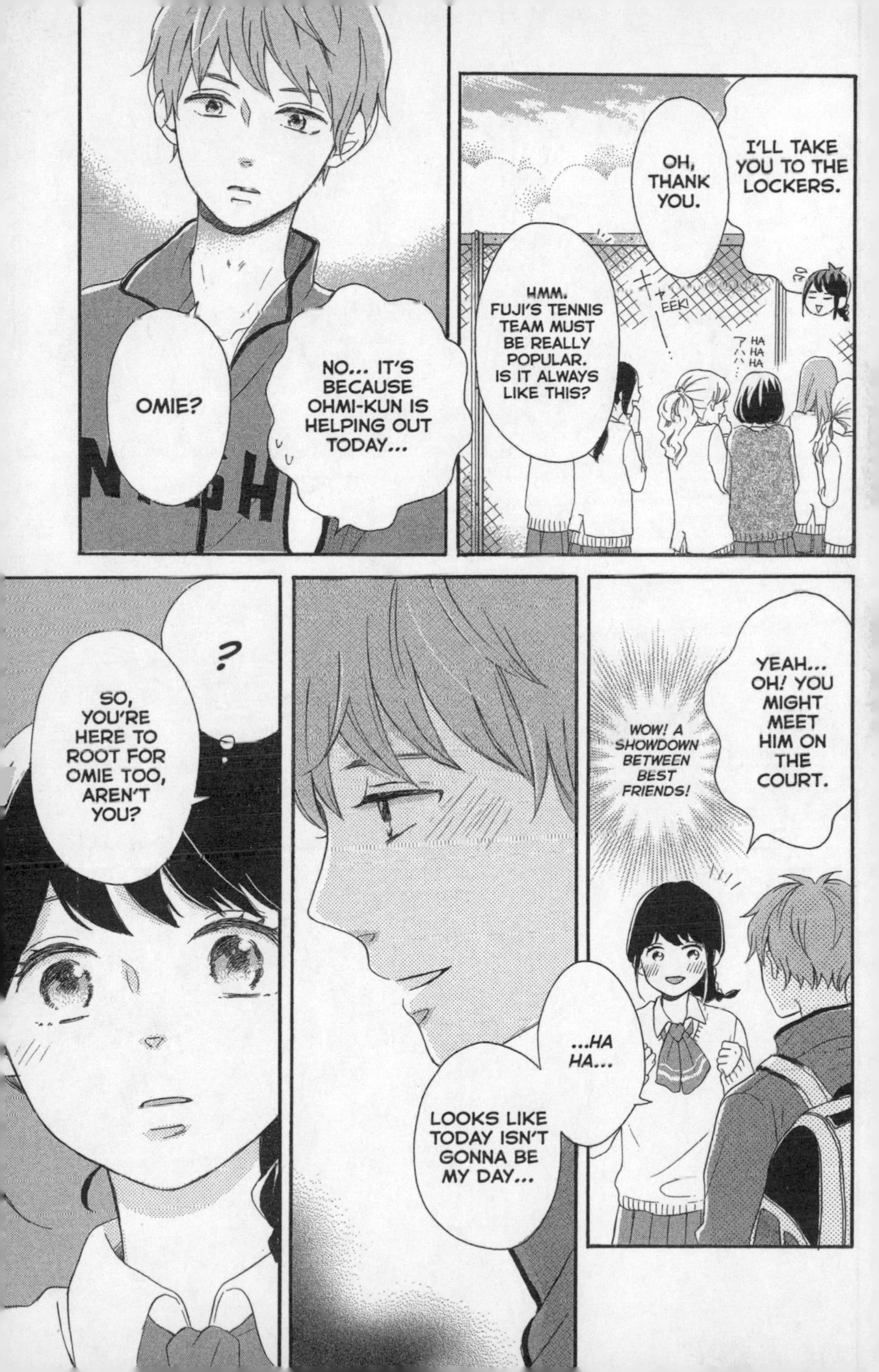
I'LL TAKE YOU TO THE LOCKERS.
OH, THANK YOU.
HMM. FUJI'S TENNIS TEAM MUST BE REALLY POPULAR. IS IT ALWAYS LIKE THIS?
EEK!
HA HA HA
NO... IT'S BECAUSE OHMI-KUN IS HELPING OUT TODAY...
OMIE?
YEAH... OH! YOU MIGHT MEET HIM ON THE COURT.
WOW! A SHOWDOWN BETWEEN BEST FRIENDS!
...HA HA...
LOOKS LIKE TODAY ISN'T GONNA BE MY DAY...
?
SO, YOU'RE HERE TO ROOT FOR OMIE TOO, AREN'T YOU?

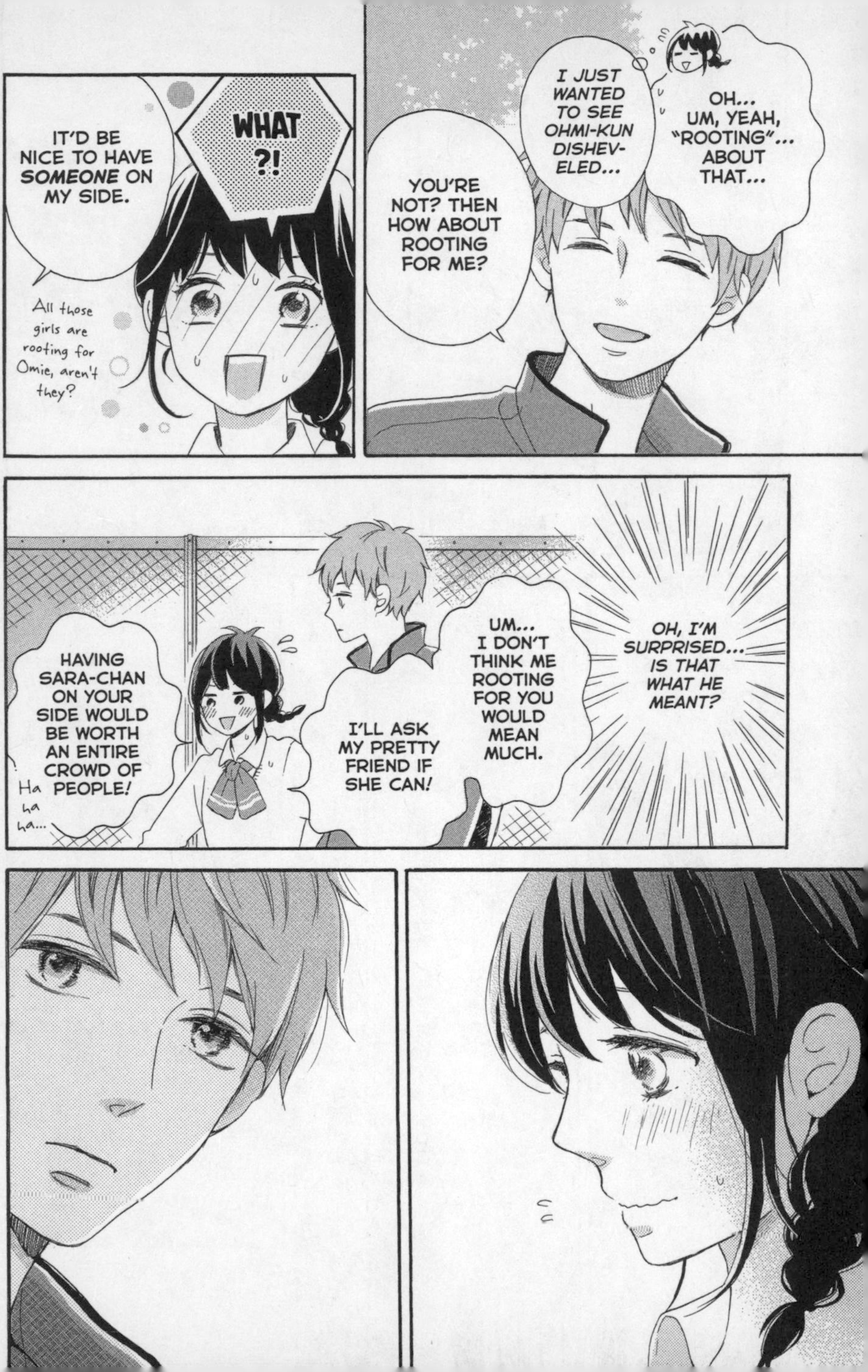

OH... UM, YEAH, "ROOTING"... ABOUT THAT...
I JUST WANTED TO SEE OHMI-KUN DISHEV-ELED...
YOU'RE NOT? THEN HOW ABOUT ROOTING FOR ME?
WHAT ?!
IT'D BE NICE TO HAVE *SOMEONE* ON MY SIDE.
All those girls are rooting for Omie, aren't they?
OH, I'M SURPRISED... IS THAT WHAT HE MEANT?
UM... I DON'T THINK ME ROOTING FOR YOU WOULD MEAN MUCH.
I'LL ASK MY PRETTY FRIEND IF SHE CAN!
HAVING SARA-CHAN ON YOUR SIDE WOULD BE WORTH AN ENTIRE CROWD OF PEOPLE!
Ha ha ha...

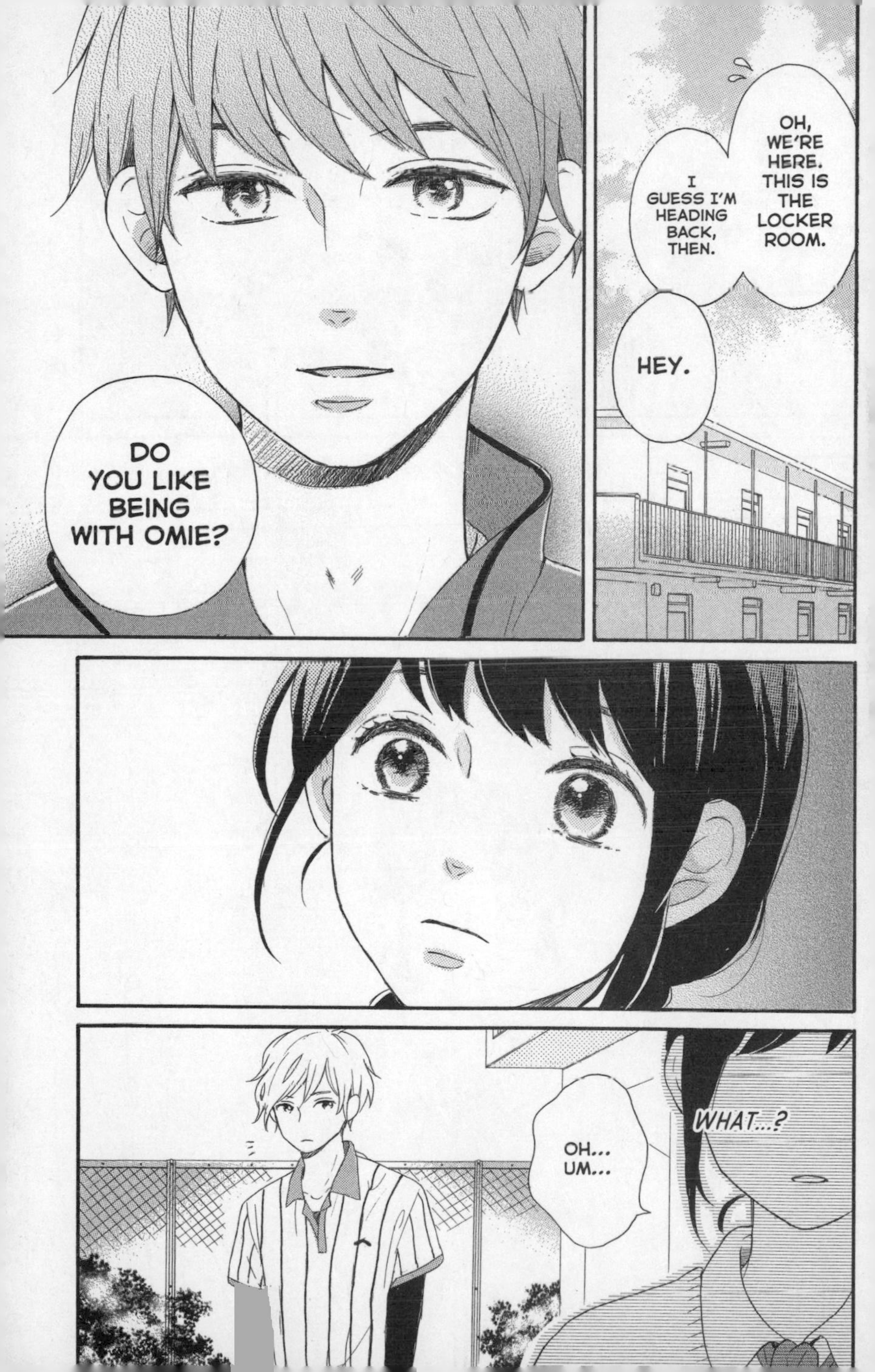
OH, WE'RE HERE. THIS IS THE LOCKER ROOM.
I GUESS I'M HEADING BACK, THEN.
HEY.
DO YOU LIKE BEING WITH OMIE?
WHAT...?
OH... UM...

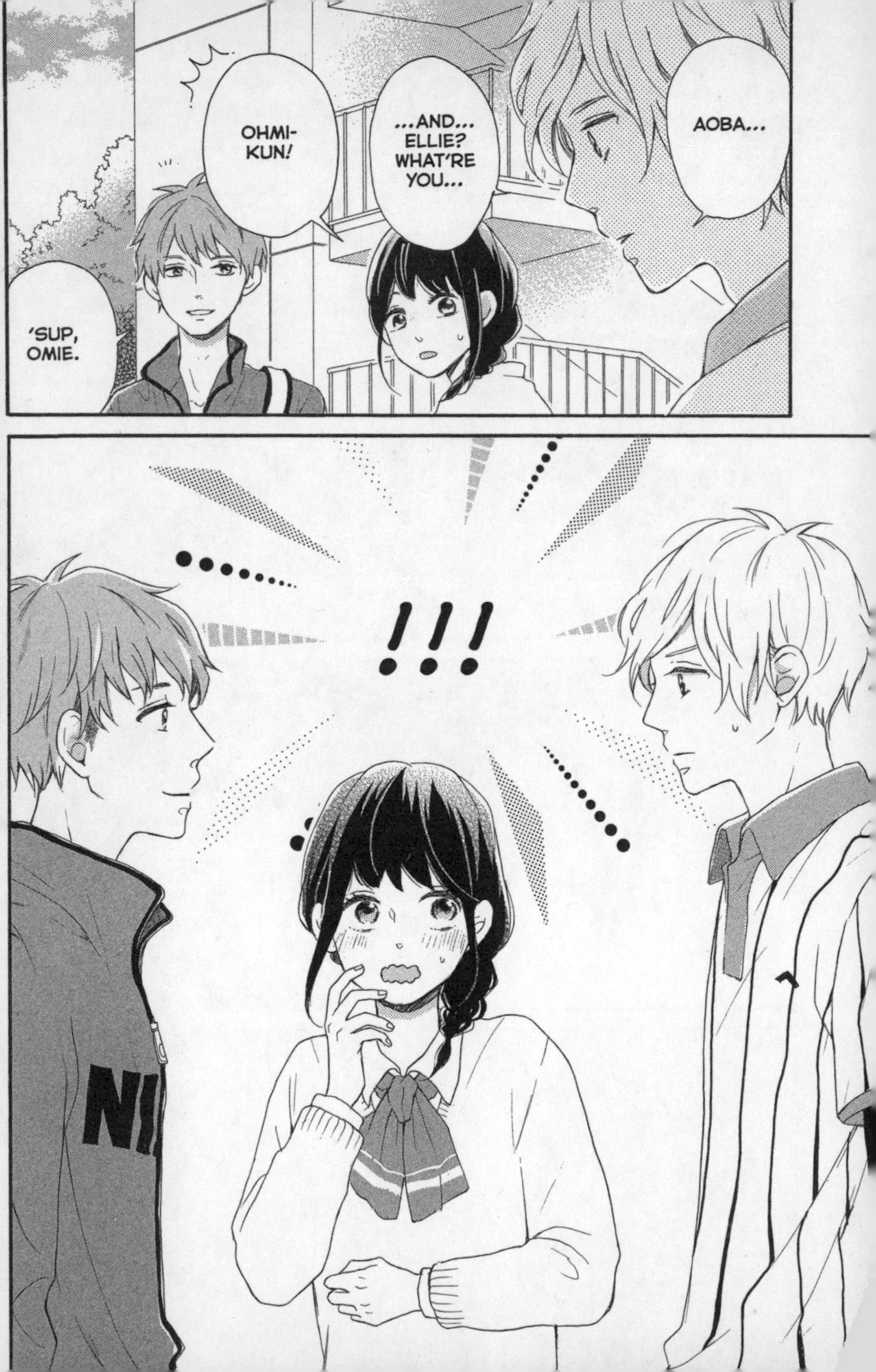
AOBA...
...AND... ELLIE? WHAT'RE YOU...
OHMI-KUN!
'SUP, OMIE.
!!!

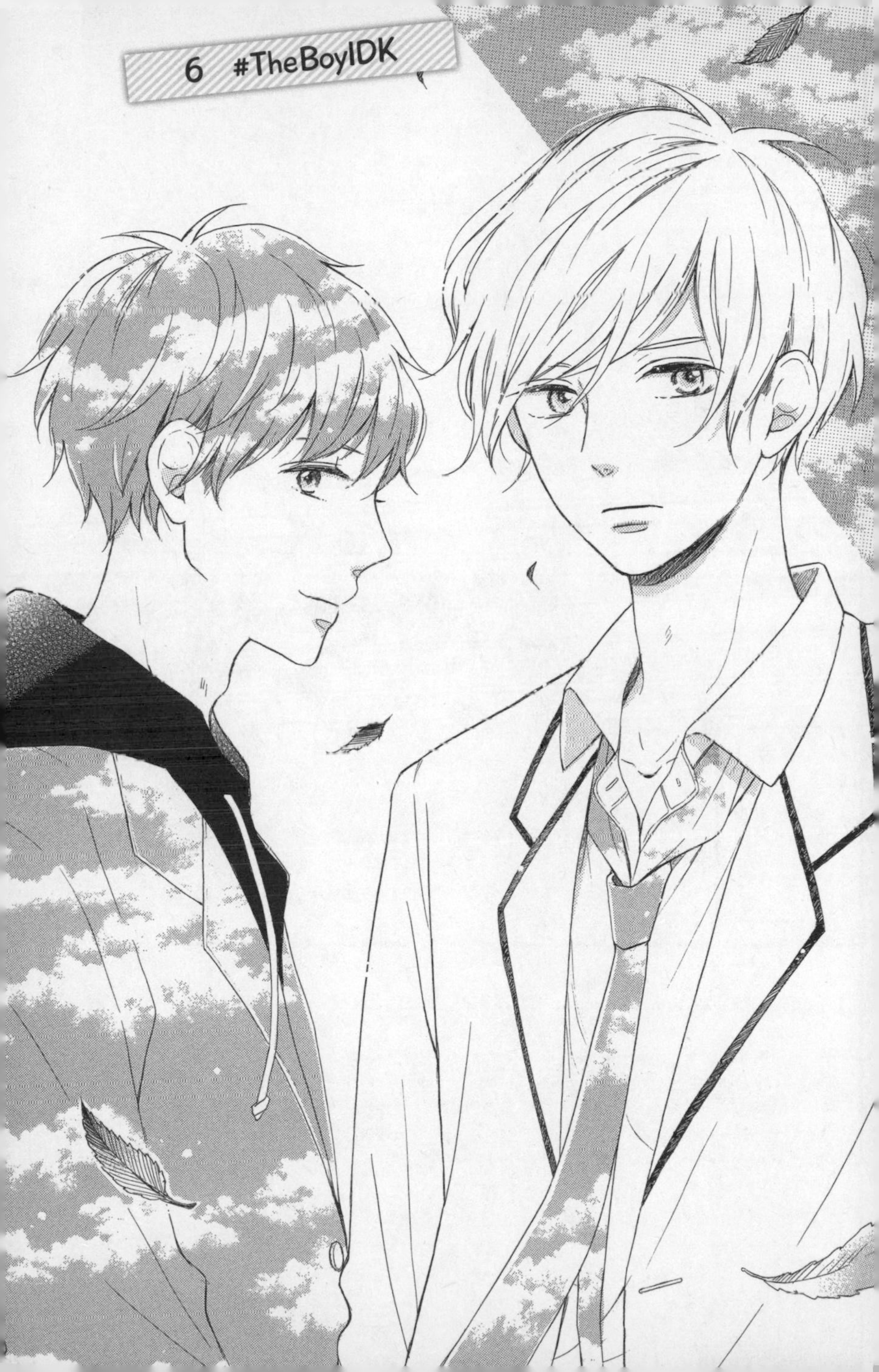
6 #TheBoyIDK

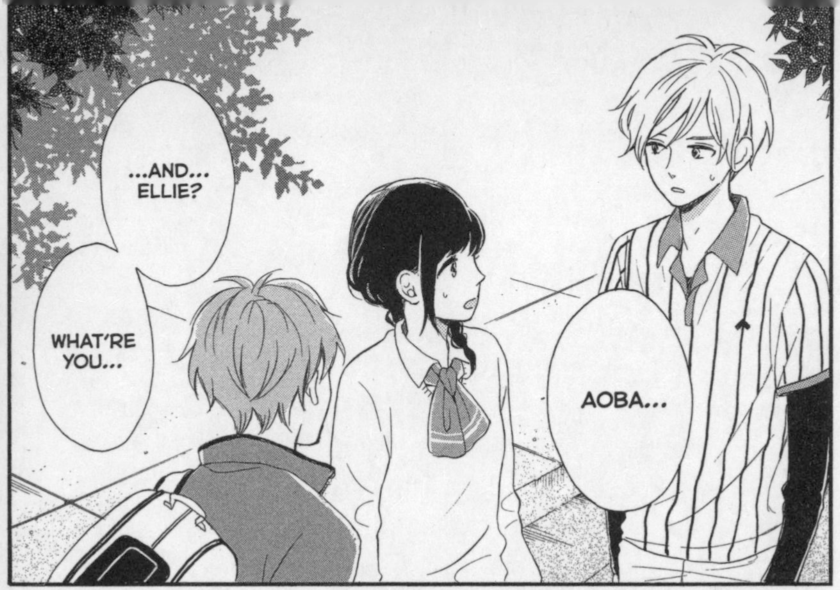
AOBA...
WHAT'RE YOU...
...AND... ELLIE?

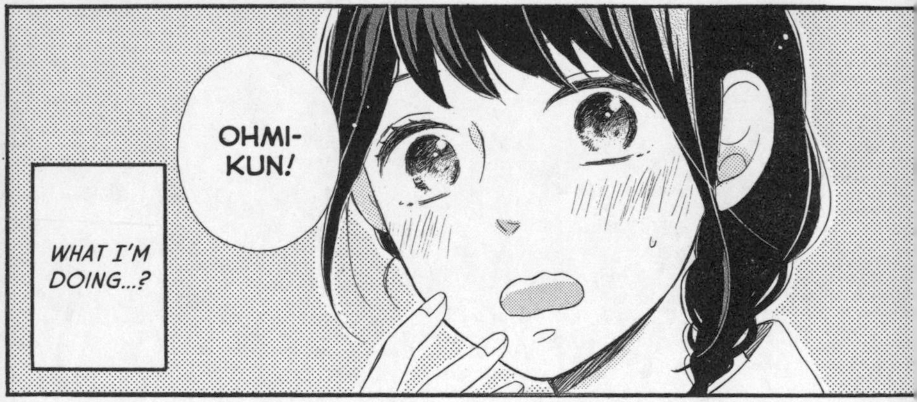
OHMI-KUN!
WHAT I'M DOING...?

Thank you for picking up the second volume of *Lovesick Ellie!*
I'm happy that some fans said the first volume sent their hearts aflutter!
But recently I've been getting a lot of comments from people who laugh at how perverted Ellie is. Those make me really happy too blush
By a fantasizing pervert, for fantasizing perverts: Volume 2!!
I hope you enjoy it!

Fujimomo

Thank you

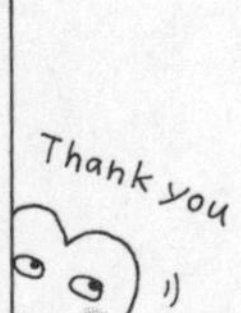

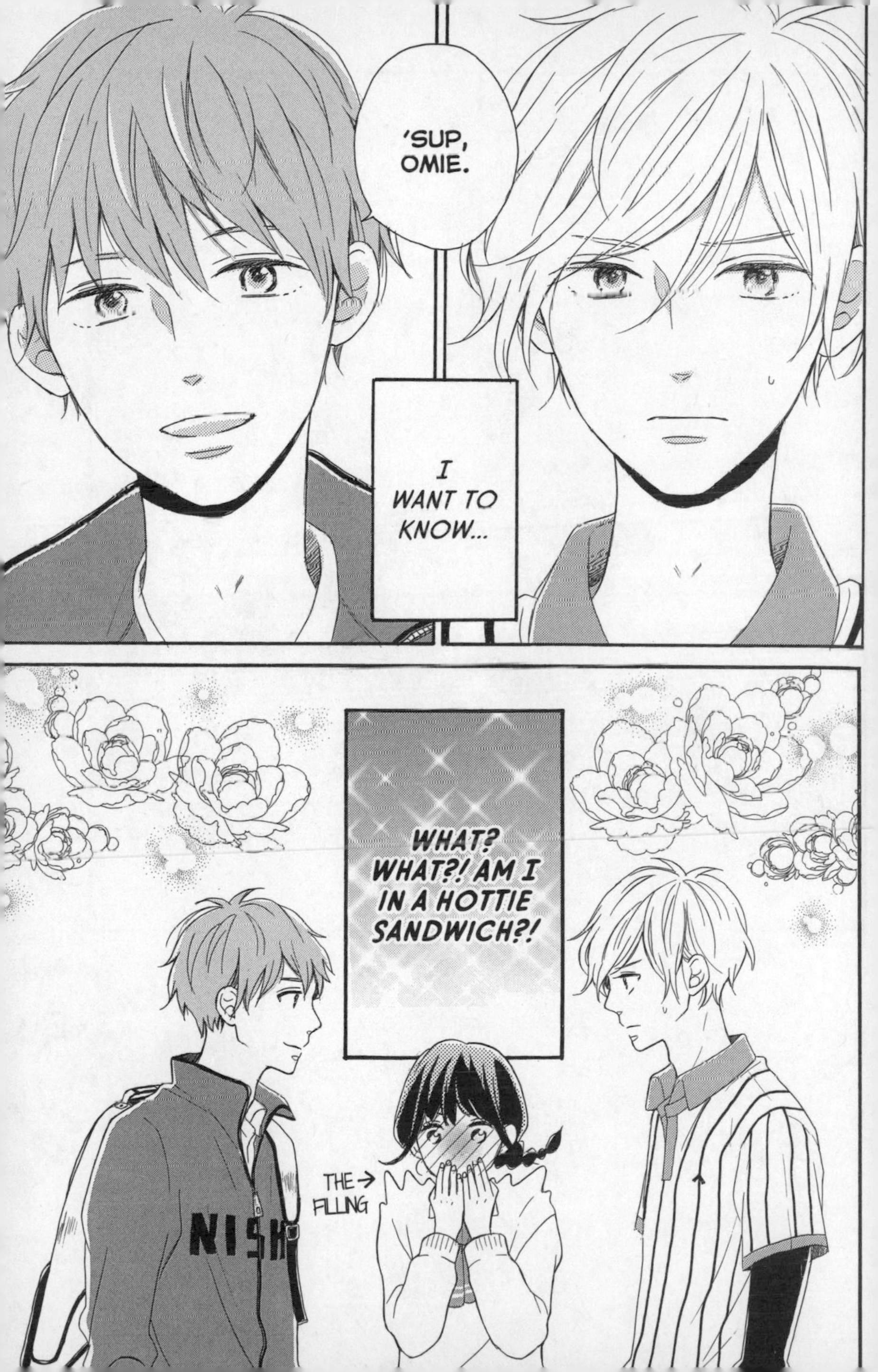
'SUP, OMIE.
I WANT TO KNOW...
WHAT? WHAT?! AM I IN A HOTTIE SANDWICH?!
THE → FILLING

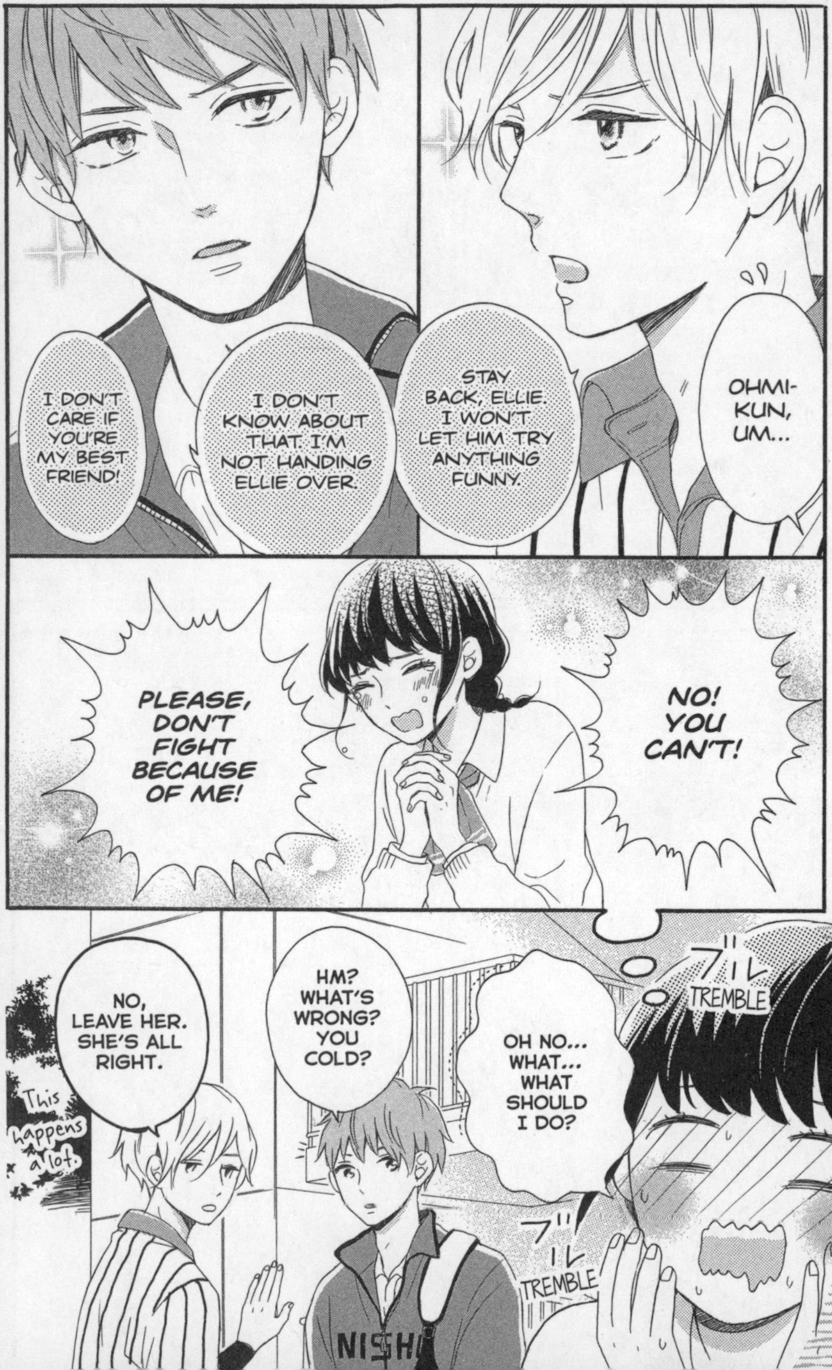
OHMI-KUN, UM...
STAY BACK, ELLIE. I WON'T LET HIM TRY ANYTHING FUNNY.
I DON'T KNOW ABOUT THAT. I'M NOT HANDING ELLIE OVER.
I DON'T CARE IF YOU'RE MY BEST FRIEND!
NO! YOU CAN'T!
PLEASE, DON'T FIGHT BECAUSE OF ME!
ブル TREMBLE
OH NO... WHAT... WHAT SHOULD I DO?
ブル TREMBLE
HM? WHAT'S WRONG? YOU COLD?
NO, LEAVE HER. SHE'S ALL RIGHT.
This happens a lot.
NISHI

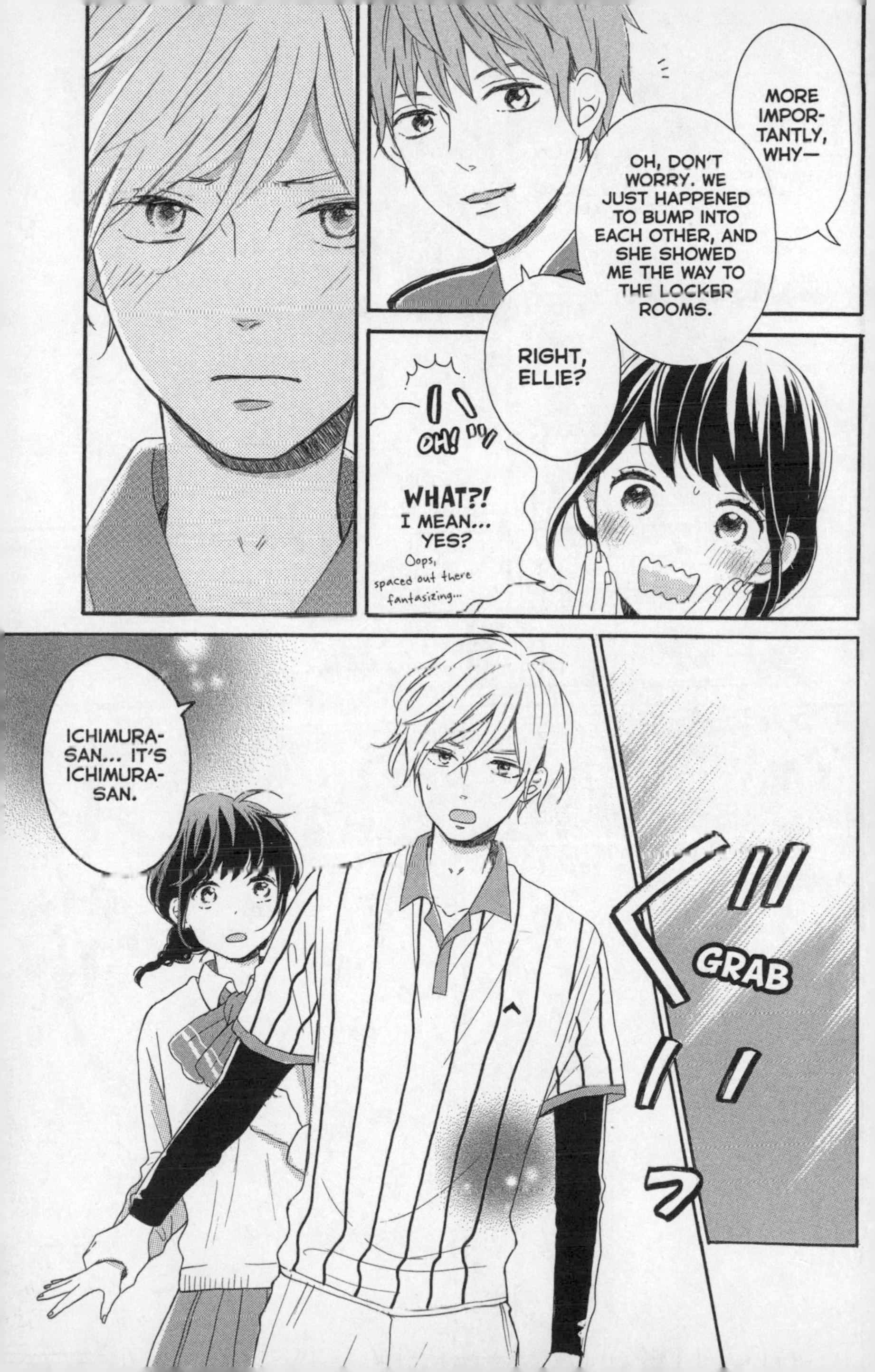
MORE IMPORTANTLY, WHY—
OH, DON'T WORRY. WE JUST HAPPENED TO BUMP INTO EACH OTHER, AND SHE SHOWED ME THE WAY TO THE LOCKER ROOMS.
RIGHT, ELLIE?
OH!
WHAT?! I MEAN... YES?
Oops, spaced out there fantasizing...
GRAB
ICHIMURA-SAN... IT'S ICHIMURA-SAN.

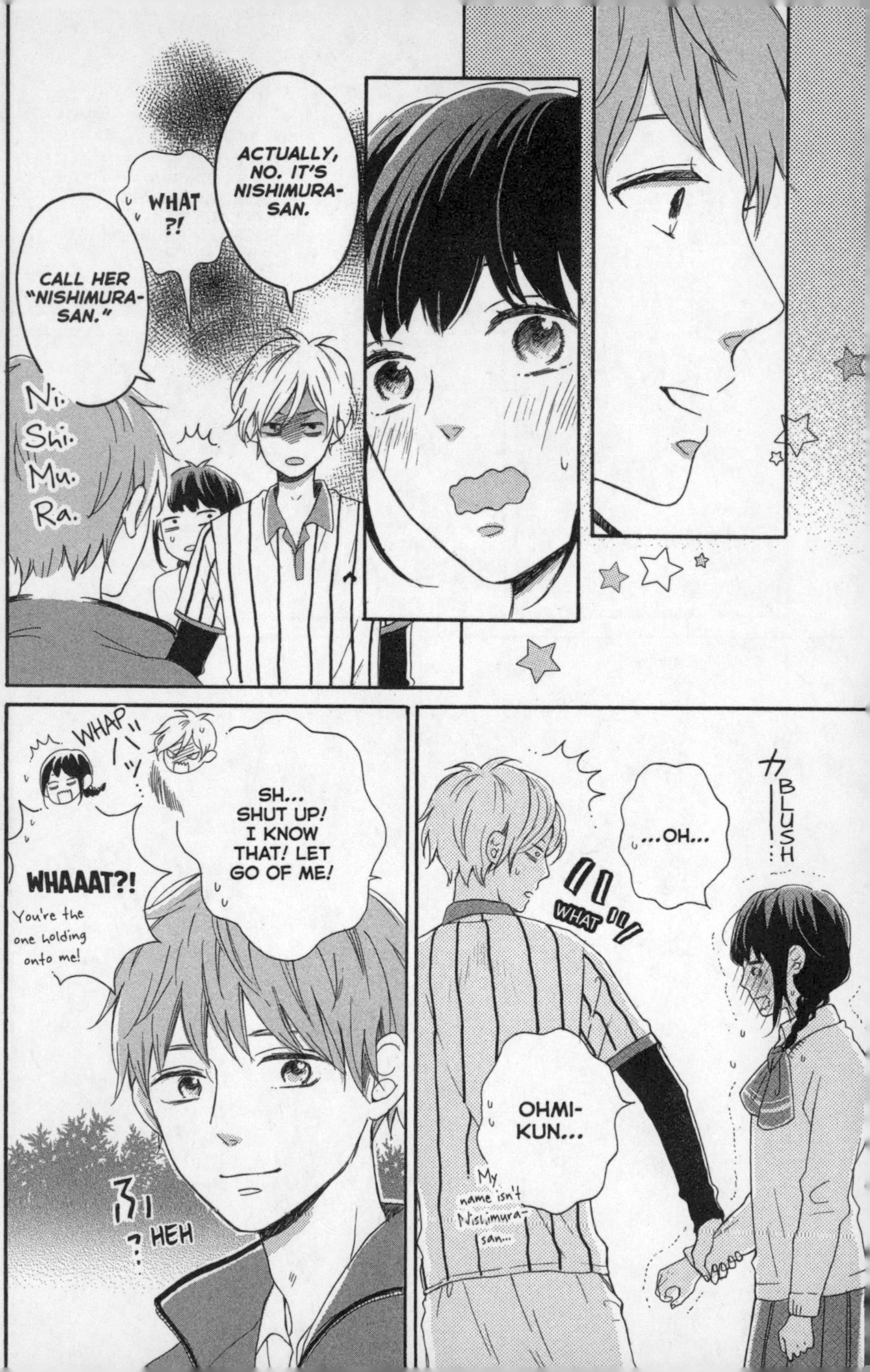
ACTUALLY, NO. IT'S NISHIMURA-SAN.
WHAT ?!
CALL HER "NISHIMURA-SAN."
Ni. Shi. Mu. Ra.
BLUSH
...OH...
WHAT
OHMI-KUN...
My name isn't Nishimura-san...
WHAP
SH... SHUT UP! I KNOW THAT! LET GO OF ME!
WHAAAT?!
You're the one holding onto me!
HEH

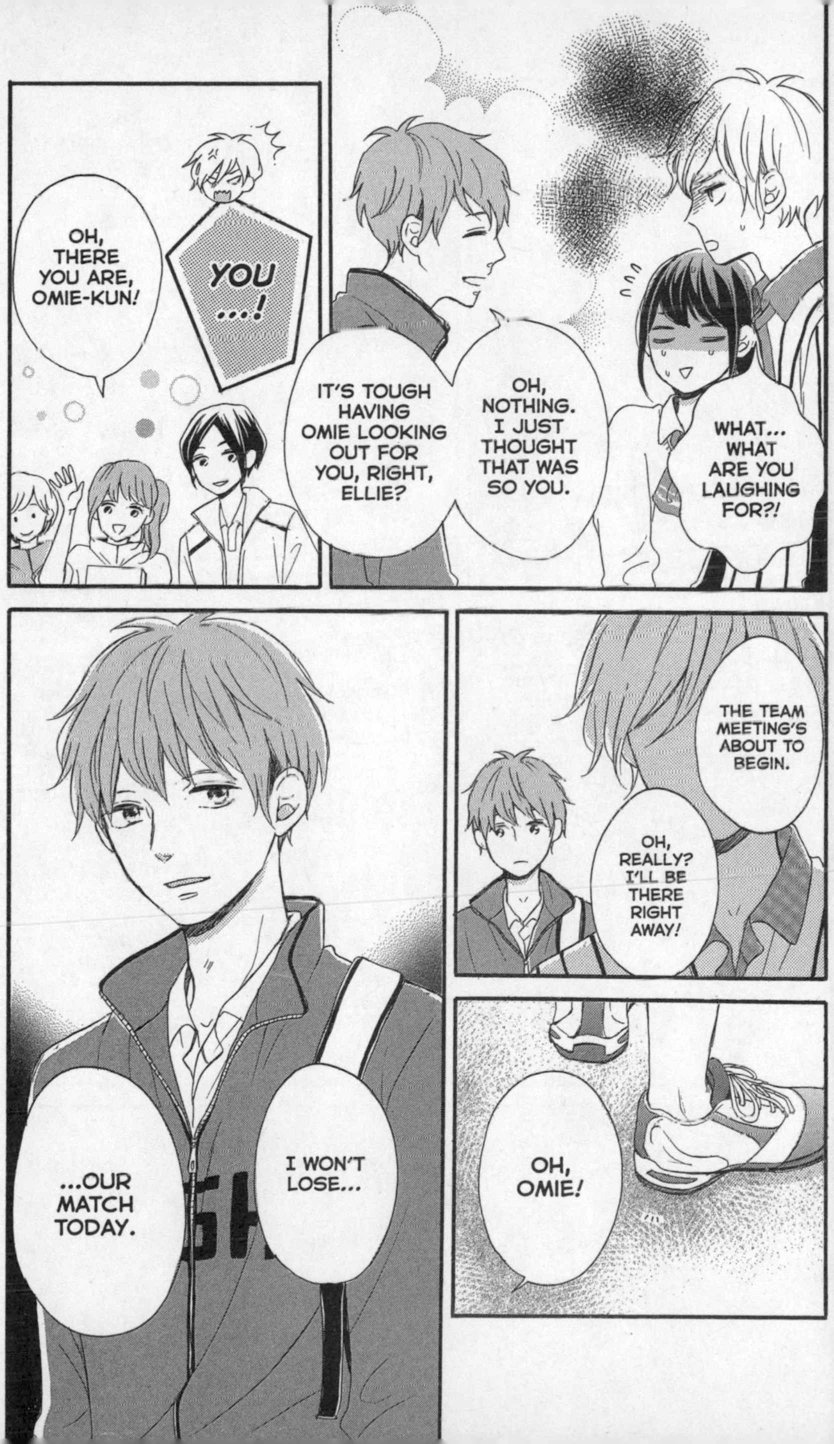
WHAT... WHAT ARE YOU LAUGHING FOR?!
OH, NOTHING. I JUST THOUGHT THAT WAS SO YOU.
IT'S TOUGH HAVING OMIE LOOKING OUT FOR YOU, RIGHT, ELLIE?
YOU ...!
OH, THERE YOU ARE, OMIE-KUN!
THE TEAM MEETING'S ABOUT TO BEGIN.
OH, REALLY? I'LL BE THERE RIGHT AWAY!
OH, OMIE!
I WON'T LOSE...
...OUR MATCH TODAY.

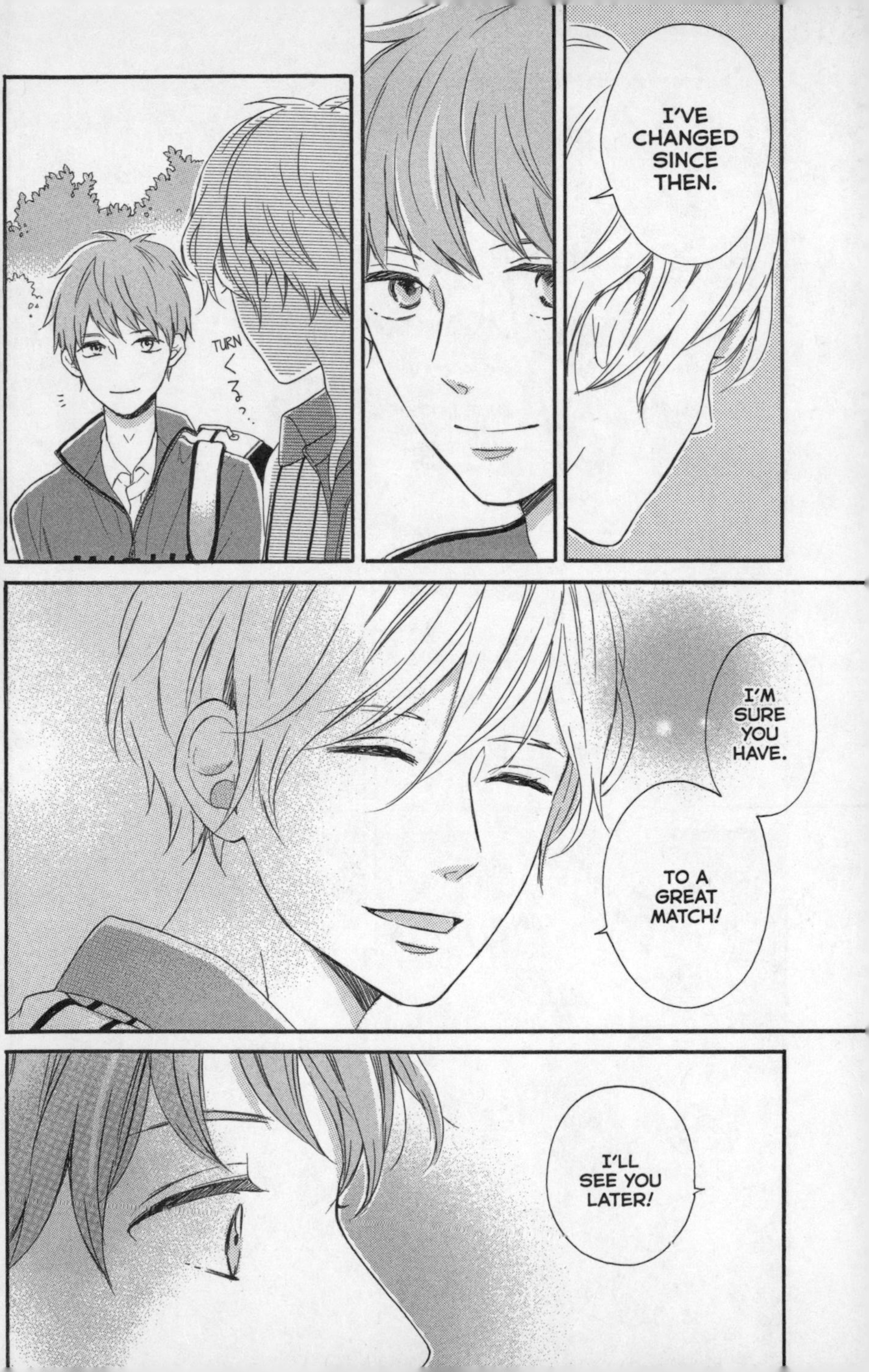
I'VE CHANGED SINCE THEN.
TURN
くるっ
I'M SURE YOU HAVE.
TO A GREAT MATCH!
I'LL SEE YOU LATER!

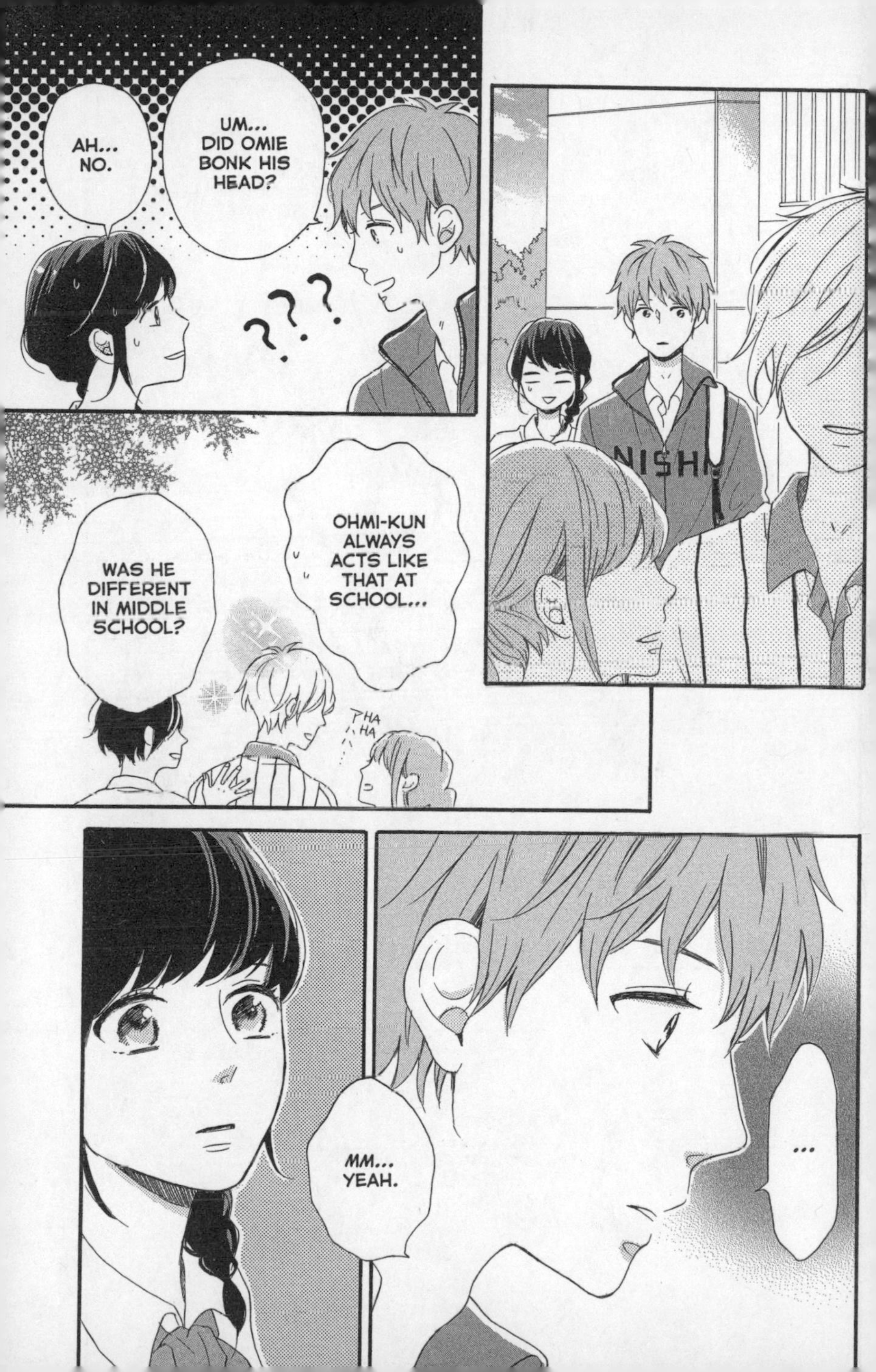
UM... DID OMIE BONK HIS HEAD?
AH... NO.
OHMI-KUN ALWAYS ACTS LIKE THAT AT SCHOOL...
WAS HE DIFFERENT IN MIDDLE SCHOOL?
HA HA
...
MM... YEAH.

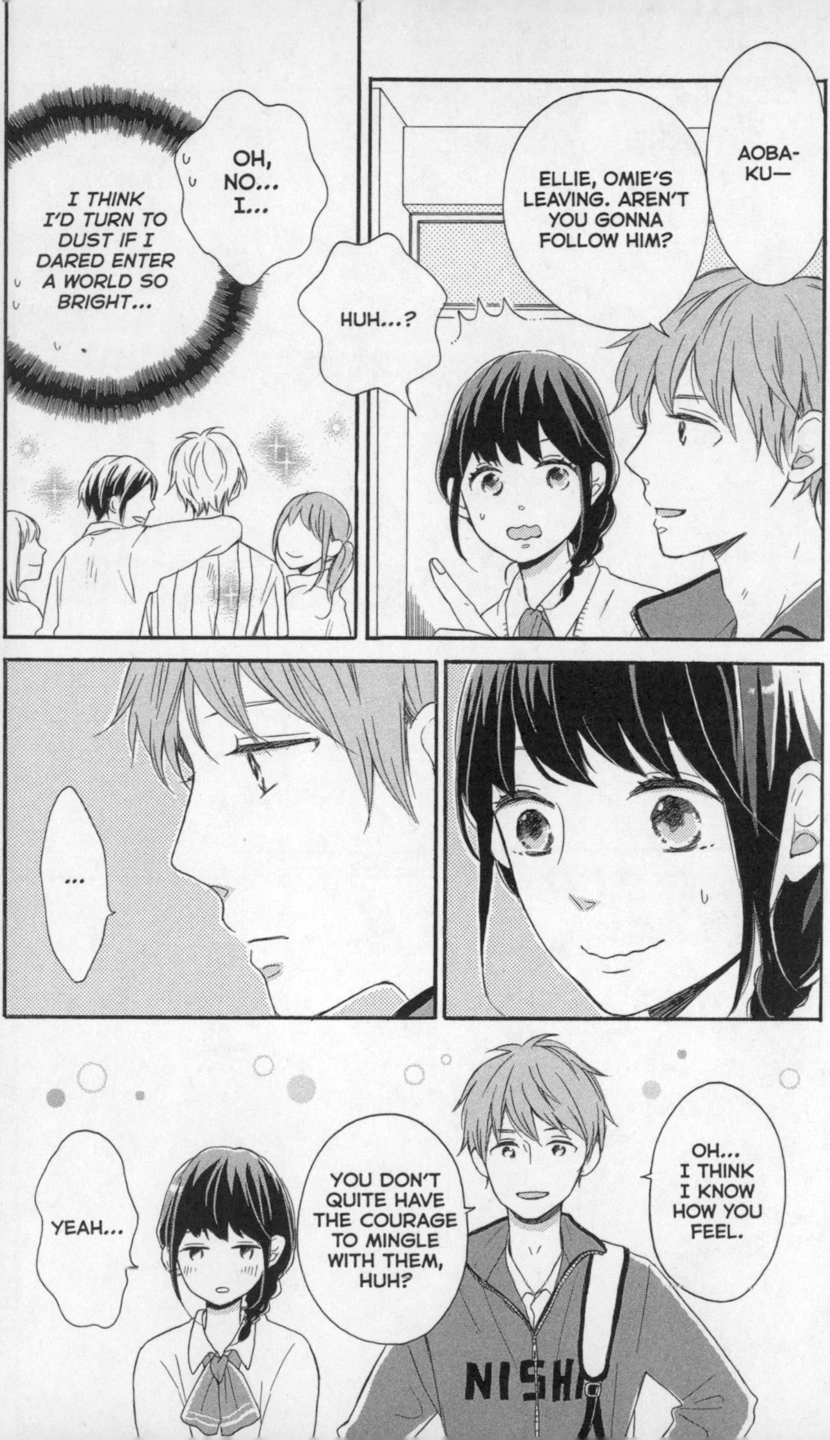
AOBA-KU—
ELLIE, OMIE'S LEAVING. AREN'T YOU GONNA FOLLOW HIM?
HUH...?
OH, NO... I...
I THINK I'D TURN TO DUST IF I DARED ENTER A WORLD SO BRIGHT...
...
OH... I THINK I KNOW HOW YOU FEEL.
YOU DON'T QUITE HAVE THE COURAGE TO MINGLE WITH THEM, HUH?
YEAH...
NISHI

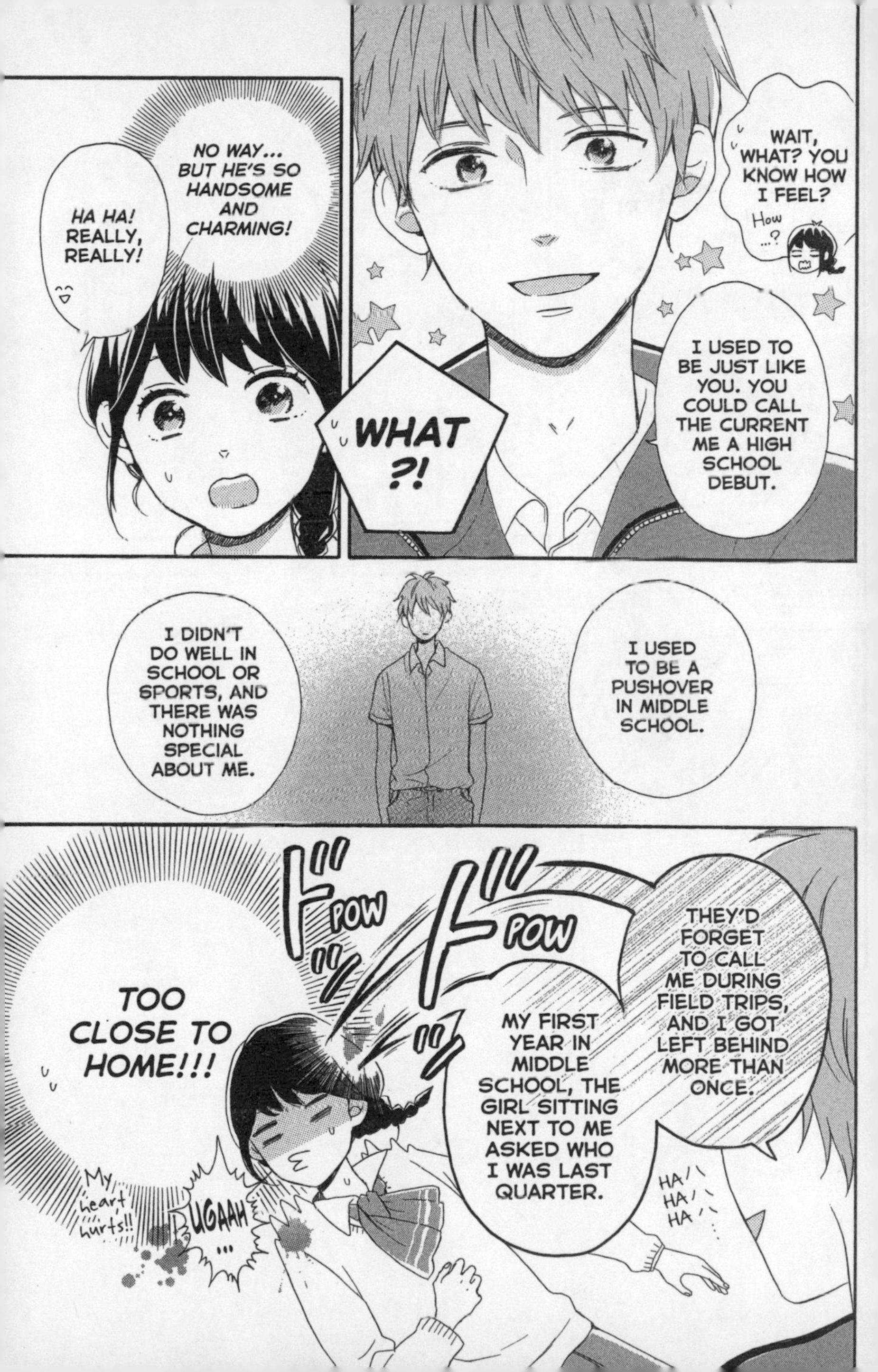
WAIT, WHAT? YOU KNOW HOW I FEEL?
How ...?
I USED TO BE JUST LIKE YOU. YOU COULD CALL THE CURRENT ME A HIGH SCHOOL DEBUT.
WHAT ?!
NO WAY... BUT HE'S SO HANDSOME AND CHARMING!
HA HA! REALLY, REALLY!
I USED TO BE A PUSHOVER IN MIDDLE SCHOOL.
I DIDN'T DO WELL IN SCHOOL OR SPORTS, AND THERE WAS NOTHING SPECIAL ABOUT ME.
THEY'D FORGET TO CALL ME DURING FIELD TRIPS, AND I GOT LEFT BEHIND MORE THAN ONCE.
MY FIRST YEAR IN MIDDLE SCHOOL, THE GIRL SITTING NEXT TO ME ASKED WHO I WAS LAST QUARTER.
HA HA HA
POW
POW
TOO CLOSE TO HOME!!!
UGAAH ...
My heart hurts!!

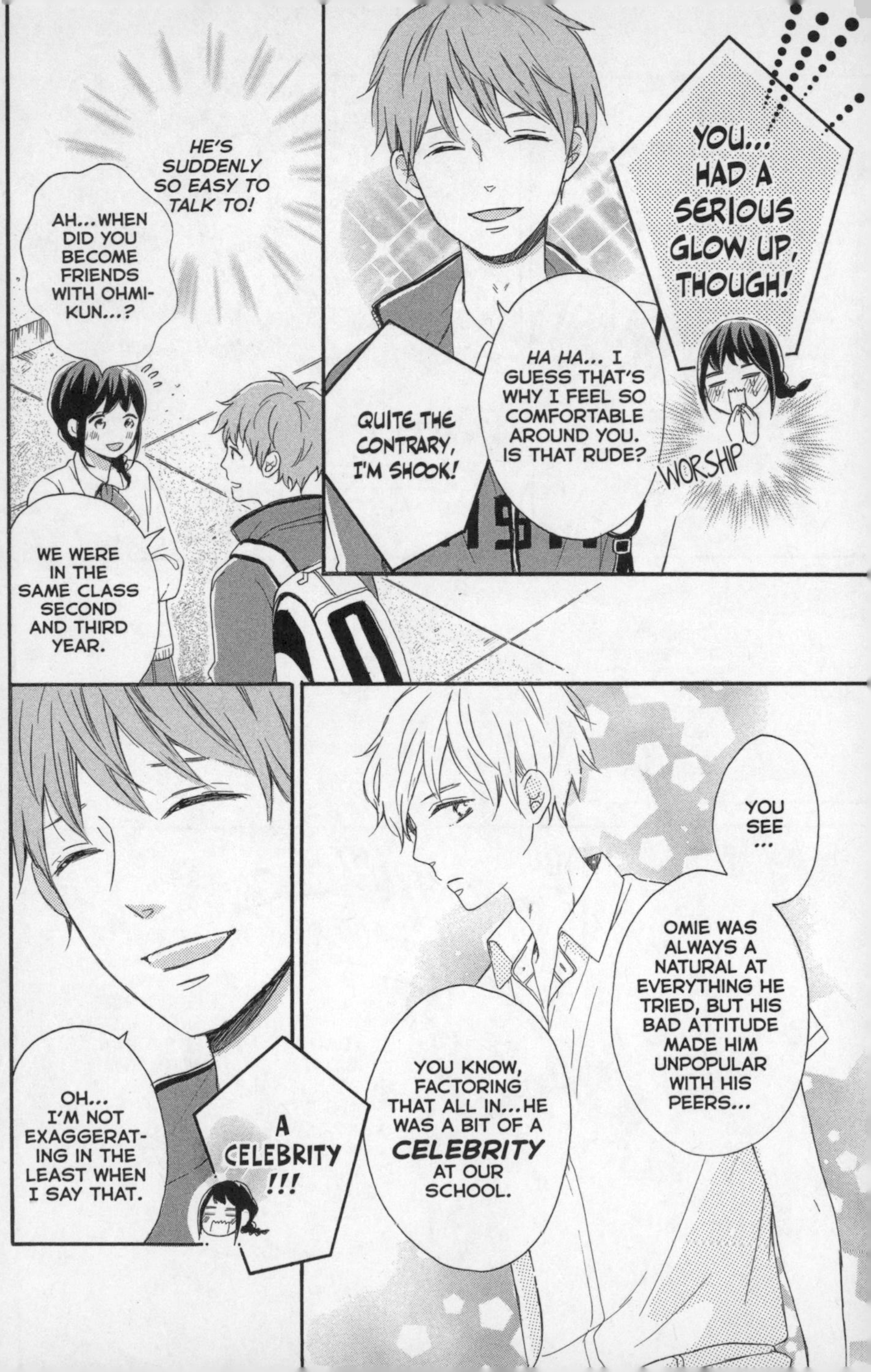
YOU... HAD A SERIOUS GLOW UP, THOUGH!
HA HA... I GUESS THAT'S WHY I FEEL SO COMFORTABLE AROUND YOU. IS THAT RUDE?
QUITE THE CONTRARY, I'M SHOOK!
WORSHIP
HE'S SUDDENLY SO EASY TO TALK TO!
AH...WHEN DID YOU BECOME FRIENDS WITH OHMI-KUN...?
WE WERE IN THE SAME CLASS SECOND AND THIRD YEAR.
YOU SEE...
OMIE WAS ALWAYS A NATURAL AT EVERYTHING HE TRIED, BUT HIS BAD ATTITUDE MADE HIM UNPOPULAR WITH HIS PEERS...
YOU KNOW, FACTORING THAT ALL IN...HE WAS A BIT OF A CELEBRITY AT OUR SCHOOL.
A CELEBRITY!!!
OH... I'M NOT EXAGGERATING IN THE LEAST WHEN I SAY THAT.

HE WAS PURPOSELY AWFUL TO GIRLS WHO TRIED TO TALK TO HIM, JUST TO MAKE THEM HATE HIM.
GET OUT OF MY WAY. YOU'RE ANNOYING.
EEEK
HE WAS GOOD ENOUGH AT TENNIS TO QUALIFY FOR THE REGIONALS, AND HE STILL QUIT JUST BECAUSE HE COULD.
I'M SICK OF THIS.
Bye.
What?!
WHETHER HE WAS A FREE SPIRIT...
...OR JUST A CONTRARIAN...
Ha ha ha.
HE TALKS ABOUT OHMI-KUN SO FONDLY...
...I REALLY...
...HAVE NO IDEA WHY HE DECIDED I, OF ALL PEOPLE, SHOULD BE HIS FRIEND.

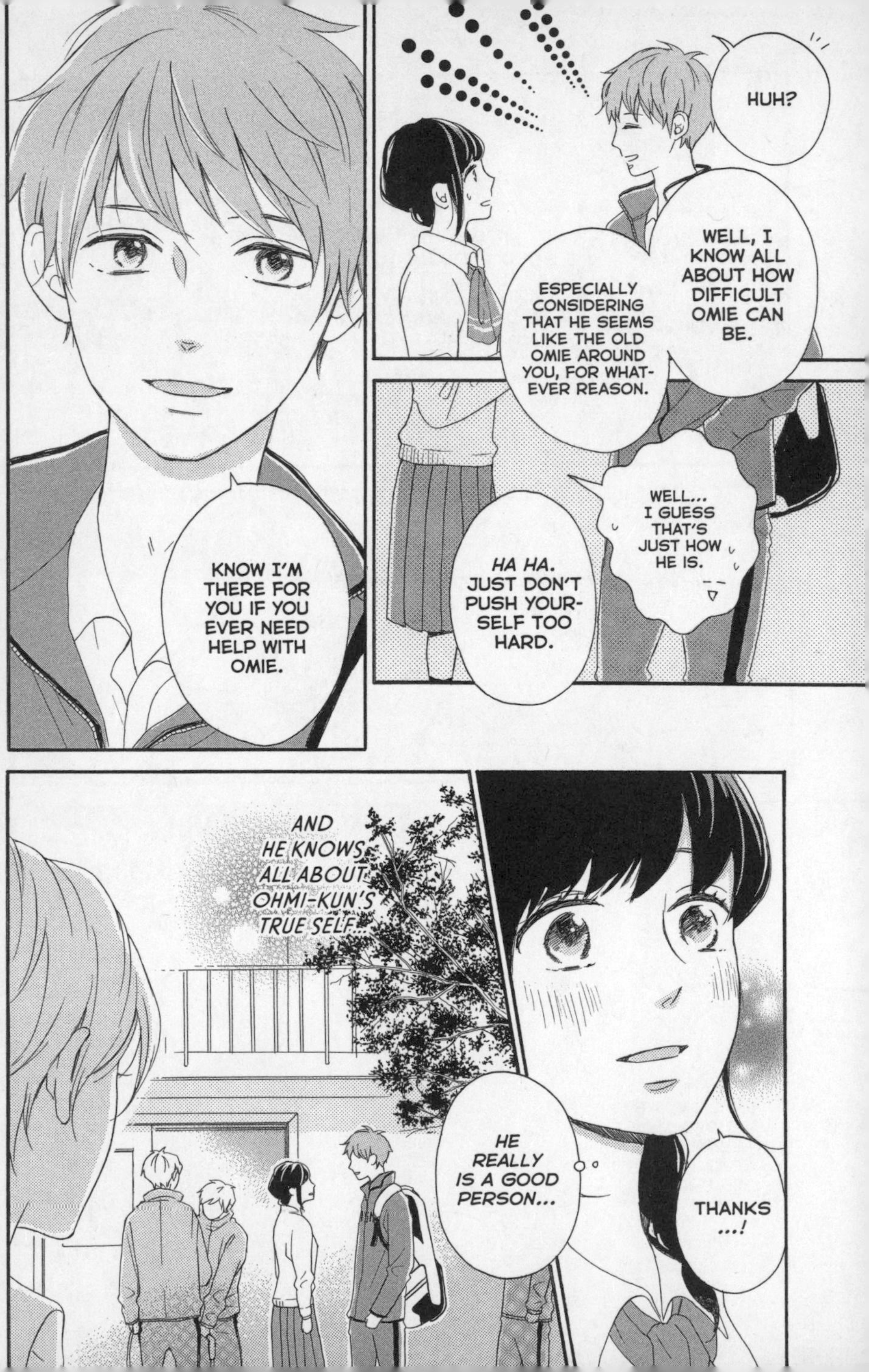
HUH?
WELL, I KNOW ALL ABOUT HOW DIFFICULT OMIE CAN BE.
ESPECIALLY CONSIDERING THAT HE SEEMS LIKE THE OLD OMIE AROUND YOU, FOR WHAT-EVER REASON.
WELL... I GUESS THAT'S JUST HOW HE IS.
HA HA. JUST DON'T PUSH YOUR-SELF TOO HARD.
KNOW I'M THERE FOR YOU IF YOU EVER NEED HELP WITH OMIE.
THANKS ...!
HE REALLY IS A GOOD PERSON...
AND HE KNOWS ALL ABOUT OHMI-KUN'S TRUE SELF...

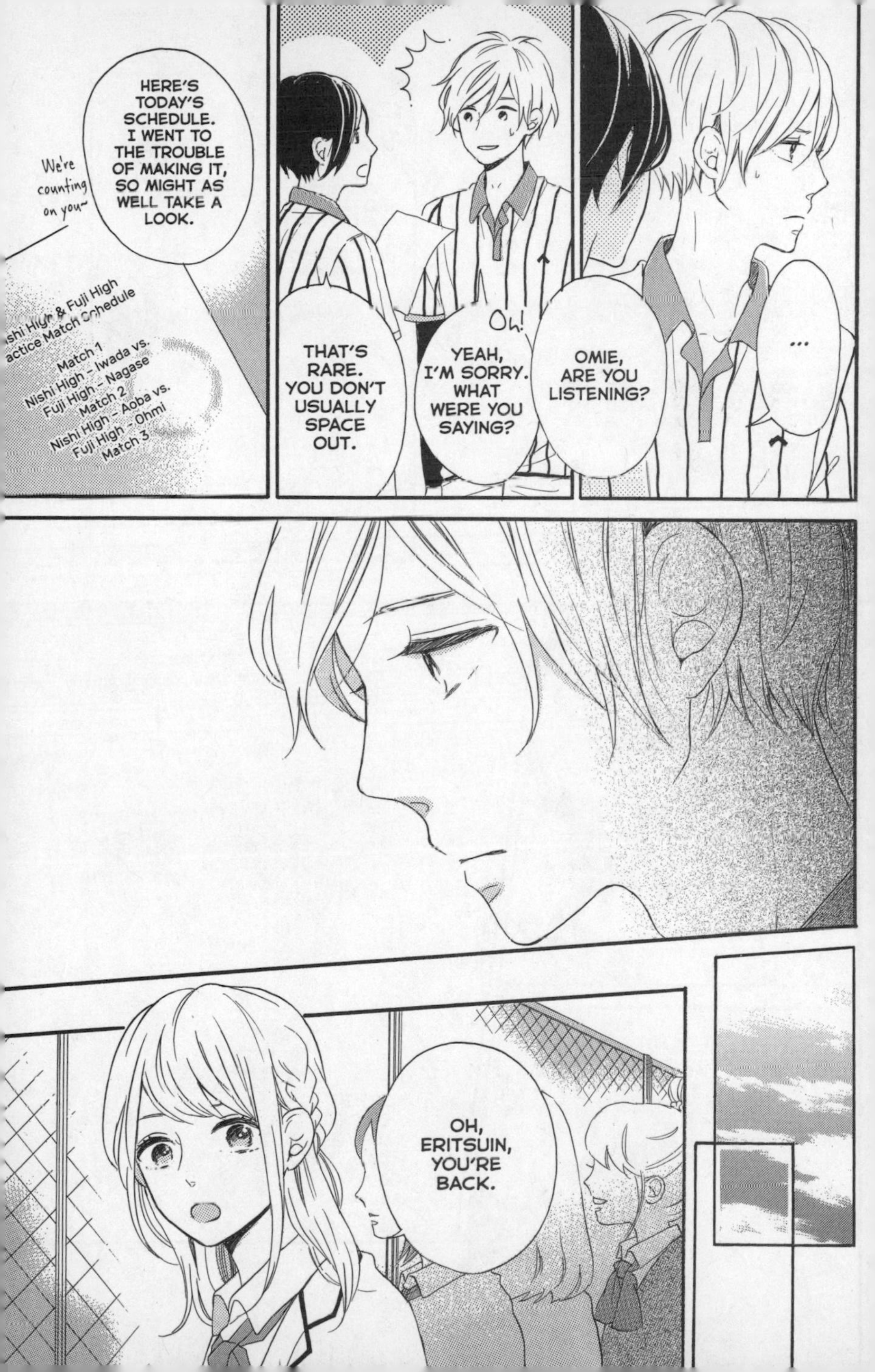
...
OMIE, ARE YOU LISTENING?
Oh!
YEAH, I'M SORRY. WHAT WERE YOU SAYING?
THAT'S RARE. YOU DON'T USUALLY SPACE OUT.
HERE'S TODAY'S SCHEDULE. I WENT TO THE TROUBLE OF MAKING IT, SO MIGHT AS WELL TAKE A LOOK.
We're counting on you~
ishi High & Fuji High
actice Match Schedule
Match 1
Nishi High - Iwada vs.
Fuji High - Nagase
Match 2
Nishi High - Aoba vs.
Fuji High - Ohmi
Match 3
OH, ERITSUIN, YOU'RE BACK.

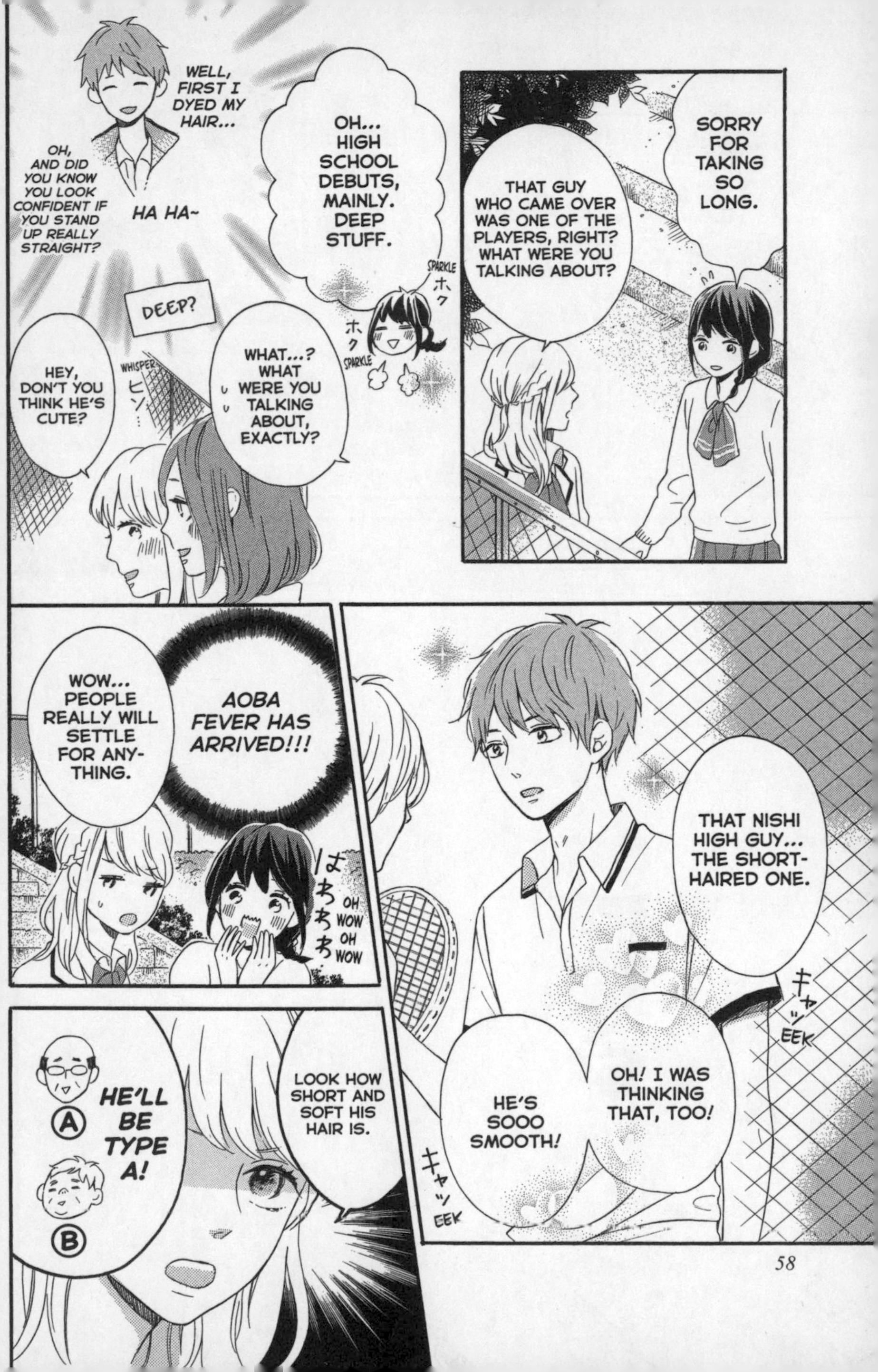
SORRY FOR TAKING SO LONG.
THAT GUY WHO CAME OVER WAS ONE OF THE PLAYERS, RIGHT? WHAT WERE YOU TALKING ABOUT?
OH... HIGH SCHOOL DEBUTS, MAINLY. DEEP STUFF.
SPARKLE ホク
ホク SPARKLE
WELL, FIRST I DYED MY HAIR...
OH, AND DID YOU KNOW YOU LOOK CONFIDENT IF YOU STAND UP REALLY STRAIGHT?
HA HA~
DEEP?
WHAT...? WHAT WERE YOU TALKING ABOUT, EXACTLY?
WHISPER ヒソ…
HEY, DON'T YOU THINK HE'S CUTE?
THAT NISHI HIGH GUY... THE SHORT-HAIRED ONE.
キャッ EEK
OH! I WAS THINKING THAT, TOO!
HE'S SOOO SMOOTH!
キャッ EEK
AOBA FEVER HAS ARRIVED!!!
WOW... PEOPLE REALLY WILL SETTLE FOR ANY-THING.
はわわわ OH WOW OH WOW
LOOK HOW SHORT AND SOFT HIS HAIR IS.
HE'LL BE TYPE A!
A
B

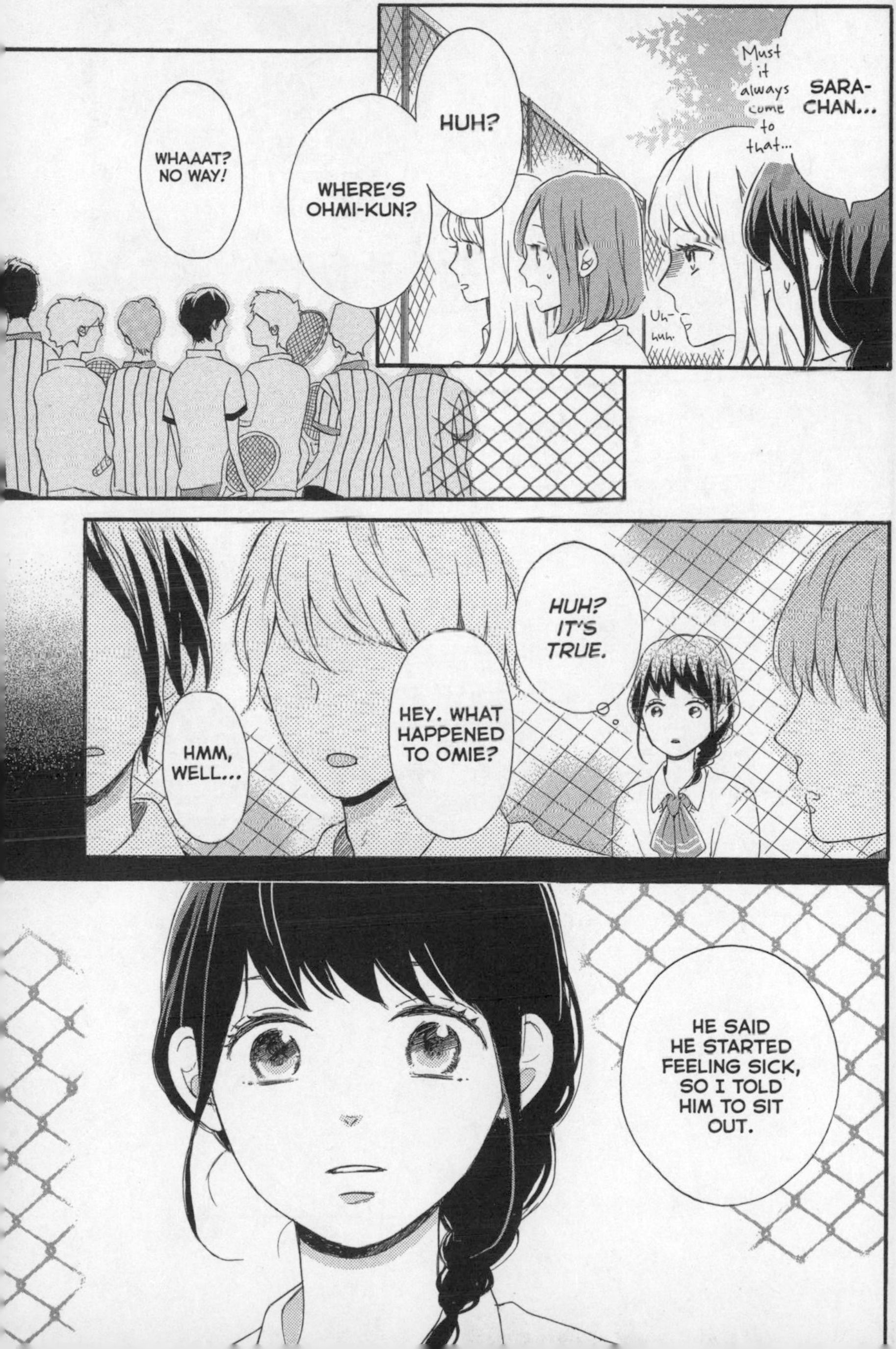
SARA-CHAN...
Must it always come to that...
Uh-huh.
HUH?
WHERE'S OHMI-KUN?
WHAAAT? NO WAY!
HUH? IT'S TRUE.
HEY. WHAT HAPPENED TO OMIE?
HMM, WELL...
HE SAID HE STARTED FEELING SICK, SO I TOLD HIM TO SIT OUT.

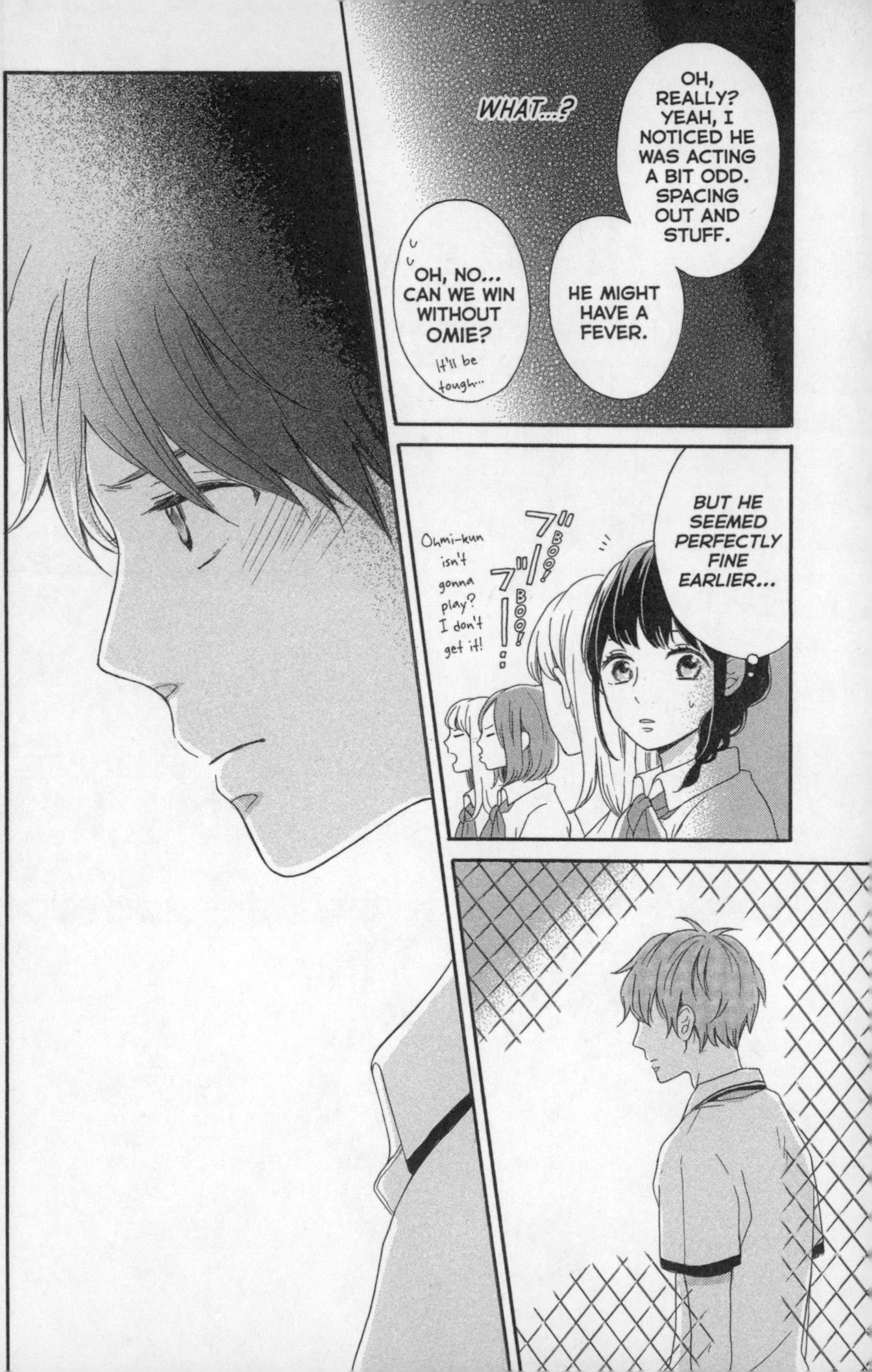
OH, REALLY? YEAH, I NOTICED HE WAS ACTING A BIT ODD. SPACING OUT AND STUFF.
WHAT...?
HE MIGHT HAVE A FEVER.
OH, NO... CAN WE WIN WITHOUT OMIE?
It'll be tough...
BUT HE SEEMED PERFECTLY FINE EARLIER...
BOO! BOO!
Ohmi-kun isn't gonna play? I don't get it!

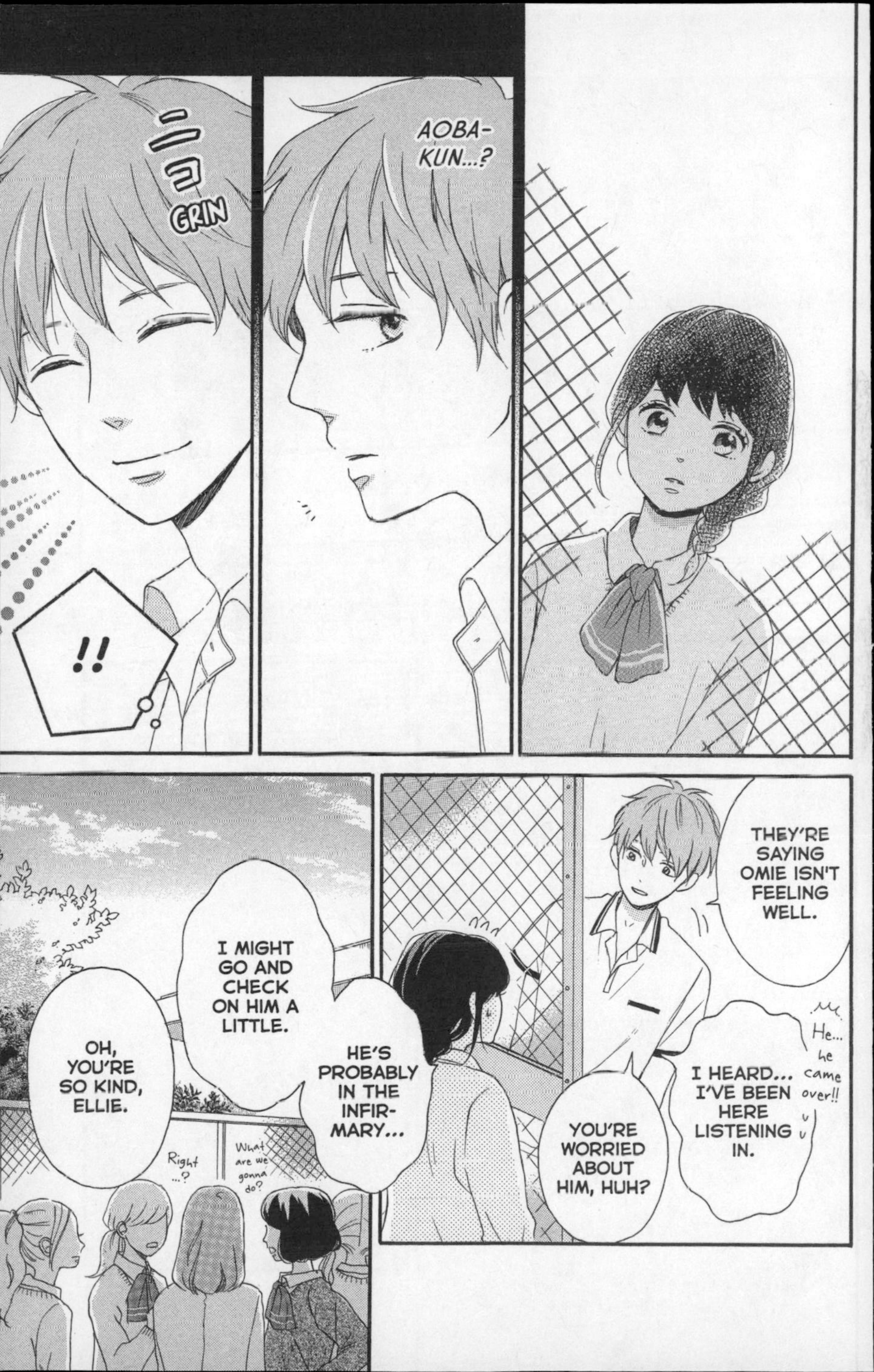
AOBA-KUN...?
ニコ
GRIN
!!
THEY'RE SAYING OMIE ISN'T FEELING WELL.
I HEARD... I'VE BEEN HERE LISTENING IN.
He... he came over!!
YOU'RE WORRIED ABOUT HIM, HUH?
HE'S PROBABLY IN THE INFIRMARY...
I MIGHT GO AND CHECK ON HIM A LITTLE.
OH, YOU'RE SO KIND, ELLIE.
What are we gonna do?
Right ...?

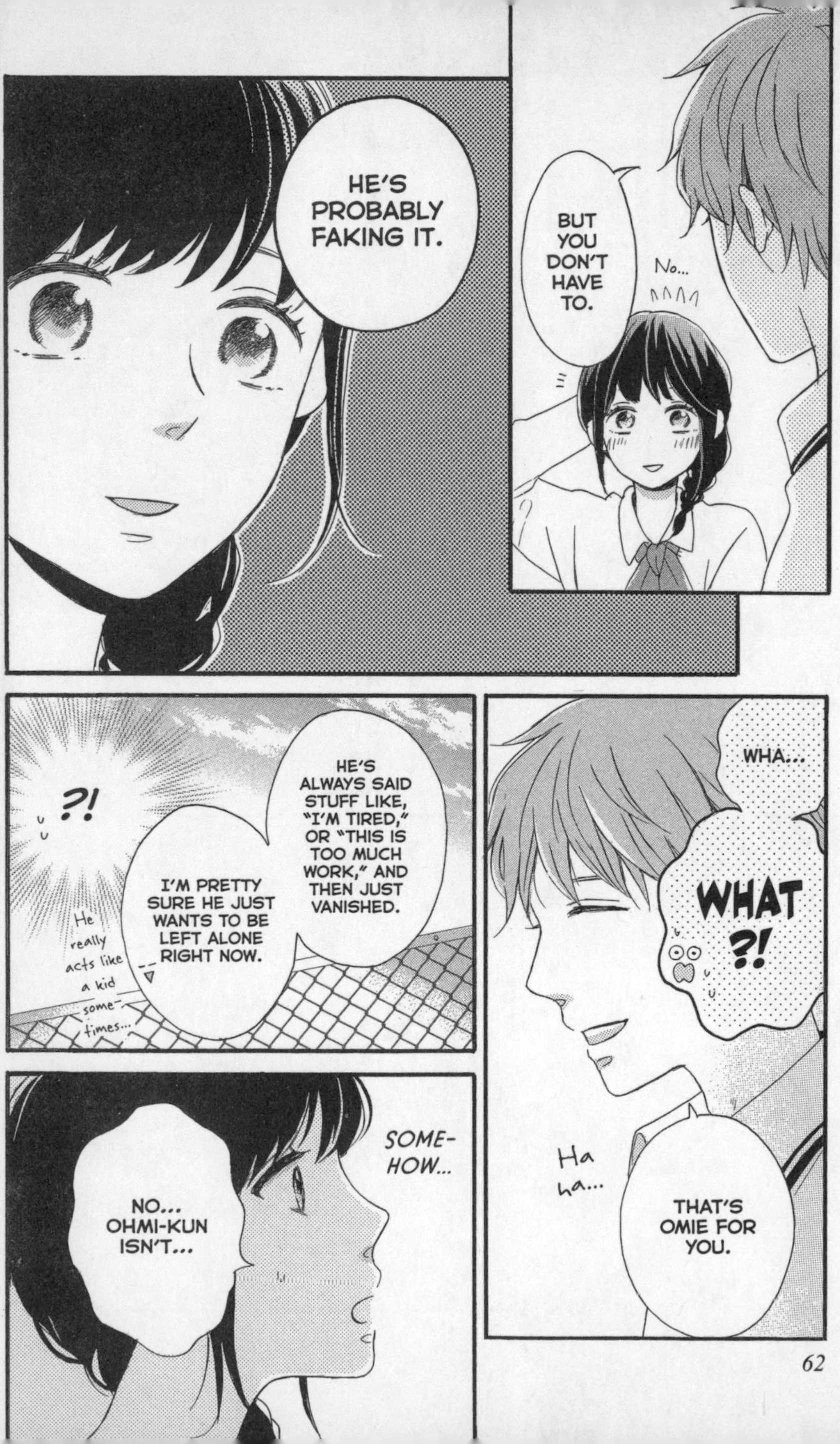

BUT YOU DON'T HAVE TO.
No...
HE'S PROBABLY FAKING IT.
WHA...
WHAT?!
Ha ha...
THAT'S OMIE FOR YOU.
HE'S ALWAYS SAID STUFF LIKE, "I'M TIRED," OR "THIS IS TOO MUCH WORK," AND THEN JUST VANISHED.
I'M PRETTY SURE HE JUST WANTS TO BE LEFT ALONE RIGHT NOW.
?!
He really acts like a kid some-times...
SOME-HOW...
NO... OHMI-KUN ISN'T...

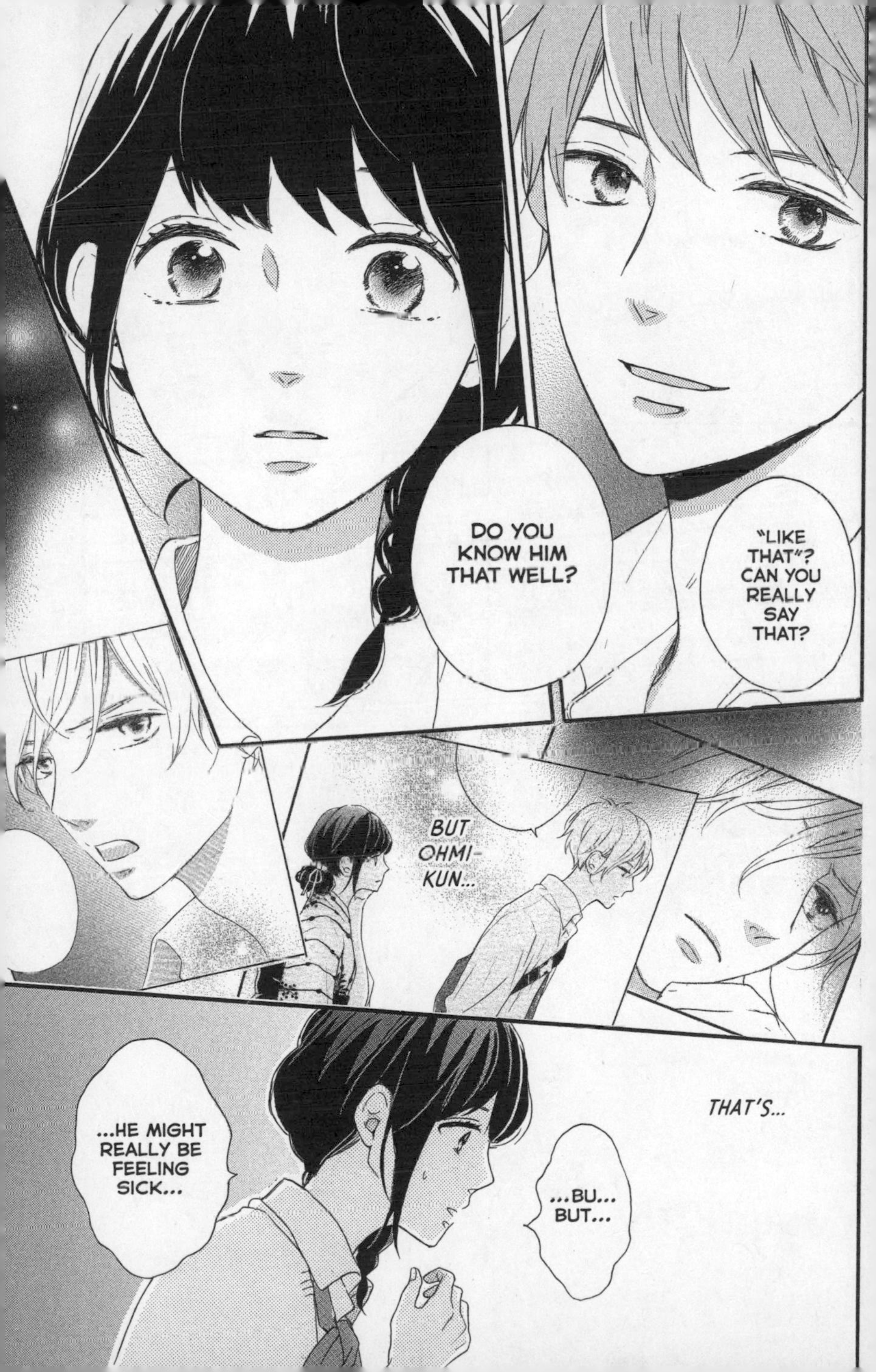
"LIKE THAT"? CAN YOU REALLY SAY THAT?
DO YOU KNOW HIM THAT WELL?
BUT OHMI-KUN...
THAT'S...
...BU... BUT...
...HE MIGHT REALLY BE FEELING SICK...

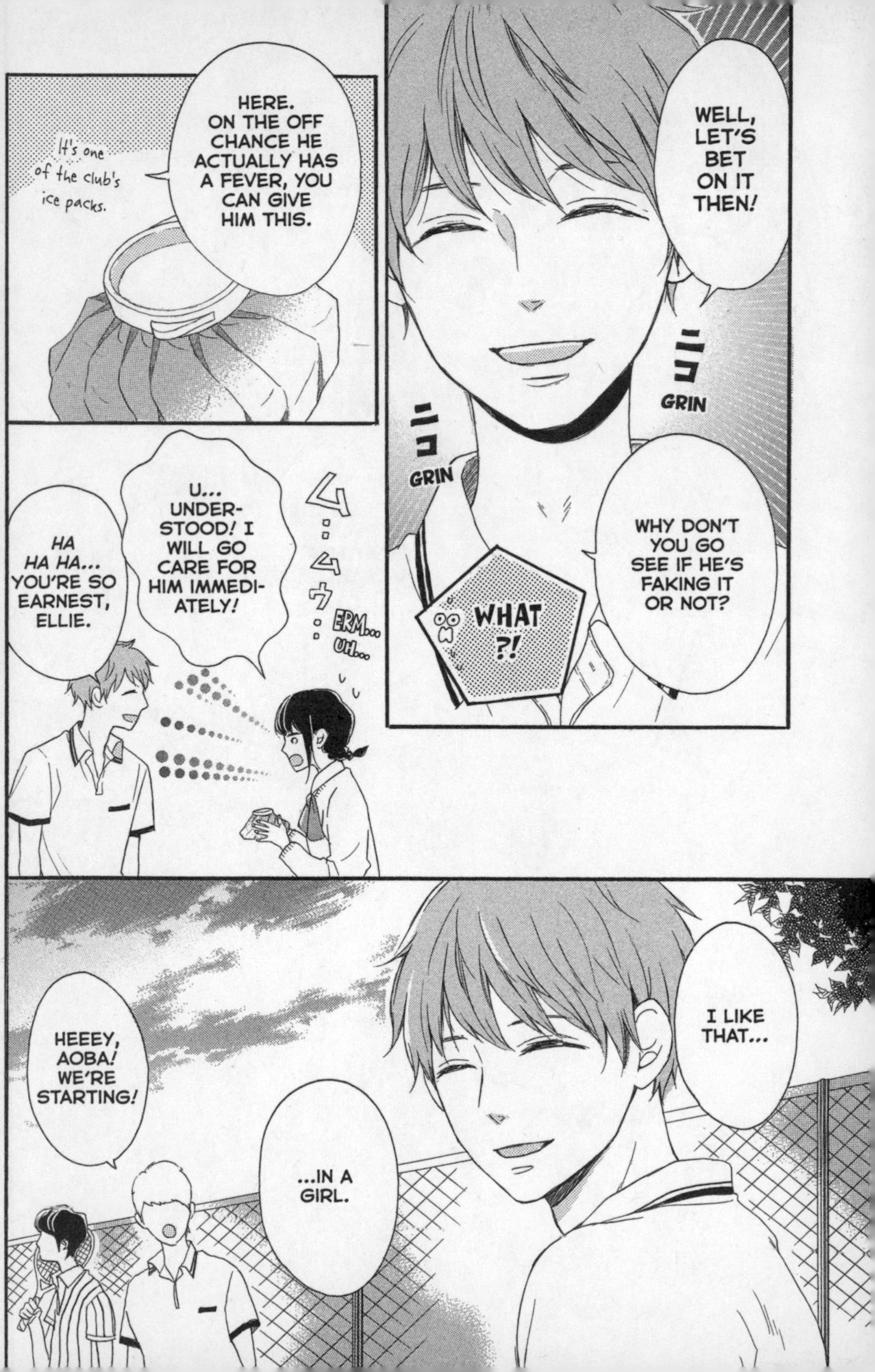
WELL, LET'S BET ON IT THEN!
ニコ GRIN
ニコ GRIN
WHY DON'T YOU GO SEE IF HE'S FAKING IT OR NOT?
WHAT ?!
HERE. ON THE OFF CHANCE HE ACTUALLY HAS A FEVER, YOU CAN GIVE HIM THIS.
It's one of the club's ice packs.
ム…ムウ… ERM... UH...
U... UNDERSTOOD! I WILL GO CARE FOR HIM IMMEDIATELY!
HA HA HA... YOU'RE SO EARNEST, ELLIE.
I LIKE THAT...
...IN A GIRL.
HEEEY, AOBA! WE'RE STARTING!

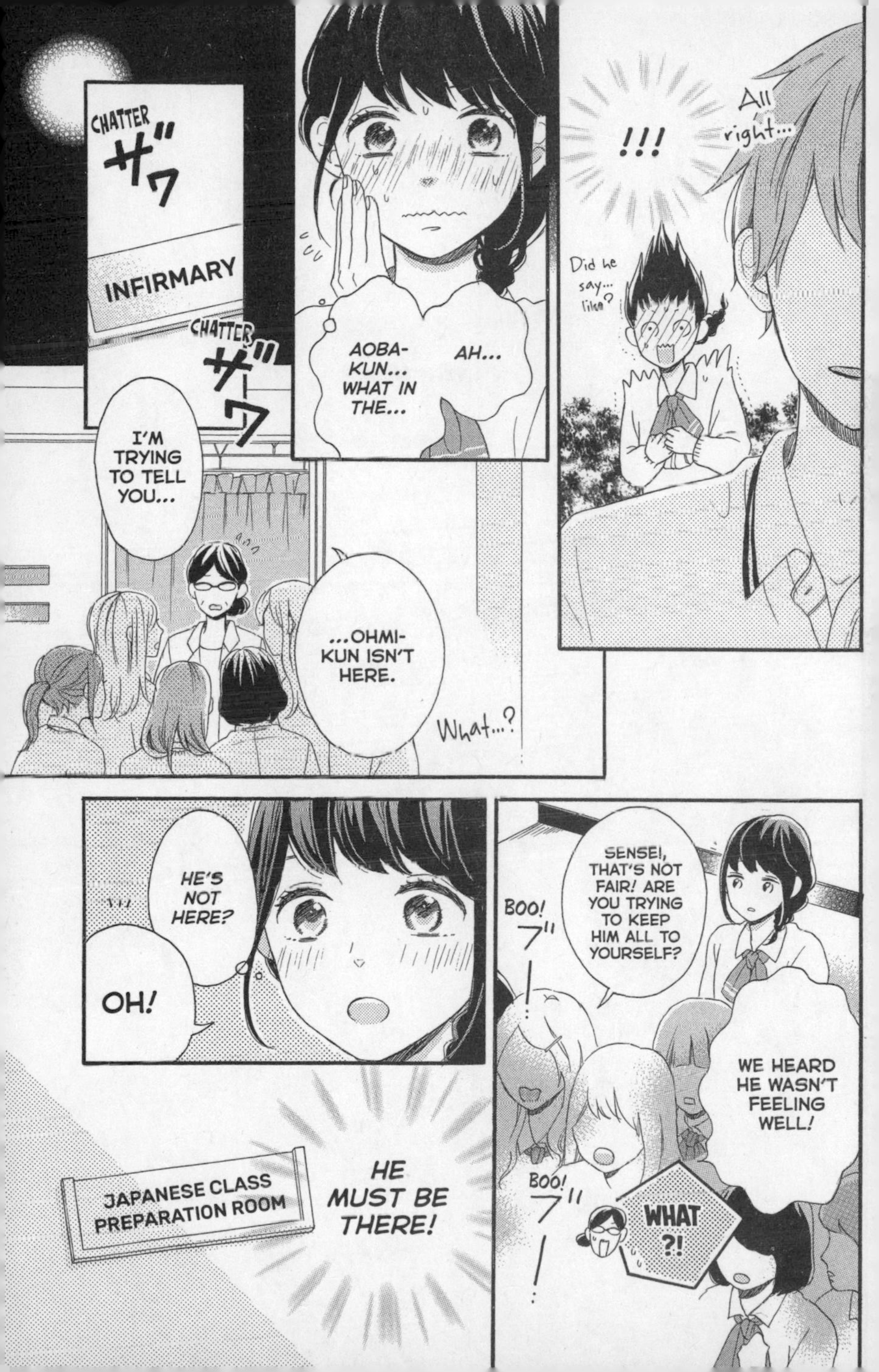
All right...
!!!
Did he say... like?
AOBA-KUN... WHAT IN THE...
AH...
CHATTER ザワ
INFIRMARY
CHATTER ザワ
I'M TRYING TO TELL YOU...
...OHMI-KUN ISN'T HERE.
What...?
SENSEI, THAT'S NOT FAIR! ARE YOU TRYING TO KEEP HIM ALL TO YOURSELF?
BOO! ブ!
WE HEARD HE WASN'T FEELING WELL!
BOO! ブ!
WHAT ?!
HE'S NOT HERE?
OH!
JAPANESE CLASS PREPARATION ROOM
HE MUST BE THERE!

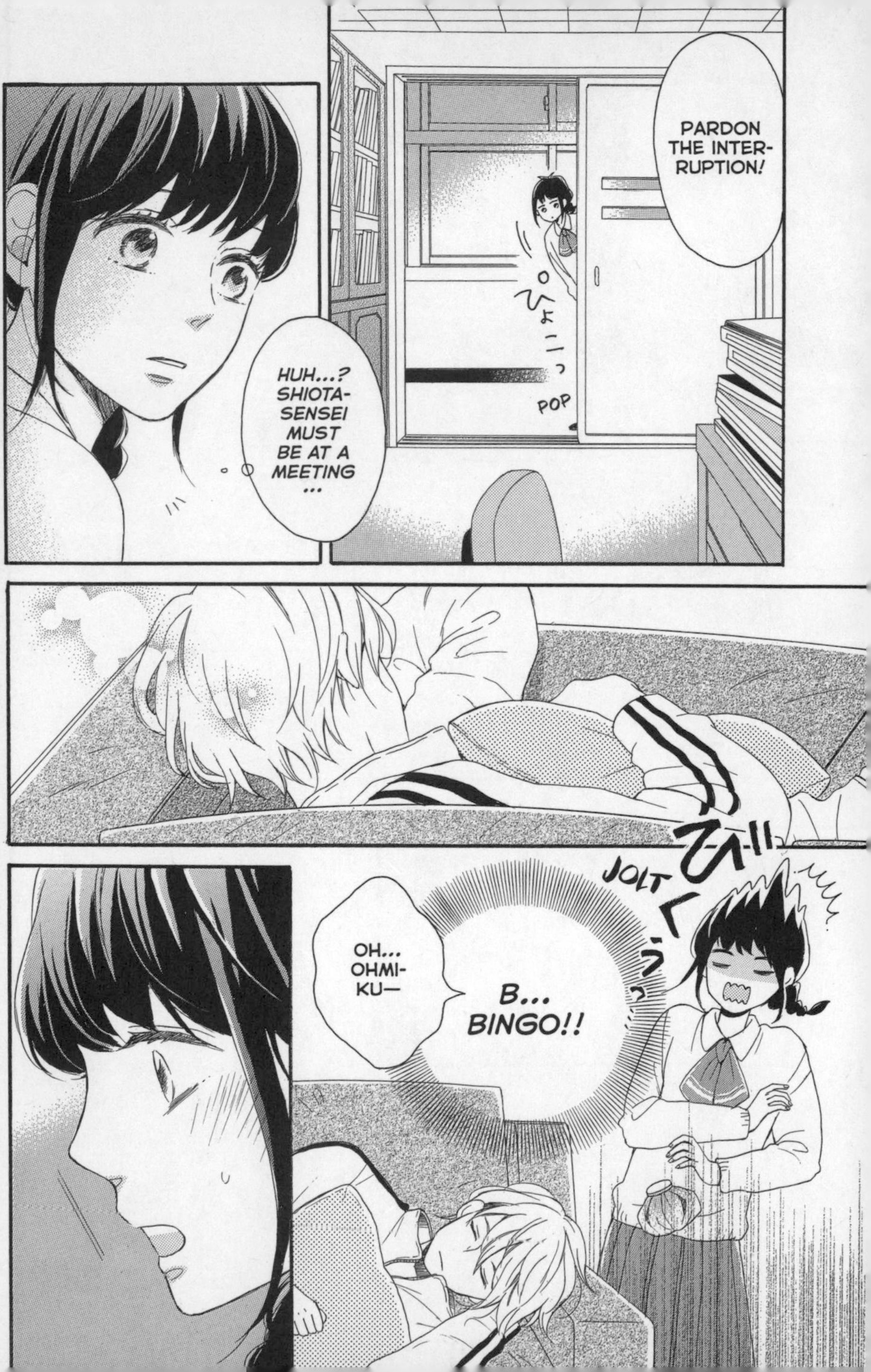
PARDON THE INTER-RUPTION!
POP
HUH...? SHIOTA-SENSEI MUST BE AT A MEETING ...
JOLT
B... BINGO!!
OH... OHMI-KU—

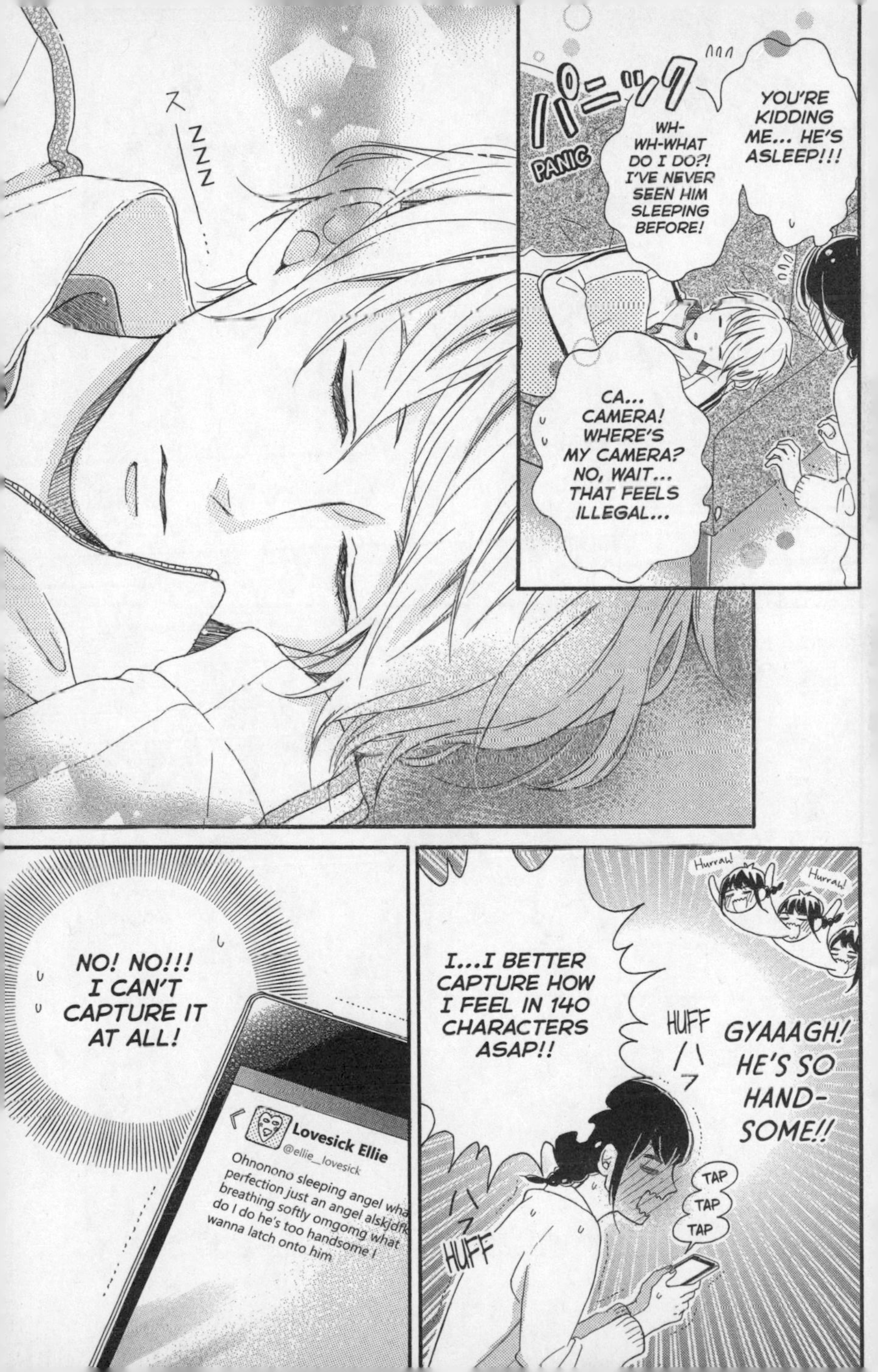
YOU'RE KIDDING ME... HE'S ASLEEP!!!
パニック
PANIC
WH- WH-WHAT DO I DO?! I'VE NEVER SEEN HIM SLEEPING BEFORE!
CA... CAMERA! WHERE'S MY CAMERA? NO, WAIT... THAT FEELS ILLEGAL...
ス
ZZZ
Hurrah!
Hurrah!
GYAAAGH! HE'S SO HAND-SOME!!
I...I BETTER CAPTURE HOW I FEEL IN 140 CHARACTERS ASAP!!
HUFF
TAP TAP TAP
HUFF
NO! NO!!! I CAN'T CAPTURE IT AT ALL!
Lovesick Ellie
@ellie__lovesick
Ohnonono sleeping angel what perfection just an angel alskjdfk breathing softly omgomg what do I do he's too handsome I wanna latch onto him

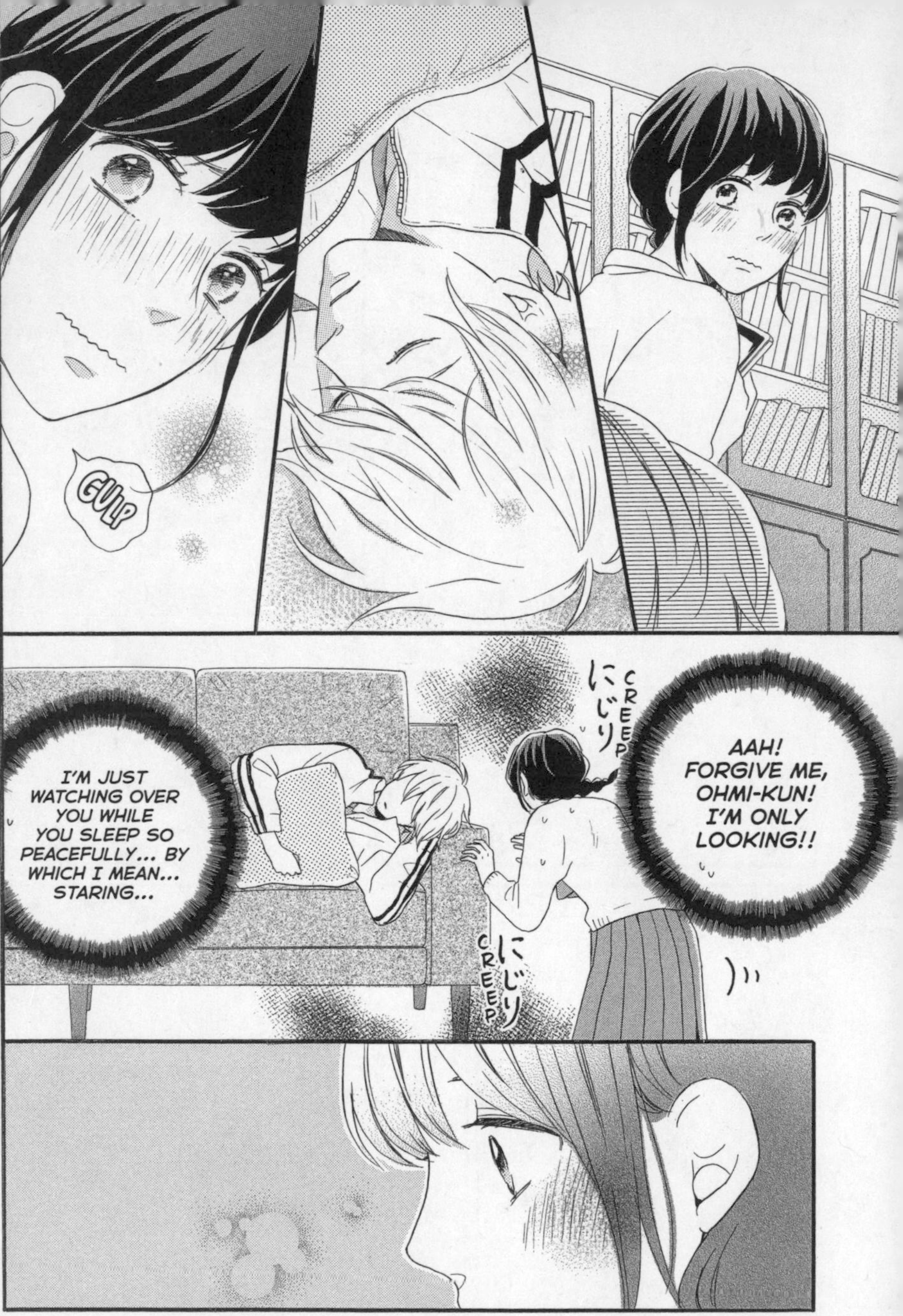
GULP
AAH! FORGIVE ME, OHMI-KUN! I'M ONLY LOOKING!!
にじり CREEP
I'M JUST WATCHING OVER YOU WHILE YOU SLEEP SO PEACEFULLY... BY WHICH I MEAN... STARING...
にじり CREEP

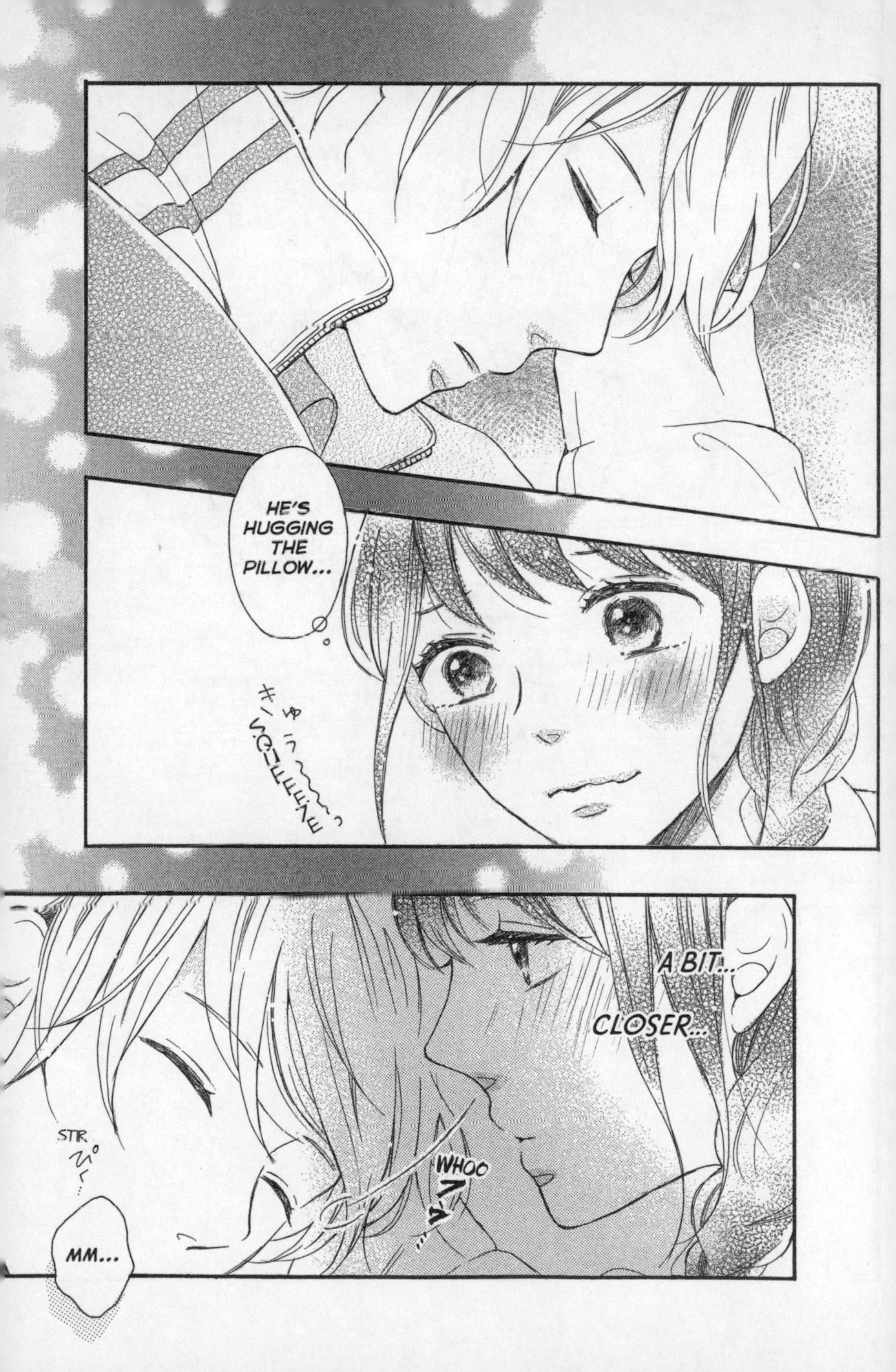
HE'S HUGGING THE PILLOW...
きゅう〜〜っ
SQUEEEEZE
A BIT...
CLOSER...
WHOO
STIR
MM...

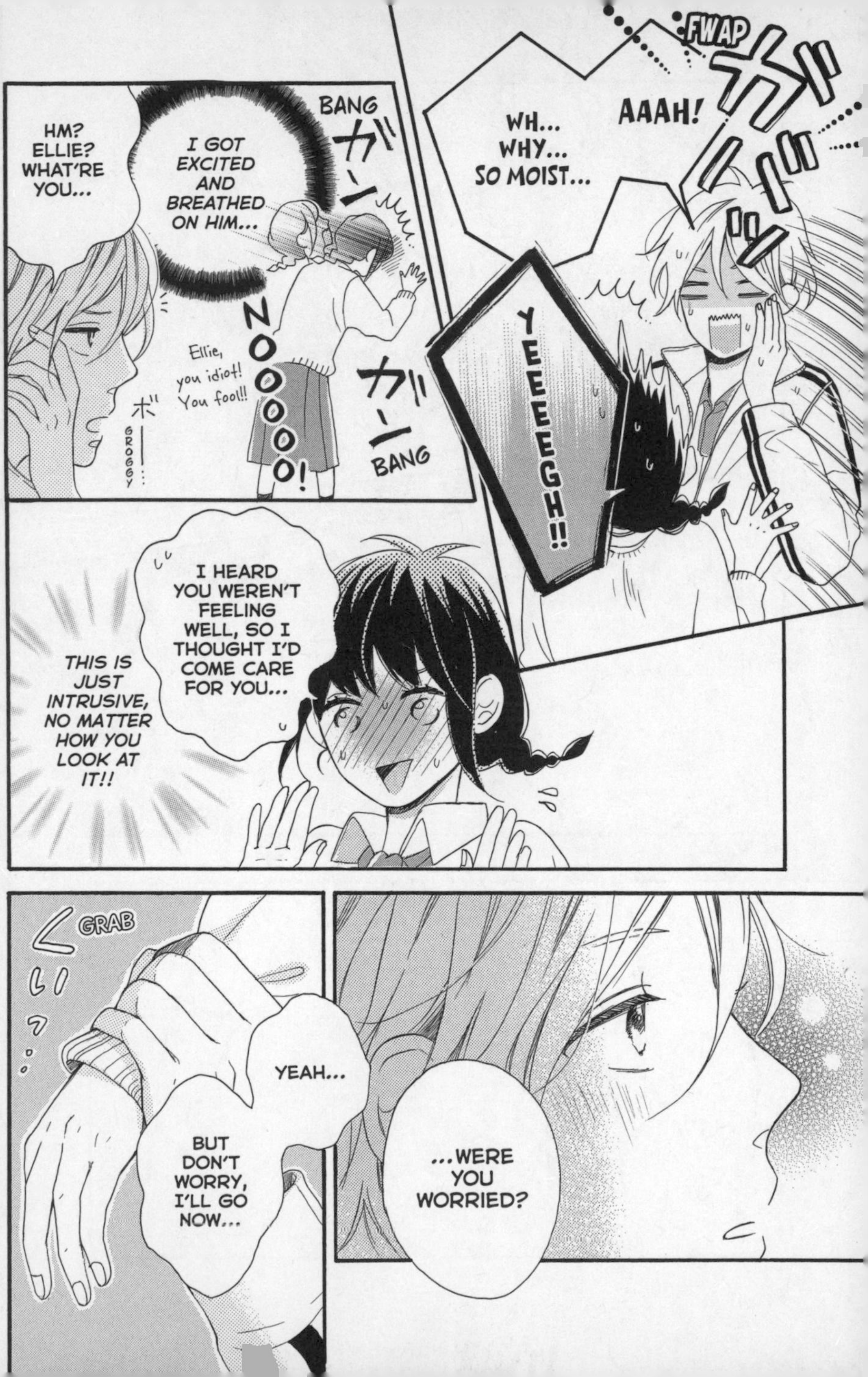

FWAP
AAAH!
WH... WHY... SO MOIST...
YEEEEEGH!!
HM? ELLIE? WHAT'RE YOU...
BANG
I GOT EXCITED AND BREATHED ON HIM...
NOOOOOO!
Ellie, you idiot! You fool!!
GROGGY
BANG
I HEARD YOU WEREN'T FEELING WELL, SO I THOUGHT I'D COME CARE FOR YOU...
THIS IS JUST INTRUSIVE, NO MATTER HOW YOU LOOK AT IT!!
...WERE YOU WORRIED?
GRAB
YEAH...
BUT DON'T WORRY, I'LL GO NOW...

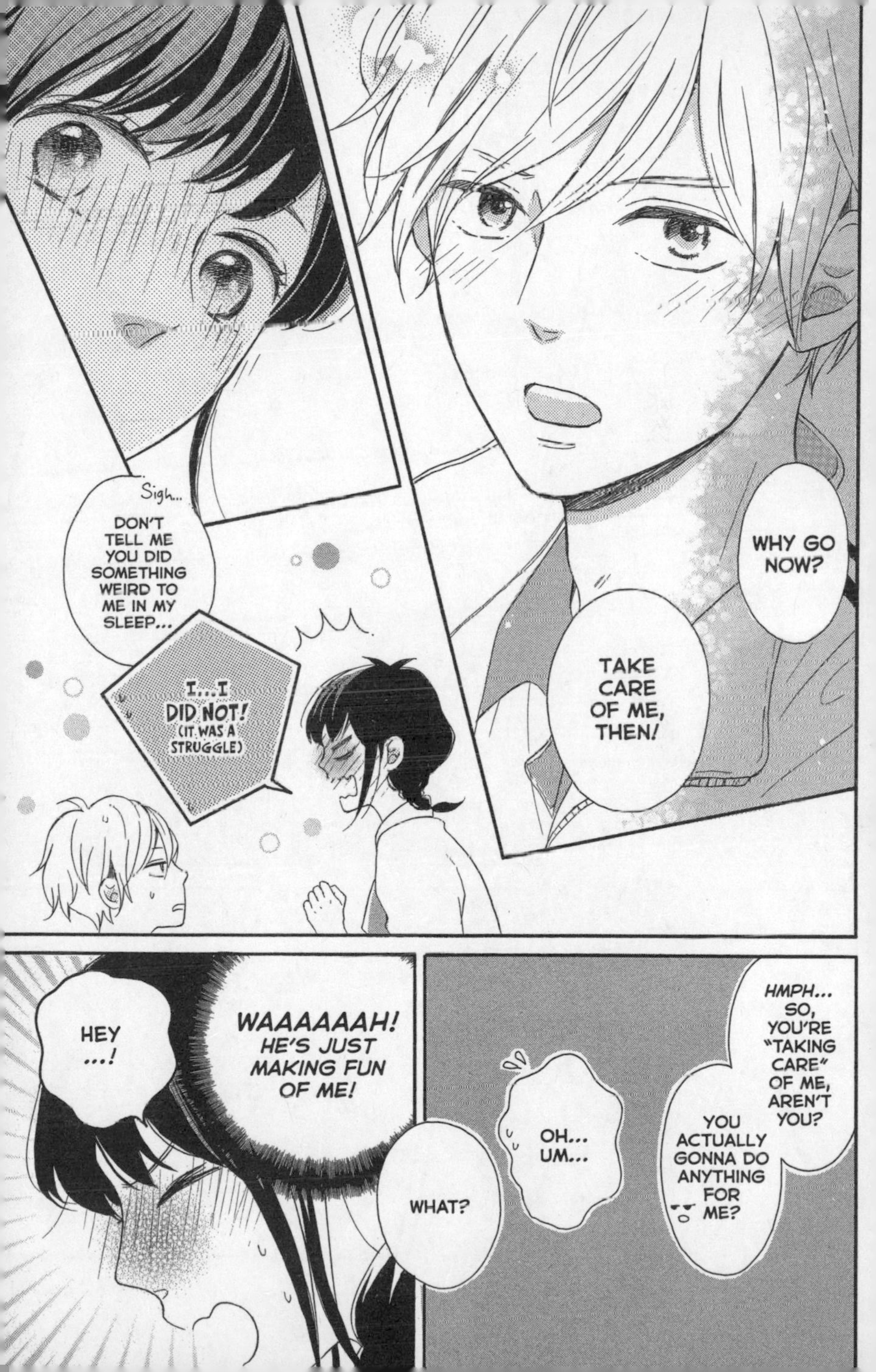
WHY GO NOW?
TAKE CARE OF ME, THEN!
Sigh...
DON'T TELL ME YOU DID SOMETHING WEIRD TO ME IN MY SLEEP...
I...I DID NOT! (IT WAS A STRUGGLE)
HMPH... SO, YOU'RE "TAKING CARE" OF ME, AREN'T YOU?
YOU ACTUALLY GONNA DO ANYTHING FOR ME?
OH... UM...
WHAT?
WAAAAAAH! HE'S JUST MAKING FUN OF ME!
HEY ...!

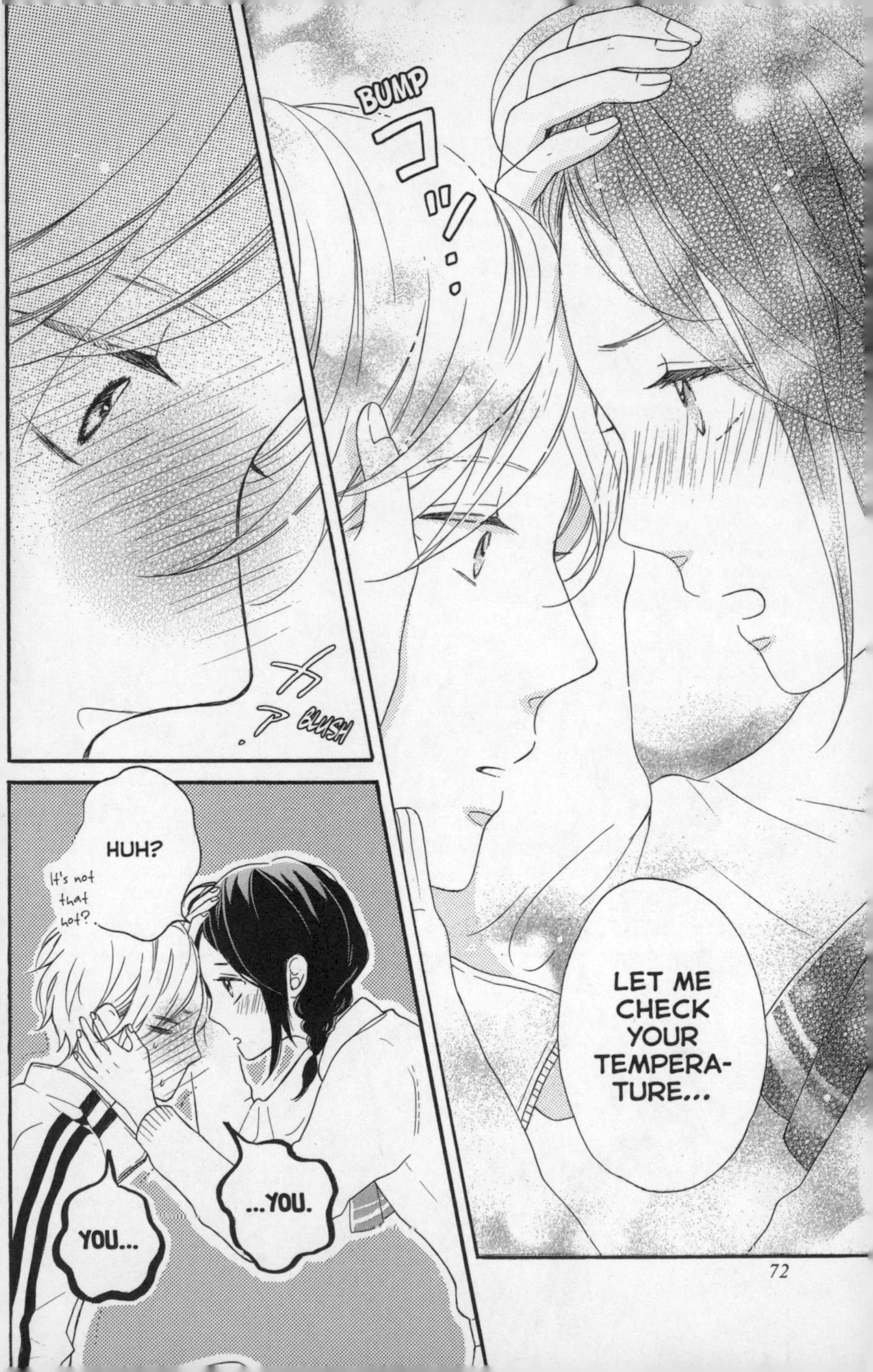
BUMP
LET ME CHECK YOUR TEMPERATURE...
BLUSH
HUH?
It's not that hot?..
...YOU.
YOU...

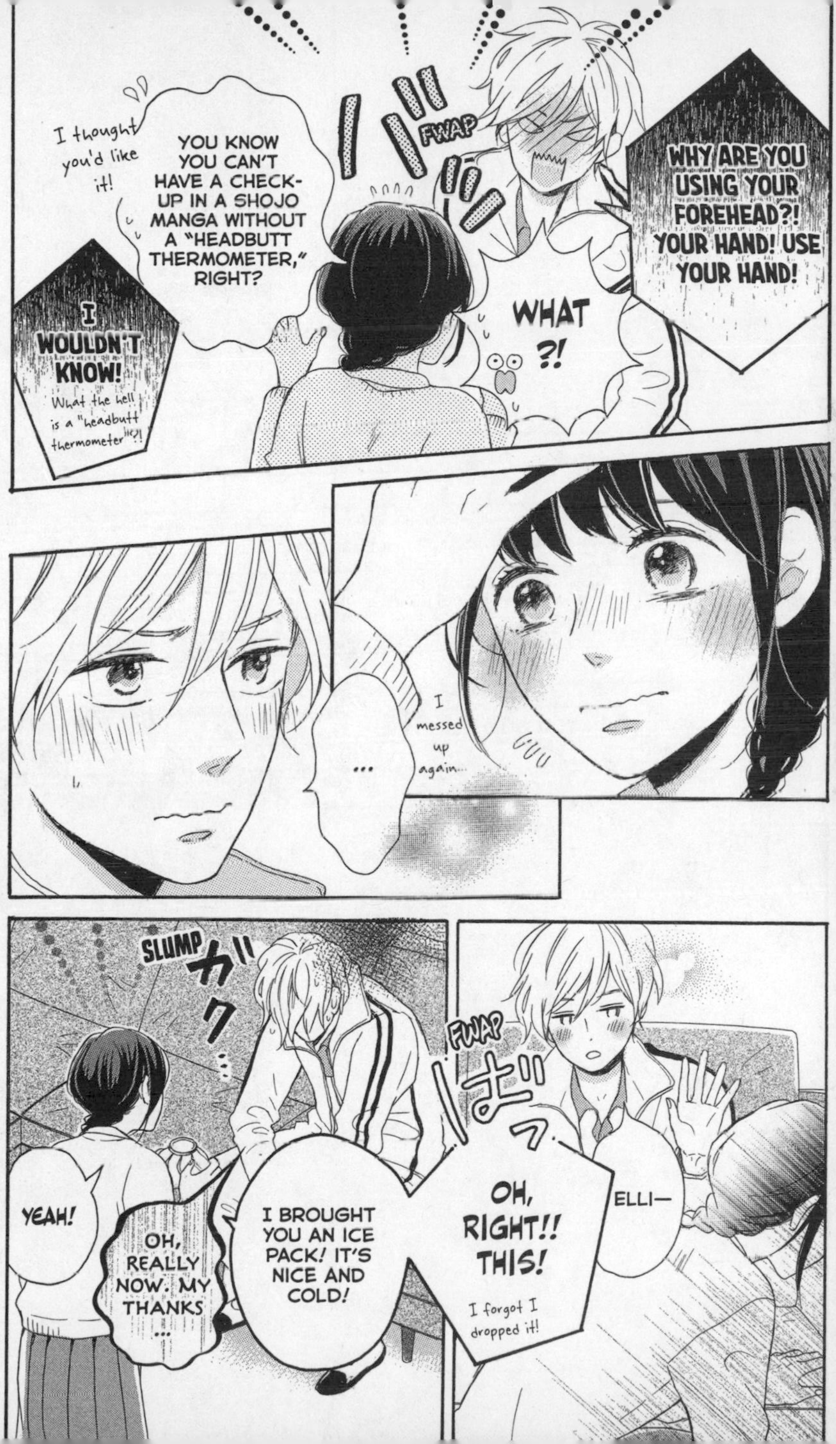
WHY ARE YOU USING YOUR FOREHEAD?! YOUR HAND! USE YOUR HAND!
FWAP
WHAT ?!
YOU KNOW YOU CAN'T HAVE A CHECK-UP IN A SHOJO MANGA WITHOUT A "HEADBUTT THERMOMETER," RIGHT?
I thought you'd like it!
I WOULDN'T KNOW!
What the hell is a "headbutt thermometer"?!
I messed up again...
...
FWAP
ELLI—
OH, RIGHT!! THIS!
I forgot I dropped it!
SLUMP
I BROUGHT YOU AN ICE PACK! IT'S NICE AND COLD!
OH, REALLY NOW. MY THANKS...
YEAH!

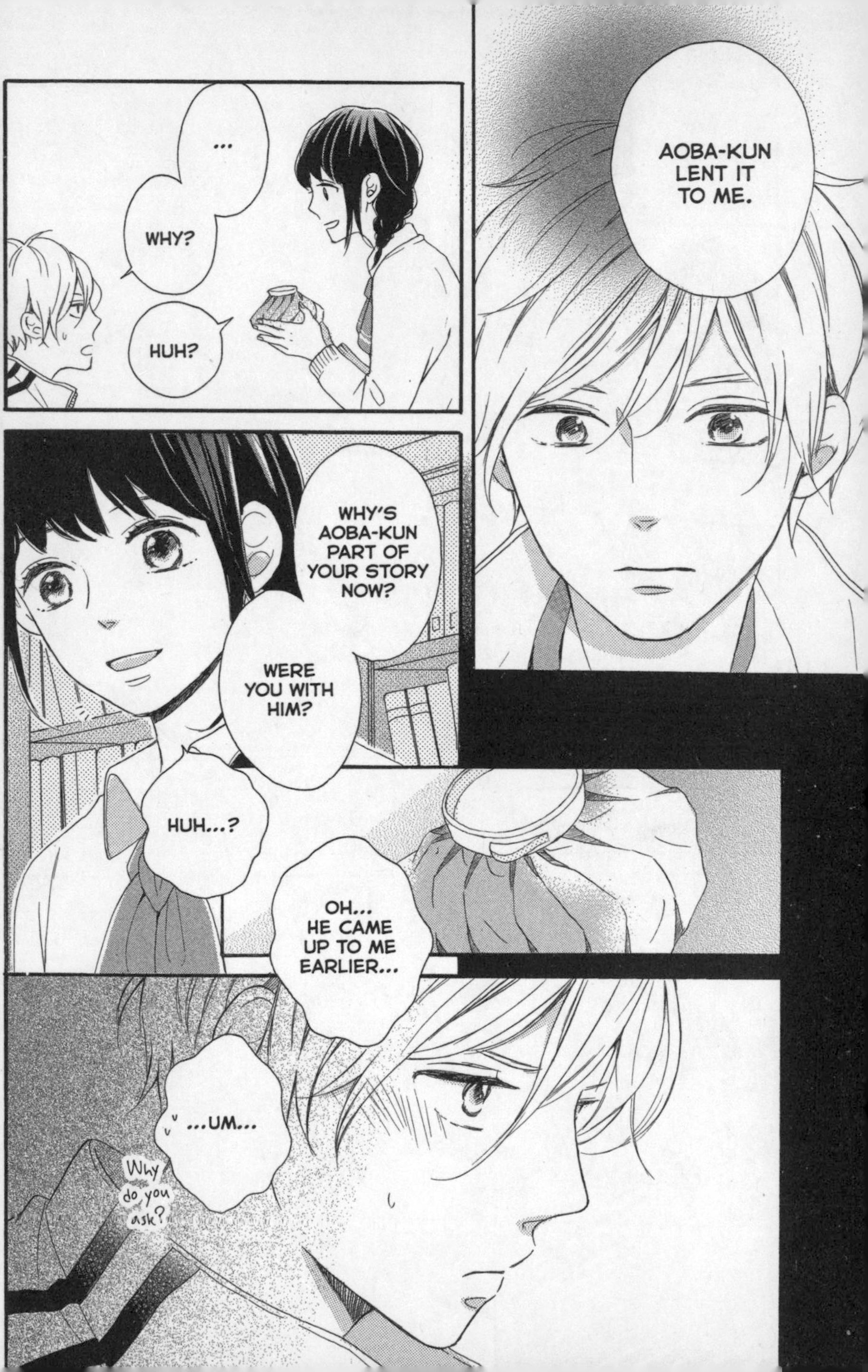
AOBA-KUN LENT IT TO ME.
...
WHY?
HUH?
WHY'S AOBA-KUN PART OF YOUR STORY NOW?
WERE YOU WITH HIM?
HUH...?
OH... HE CAME UP TO ME EARLIER...
...UM...
Why do you ask?

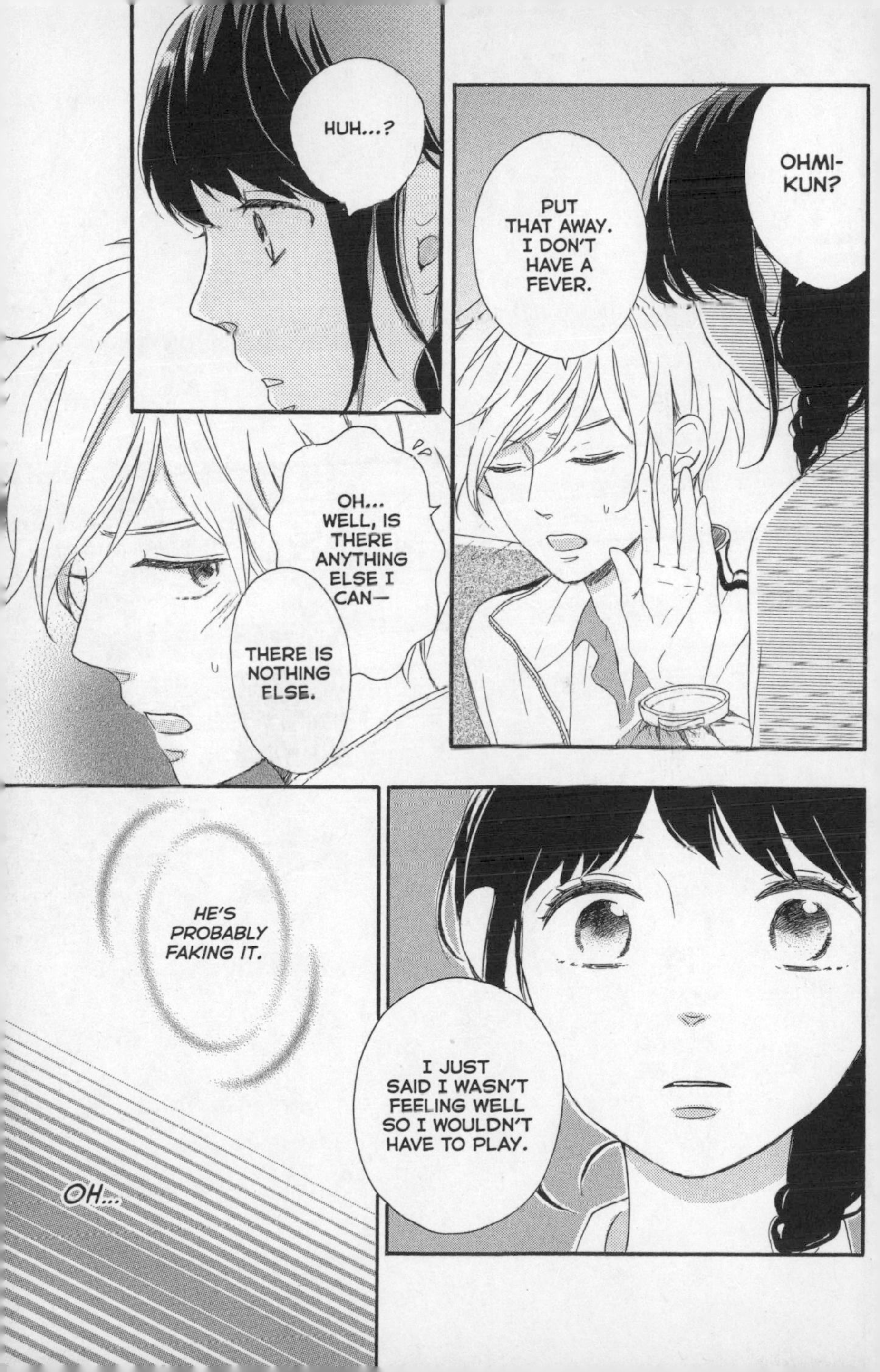
OHMI-KUN?
PUT THAT AWAY. I DON'T HAVE A FEVER.
HUH...?
OH... WELL, IS THERE ANYTHING ELSE I CAN—
THERE IS NOTHING ELSE.
I JUST SAID I WASN'T FEELING WELL SO I WOULDN'T HAVE TO PLAY.
HE'S PROBABLY FAKING IT.
OH...

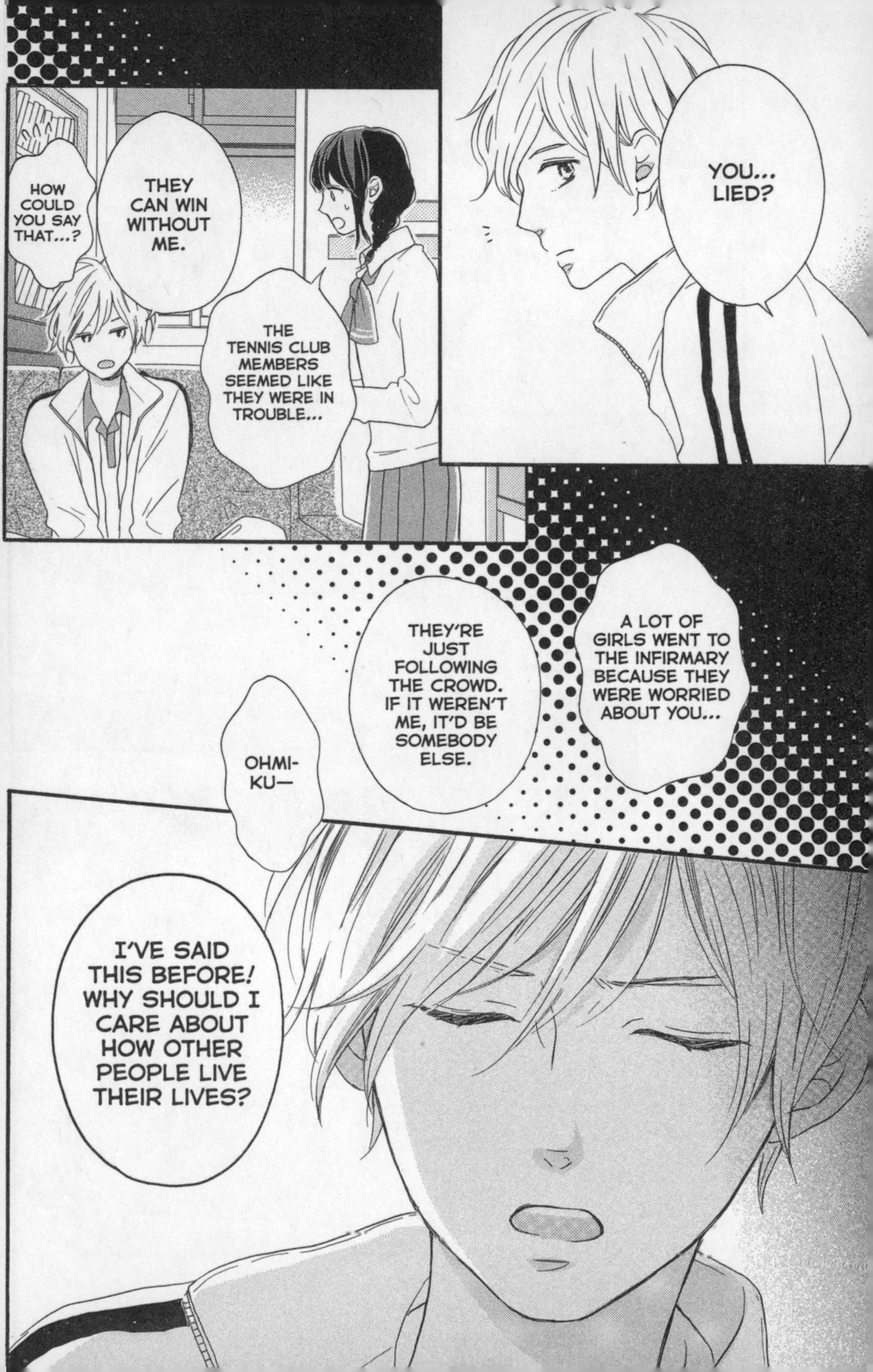
YOU... LIED?
THEY CAN WIN WITHOUT ME.
HOW COULD YOU SAY THAT...?
THE TENNIS CLUB MEMBERS SEEMED LIKE THEY WERE IN TROUBLE...
A LOT OF GIRLS WENT TO THE INFIRMARY BECAUSE THEY WERE WORRIED ABOUT YOU...
THEY'RE JUST FOLLOWING THE CROWD. IF IT WEREN'T ME, IT'D BE SOMEBODY ELSE.
OHMI-KU—
I'VE SAID THIS BEFORE! WHY SHOULD I CARE ABOUT HOW OTHER PEOPLE LIVE THEIR LIVES?

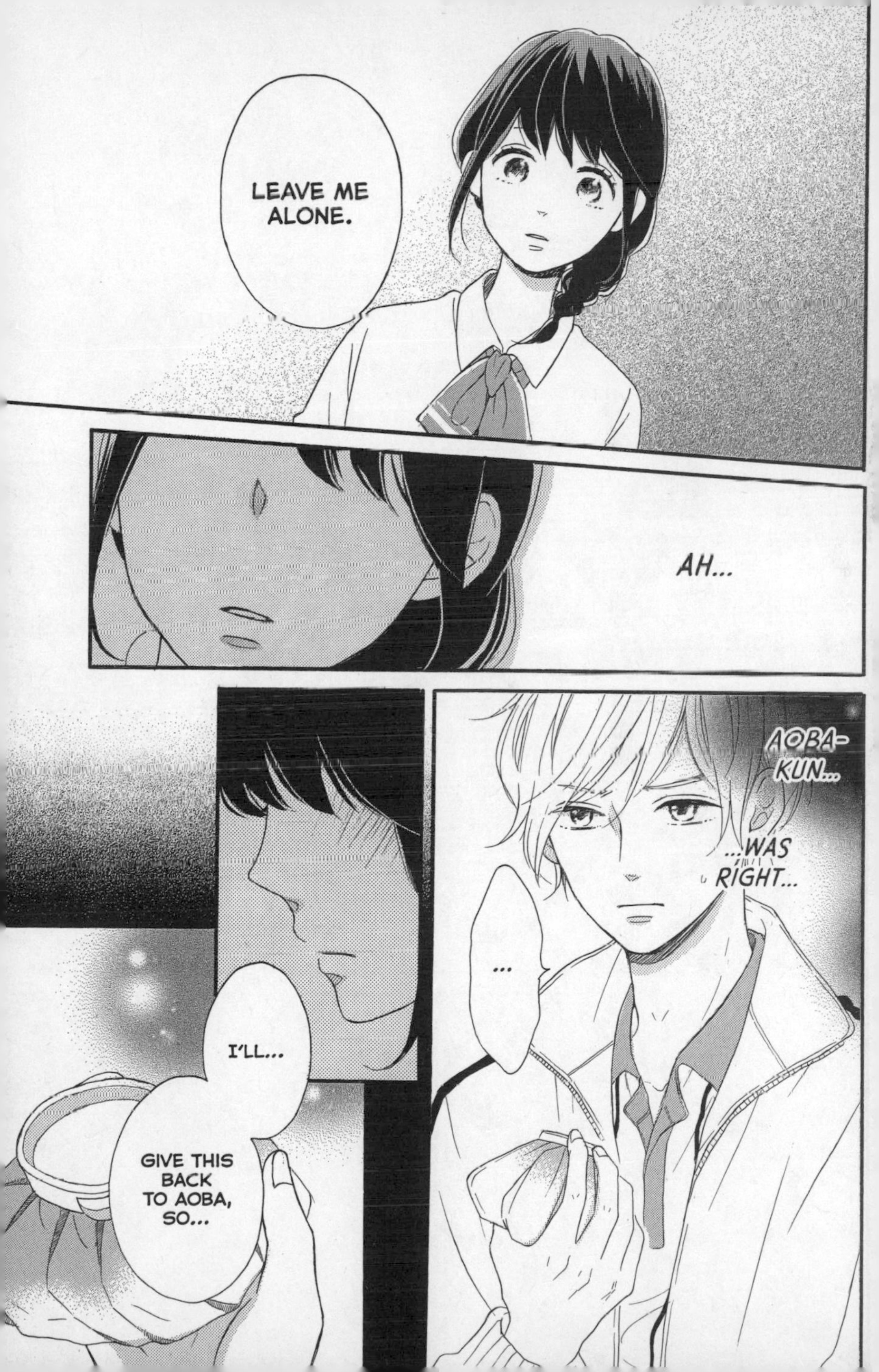
LEAVE ME ALONE.
AH...
AOBA-KUN...
...WAS RIGHT...
...
I'LL...
GIVE THIS BACK TO AOBA, SO...

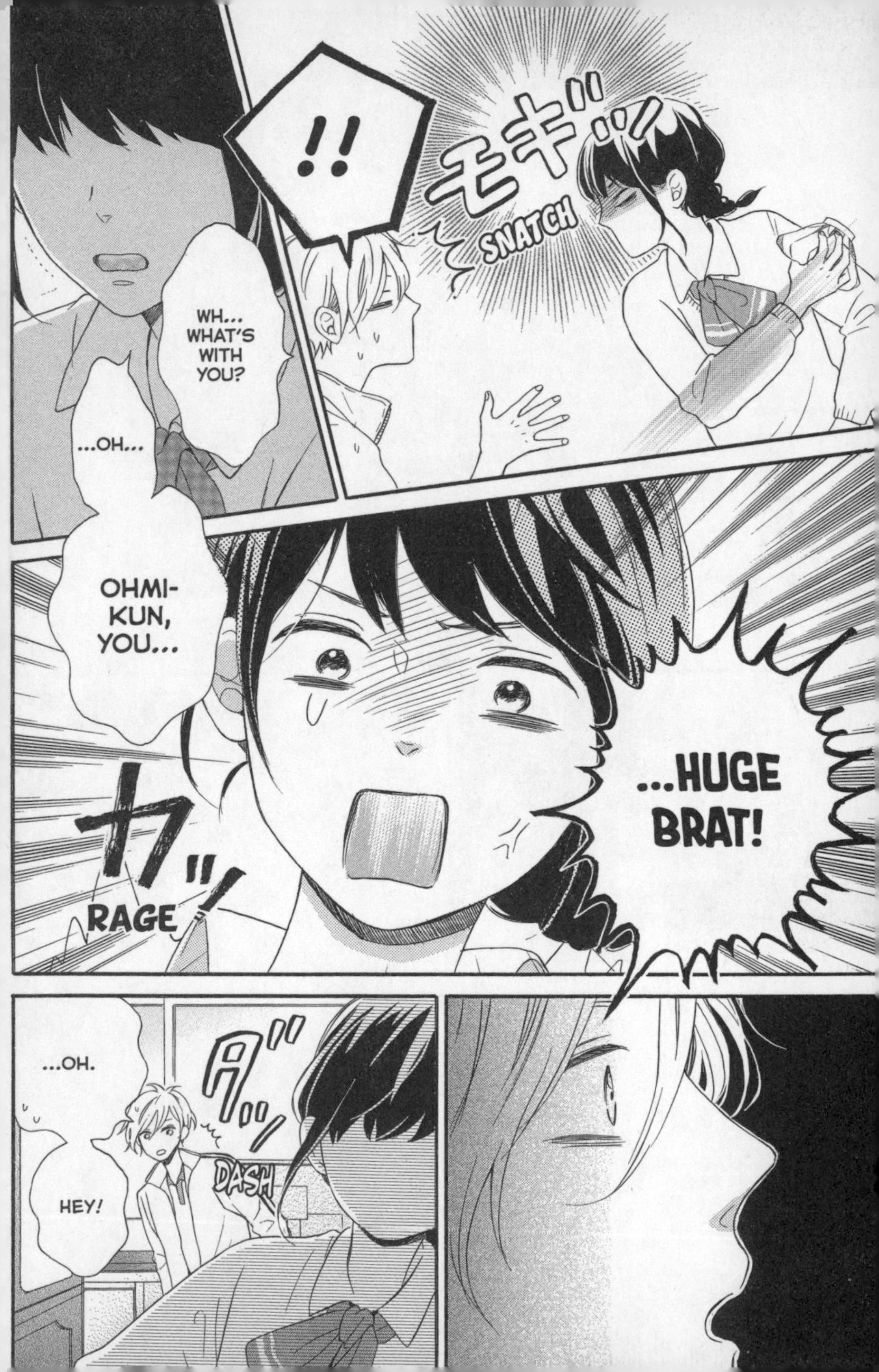
モギッ
SNATCH
!!
WH... WHAT'S WITH YOU?
...OH...
OHMI-KUN, YOU...
...HUGE BRAT!
カッ
RAGE
ダッ
DASH
...OH.
HEY!

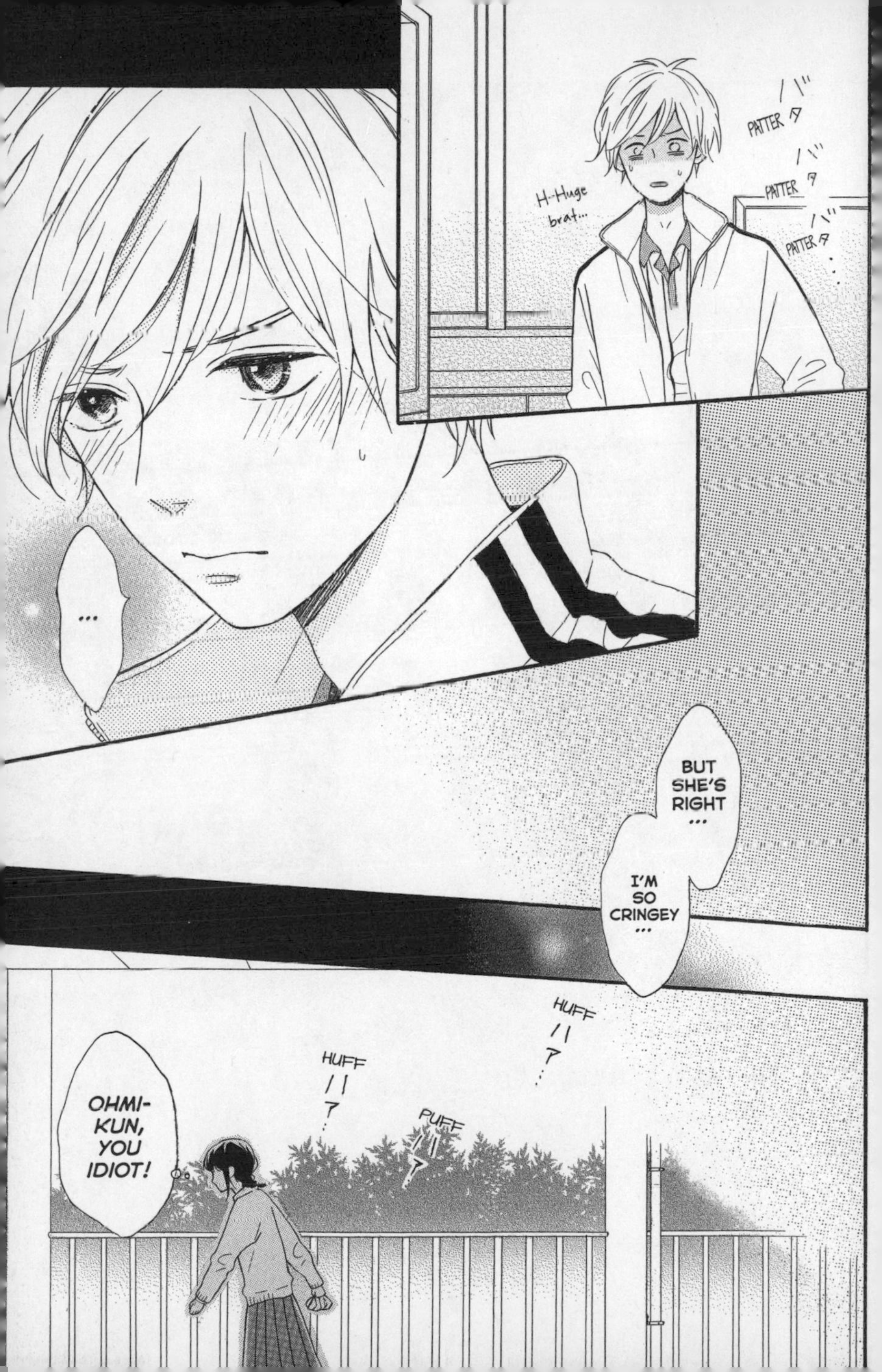
PATTER
PATTER
PATTER
H-Huge brat...
...
BUT SHE'S RIGHT...
I'M SO CRINGEY...
HUFF
HUFF
PUFF
OHMI-KUN, YOU IDIOT!

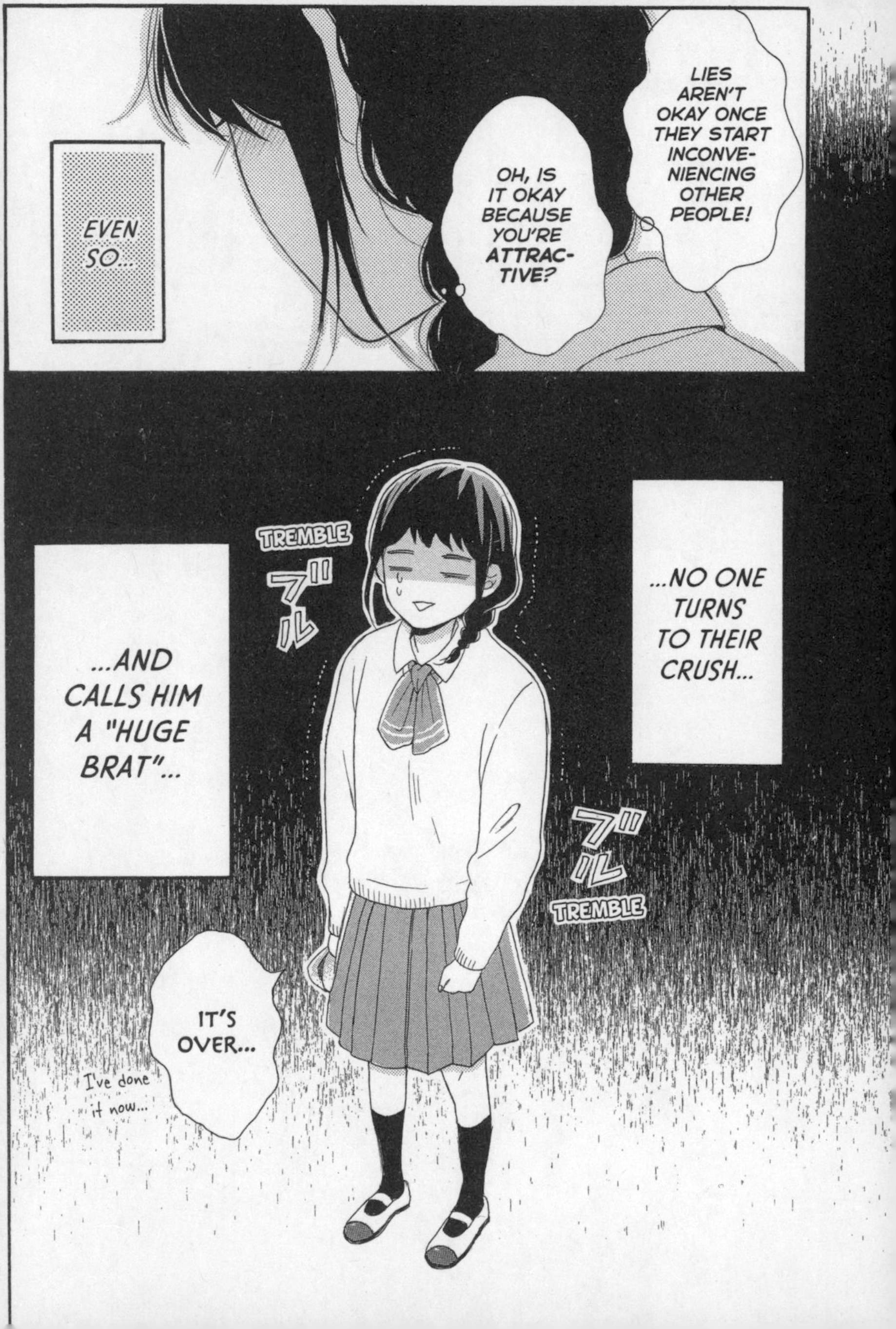
LIES AREN'T OKAY ONCE THEY START INCONVE-NIENCING OTHER PEOPLE!
OH, IS IT OKAY BECAUSE YOU'RE ATTRAC-TIVE?
EVEN SO...
...NO ONE TURNS TO THEIR CRUSH...
ブル
TREMBLE
ブル
TREMBLE
...AND CALLS HIM A "HUGE BRAT"...
IT'S OVER...
I've done it now...

7 #uncool

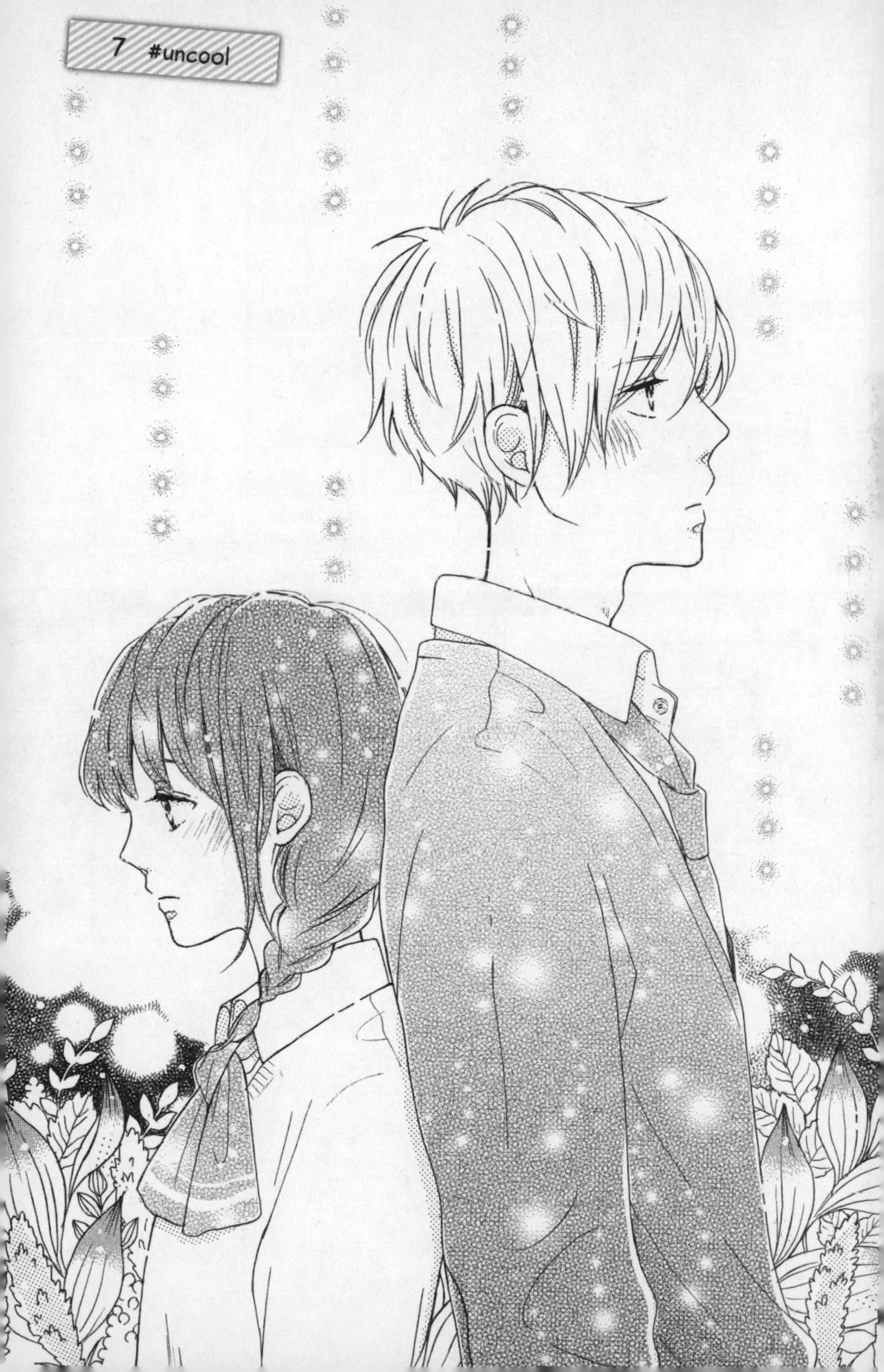

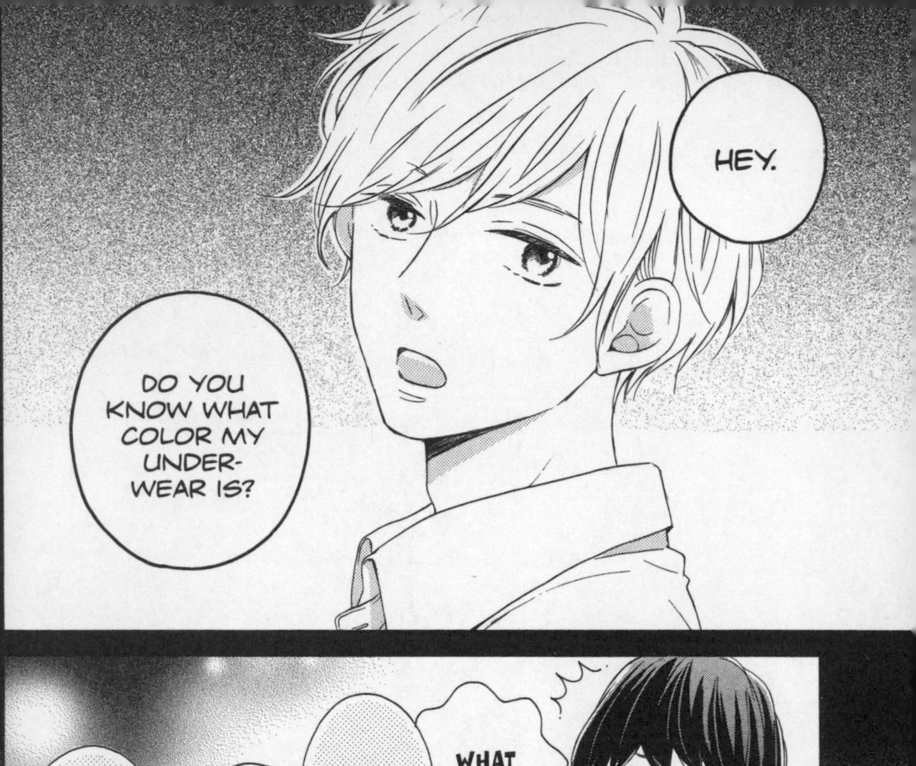
HEY.
DO YOU KNOW WHAT COLOR MY UNDER-WEAR IS?
WHAT ...?!
HOW ABOUT MY BLOOD TYPE?
MY FAVORITE FOOD?
THE SONG I ALWAYS SING AT KARAOKE?

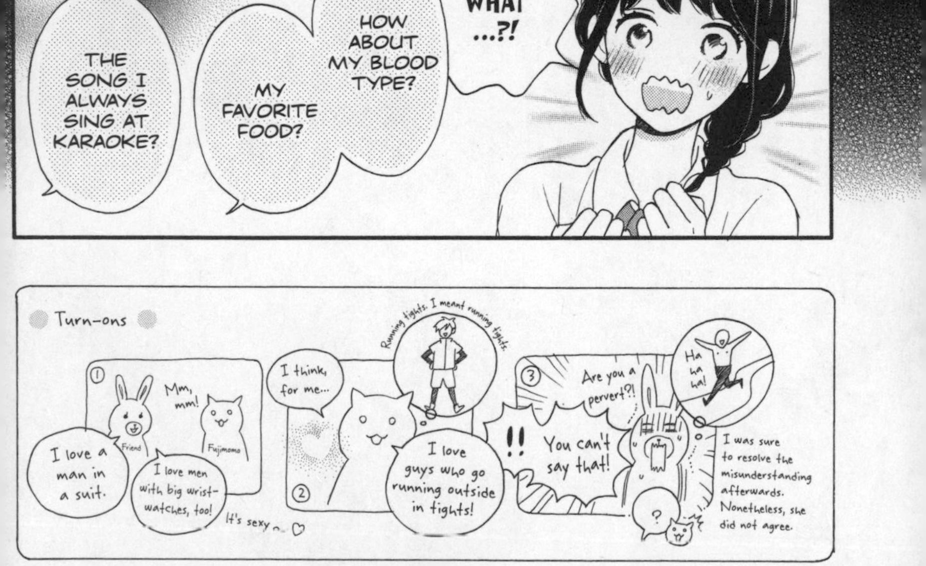
Turn-ons
1
Mm, mm!
I love a man in a suit.
Friend
Fujimomo
I love men with big wrist-watches, too!
It's sexy ~ ♡
2
I think, for me...
Running tights. I meant running tights.
I love guys who go running outside in tights!
3
Are you a pervert?!
You can't say that!
!!
Ha ha ha!
?
I was sure to resolve the misunderstanding afterwards. Nonetheless, she did not agree.

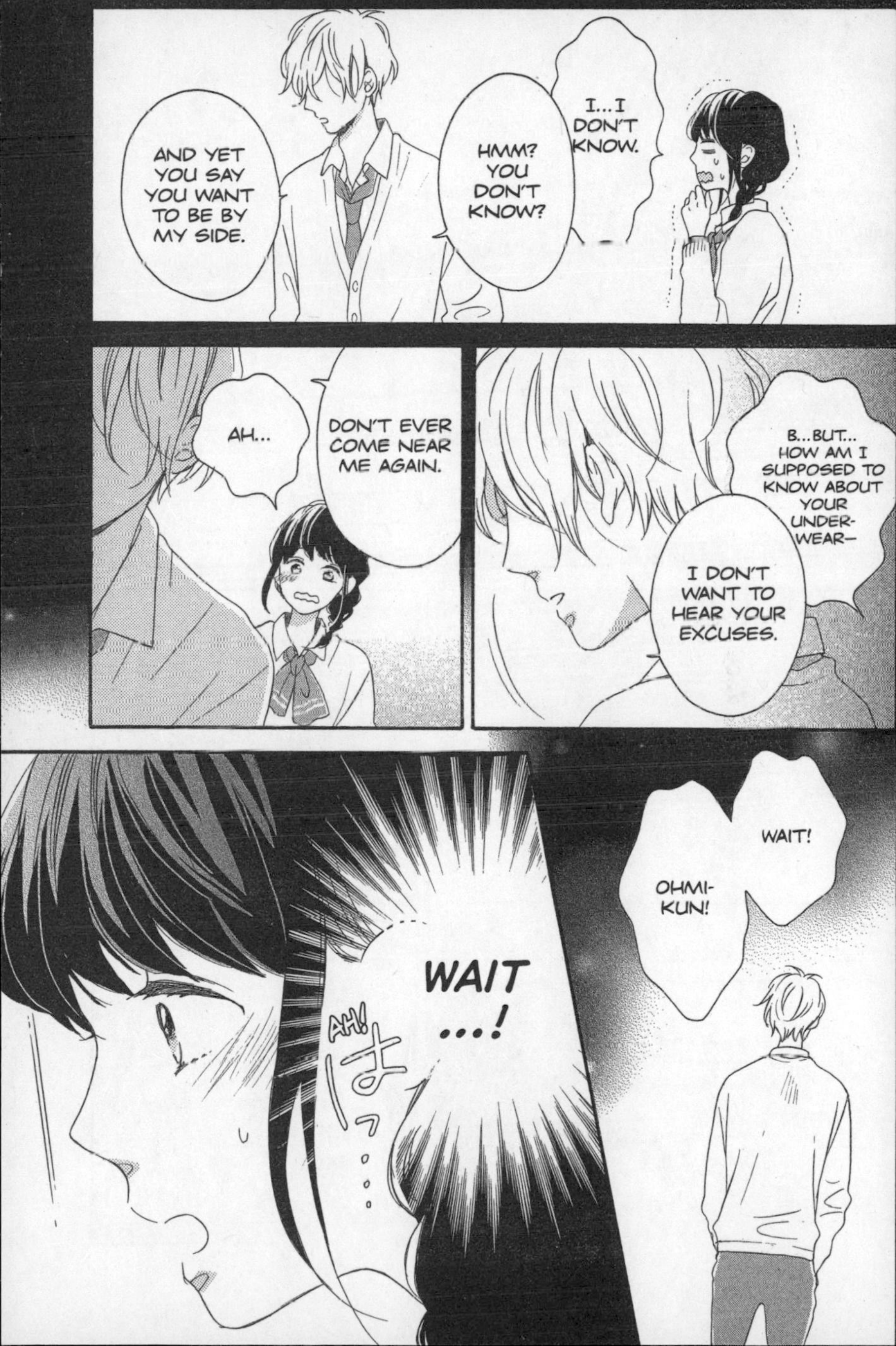
I...I DON'T KNOW.
HMM? YOU DON'T KNOW?
AND YET YOU SAY YOU WANT TO BE BY MY SIDE.
B...BUT... HOW AM I SUPPOSED TO KNOW ABOUT YOUR UNDER-WEAR—
I DON'T WANT TO HEAR YOUR EXCUSES.
DON'T EVER COME NEAR ME AGAIN.
AH...
WAIT!
OHMI-KUN!
WAIT ...!
AH!
はっ

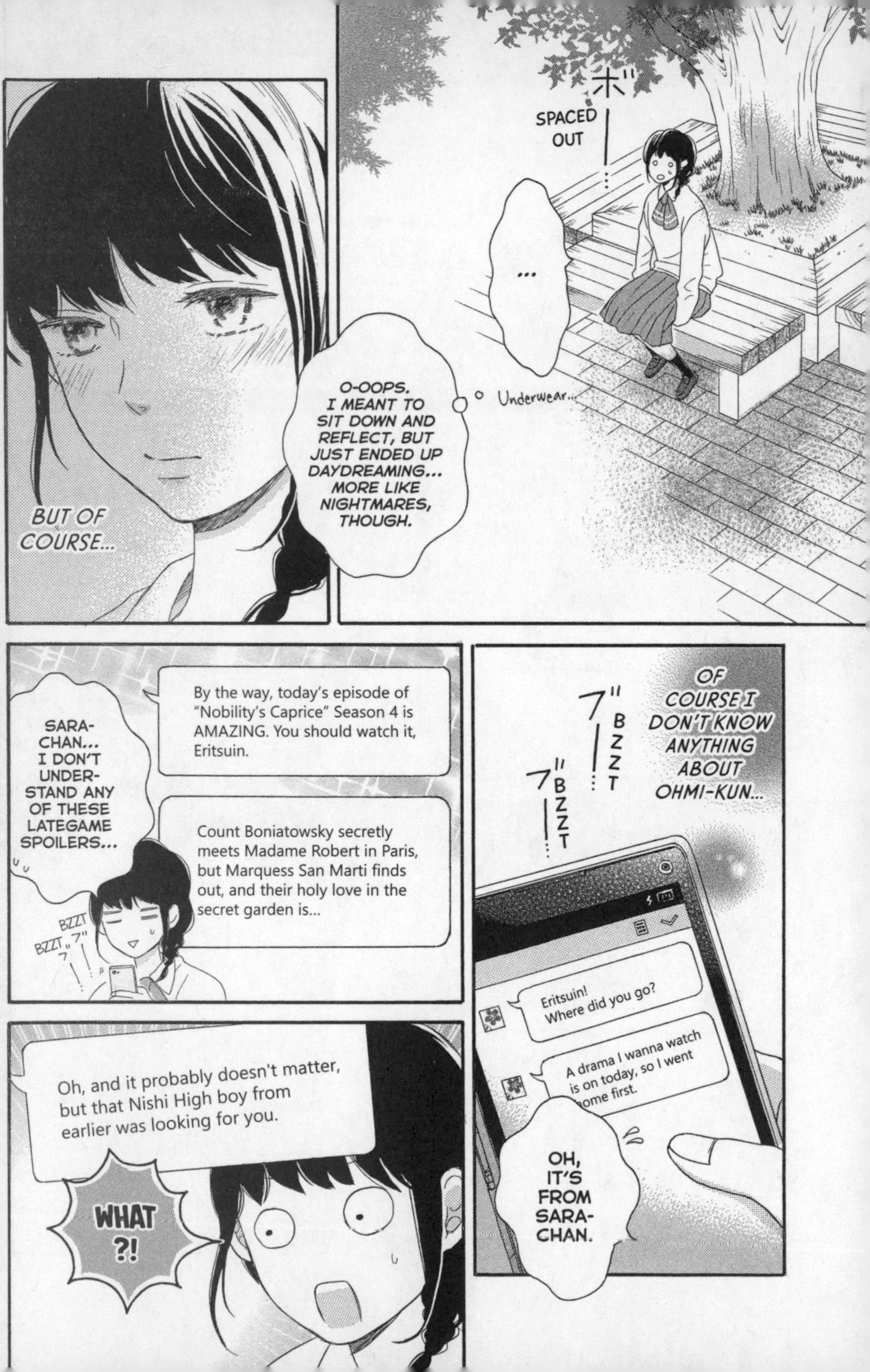
SPACED OUT
...
Underwear...
O-OOPS. I MEANT TO SIT DOWN AND REFLECT, BUT JUST ENDED UP DAYDREAMING... MORE LIKE NIGHTMARES, THOUGH.
BUT OF COURSE...
OF COURSE I DON'T KNOW ANYTHING ABOUT OHMI-KUN...
BZZT
BZZT
Eritsuin! Where did you go?
A drama I wanna watch is on today, so I went home first.
OH, IT'S FROM SARA-CHAN.
By the way, today's episode of "Nobility's Caprice" Season 4 is AMAZING. You should watch it, Eritsuin.
Count Boniatowsky secretly meets Madame Robert in Paris, but Marquess San Marti finds out, and their holy love in the secret garden is...
SARA-CHAN... I DON'T UNDERSTAND ANY OF THESE LATEGAME SPOILERS...
BZZT BZZT
Oh, and it probably doesn't matter, but that Nishi High boy from earlier was looking for you.
WHAT?!

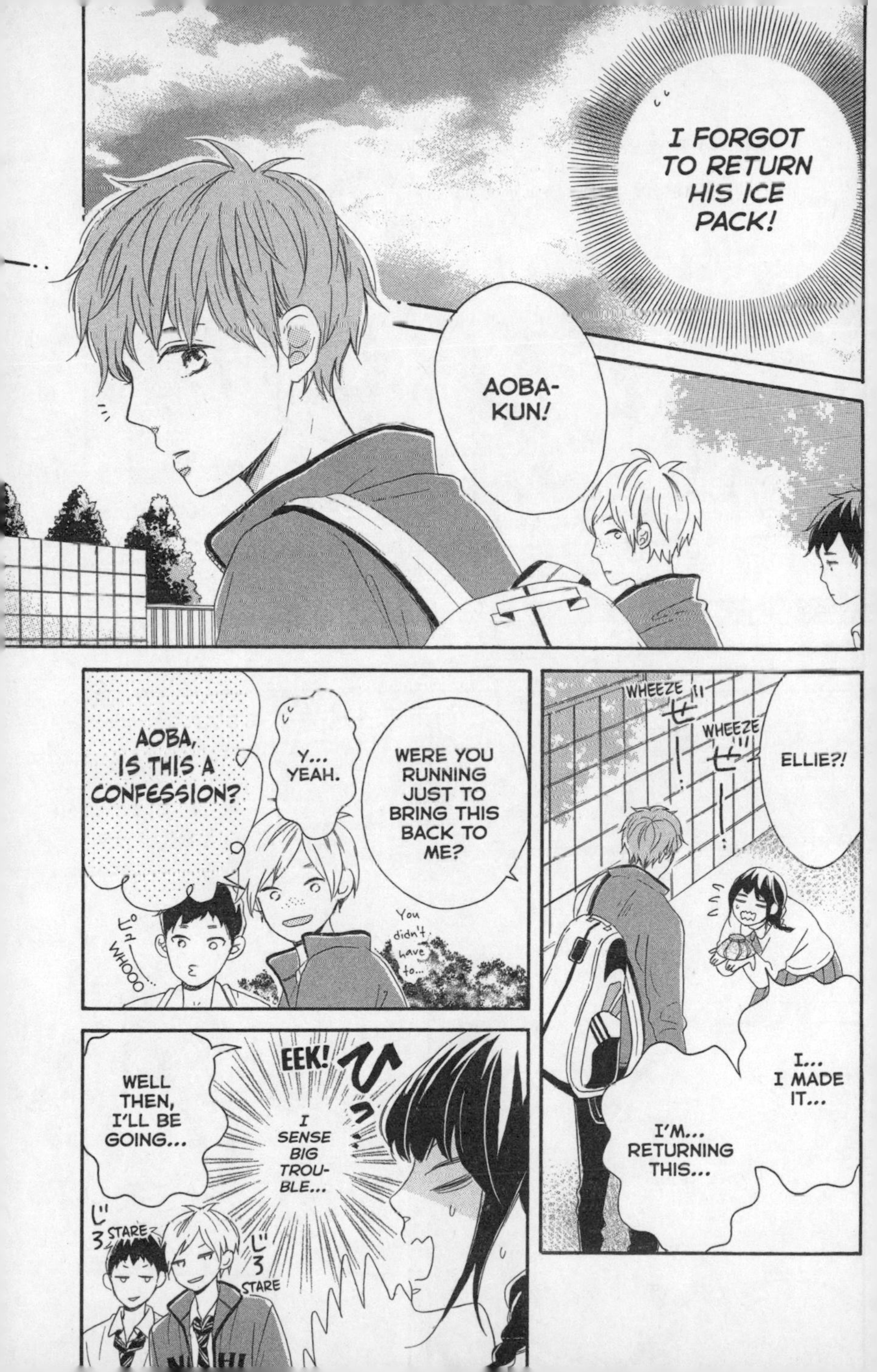
I FORGOT TO RETURN HIS ICE PACK!
AOBA-KUN!
ELLIE?!
WHEEZE
WHEEZE
I... I MADE IT...
I'M... RETURNING THIS...
WERE YOU RUNNING JUST TO BRING THIS BACK TO ME?
Y... YEAH.
AOBA, IS THIS A CONFESSION?
WHOOO
You didn't have to...
EEK!
I SENSE BIG TROUBLE...
WELL THEN, I'LL BE GOING...
STARE
STARE

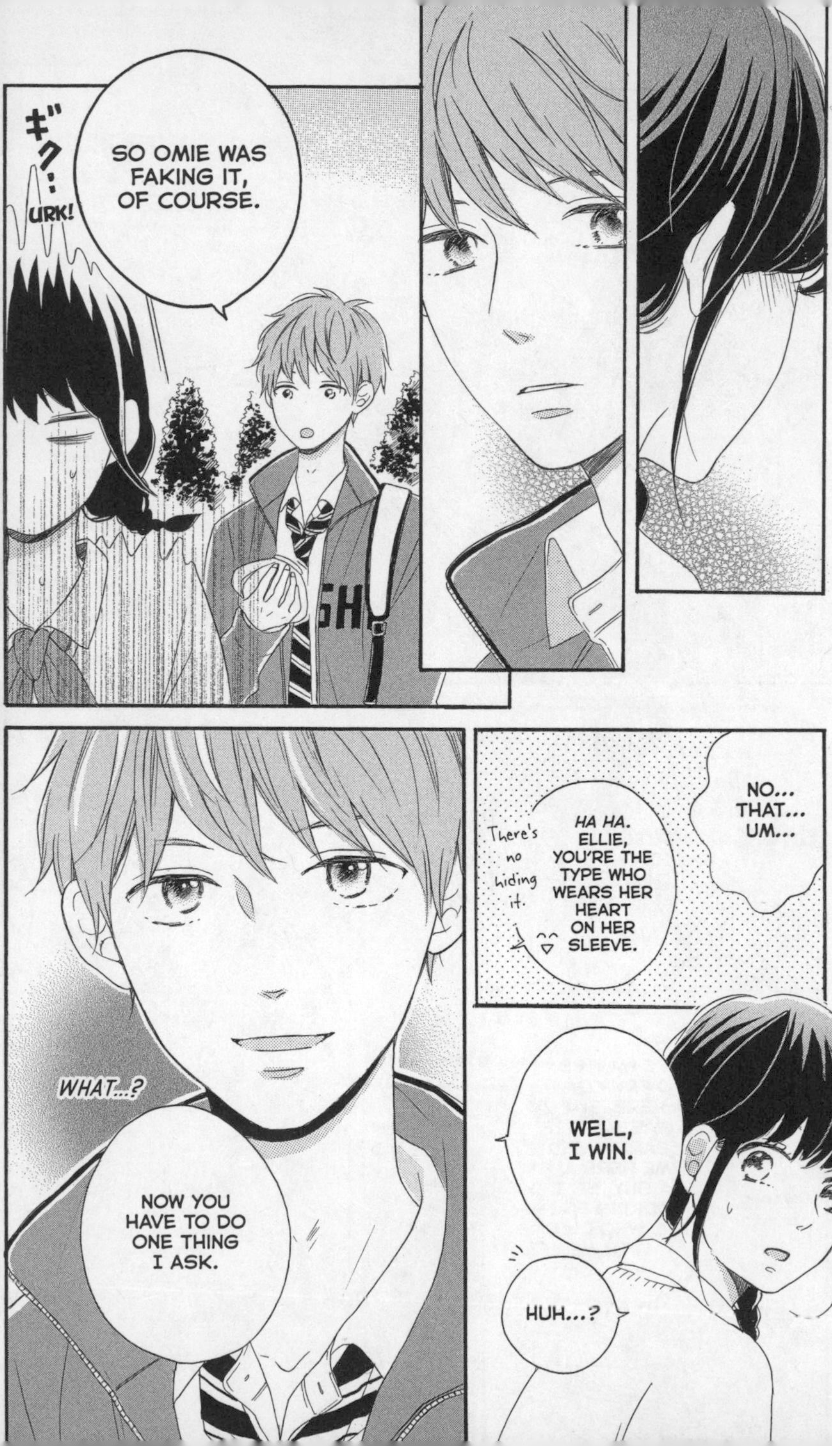
SO OMIE WAS FAKING IT, OF COURSE.
ギク…
URK!
NO... THAT... UM...
HA HA. ELLIE, YOU'RE THE TYPE WHO WEARS HER HEART ON HER SLEEVE.
There's no hiding it.
WELL, I WIN.
HUH...?
WHAT...?
NOW YOU HAVE TO DO ONE THING I ASK.

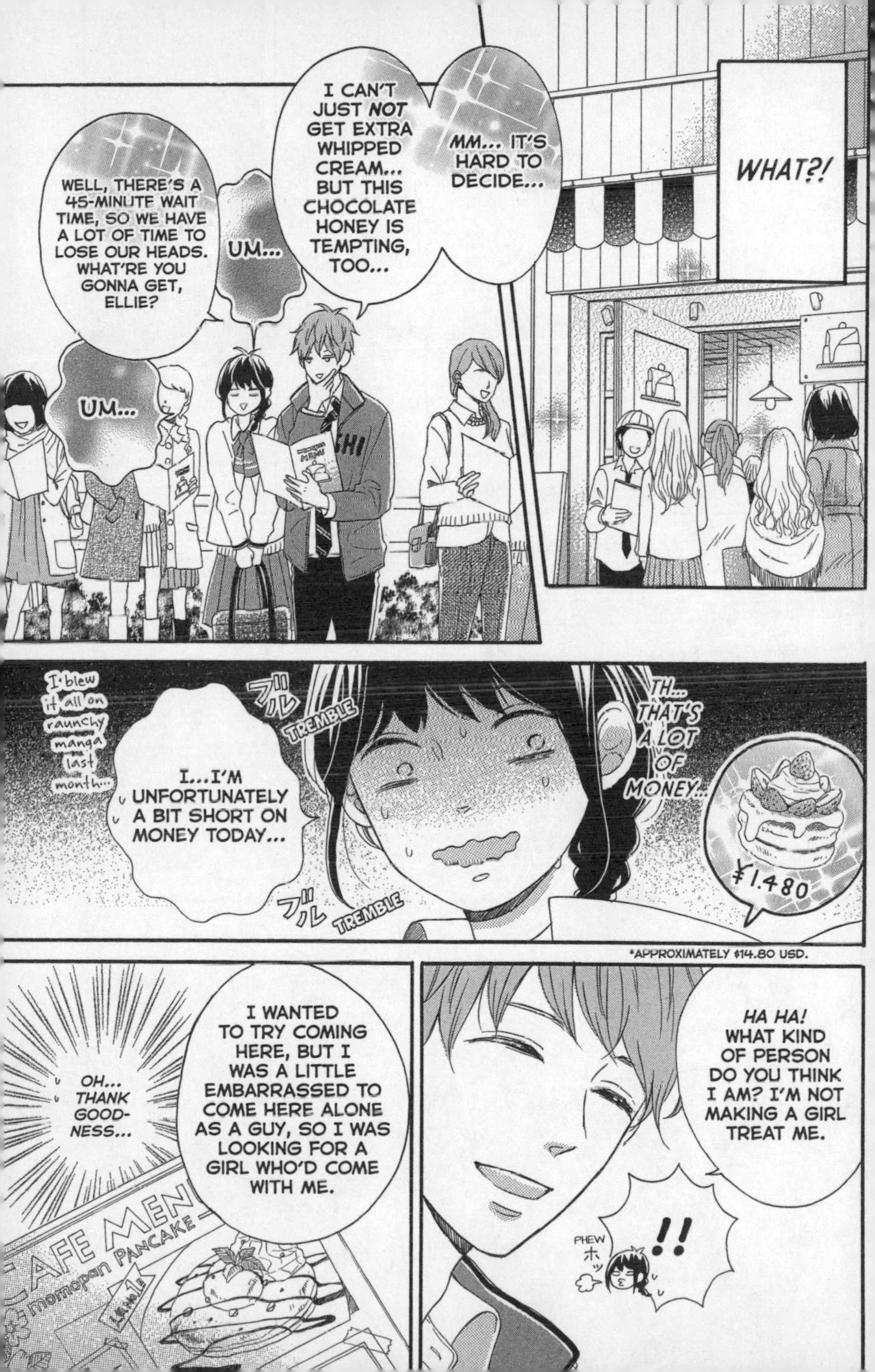
WHAT?!
MM... IT'S HARD TO DECIDE...
I CAN'T JUST *NOT* GET EXTRA WHIPPED CREAM... BUT THIS CHOCOLATE HONEY IS TEMPTING, TOO...
UM...
WELL, THERE'S A 45-MINUTE WAIT TIME, SO WE HAVE A LOT OF TIME TO LOSE OUR HEADS. WHAT'RE YOU GONNA GET, ELLIE?
UM...
MENU
TH... THAT'S A LOT OF MONEY...
¥1,480
ブル TREMBLE
I...I'M UNFORTUNATELY A BIT SHORT ON MONEY TODAY...
ブル TREMBLE
I blew it all on raunchy manga last month...
HA HA! WHAT KIND OF PERSON DO YOU THINK I AM? I'M NOT MAKING A GIRL TREAT ME.
!!
PHEW ホッ
I WANTED TO TRY COMING HERE, BUT I WAS A LITTLE EMBARRASSED TO COME HERE ALONE AS A GUY, SO I WAS LOOKING FOR A GIRL WHO'D COME WITH ME.
OH... THANK GOODNESS...
CAFE MEN
momopan PANCAKE

*APPROXIMATELY $14.80 USD.

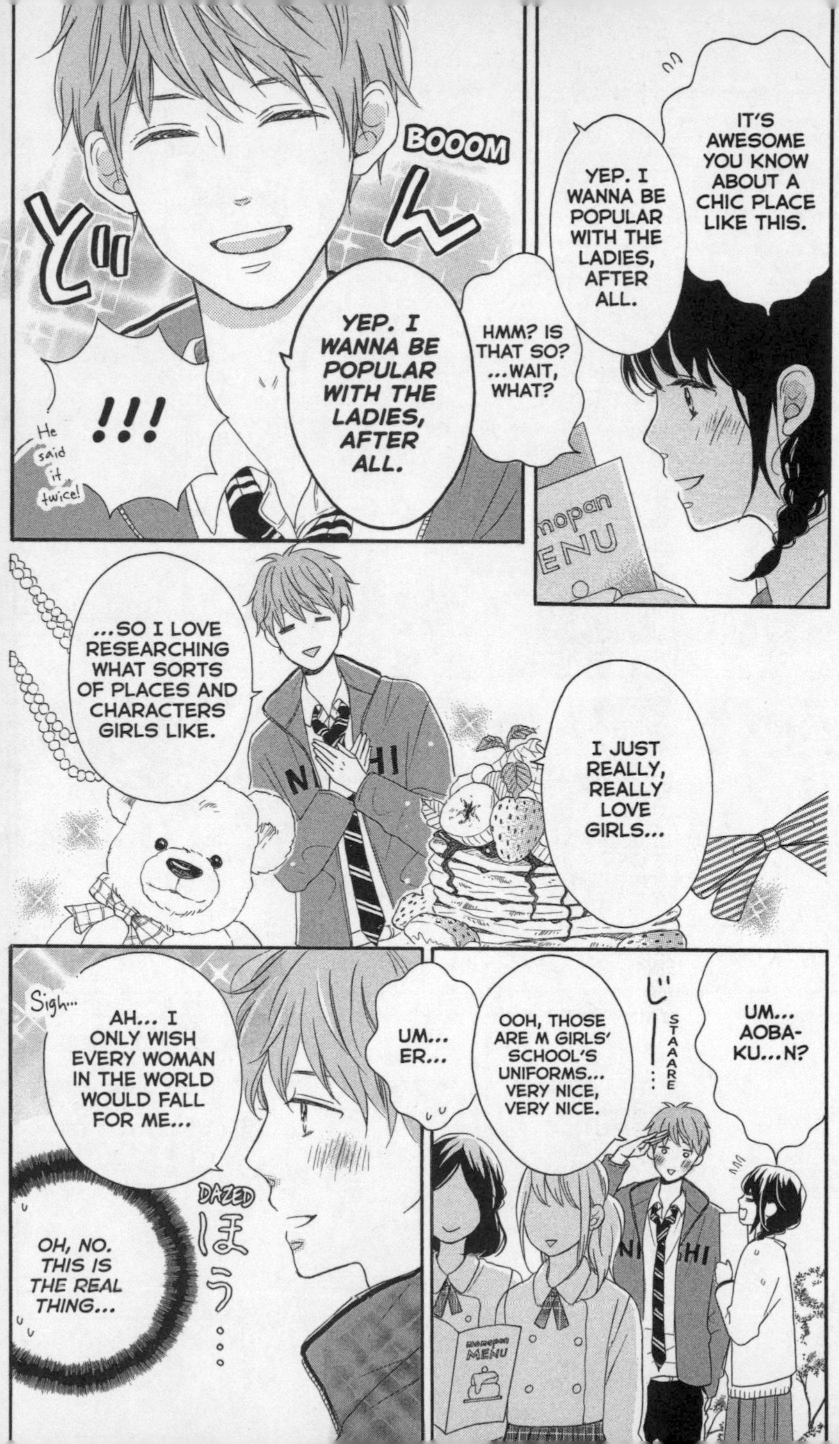
IT'S AWESOME YOU KNOW ABOUT A CHIC PLACE LIKE THIS.
YEP. I WANNA BE POPULAR WITH THE LADIES, AFTER ALL.
HMM? IS THAT SO? ...WAIT, WHAT?
mopan MENU
YEP. I WANNA BE POPULAR WITH THE LADIES, AFTER ALL.
BOOOM
!!!
He said it twice!
...SO I LOVE RESEARCHING WHAT SORTS OF PLACES AND CHARACTERS GIRLS LIKE.
I JUST REALLY, REALLY LOVE GIRLS...
NISHI
UM... AOBA-KU...N?
STAAARE
OOH, THOSE ARE M GIRLS' SCHOOL'S UNIFORMS... VERY NICE, VERY NICE.
UM... ER...
NISHI
MENU
Sigh...
AH... I ONLY WISH EVERY WOMAN IN THE WORLD WOULD FALL FOR ME...
DAZED
OH, NO. THIS IS THE REAL THING...

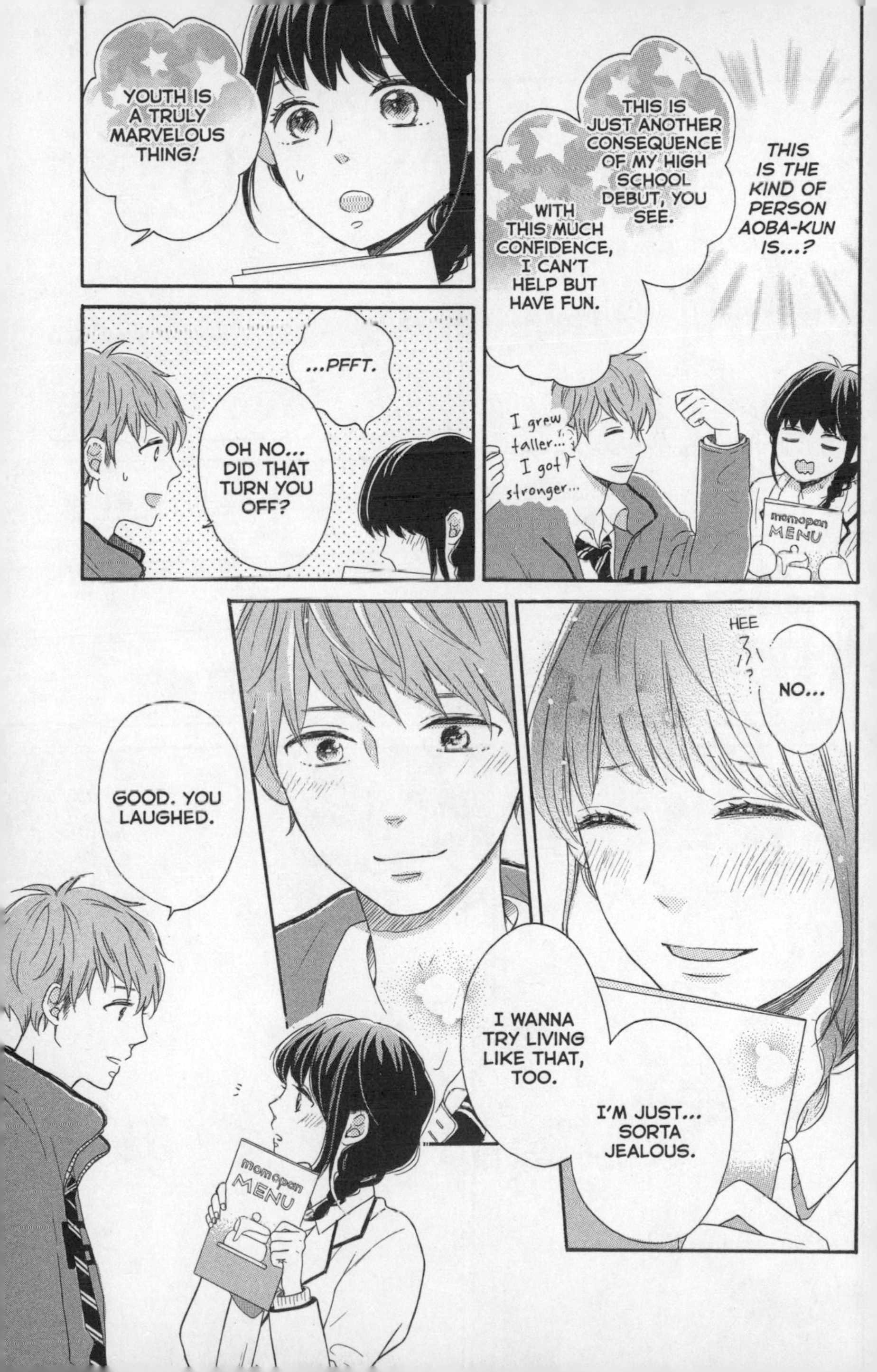
THIS IS THE KIND OF PERSON AOBA-KUN IS...?
THIS IS JUST ANOTHER CONSEQUENCE OF MY HIGH SCHOOL DEBUT, YOU SEE.
WITH THIS MUCH CONFIDENCE, I CAN'T HELP BUT HAVE FUN.
I grew taller... I got stronger...
momopan MENU
YOUTH IS A TRULY MARVELOUS THING!
...PFFT.
OH NO... DID THAT TURN YOU OFF?
HEE
NO...
I WANNA TRY LIVING LIKE THAT, TOO.
I'M JUST... SORTA JEALOUS.
GOOD. YOU LAUGHED.
momopan MENU

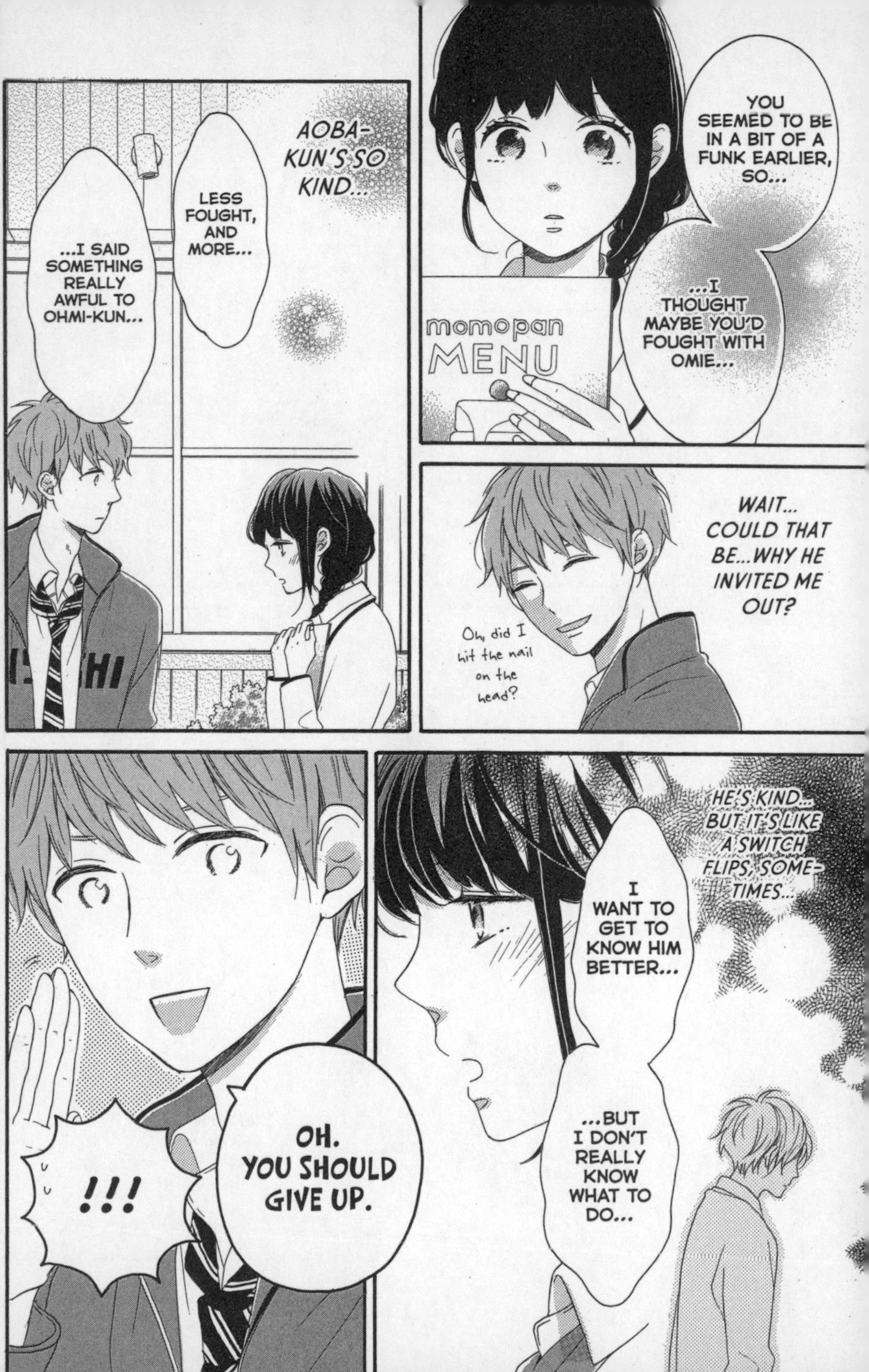
YOU SEEMED TO BE IN A BIT OF A FUNK EARLIER, SO...
...I THOUGHT MAYBE YOU'D FOUGHT WITH OMIE...
momopan MENU
WAIT... COULD THAT BE...WHY HE INVITED ME OUT?
Oh, did I hit the nail on the head?
AOBA-KUN'S SO KIND...
LESS FOUGHT, AND MORE...
...I SAID SOMETHING REALLY AWFUL TO OHMI-KUN...
HE'S KIND... BUT IT'S LIKE A SWITCH FLIPS, SOMETIMES...
I WANT TO GET TO KNOW HIM BETTER...
...BUT I DON'T REALLY KNOW WHAT TO DO...
OH. YOU SHOULD GIVE UP.
!!!

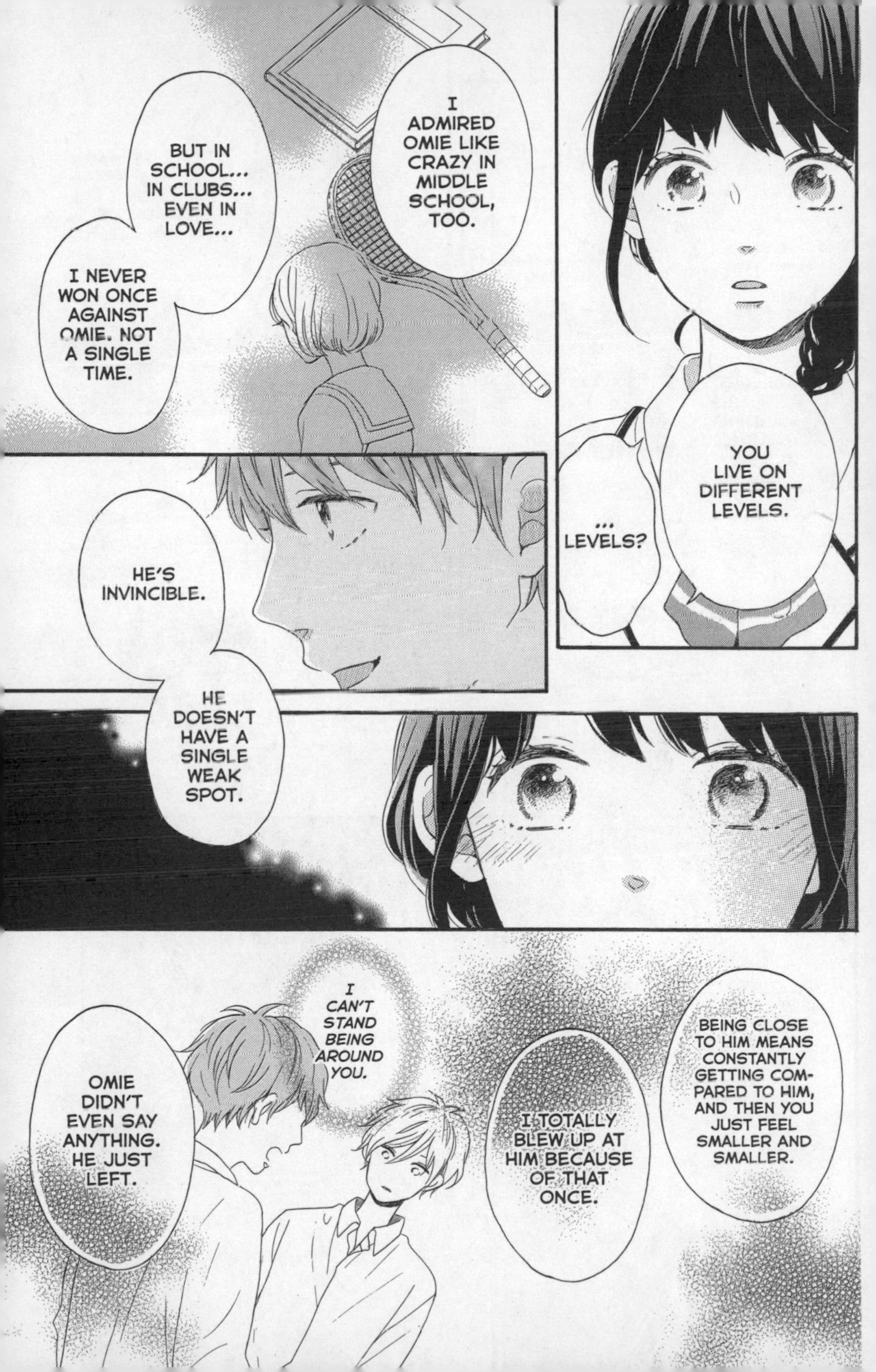

YOU LIVE ON DIFFERENT LEVELS.
...LEVELS?
I ADMIRED OMIE LIKE CRAZY IN MIDDLE SCHOOL, TOO.
BUT IN SCHOOL... IN CLUBS... EVEN IN LOVE...
I NEVER WON ONCE AGAINST OMIE. NOT A SINGLE TIME.
HE'S INVINCIBLE.
HE DOESN'T HAVE A SINGLE WEAK SPOT.
BEING CLOSE TO HIM MEANS CONSTANTLY GETTING COMPARED TO HIM, AND THEN YOU JUST FEEL SMALLER AND SMALLER.
I TOTALLY BLEW UP AT HIM BECAUSE OF THAT ONCE.
I CAN'T STAND BEING AROUND YOU.
OMIE DIDN'T EVEN SAY ANYTHING. HE JUST LEFT.

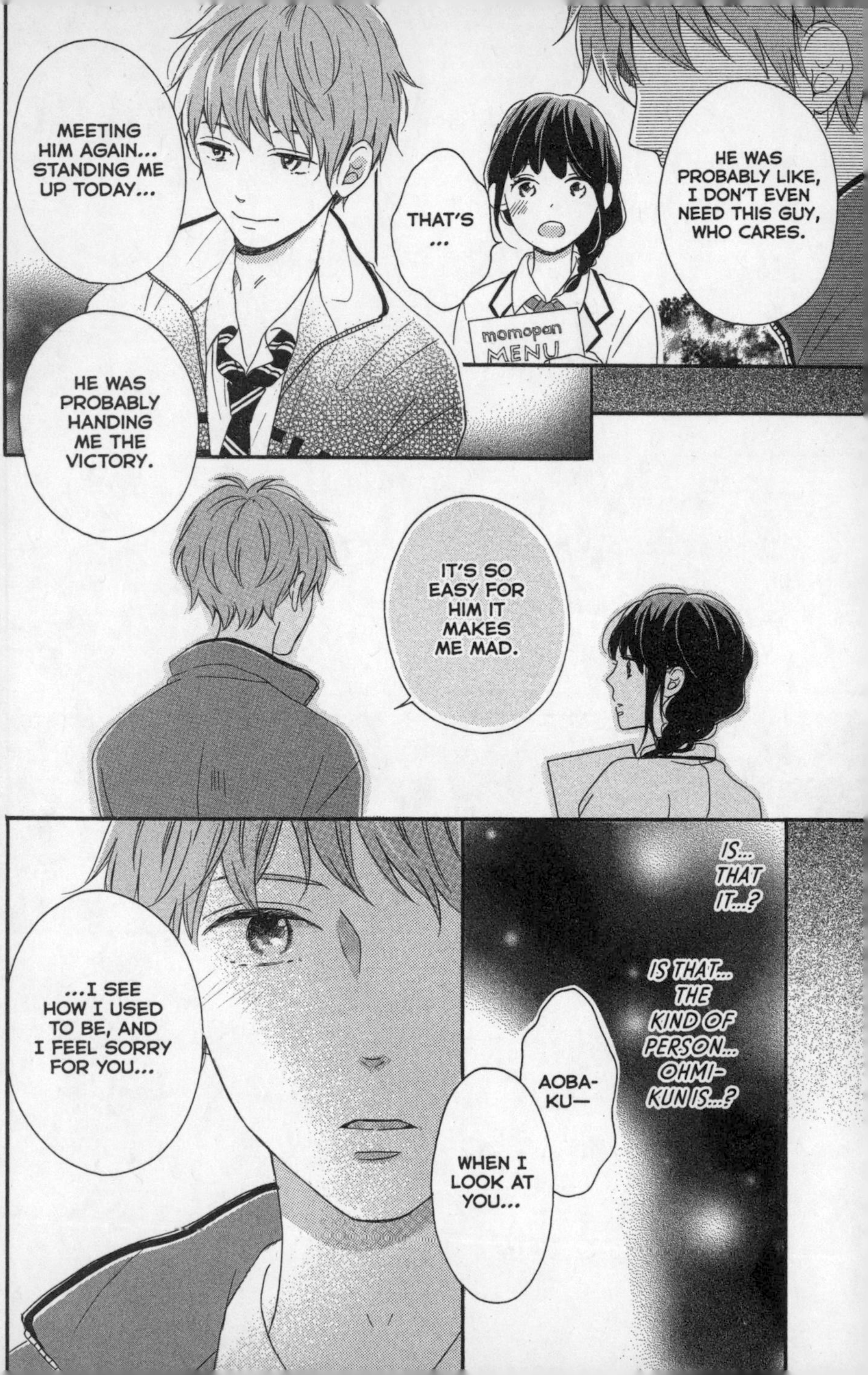
HE WAS PROBABLY LIKE, I DON'T EVEN NEED THIS GUY, WHO CARES.
momopan MENU
THAT'S ...
MEETING HIM AGAIN... STANDING ME UP TODAY...
HE WAS PROBABLY HANDING ME THE VICTORY.
IT'S SO EASY FOR HIM IT MAKES ME MAD.
IS... THAT IT...?
IS THAT... THE KIND OF PERSON... OHMI-KUN IS...?
AOBA-KU—
WHEN I LOOK AT YOU...
...I SEE HOW I USED TO BE, AND I FEEL SORRY FOR YOU...

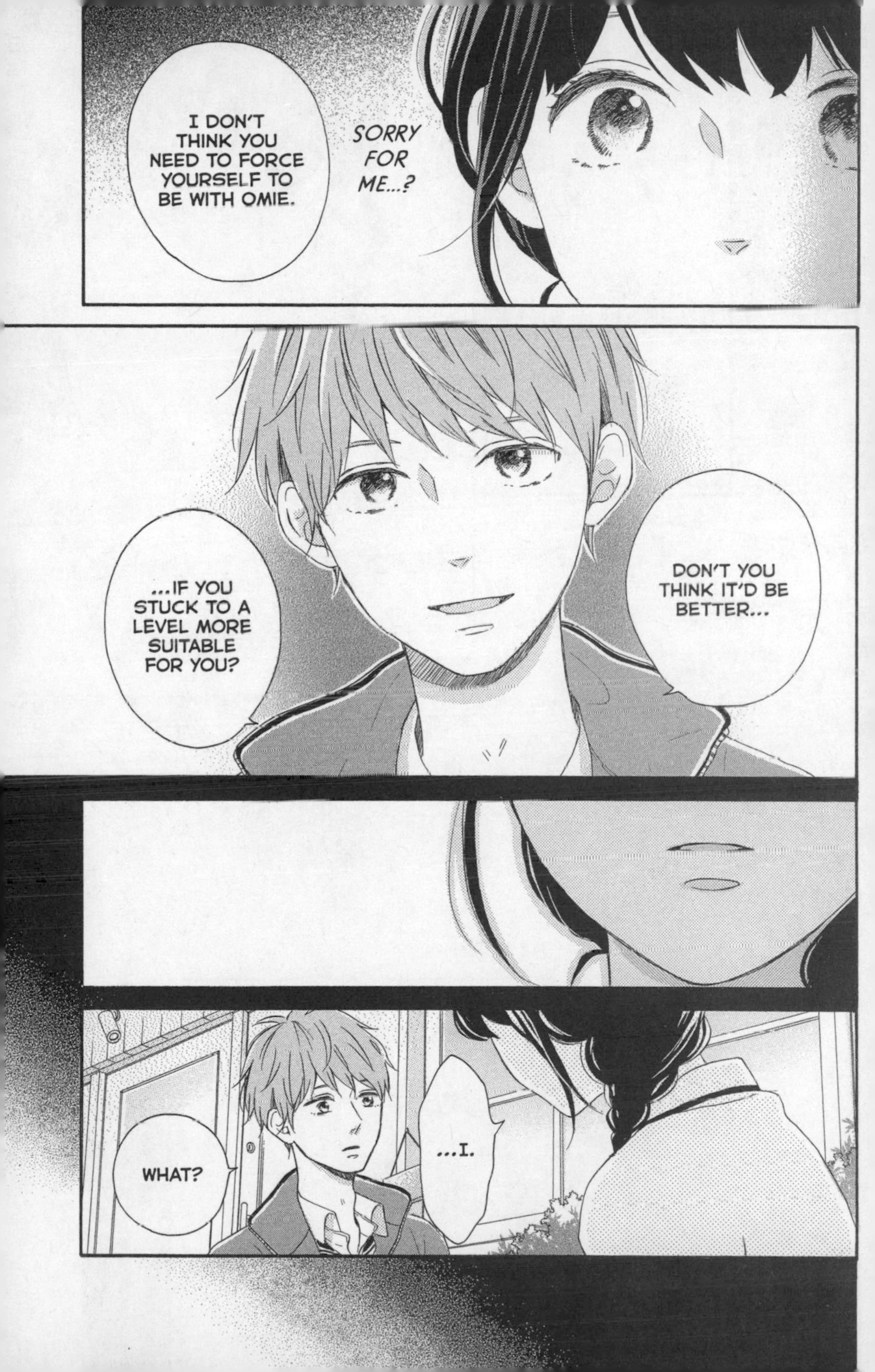
SORRY FOR ME...?
I DON'T THINK YOU NEED TO FORCE YOURSELF TO BE WITH OMIE.
DON'T YOU THINK IT'D BE BETTER...
...IF YOU STUCK TO A LEVEL MORE SUITABLE FOR YOU?
...I.
WHAT?

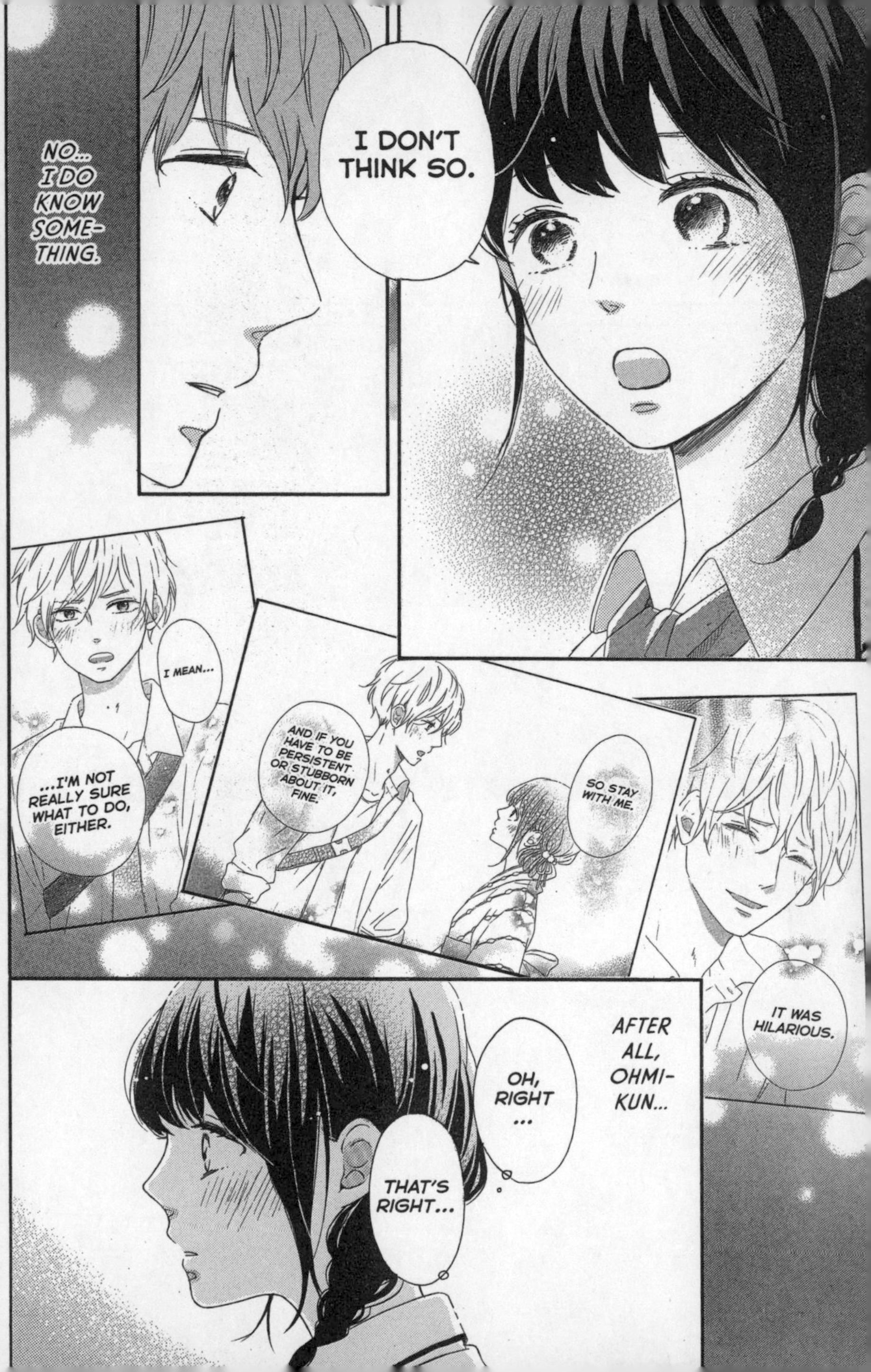
I DON'T THINK SO.
NO... I DO KNOW SOME-THING.
I MEAN...
...I'M NOT REALLY SURE WHAT TO DO, EITHER.
AND IF YOU HAVE TO BE PERSISTENT OR STUBBORN ABOUT IT, FINE.
SO STAY WITH ME.
IT WAS HILARIOUS.
AFTER ALL, OHMI-KUN...
OH, RIGHT ...
THAT'S RIGHT...

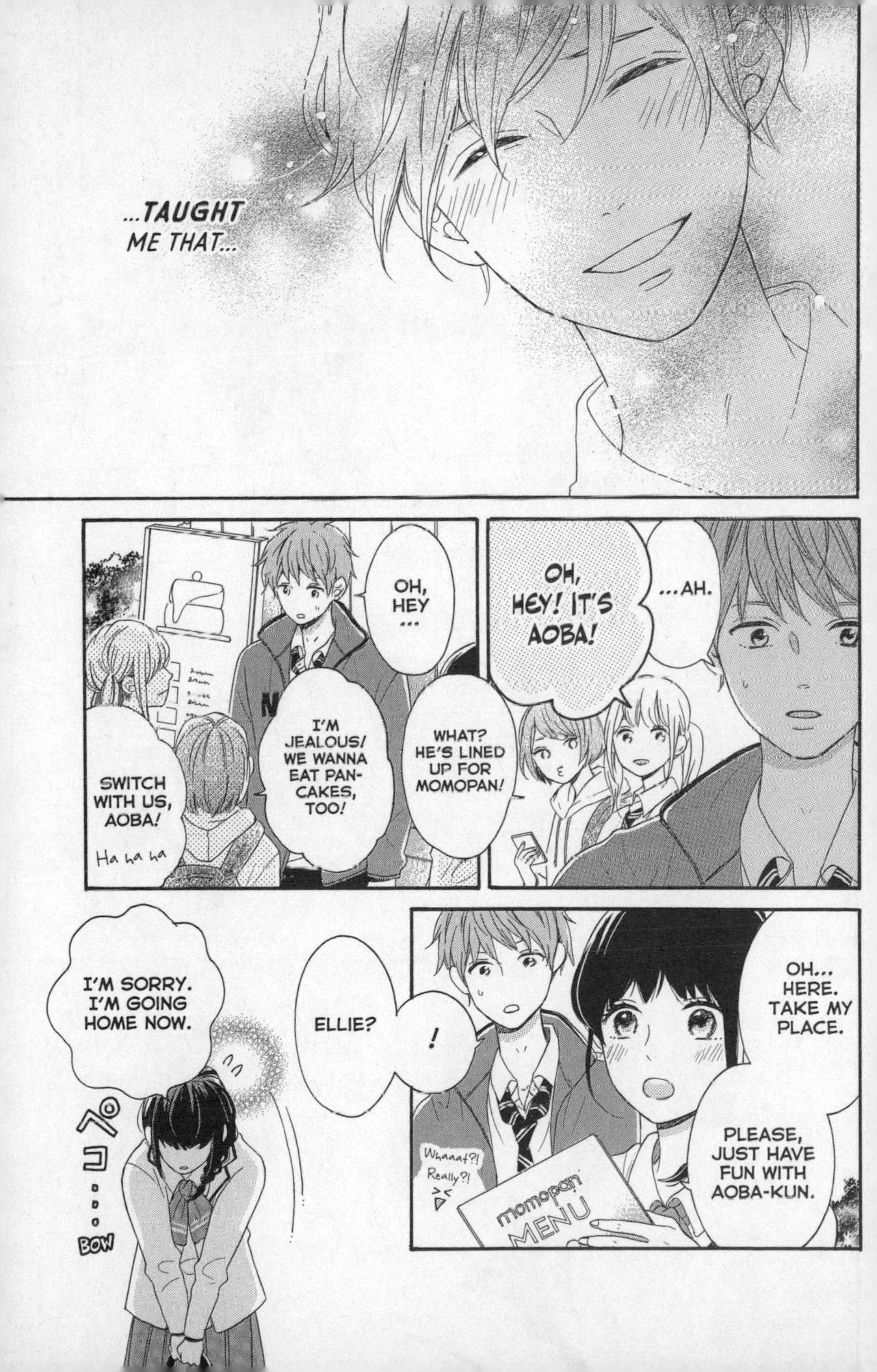
...TAUGHT ME THAT...
...AH.
OH, HEY! IT'S AOBA!
OH, HEY ...
WHAT? HE'S LINED UP FOR MOMOPAN!
I'M JEALOUS! WE WANNA EAT PAN-CAKES, TOO!
SWITCH WITH US, AOBA!
Ha ha ha
OH... HERE. TAKE MY PLACE.
!
ELLIE?
PLEASE, JUST HAVE FUN WITH AOBA-KUN.
Whaaat?! Really?!
momopan MENU
I'M SORRY. I'M GOING HOME NOW.
ペコ
BOW

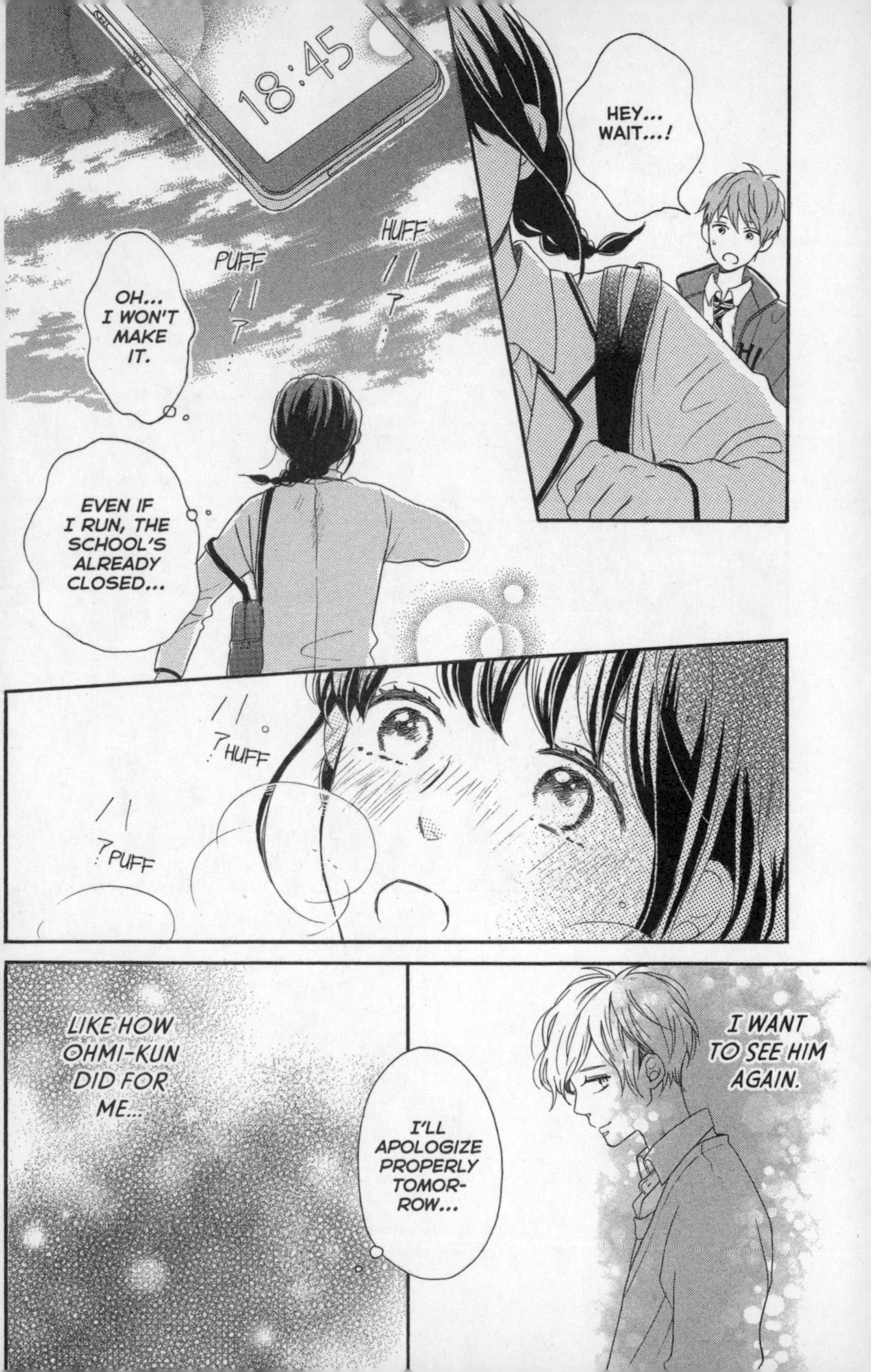
HEY... WAIT...!
HUFF
PUFF
OH... I WON'T MAKE IT.
EVEN IF I RUN, THE SCHOOL'S ALREADY CLOSED...
HUFF
PUFF
I WANT TO SEE HIM AGAIN.
I'LL APOLOGIZE PROPERLY TOMORROW...
LIKE HOW OHMI-KUN DID FOR ME...

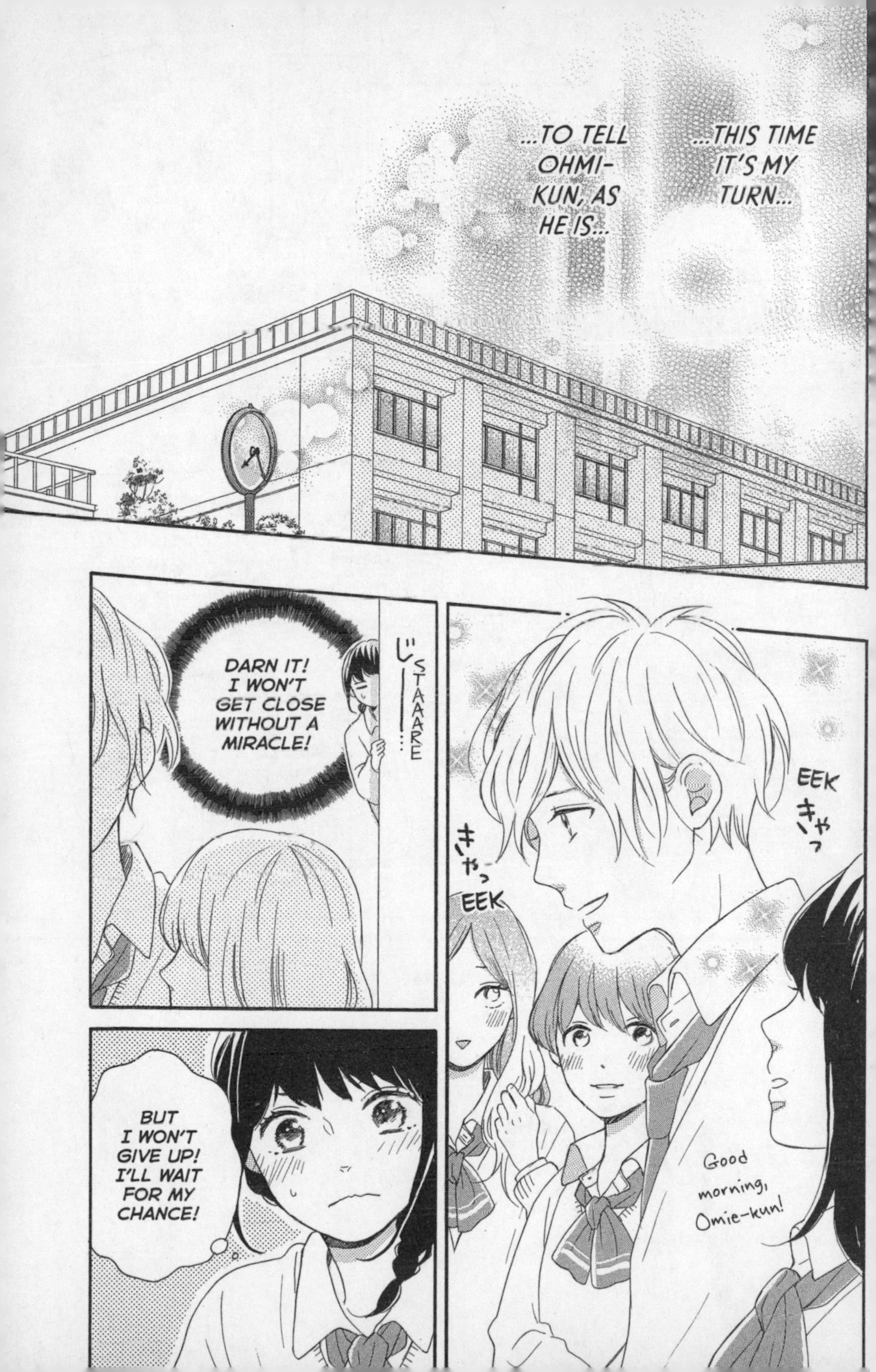
...THIS TIME IT'S MY TURN...
...TO TELL OHMI-KUN, AS HE IS...
EEK
きゃっ
きゃっ
EEK
Good morning, Omie-kun!
じー
STAAARE
DARN IT! I WON'T GET CLOSE WITHOUT A MIRACLE!
BUT I WON'T GIVE UP! I'LL WAIT FOR MY CHANCE!

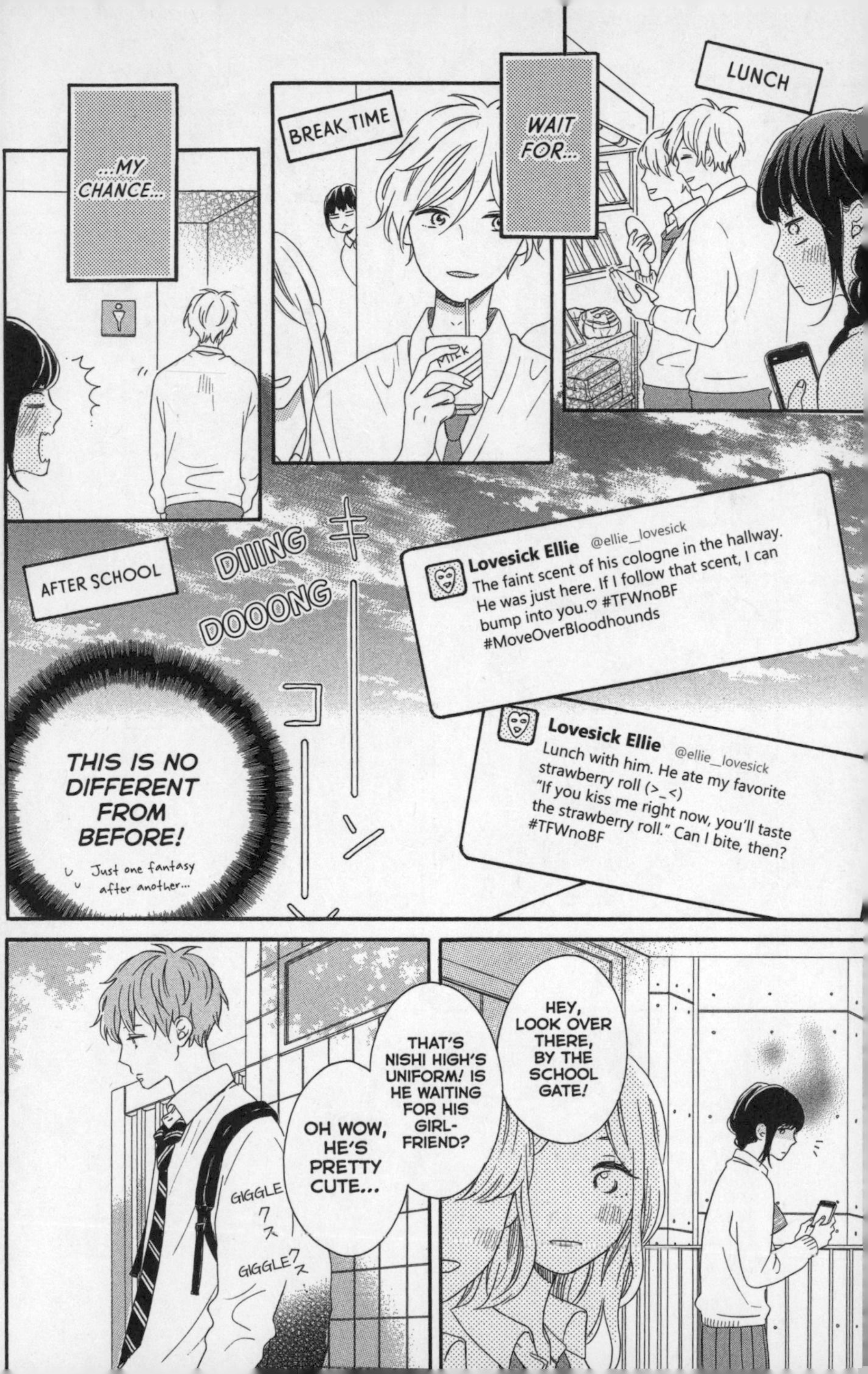
LUNCH
WAIT FOR...
BREAK TIME
MILK
...MY CHANCE...
Lovesick Ellie @ellie__lovesick
The faint scent of his cologne in the hallway. He was just here. If I follow that scent, I can bump into you.♡ #TFWnoBF #MoveOverBloodhounds
Lovesick Ellie @ellie__lovesick
Lunch with him. He ate my favorite strawberry roll (>_<) "If you kiss me right now, you'll taste the strawberry roll." Can I bite, then? #TFWnoBF
キーンコーン
DIIING DOOONG
AFTER SCHOOL
THIS IS NO DIFFERENT FROM BEFORE!
Just one fantasy after another...
HEY, LOOK OVER THERE, BY THE SCHOOL GATE!
THAT'S NISHI HIGH'S UNIFORM! IS HE WAITING FOR HIS GIRL-FRIEND?
OH WOW, HE'S PRETTY CUTE...
GIGGLE クス
GIGGLE クス

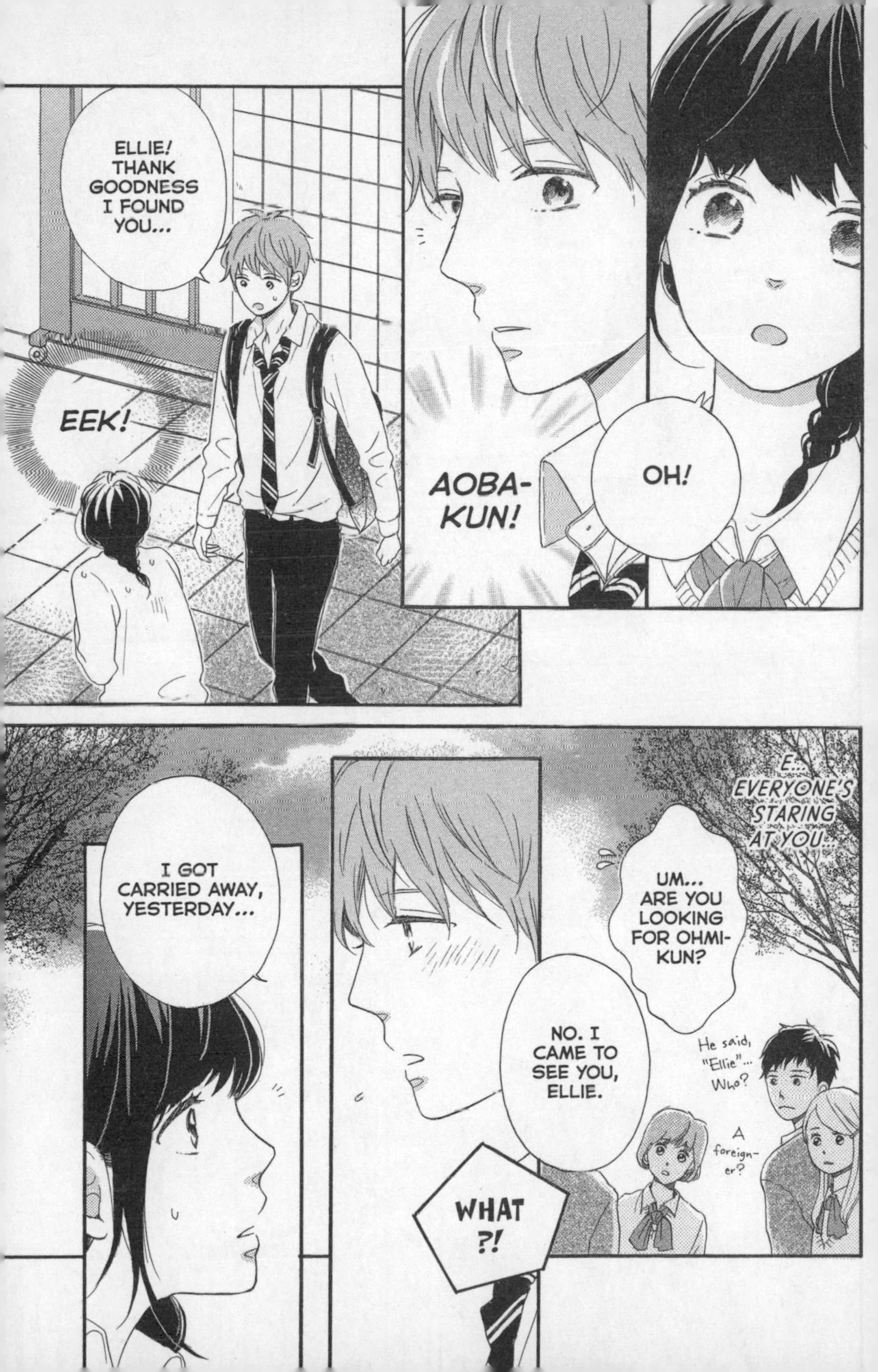
OH!
AOBA-KUN!
ELLIE! THANK GOODNESS I FOUND YOU...
EEK!
E... EVERYONE'S STARING AT YOU...
UM... ARE YOU LOOKING FOR OHMI-KUN?
He said, "Ellie"... Who?
A foreigner?
NO. I CAME TO SEE YOU, ELLIE.
WHAT ?!
I GOT CARRIED AWAY, YESTERDAY...

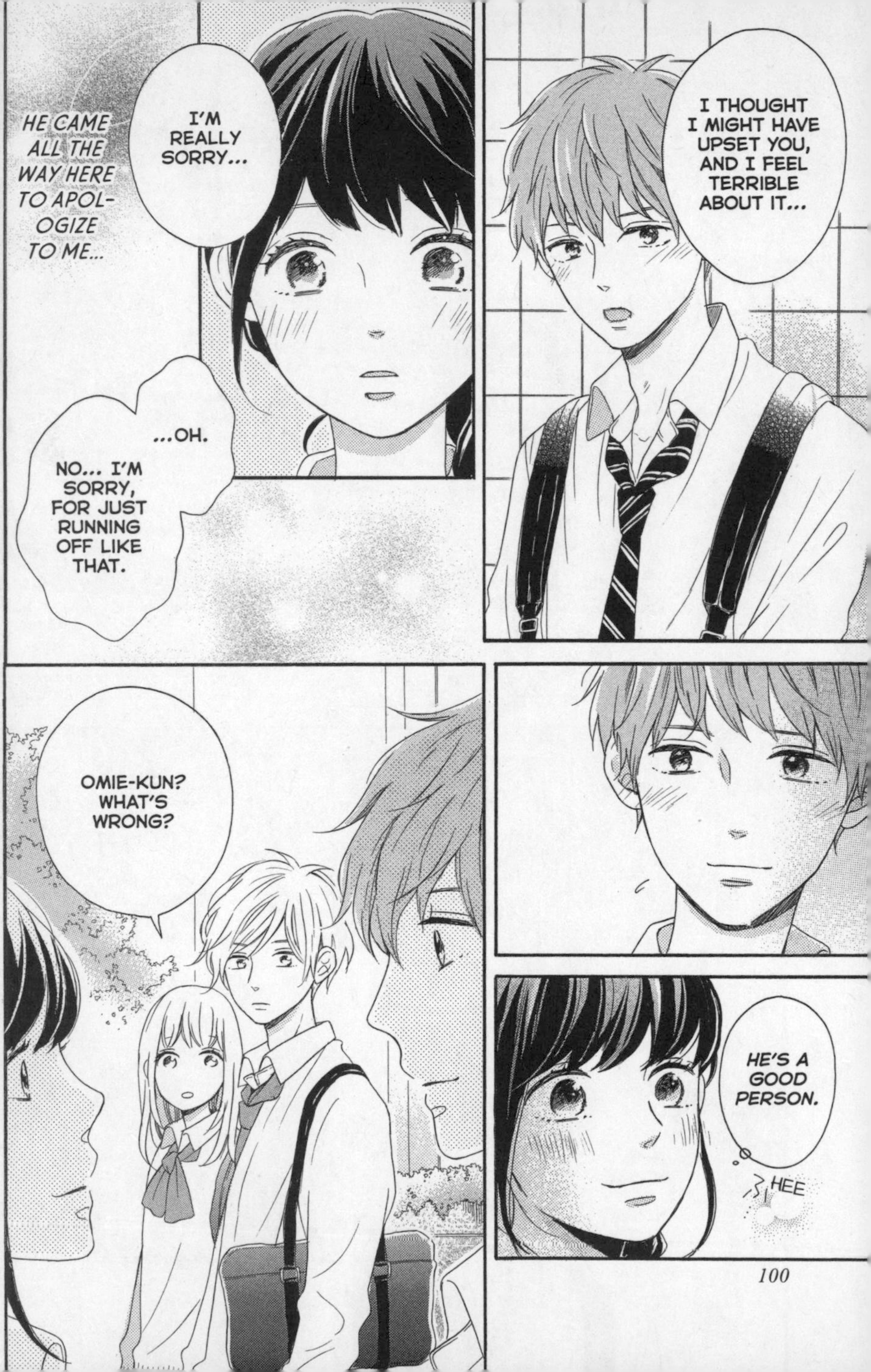
I THOUGHT I MIGHT HAVE UPSET YOU, AND I FEEL TERRIBLE ABOUT IT...
I'M REALLY SORRY...
HE CAME ALL THE WAY HERE TO APOLOGIZE TO ME...
...OH.
NO... I'M SORRY, FOR JUST RUNNING OFF LIKE THAT.
HE'S A GOOD PERSON.
HEE
OMIE-KUN? WHAT'S WRONG?

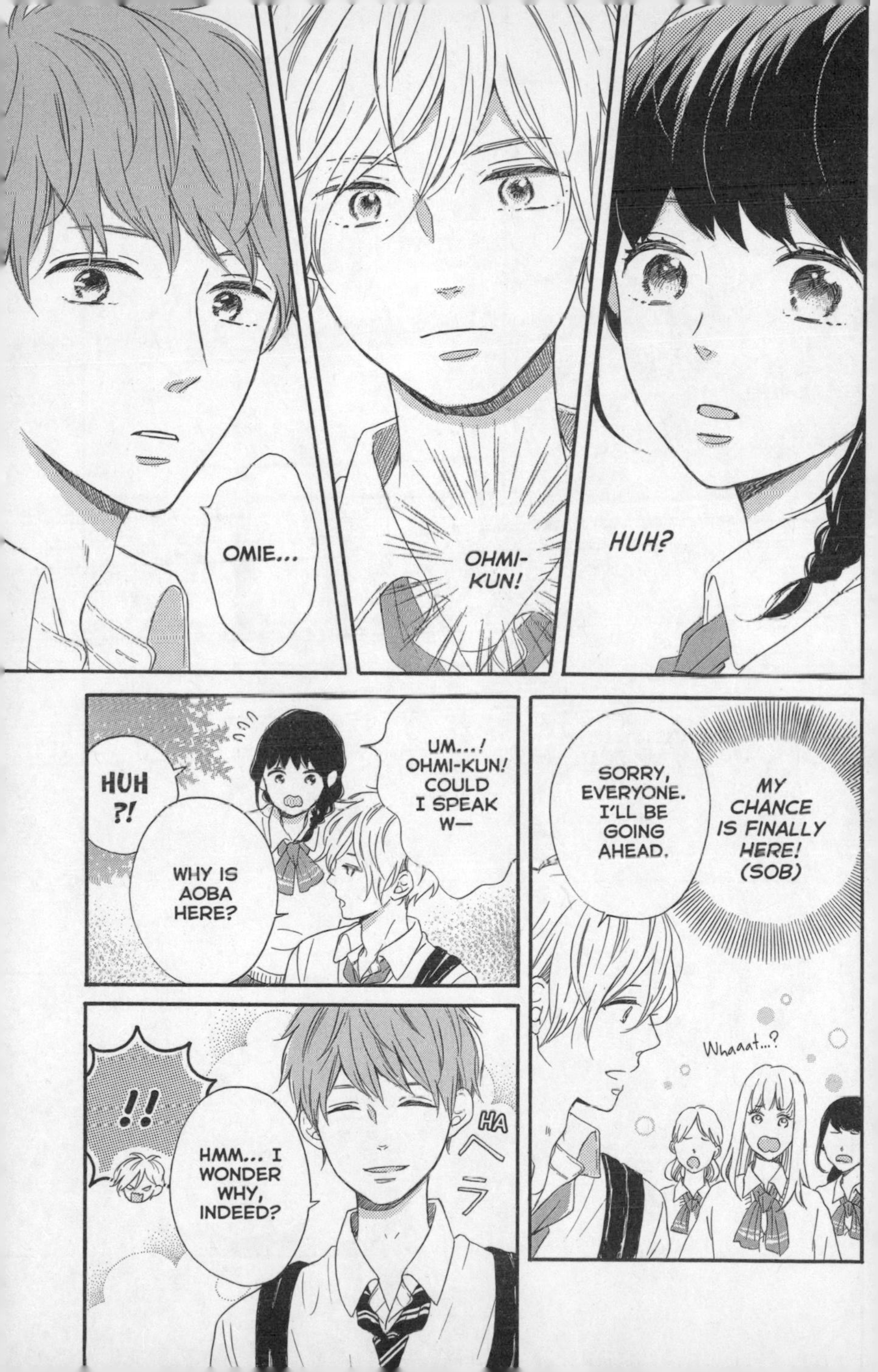
HUH?
OHMI-KUN!
OMIE...
MY CHANCE IS FINALLY HERE! (SOB)
SORRY, EVERYONE. I'LL BE GOING AHEAD.
Whaaat...?
UM...! OHMI-KUN! COULD I SPEAK W—
HUH ?!
WHY IS AOBA HERE?
HA
HMM... I WONDER WHY, INDEED?
!!

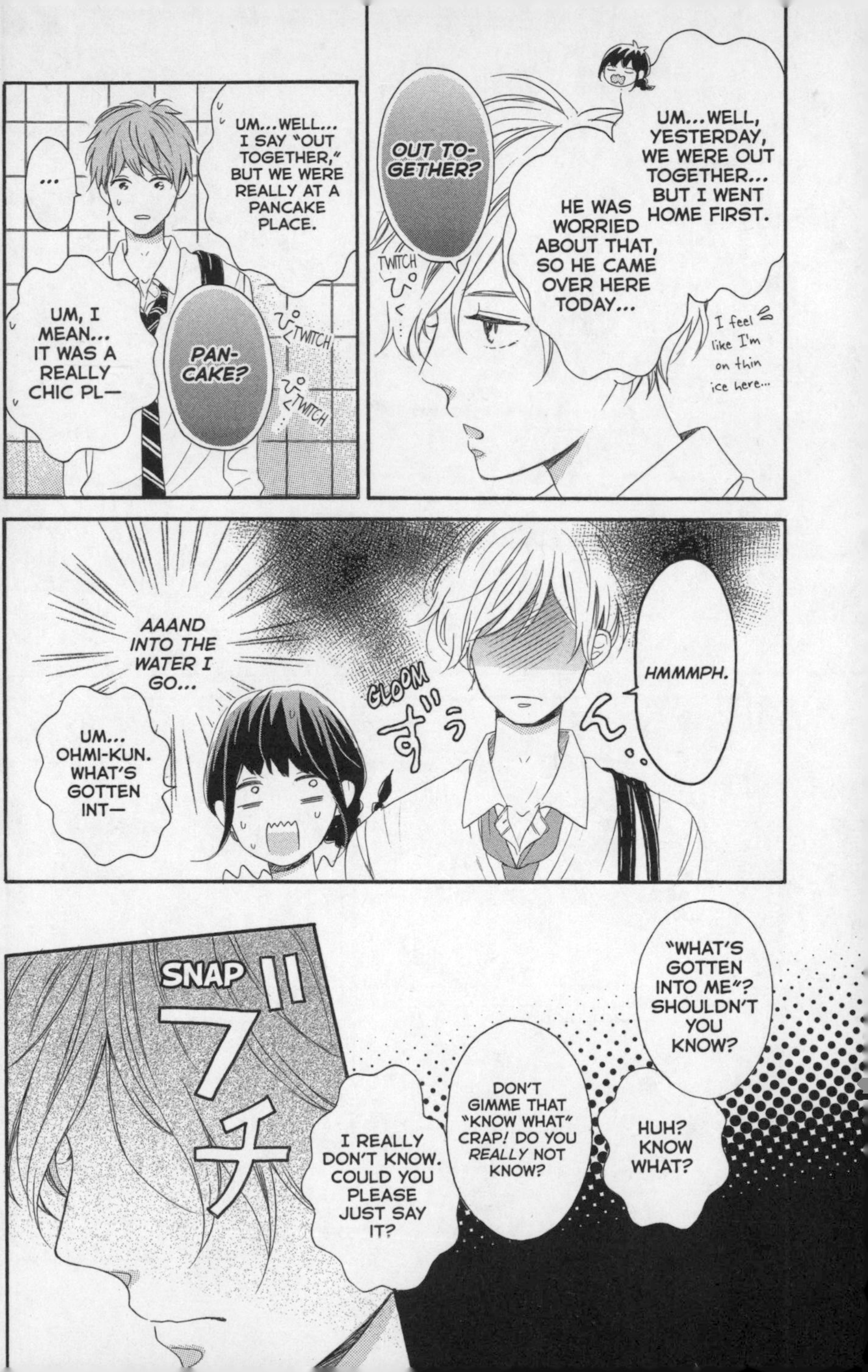

UM...WELL, YESTERDAY, WE WERE OUT TOGETHER... BUT I WENT HOME FIRST.
HE WAS WORRIED ABOUT THAT, SO HE CAME OVER HERE TODAY...
OUT TO-GETHER?
TWITCH
I feel like I'm on thin ice here...
UM...WELL... I SAY "OUT TOGETHER," BUT WE WERE REALLY AT A PANCAKE PLACE.
...
PAN-CAKE?
TWITCH
TWITCH
UM, I MEAN... IT WAS A REALLY CHIC PL—
HMMMPH.
GLOOM
AAAND INTO THE WATER I GO...
UM... OHMI-KUN. WHAT'S GOTTEN INT—
"WHAT'S GOTTEN INTO ME"? SHOULDN'T YOU KNOW?
HUH? KNOW WHAT?
DON'T GIMME THAT "KNOW WHAT" CRAP! DO YOU *REALLY* NOT KNOW?
I REALLY DON'T KNOW. COULD YOU PLEASE JUST SAY IT?
SNAP

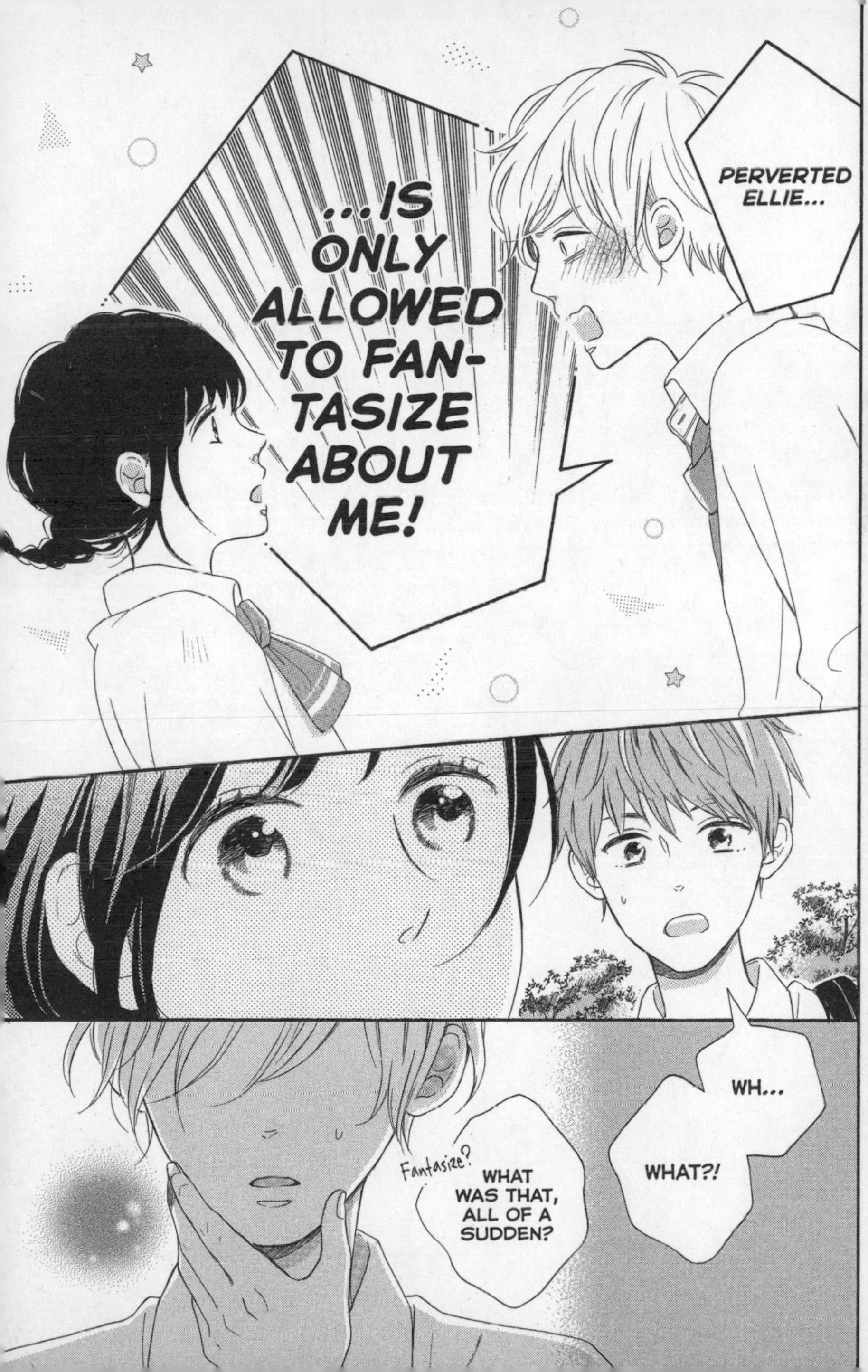
PERVERTED ELLIE...
...IS ONLY ALLOWED TO FAN-TASIZE ABOUT ME!
WH...
WHAT?!
Fantasize?
WHAT WAS THAT, ALL OF A SUDDEN?

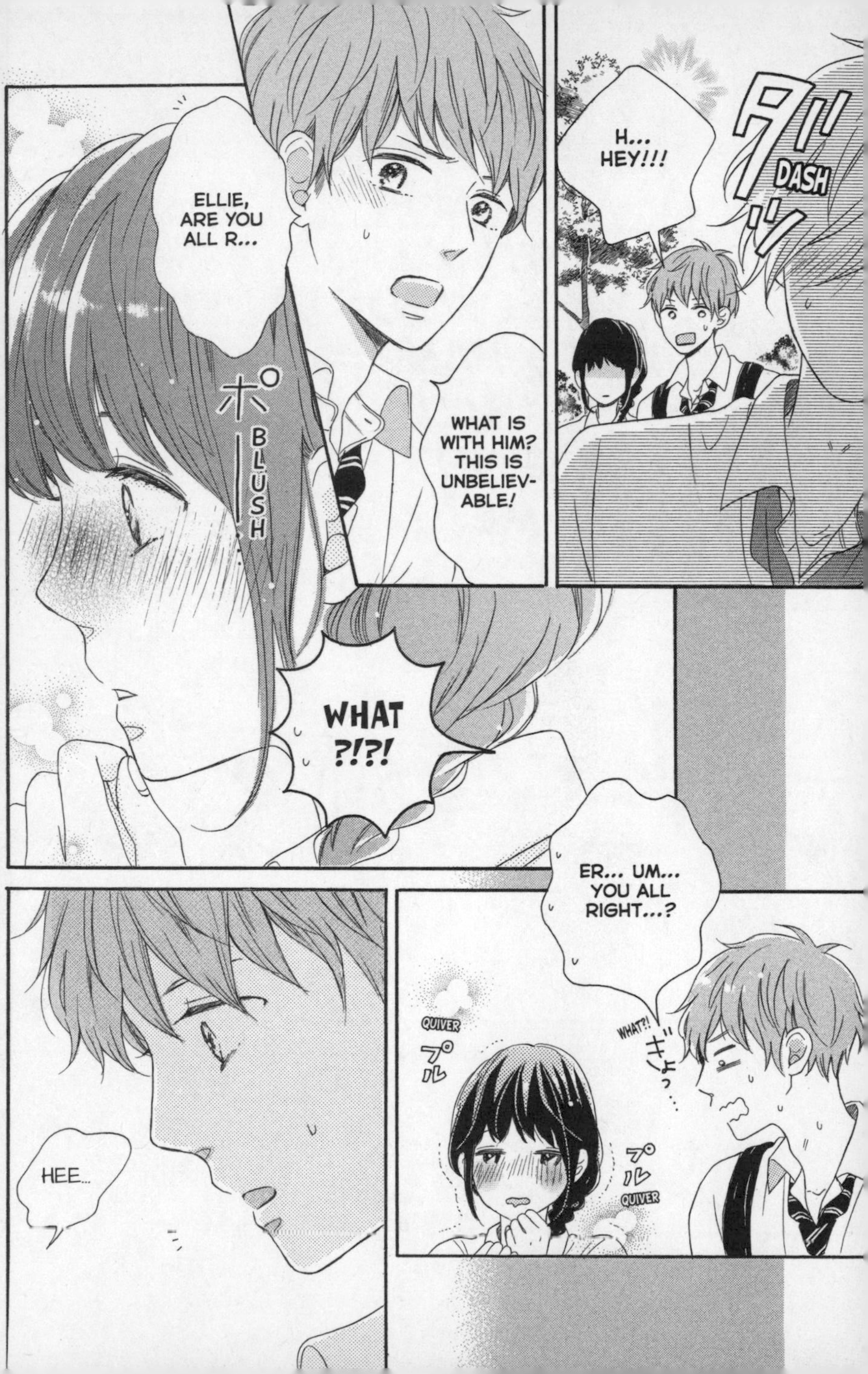
DASH
H... HEY!!!
ELLIE, ARE YOU ALL R...
WHAT IS WITH HIM? THIS IS UNBELIEVABLE!
BLUSH
WHAT ?!?!
ER... UM... YOU ALL RIGHT...?
WHAT?!
QUIVER
QUIVER
HEE...

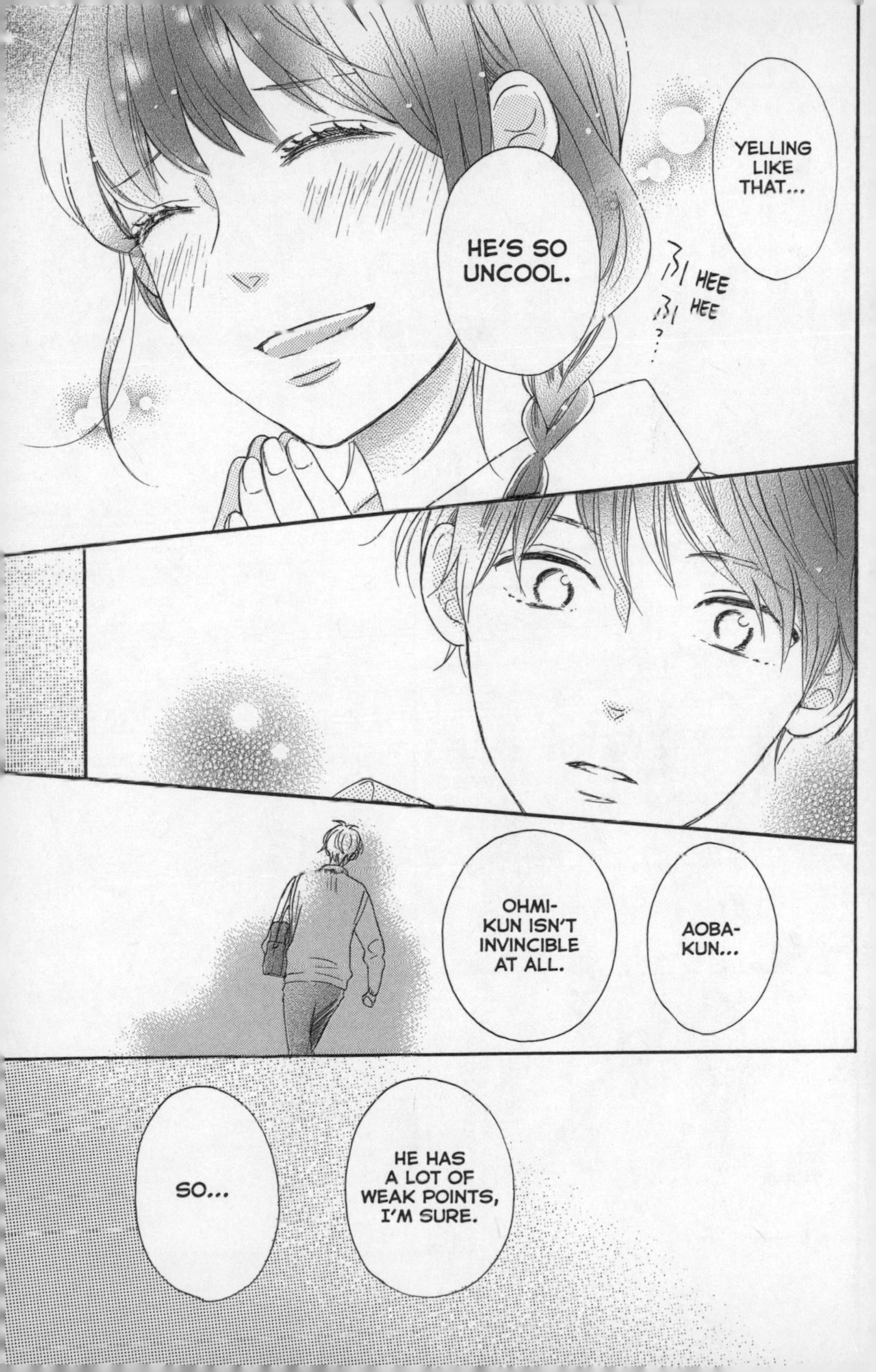
YELLING LIKE THAT...
HE'S SO UNCOOL.
HEE HEE
AOBA-KUN...
OHMI-KUN ISN'T INVINCIBLE AT ALL.
HE HAS A LOT OF WEAK POINTS, I'M SURE.
SO...

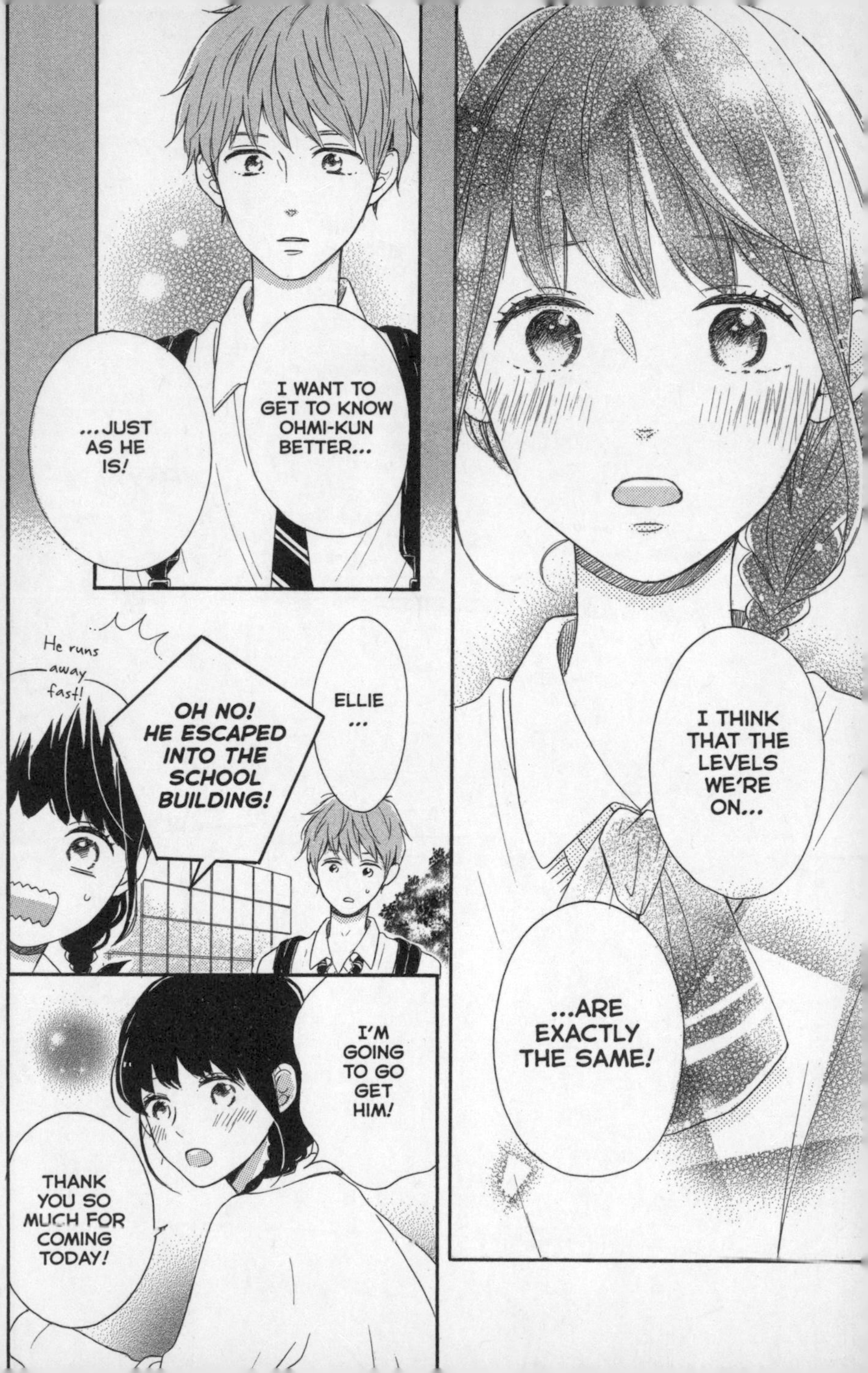
I THINK THAT THE LEVELS WE'RE ON...
...ARE EXACTLY THE SAME!
I WANT TO GET TO KNOW OHMI-KUN BETTER...
...JUST AS HE IS!
ELLIE...
OH NO! HE ESCAPED INTO THE SCHOOL BUILDING!
He runs away fast!
I'M GOING TO GO GET HIM!
THANK YOU SO MUCH FOR COMING TODAY!

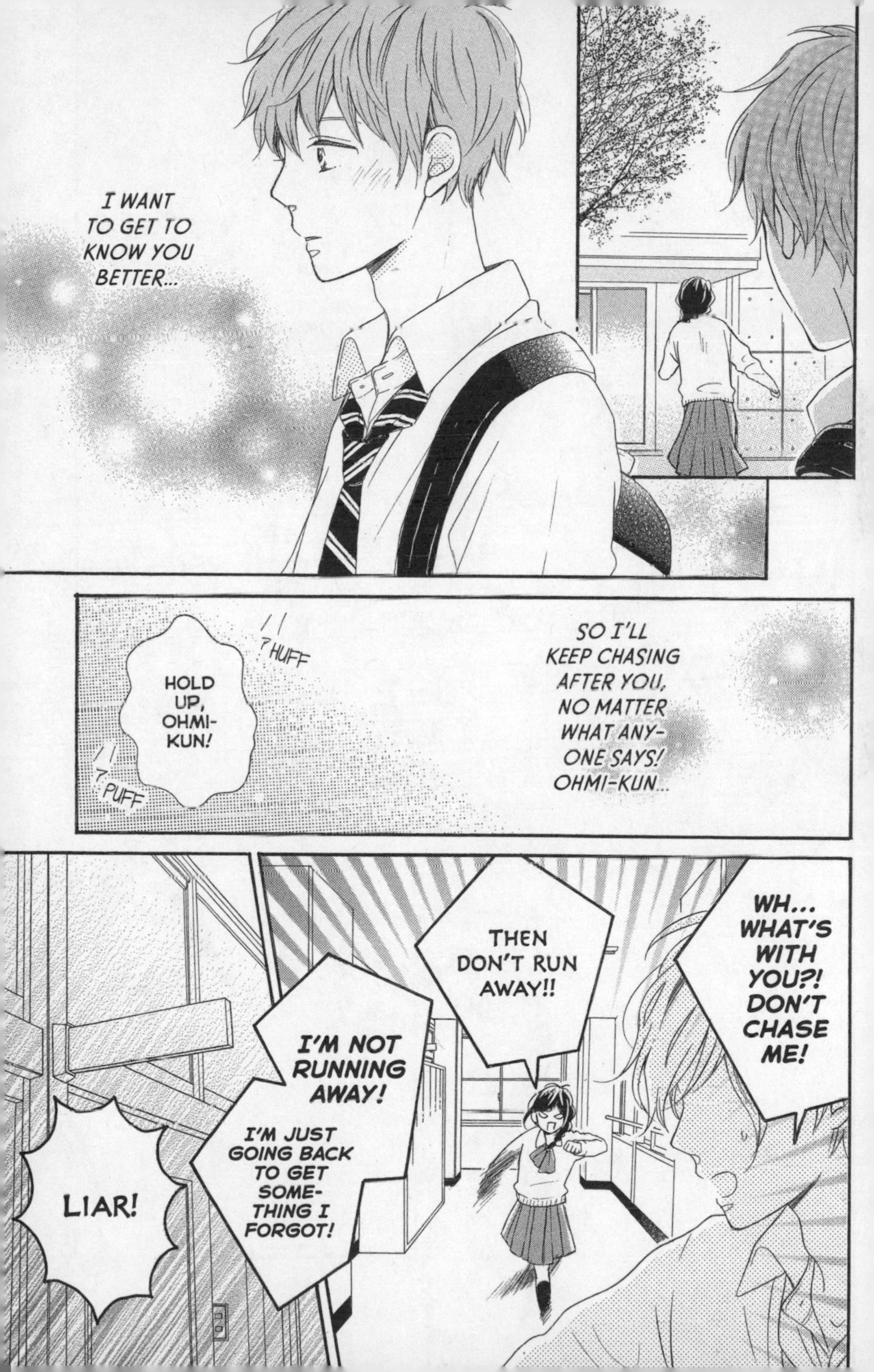
I WANT TO GET TO KNOW YOU BETTER...
SO I'LL KEEP CHASING AFTER YOU, NO MATTER WHAT ANYONE SAYS! OHMI-KUN...
HUFF
HOLD UP, OHMI-KUN!
PUFF
WH... WHAT'S WITH YOU?! DON'T CHASE ME!
THEN DON'T RUN AWAY!!
I'M NOT RUNNING AWAY!
I'M JUST GOING BACK TO GET SOMETHING I FORGOT!
LIAR!

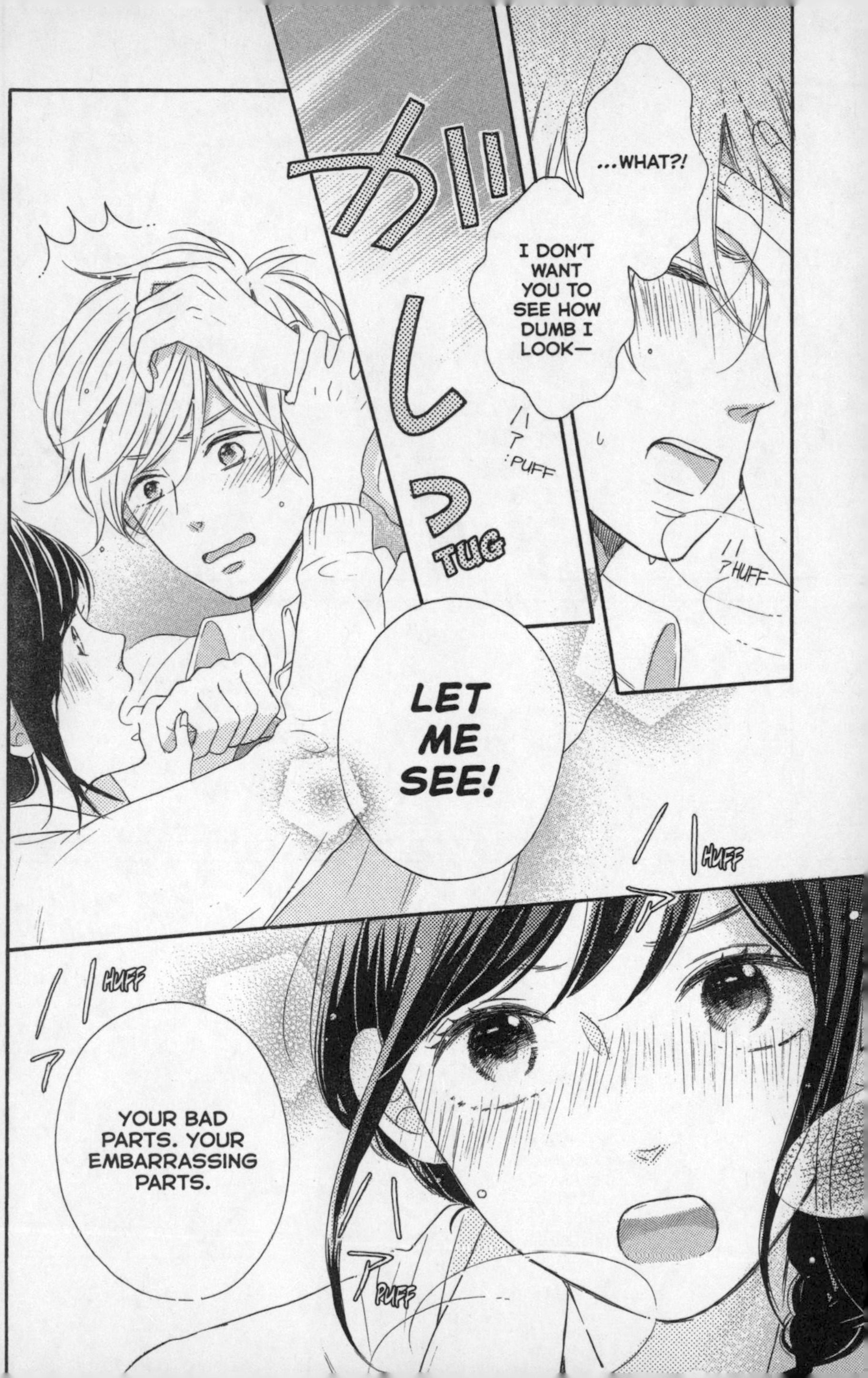
...WHAT?!
I DON'T WANT YOU TO SEE HOW DUMB I LOOK—
PUFF
HUFF
TUG
LET ME SEE!
HUFF
HUFF
YOUR BAD PARTS. YOUR EMBARRASSING PARTS.
PUFF

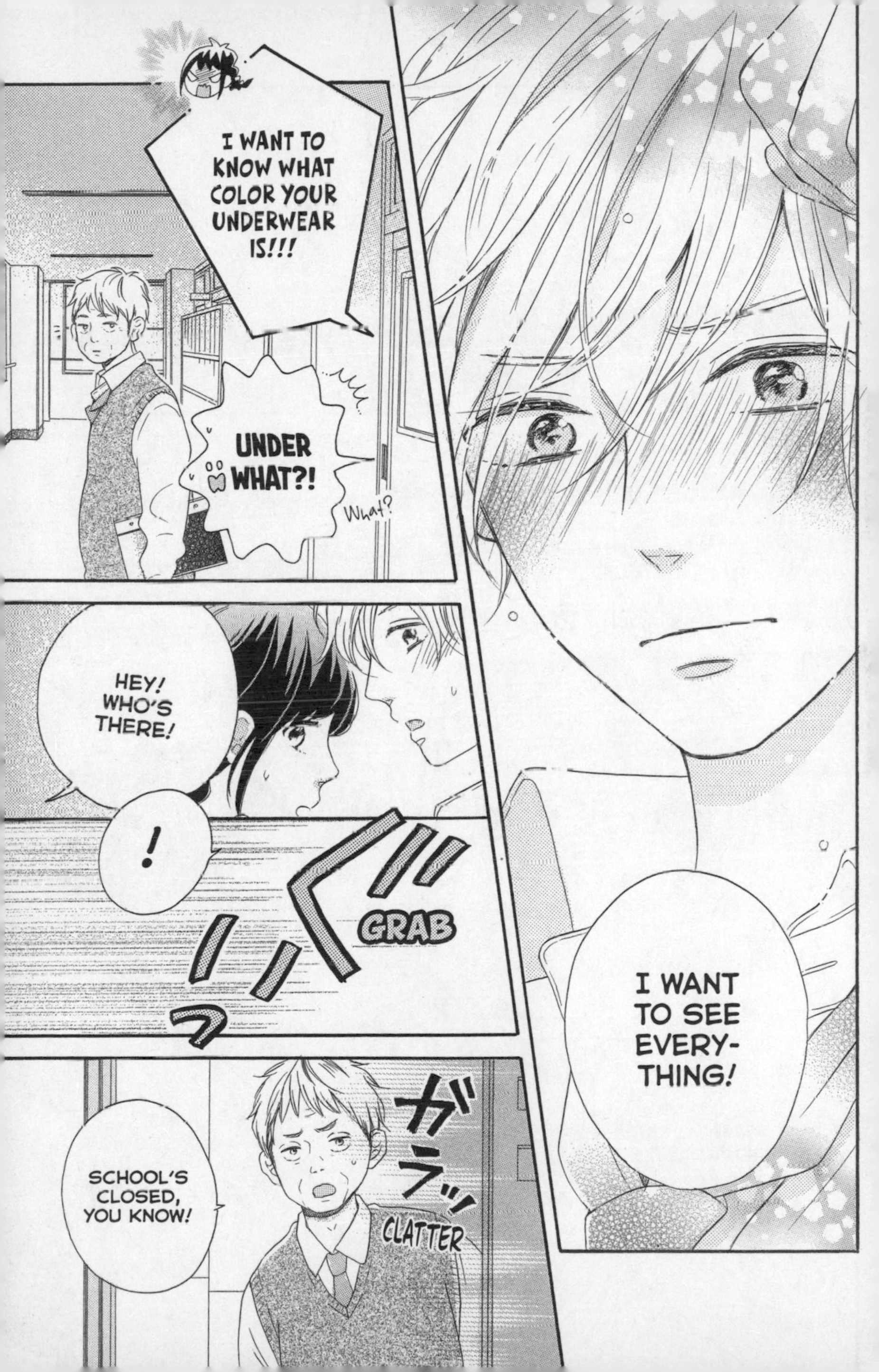
I WANT TO SEE EVERY-THING!
I WANT TO KNOW WHAT COLOR YOUR UNDERWEAR IS!!!
UNDER WHAT?!
What?
HEY! WHO'S THERE!
!
GRAB
SCHOOL'S CLOSED, YOU KNOW!
CLATTER

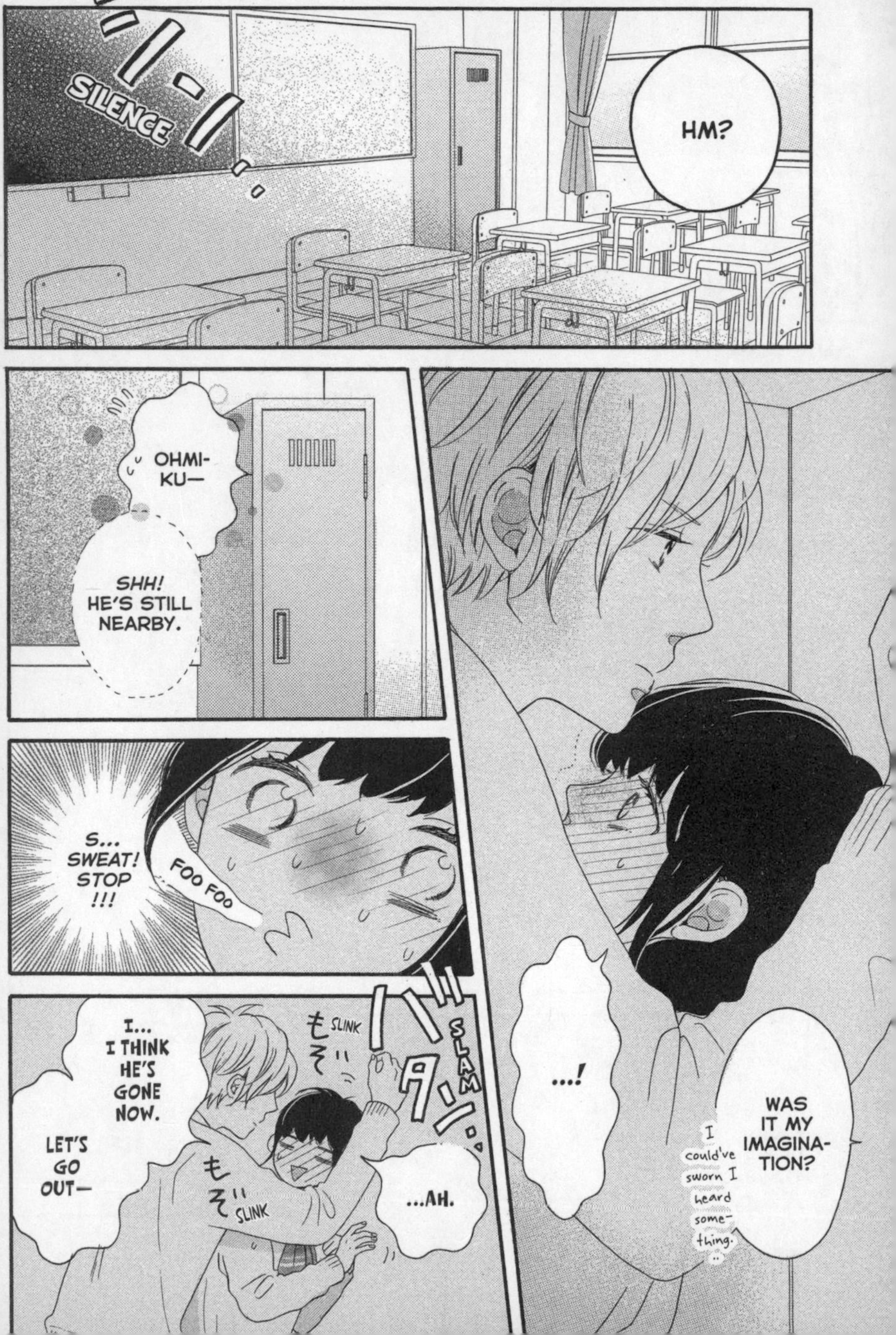
HM?
SILENCE
WAS IT MY IMAGINATION?
I could've sworn I heard some-thing...
...!
OHMI-KU—
SHH! HE'S STILL NEARBY.
FOO FOO
S... SWEAT! STOP !!!
SLAM
SLINK
...AH.
SLINK
I... I THINK HE'S GONE NOW.
LET'S GO OUT—

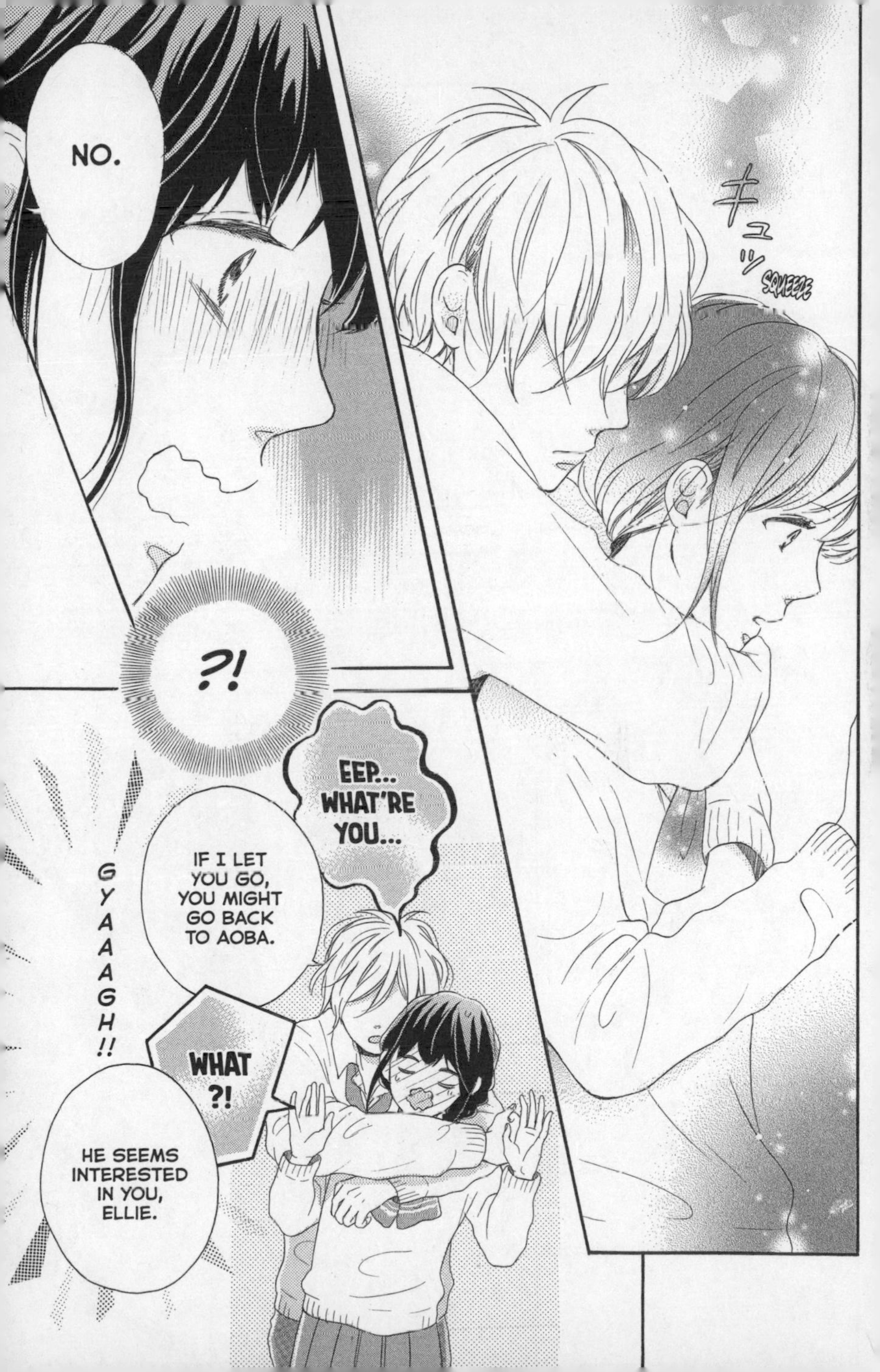
キュッ
SQUEEZE
NO.
?!
EEP... WHAT'RE YOU...
IF I LET YOU GO, YOU MIGHT GO BACK TO AOBA.
WHAT ?!
HE SEEMS INTERESTED IN YOU, ELLIE.
GYAAAGH!!

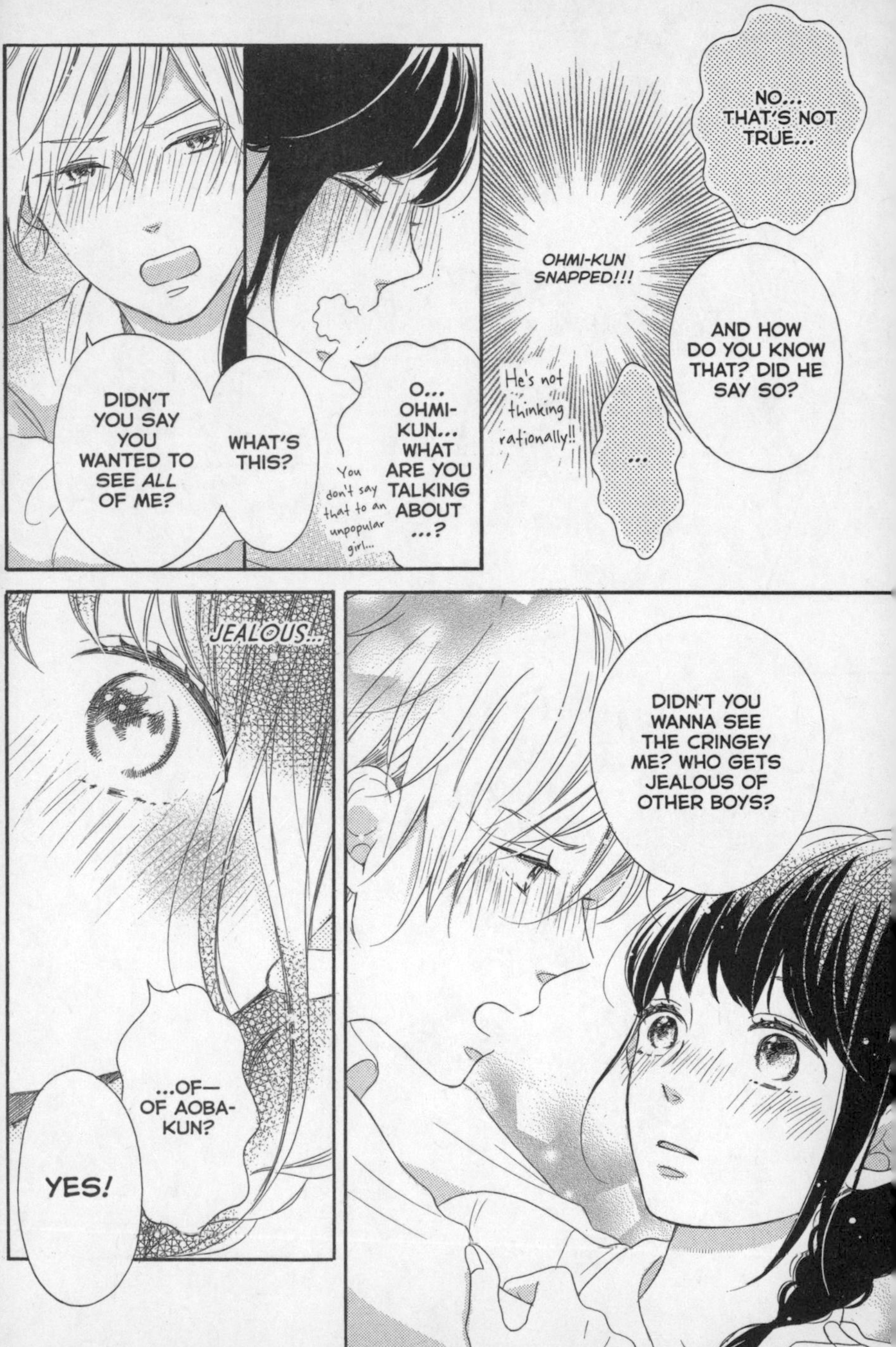
NO... THAT'S NOT TRUE...
OHMI-KUN SNAPPED!!!
AND HOW DO YOU KNOW THAT? DID HE SAY SO?
He's not thinking rationally!!
...
O... OHMI-KUN... WHAT ARE YOU TALKING ABOUT...?
You don't say that to an unpopular girl...
WHAT'S THIS?
DIDN'T YOU SAY YOU WANTED TO SEE *ALL* OF ME?
DIDN'T YOU WANNA SEE THE CRINGEY ME? WHO GETS JEALOUS OF OTHER BOYS?
JEALOUS...
...OF— OF AOBA-KUN?
YES!

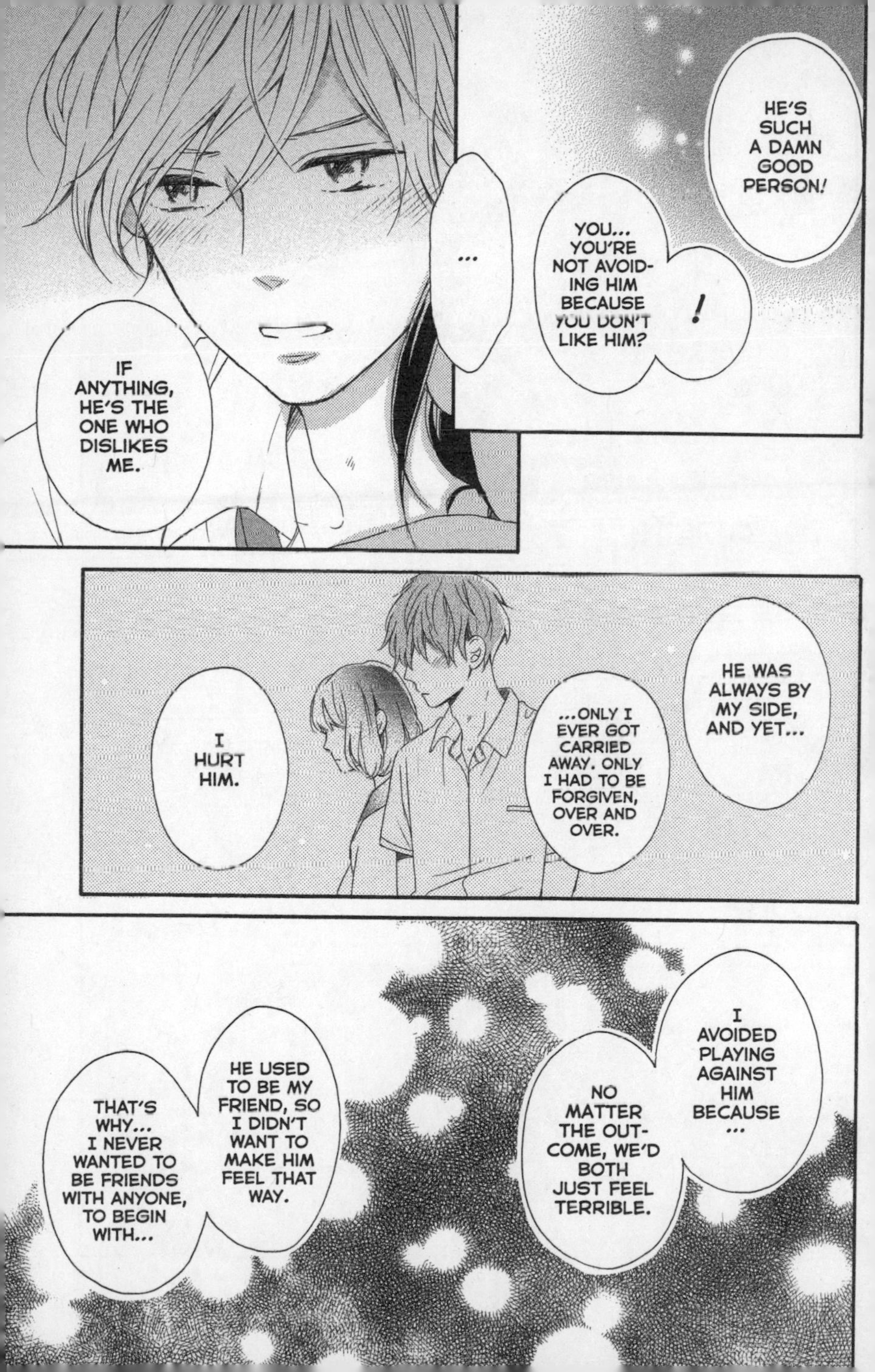
HE'S SUCH A DAMN GOOD PERSON!
YOU... YOU'RE NOT AVOIDING HIM BECAUSE YOU DON'T LIKE HIM?
!
...
IF ANYTHING, HE'S THE ONE WHO DISLIKES ME.
HE WAS ALWAYS BY MY SIDE, AND YET...
...ONLY I EVER GOT CARRIED AWAY. ONLY I HAD TO BE FORGIVEN, OVER AND OVER.
I HURT HIM.
I AVOIDED PLAYING AGAINST HIM BECAUSE...
NO MATTER THE OUTCOME, WE'D BOTH JUST FEEL TERRIBLE.
HE USED TO BE MY FRIEND, SO I DIDN'T WANT TO MAKE HIM FEEL THAT WAY.
THAT'S WHY... I NEVER WANTED TO BE FRIENDS WITH ANYONE, TO BEGIN WITH...

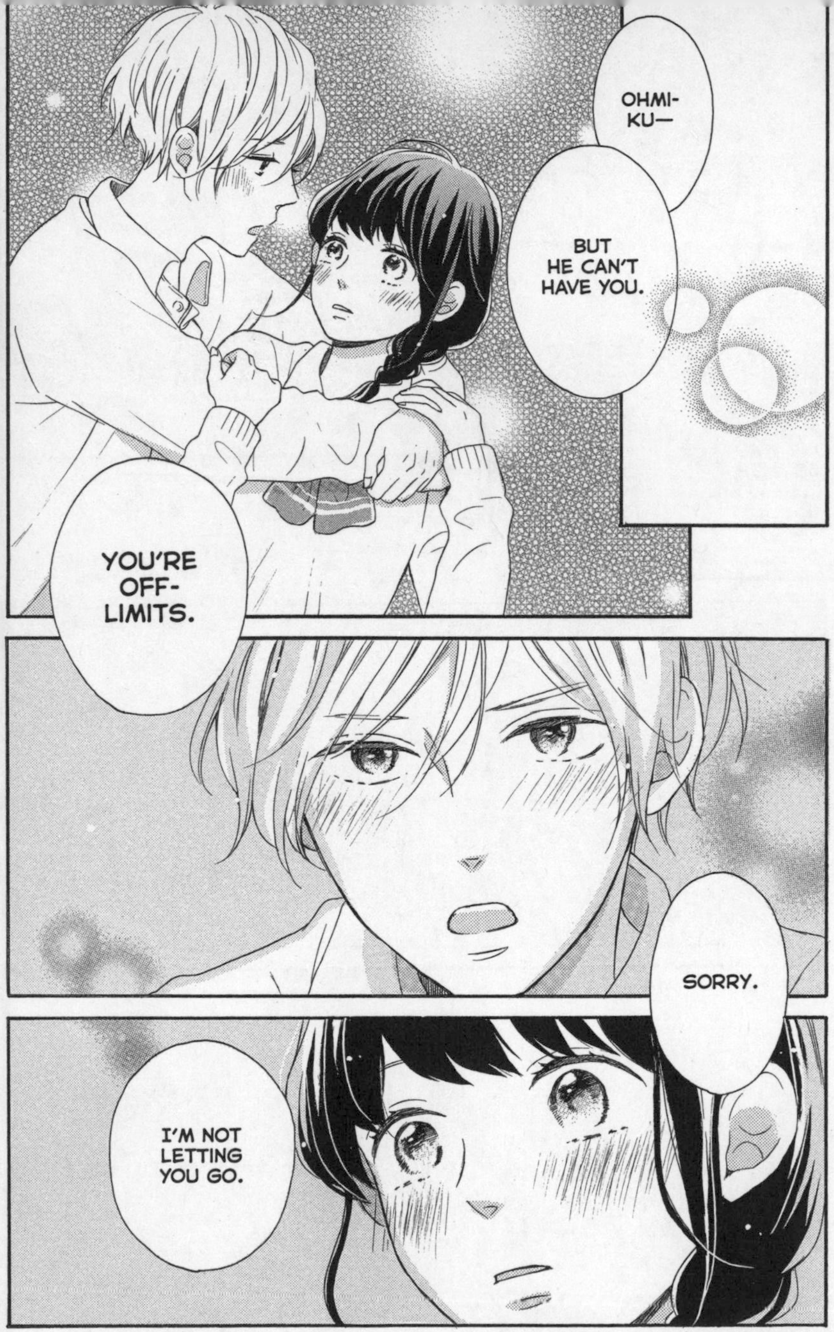
OHMI-KU—
BUT HE CAN'T HAVE YOU.
YOU'RE OFF-LIMITS.
SORRY.
I'M NOT LETTING YOU GO.

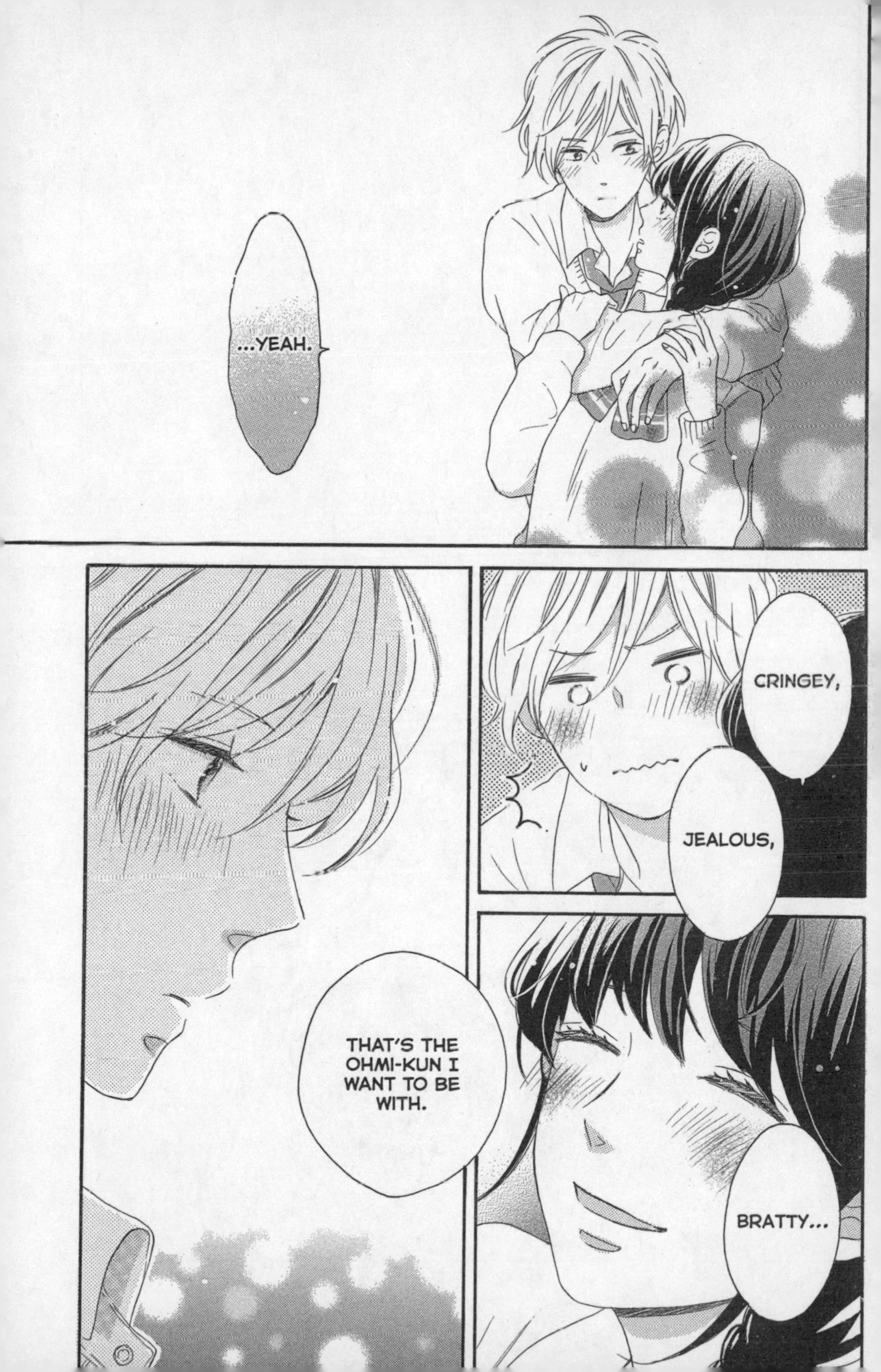
...YEAH.
CRINGEY,
JEALOUS,
BRATTY...
THAT'S THE OHMI-KUN I WANT TO BE WITH.

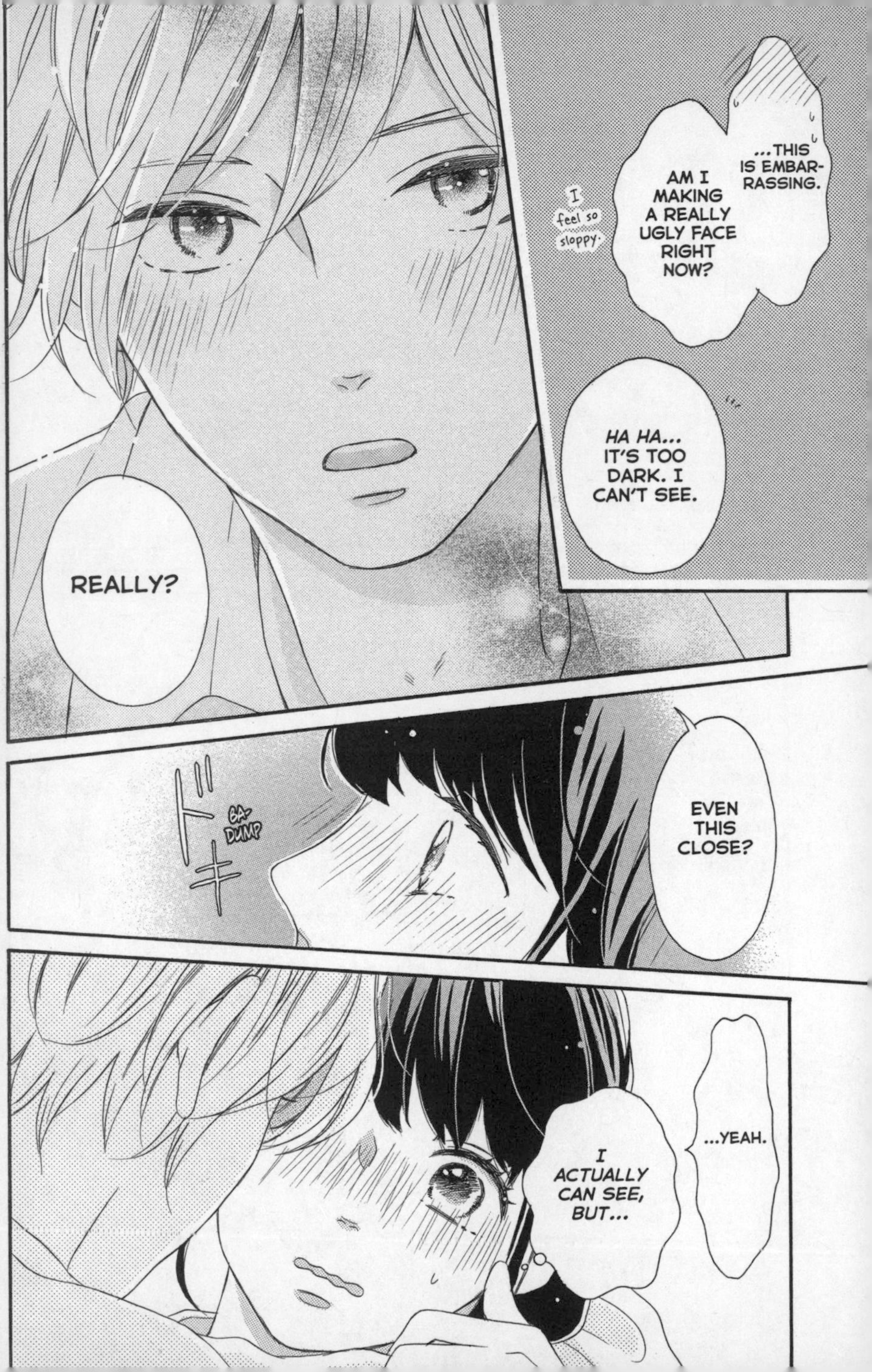
...THIS IS EMBARRASSING.
AM I MAKING A REALLY UGLY FACE RIGHT NOW?
I feel so sloppy.
HA HA... IT'S TOO DARK. I CAN'T SEE.
REALLY?
EVEN THIS CLOSE?
ドキ
BA-DUMP
...YEAH.
I ACTUALLY CAN SEE, BUT...

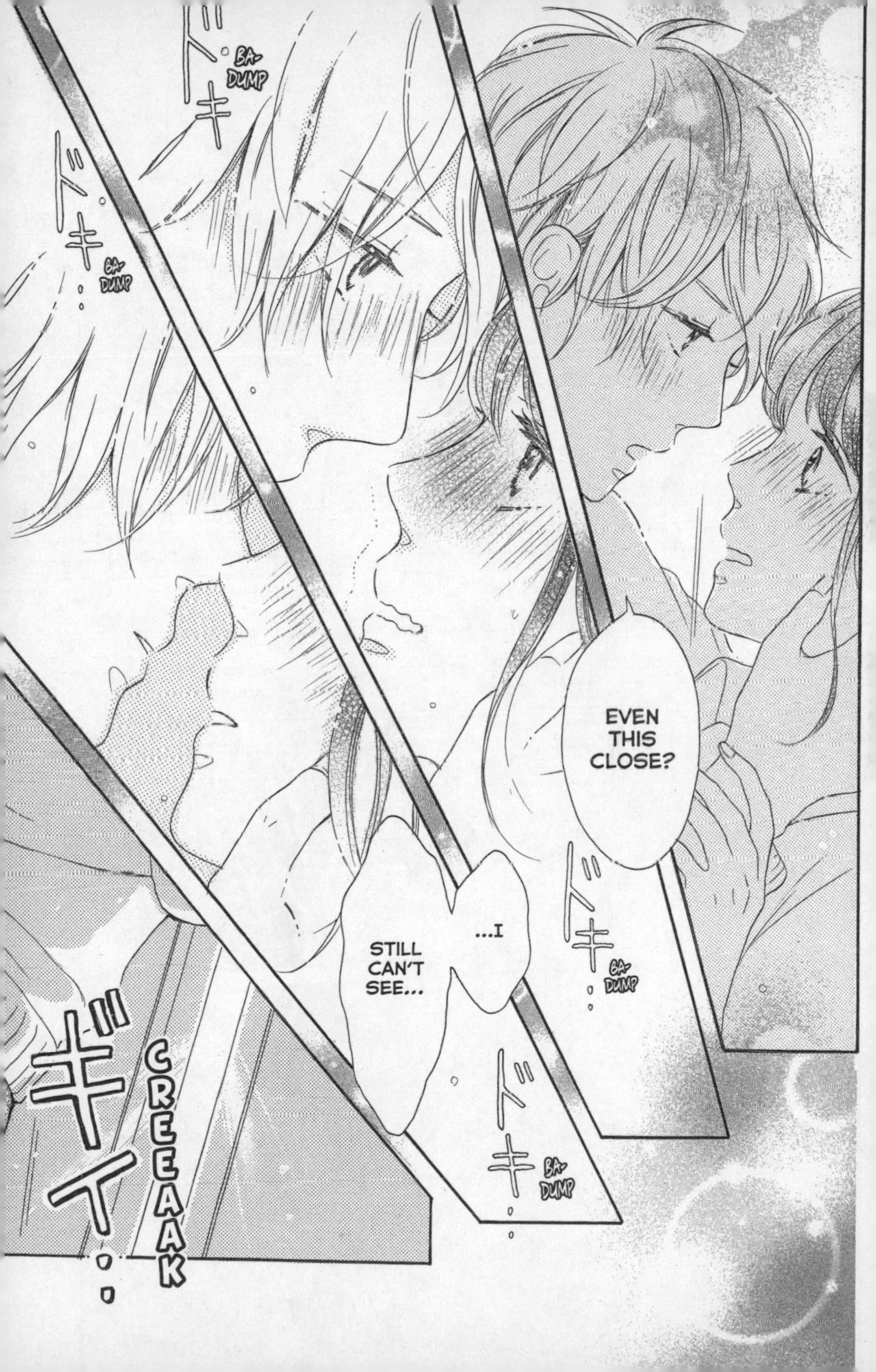
EVEN THIS CLOSE?
ドキ BA-DUMP
...I
STILL CAN'T SEE...
ドキ BA-DUMP
ドキ BA-DUMP
ドキ BA-DUMP
ギイ CREEAAK

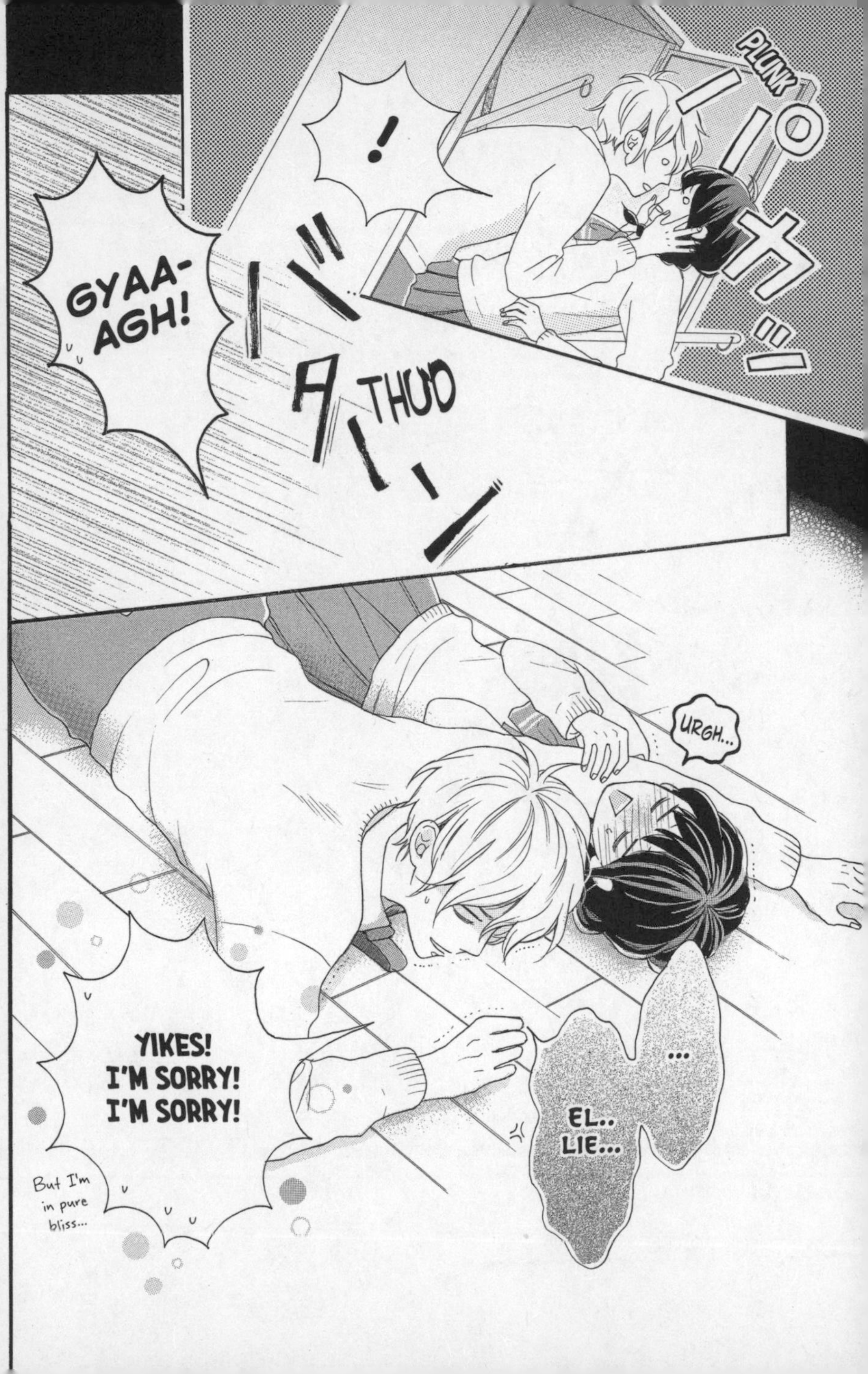
PLUNK
!
THUD
GYAA-AGH!
URGH...
...
EL.. LIE...
YIKES! I'M SORRY! I'M SORRY!
But I'm in pure bliss...

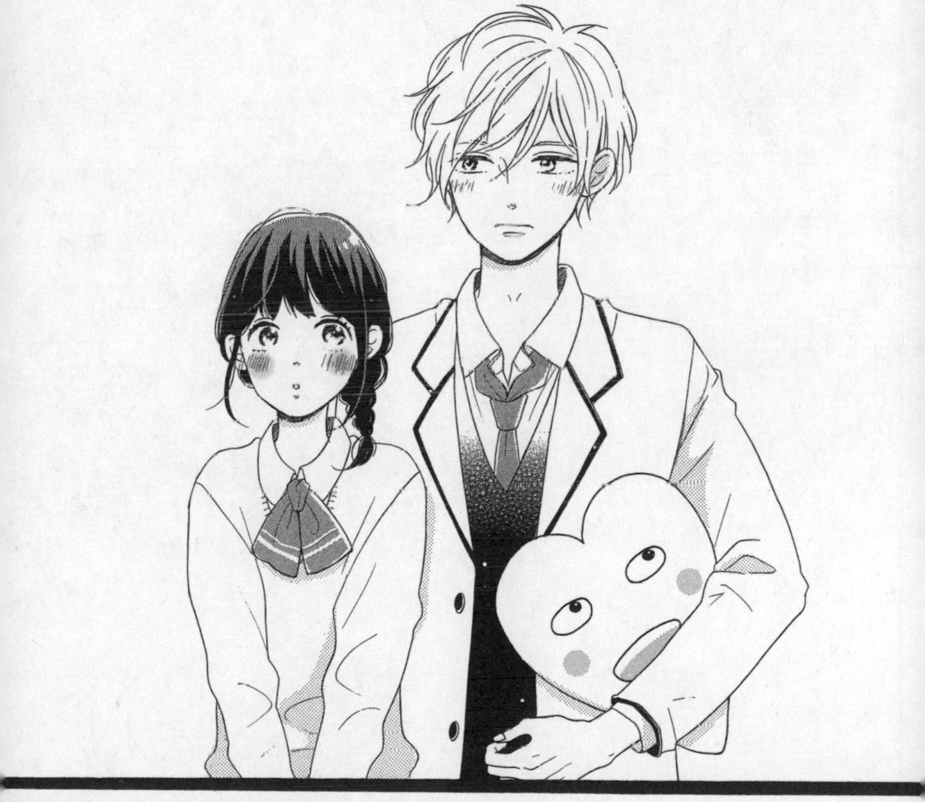

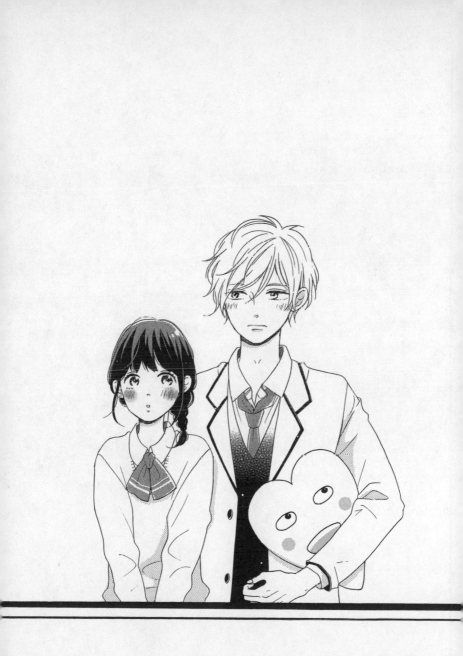

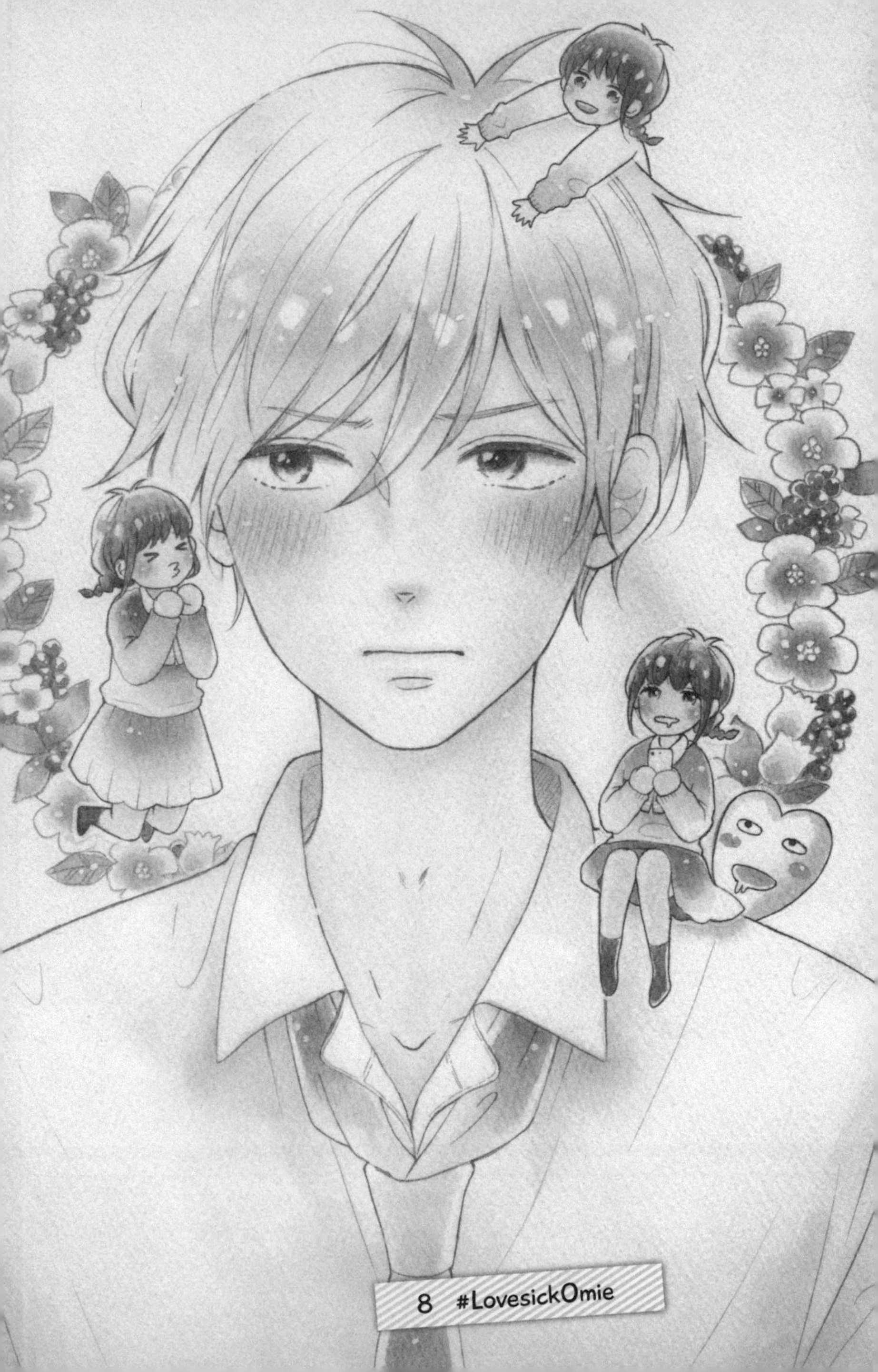
8 #LovesickOmie

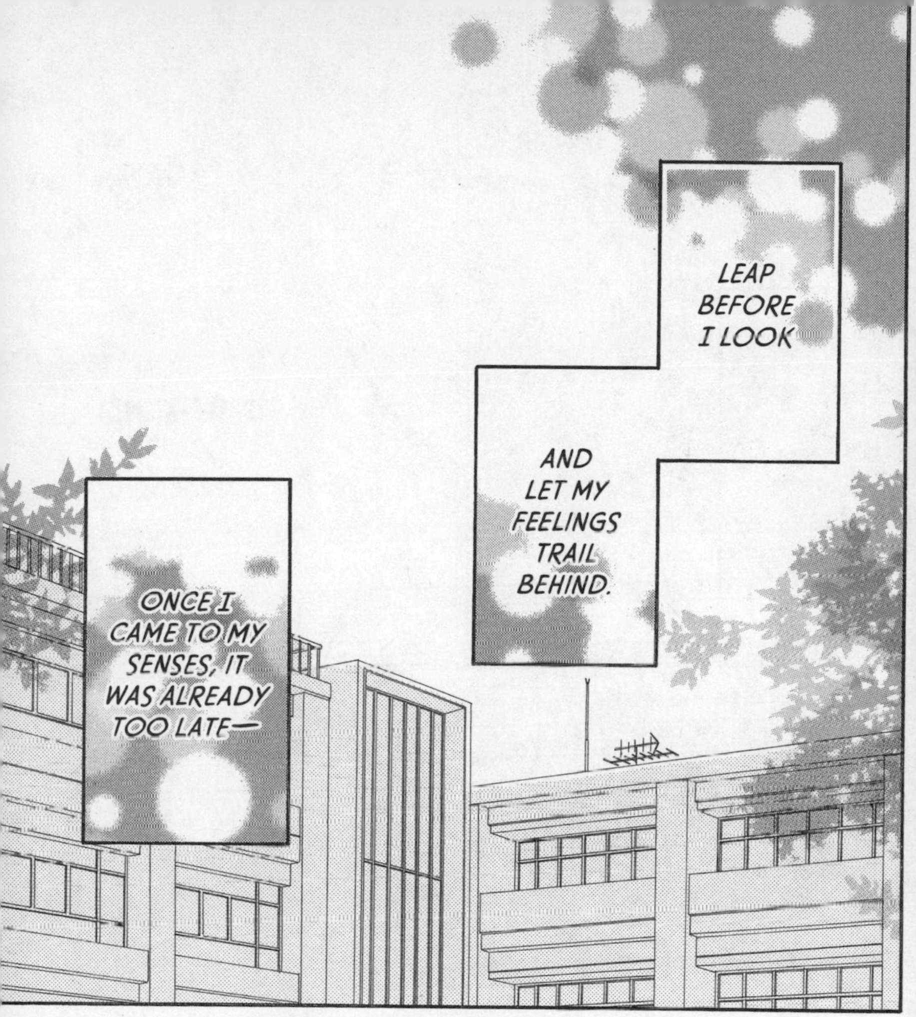
LEAP BEFORE I LOOK
AND LET MY FEELINGS TRAIL BEHIND.
ONCE I CAME TO MY SENSES, IT WAS ALREADY TOO LATE—

Special Thanks

Kuumii

Editor Minchi

Designer Osawa

Nagasaki

Dessert Editorial Department
Everyone involved in the creation of this book

Chiaki

Mechin

My friends and family

I am indebted to a great many people. I couldn't have published Volume 2 without you.
I look forward to working with you again on Volume 3.

Volume 3...
I feel like I'm dreaming.

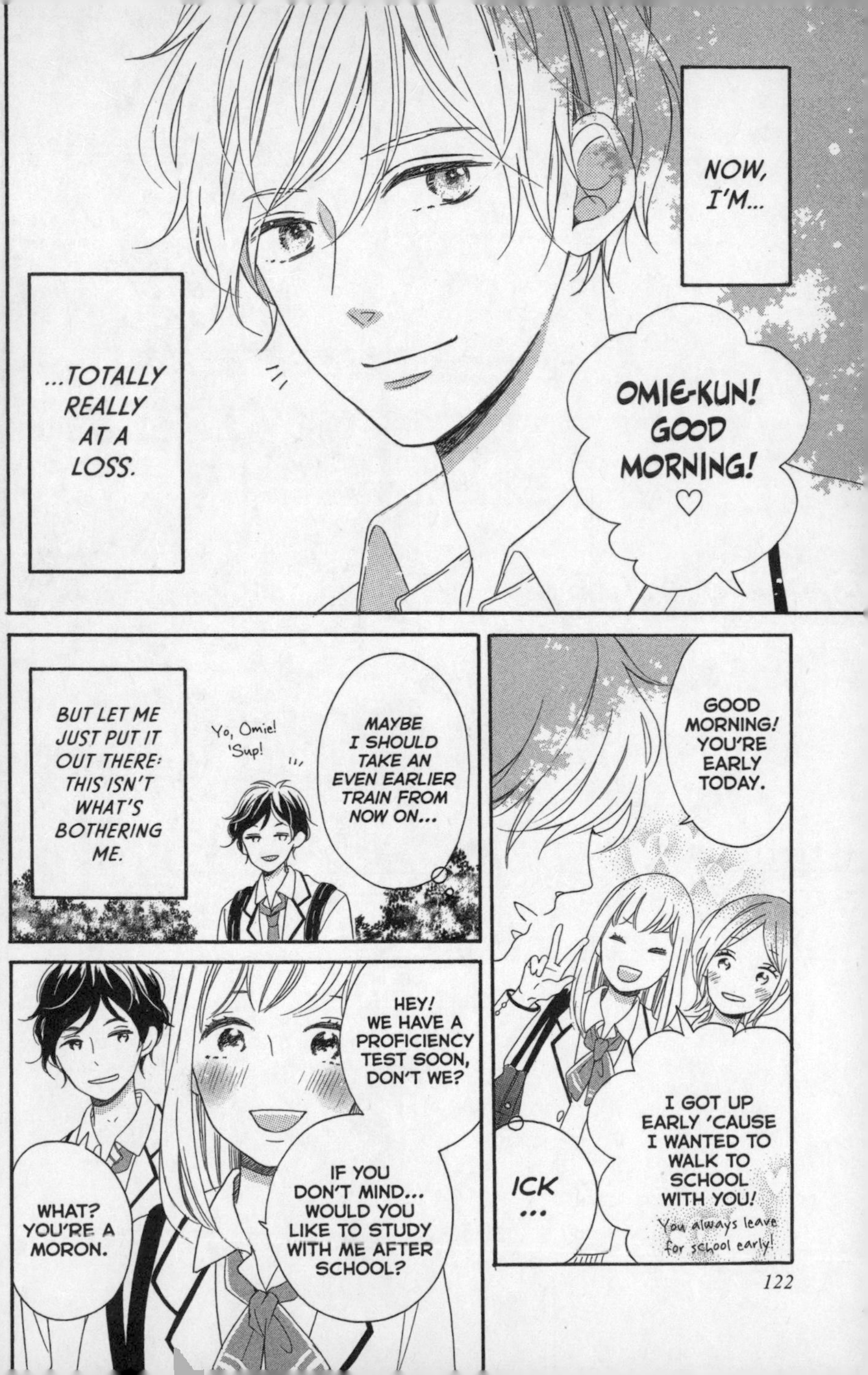
NOW, I'M...
...TOTALLY REALLY AT A LOSS.
OMIE-KUN! GOOD MORNING! ♡
GOOD MORNING! YOU'RE EARLY TODAY.
I GOT UP EARLY 'CAUSE I WANTED TO WALK TO SCHOOL WITH YOU!
You always leave for school early!
ICK...
MAYBE I SHOULD TAKE AN EVEN EARLIER TRAIN FROM NOW ON...
Yo, Omie! 'Sup!
BUT LET ME JUST PUT IT OUT THERE: THIS ISN'T WHAT'S BOTHERING ME.
HEY! WE HAVE A PROFICIENCY TEST SOON, DON'T WE?
IF YOU DON'T MIND... WOULD YOU LIKE TO STUDY WITH ME AFTER SCHOOL?
WHAT? YOU'RE A MORON.

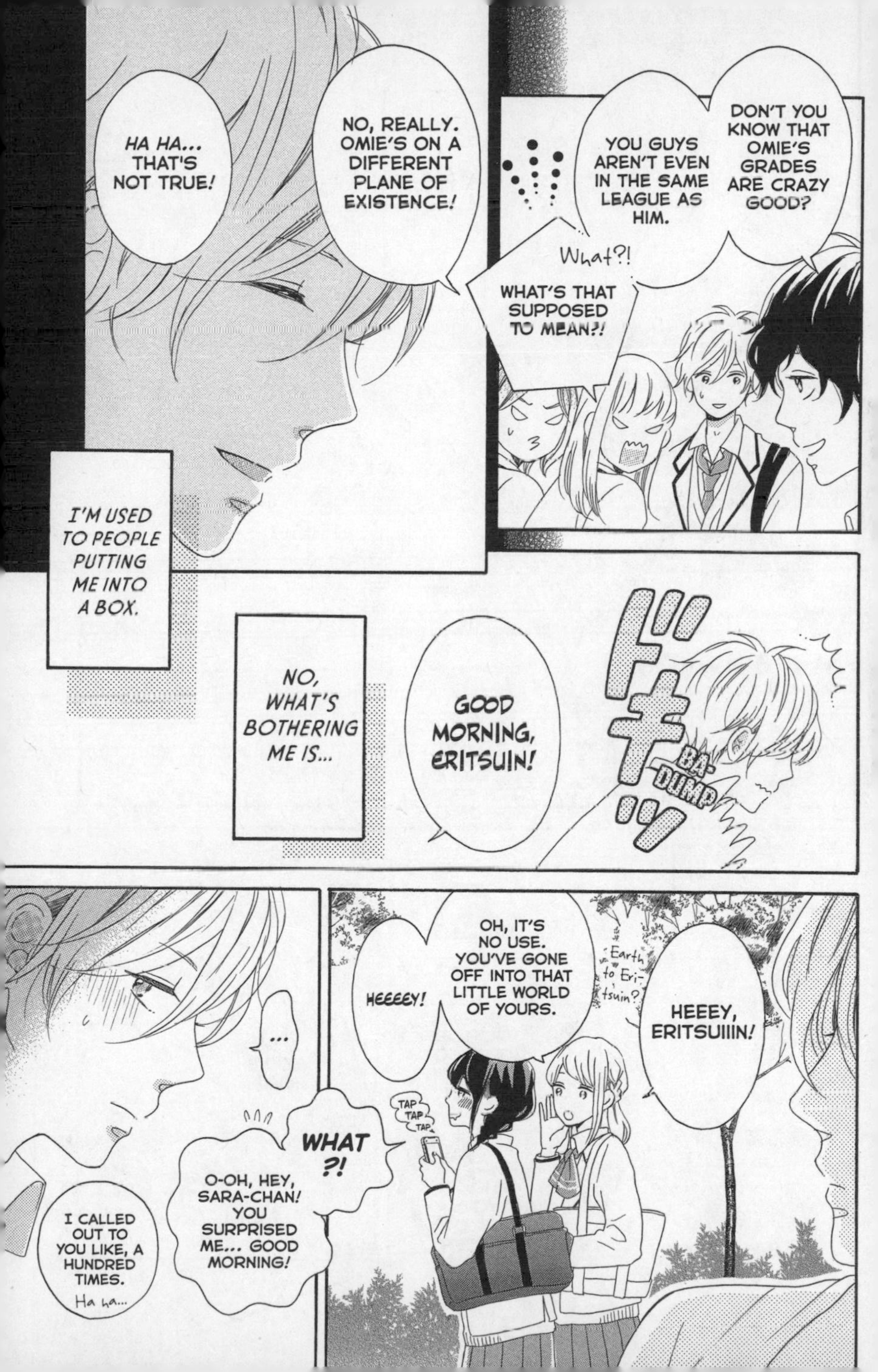
DON'T YOU KNOW THAT OMIE'S GRADES ARE CRAZY GOOD?
YOU GUYS AREN'T EVEN IN THE SAME LEAGUE AS HIM.
What?!
WHAT'S THAT SUPPOSED TO MEAN?!
NO, REALLY. OMIE'S ON A DIFFERENT PLANE OF EXISTENCE!
HA HA... THAT'S NOT TRUE!
I'M USED TO PEOPLE PUTTING ME INTO A BOX.
NO, WHAT'S BOTHERING ME IS...
GOOD MORNING, ERITSUIN!
BA-DUMP
HEEEY, ERITSUIIIN!
Earth to Eri-tsuin?
OH, IT'S NO USE. YOU'VE GONE OFF INTO THAT LITTLE WORLD OF YOURS.
HEEEEY!
TAP TAP TAP
...
WHAT ?!
O-OH, HEY, SARA-CHAN! YOU SURPRISED ME... GOOD MORNING!
I CALLED OUT TO YOU LIKE, A HUNDRED TIMES.
Ha ha...

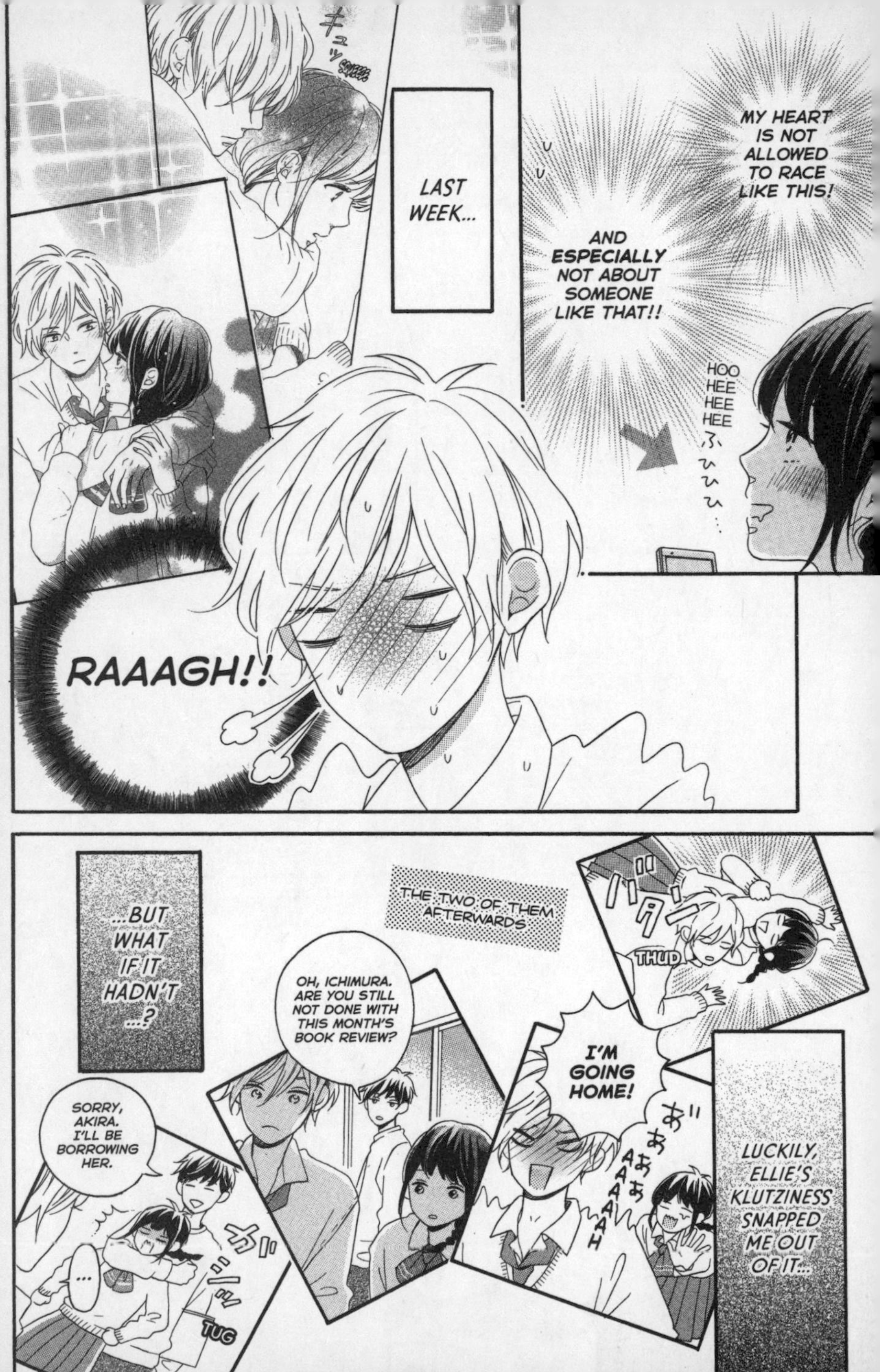
MY HEART IS NOT ALLOWED TO RACE LIKE THIS!
AND ESPECIALLY NOT ABOUT SOMEONE LIKE THAT!!
HOO HEE HEE HEE
ふひひひ…
LAST WEEK...
キュッ
SQUEEZE
RAAAGH!!
THUD
THE TWO OF THEM AFTERWARDS
LUCKILY, ELLIE'S KLUTZINESS SNAPPED ME OUT OF IT...
I'M GOING HOME!
あ゛あああ
AAAAAAH
OH, ICHIMURA. ARE YOU STILL NOT DONE WITH THIS MONTH'S BOOK REVIEW?
...BUT WHAT IF IT HADN'T ...?
SORRY, AKIRA. I'LL BE BORROWING HER.
...
TUG

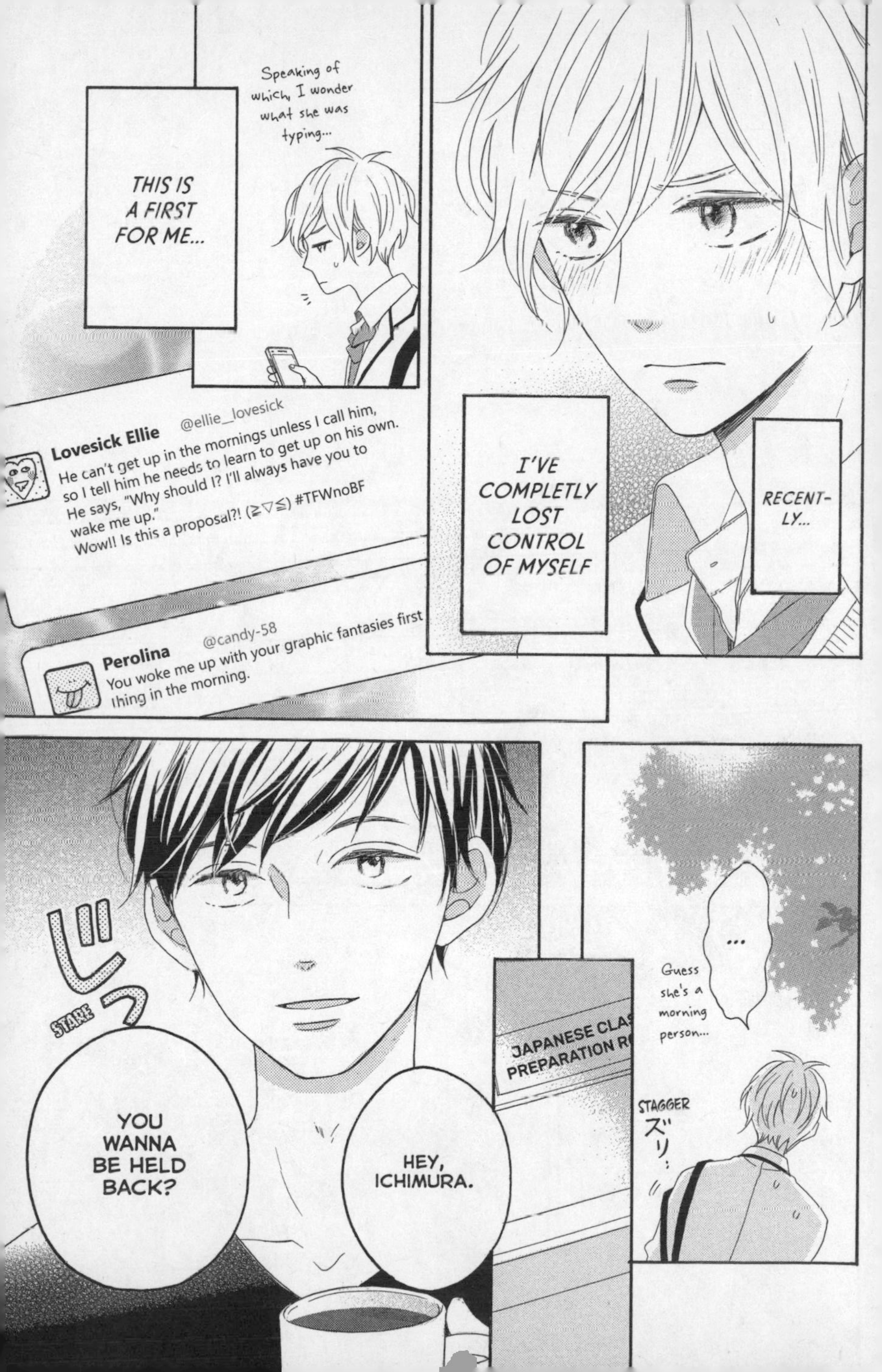
RECENT-
LY...
I'VE COMPLETLY LOST CONTROL OF MYSELF
Speaking of which, I wonder what she was typing...
THIS IS A FIRST FOR ME...
Lovesick Ellie @ellie_lovesick
He can't get up in the mornings unless I call him, so I tell him he needs to learn to get up on his own. He says, "Why should I? I'll always have you to wake me up."
Wow!! Is this a proposal?! (≧▽≦) #TFWnoBF
Perolina @candy-58
You woke me up with your graphic fantasies first thing in the morning.
...
Guess she's a morning person...
JAPANESE CLAS
PREPARATION R
STAGGER
ズリ
STARE
じっ
HEY, ICHIMURA.
YOU WANNA BE HELD BACK?

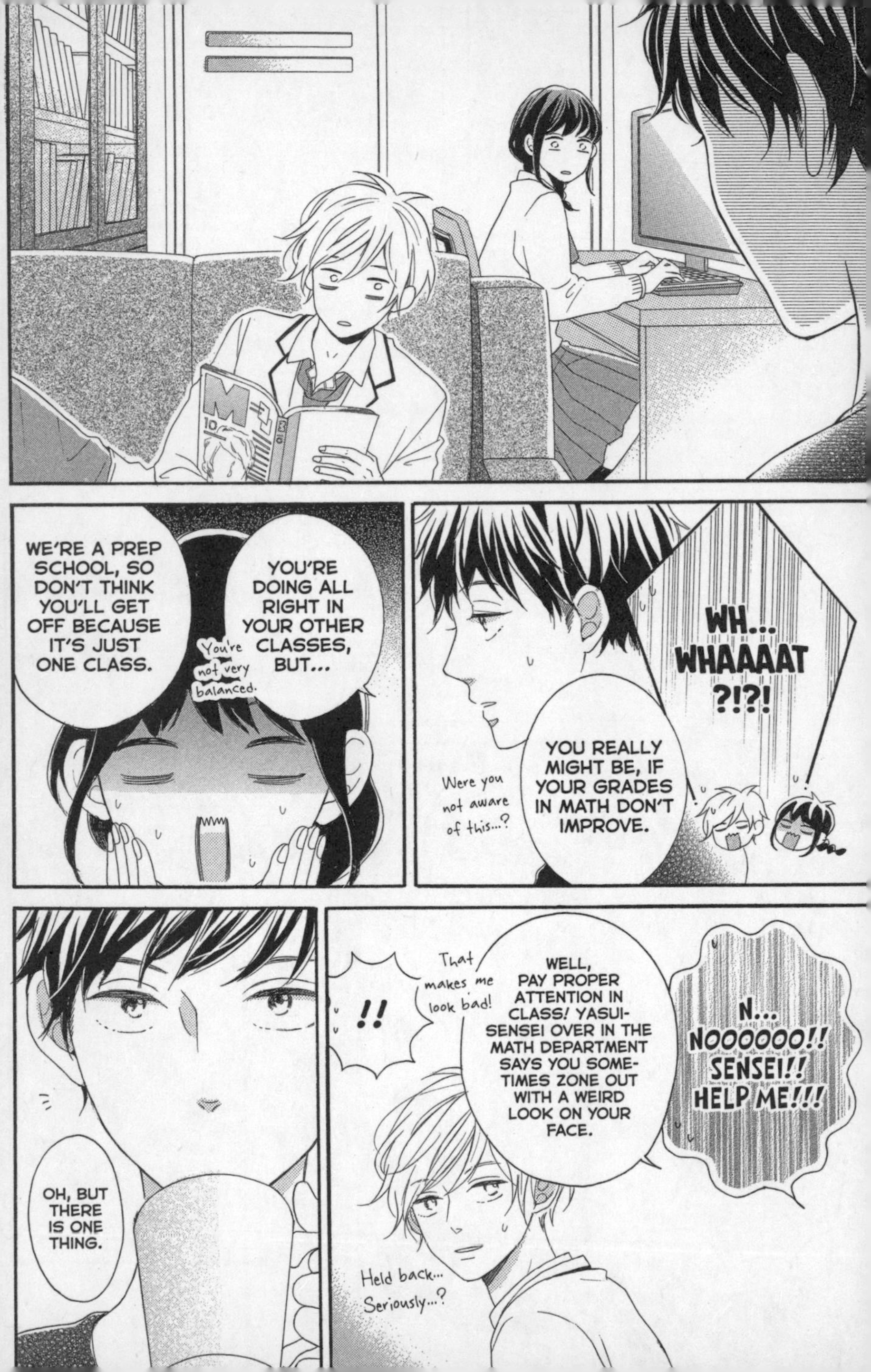
WH... WHAAAAT ?!?!
YOU REALLY MIGHT BE, IF YOUR GRADES IN MATH DON'T IMPROVE.
Were you not aware of this...?
YOU'RE DOING ALL RIGHT IN YOUR OTHER CLASSES, BUT...
You're not very balanced.
WE'RE A PREP SCHOOL, SO DON'T THINK YOU'LL GET OFF BECAUSE IT'S JUST ONE CLASS.
N... NOOOOOO!! SENSEI!! HELP ME!!!
WELL, PAY PROPER ATTENTION IN CLASS! YASUI-SENSEI OVER IN THE MATH DEPARTMENT SAYS YOU SOME-TIMES ZONE OUT WITH A WEIRD LOOK ON YOUR FACE.
That makes me look bad!
!!
Held back... Seriously...?
OH, BUT THERE IS ONE THING.

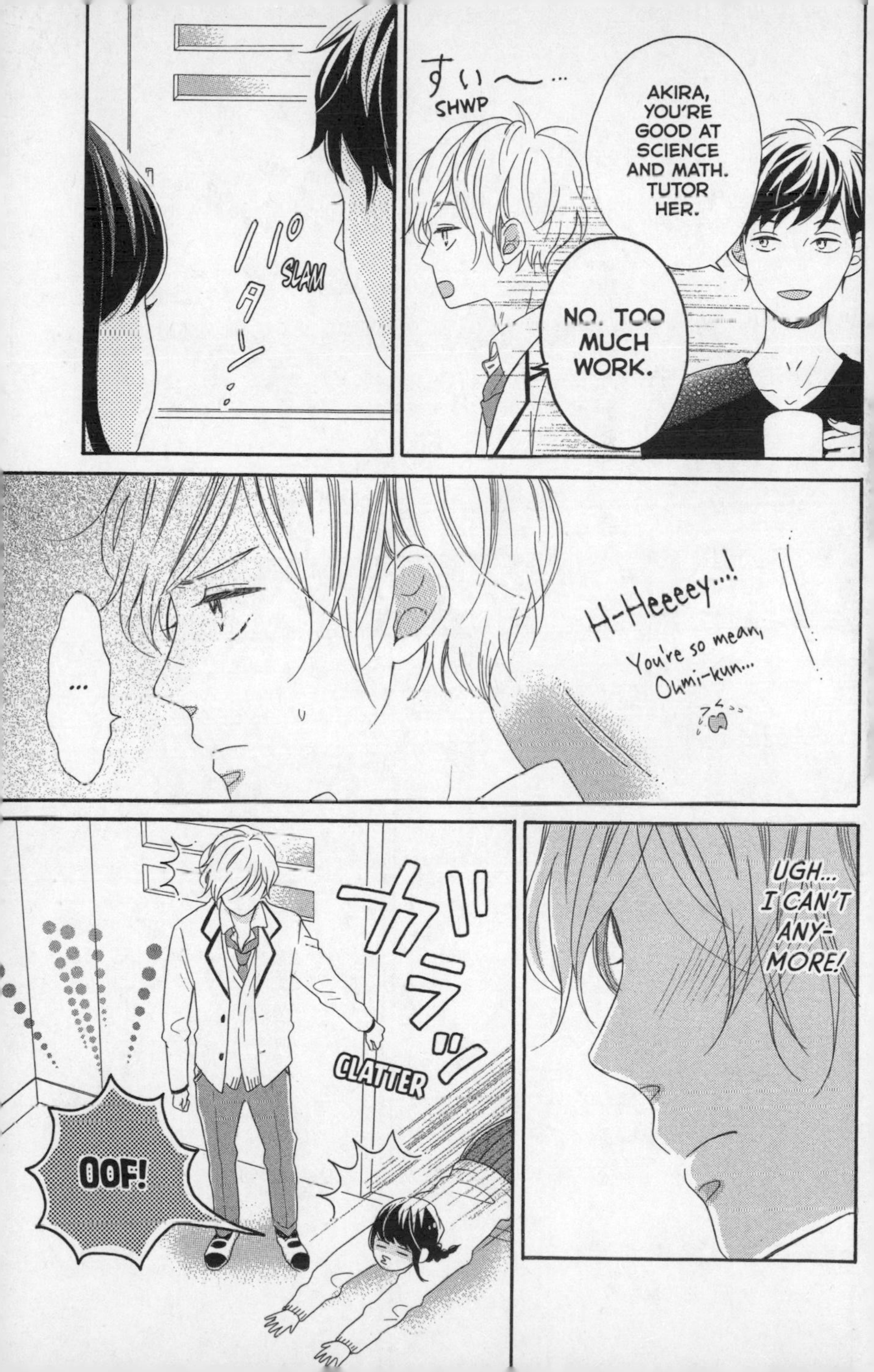
すい〜…
SHWP
AKIRA, YOU'RE GOOD AT SCIENCE AND MATH. TUTOR HER.
NO. TOO MUCH WORK.
パターン
SLAM
H-Heeeey...!
You're so mean, Ohmi-kun...
...
UGH... I CAN'T ANY-MORE!
ガラッ
CLATTER
OOF!

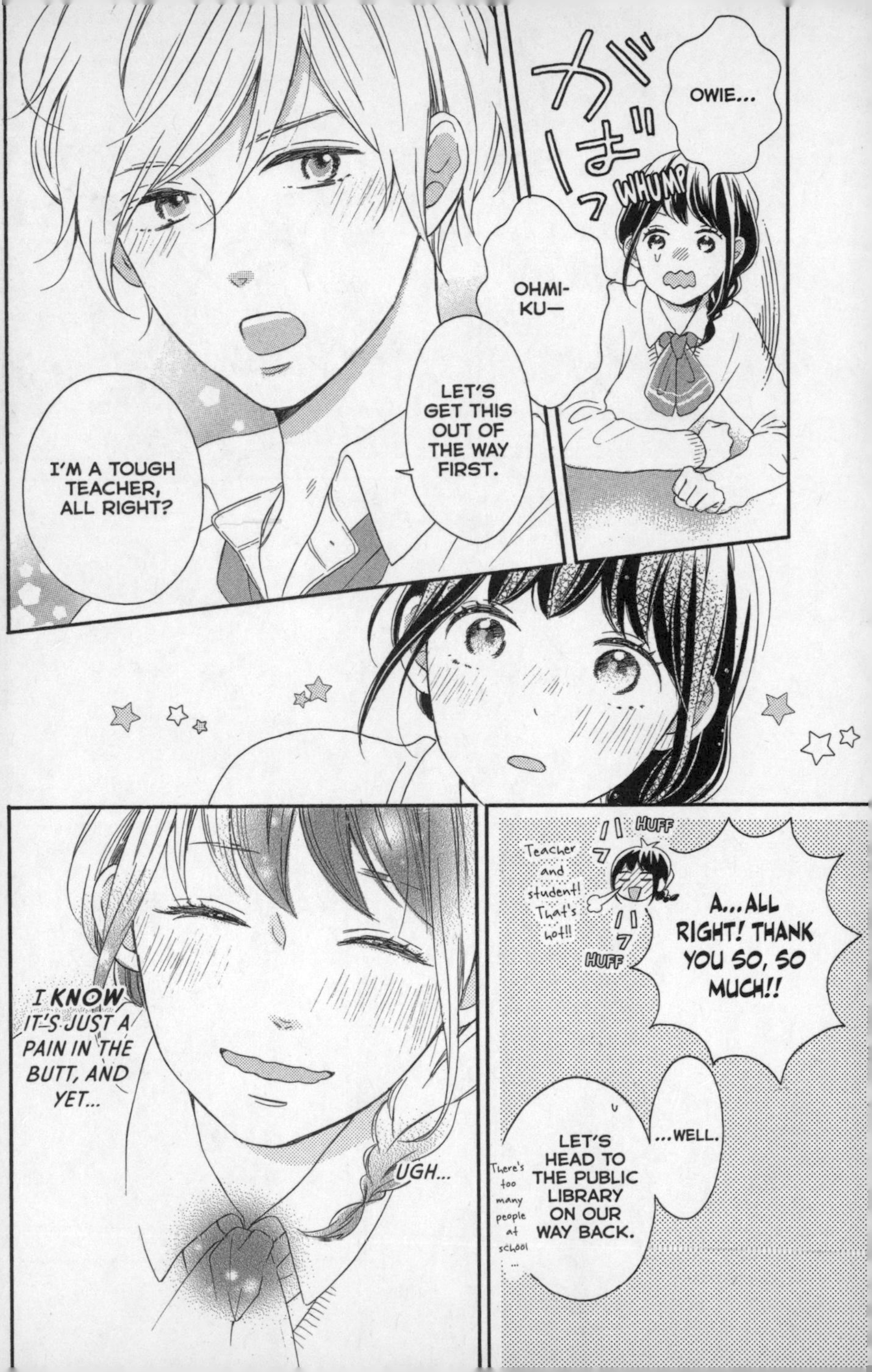

わばっ
WHUMP
OWIE...
OHMI-KU—
LET'S GET THIS OUT OF THE WAY FIRST.
I'M A TOUGH TEACHER, ALL RIGHT?
HUFF
Teacher and student! That's hot!!
HUFF
A...ALL RIGHT! THANK YOU SO, SO MUCH!!
...WELL.
LET'S HEAD TO THE PUBLIC LIBRARY ON OUR WAY BACK.
There's too many people at school...
I KNOW IT'S JUST A PAIN IN THE BUTT, AND YET...
UGH...

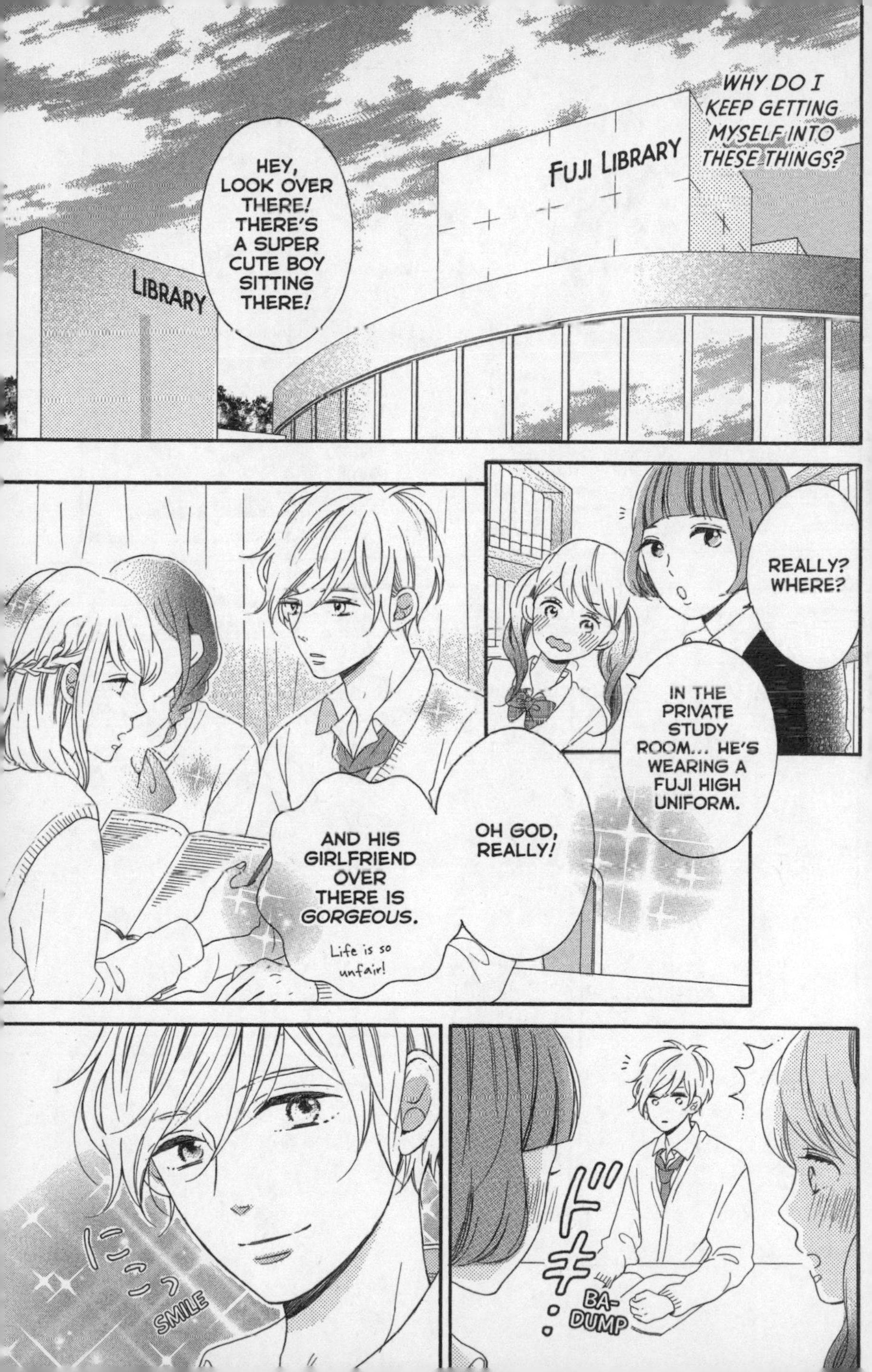
WHY DO I KEEP GETTING MYSELF INTO THESE THINGS?
FUJI LIBRARY
HEY, LOOK OVER THERE! THERE'S A SUPER CUTE BOY SITTING THERE!
LIBRARY
REALLY? WHERE?
IN THE PRIVATE STUDY ROOM... HE'S WEARING A FUJI HIGH UNIFORM.
OH GOD, REALLY!
AND HIS GIRLFRIEND OVER THERE IS GORGEOUS.
Life is so unfair!
ドキ
BA-DUMP
にこっ
SMILE

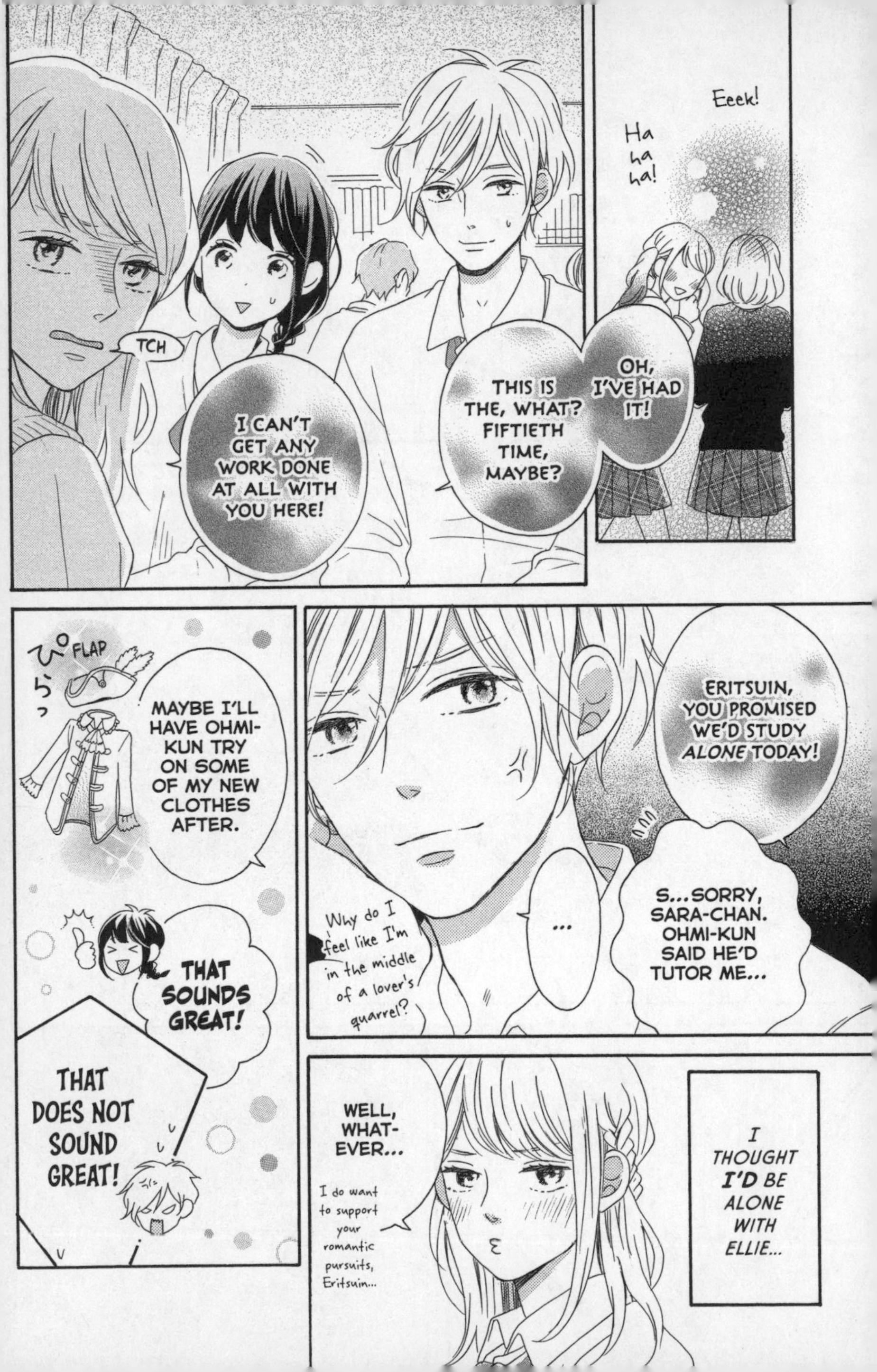
Eeek!
Ha ha ha!
OH, I'VE HAD IT!
THIS IS THE, WHAT? FIFTIETH TIME, MAYBE?
I CAN'T GET ANY WORK DONE AT ALL WITH YOU HERE!
TCH
ERITSUIN, YOU PROMISED WE'D STUDY *ALONE* TODAY!
S...SORRY, SARA-CHAN. OHMI-KUN SAID HE'D TUTOR ME...
...
Why do I feel like I'm in the middle of a lover's quarrel?
I THOUGHT **I'D** BE ALONE WITH ELLIE...
WELL, WHATEVER...
I do want to support your romantic pursuits, Eritsuin...
FLAP
MAYBE I'LL HAVE OHMI-KUN TRY ON SOME OF MY NEW CLOTHES AFTER.
THAT SOUNDS GREAT!
THAT DOES NOT SOUND GREAT!

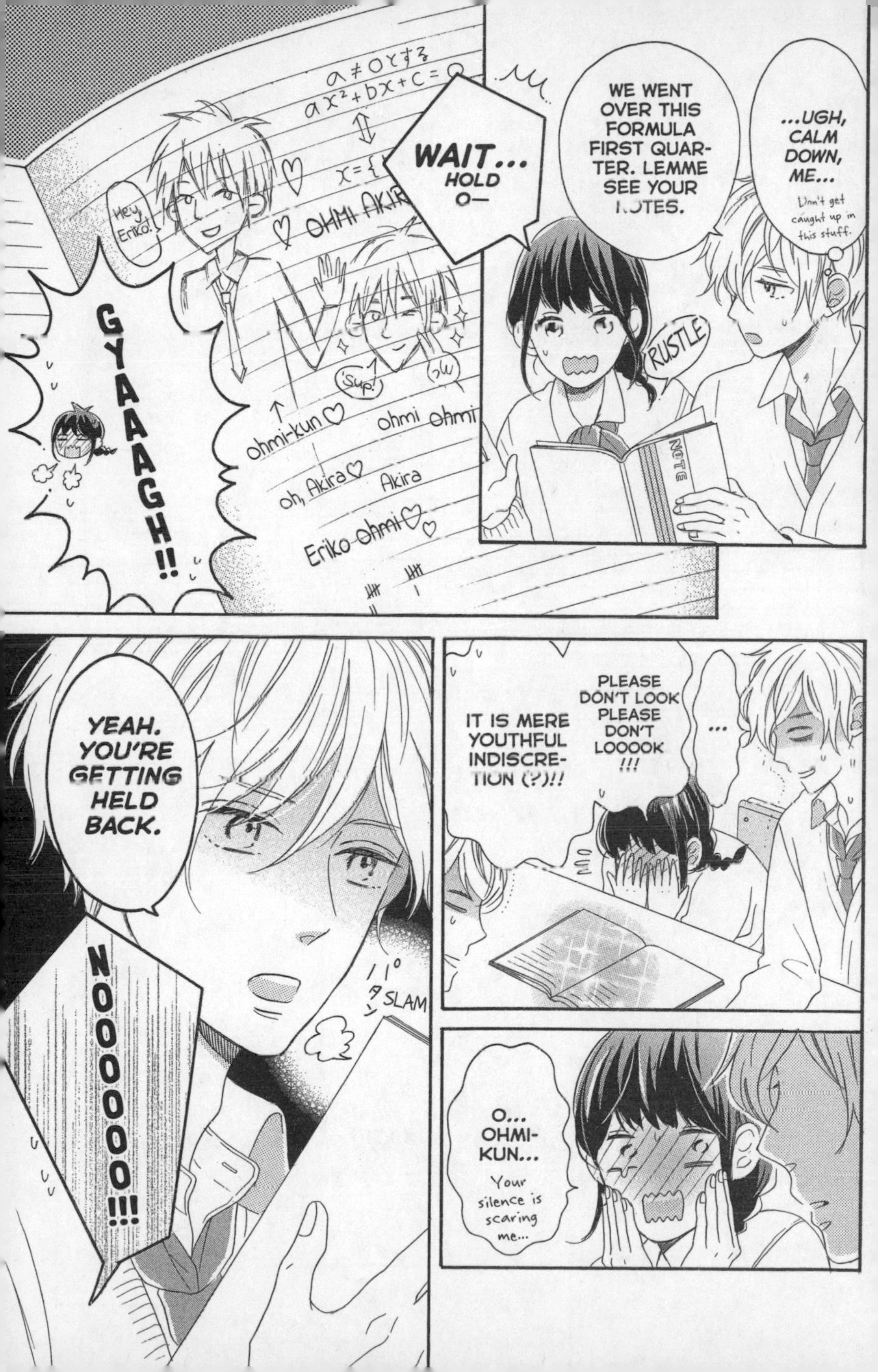
...UGH, CALM DOWN, ME...
Don't get caught up in this stuff.
WE WENT OVER THIS FORMULA FIRST QUARTER. LEMME SEE YOUR NOTES.
RUSTLE
WAIT... HOLD O—
a≠0とする
ax²+bx+c=0
x={
Hey, Eriko!
OHMI AKIRA
'Sup!
ohmi-kun
ohmi ohmi
oh, Akira
Akira
Eriko Ohmi
GYAAAGH!!
...
PLEASE DON'T LOOK PLEASE DON'T LOOOOK!!!
IT IS MERE YOUTHFUL INDISCRETION (?)!!
O... OHMI-KUN...
Your silence is scaring me...
YEAH. YOU'RE GETTING HELD BACK.
SLAM
NOOOOOOO!!!

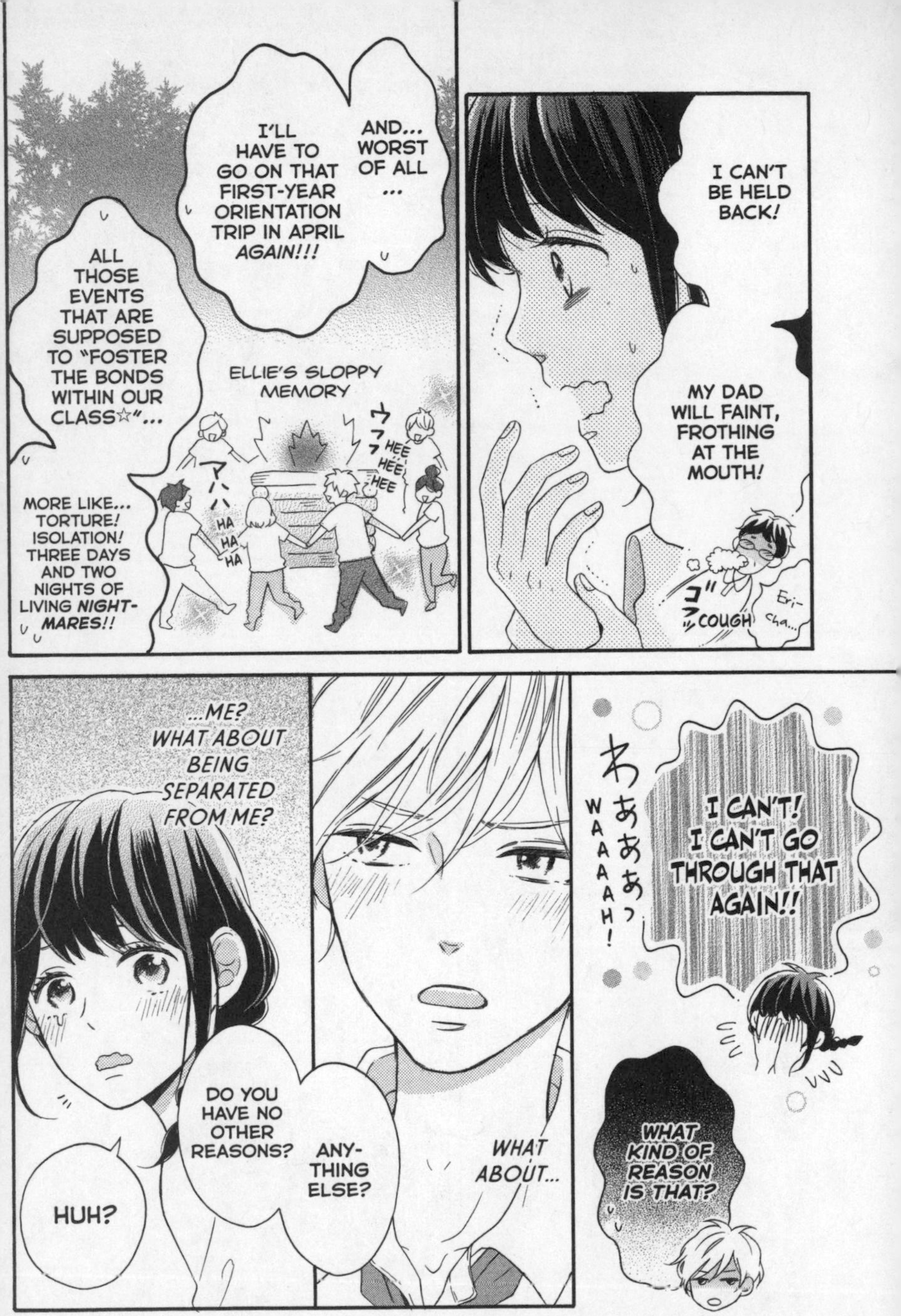
I CAN'T BE HELD BACK!
MY DAD WILL FAINT, FROTHING AT THE MOUTH!
COUGH
Eri-cha...
AND... WORST OF ALL ...
I'LL HAVE TO GO ON THAT FIRST-YEAR ORIENTATION TRIP IN APRIL AGAIN!!!
ALL THOSE EVENTS THAT ARE SUPPOSED TO "FOSTER THE BONDS WITHIN OUR CLASS☆"...
ELLIE'S SLOPPY MEMORY
HEE HEE HEE
HA HA HA
MORE LIKE... TORTURE! ISOLATION! THREE DAYS AND TWO NIGHTS OF LIVING NIGHT-MARES!!
WAAAAH!
I CAN'T! I CAN'T GO THROUGH THAT AGAIN!!
WHAT KIND OF REASON IS THAT?
WHAT ABOUT...
ANY-THING ELSE?
DO YOU HAVE NO OTHER REASONS?
...ME? WHAT ABOUT BEING SEPARATED FROM ME?
HUH?

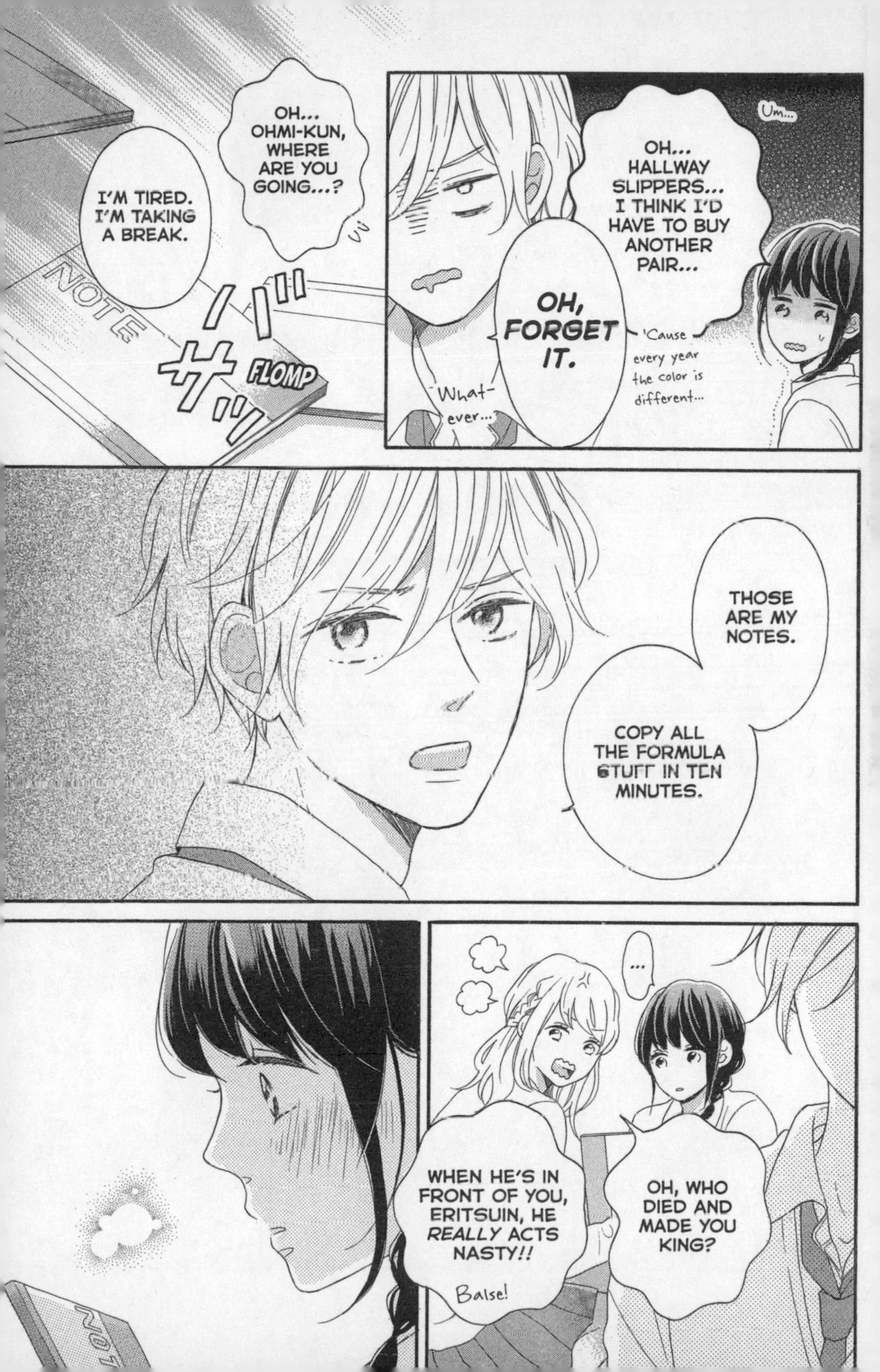
Um...
OH... HALLWAY SLIPPERS... I THINK I'D HAVE TO BUY ANOTHER PAIR...
'Cause every year the color is different...
OH, FORGET IT.
What-ever...
OH... OHMI-KUN, WHERE ARE YOU GOING...?
I'M TIRED. I'M TAKING A BREAK.
FLOMP
THOSE ARE MY NOTES.
COPY ALL THE FORMULA STUFF IN TEN MINUTES.
...
OH, WHO DIED AND MADE YOU KING?
WHEN HE'S IN FRONT OF YOU, ERITSUIN, HE REALLY ACTS NASTY!!
Balse!

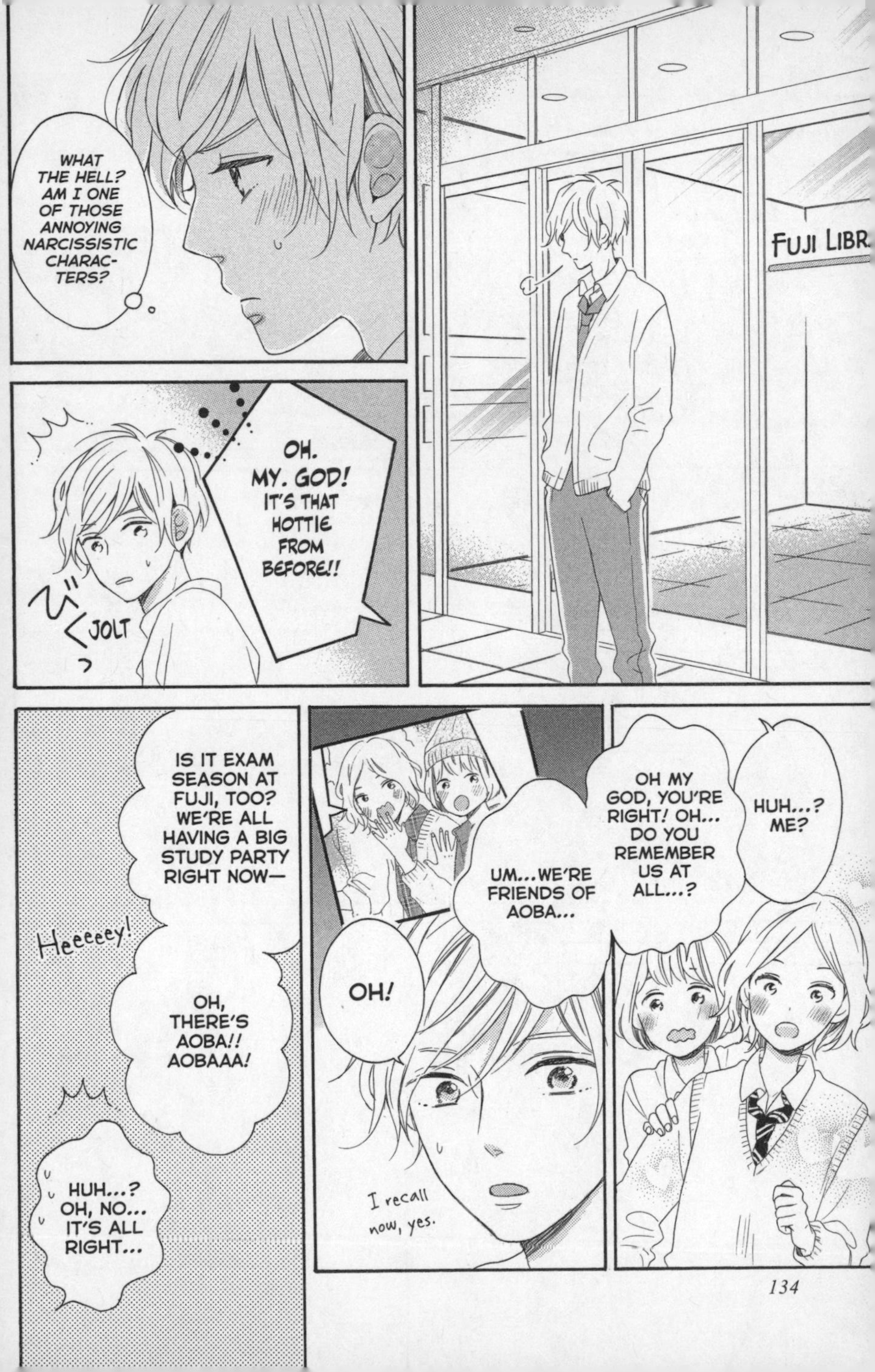
FUJI LIBR
WHAT THE HELL? AM I ONE OF THOSE ANNOYING NARCISSISTIC CHARACTERS?
JOLT
OH. MY. GOD! IT'S THAT HOTTIE FROM BEFORE!!
HUH...? ME?
OH MY GOD, YOU'RE RIGHT! OH... DO YOU REMEMBER US AT ALL...?
UM...WE'RE FRIENDS OF AOBA...
OH!
I recall now, yes.
IS IT EXAM SEASON AT FUJI, TOO? WE'RE ALL HAVING A BIG STUDY PARTY RIGHT NOW—
Heeeeey!
OH, THERE'S AOBA!! AOBAAA!
HUH...? OH, NO... IT'S ALL RIGHT...

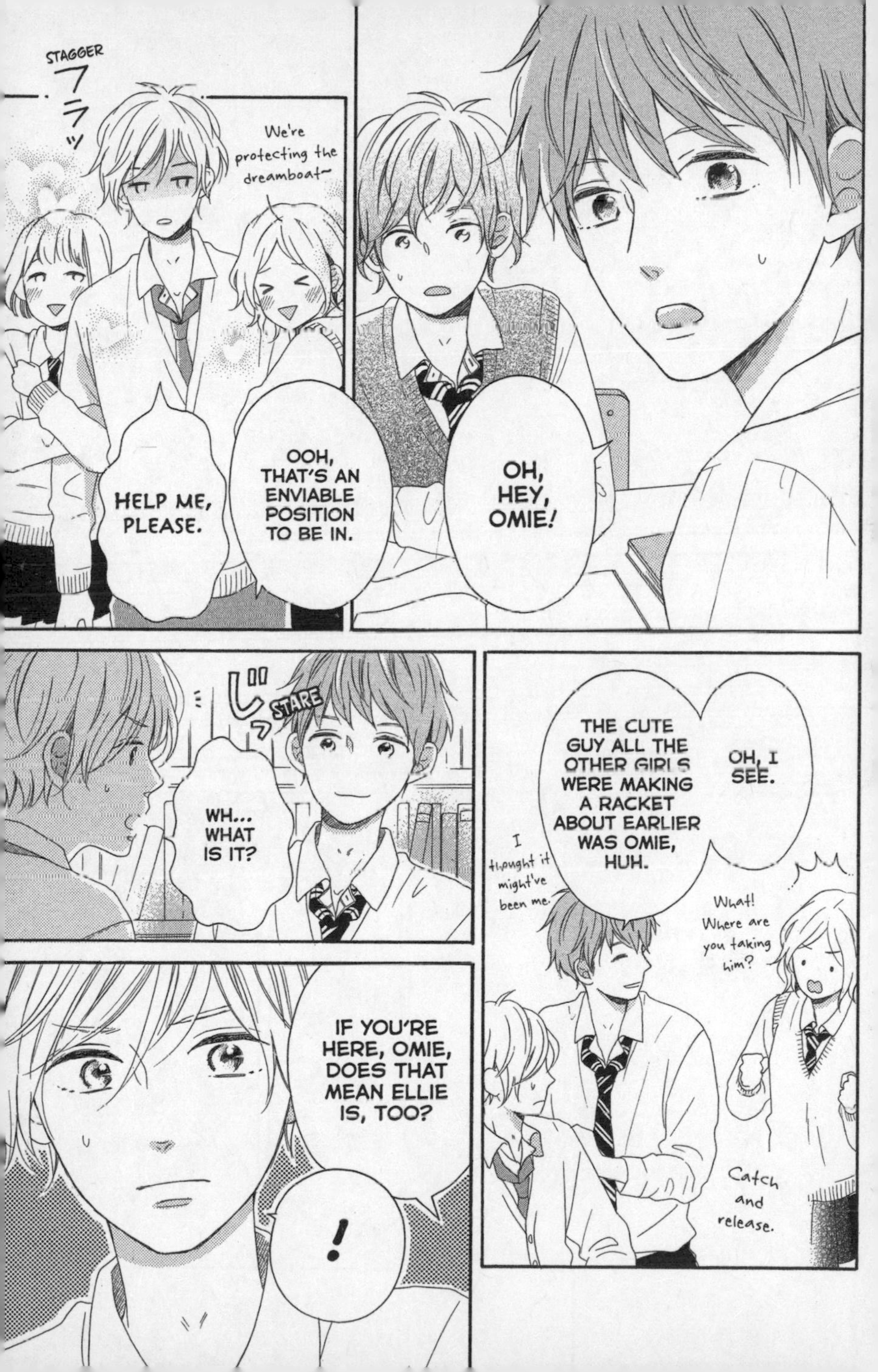
OH, HEY, OMIE!
We're protecting the dreamboat~
STAGGER
フラッ
OOH, THAT'S AN ENVIABLE POSITION TO BE IN.
HELP ME, PLEASE.
OH, I SEE.
THE CUTE GUY ALL THE OTHER GIRLS WERE MAKING A RACKET ABOUT EARLIER WAS OMIE, HUH.
I thought it might've been me.
What! Where are you taking him?
Catch and release.
じっ
STARE
WH... WHAT IS IT?
IF YOU'RE HERE, OMIE, DOES THAT MEAN ELLIE IS, TOO?
!

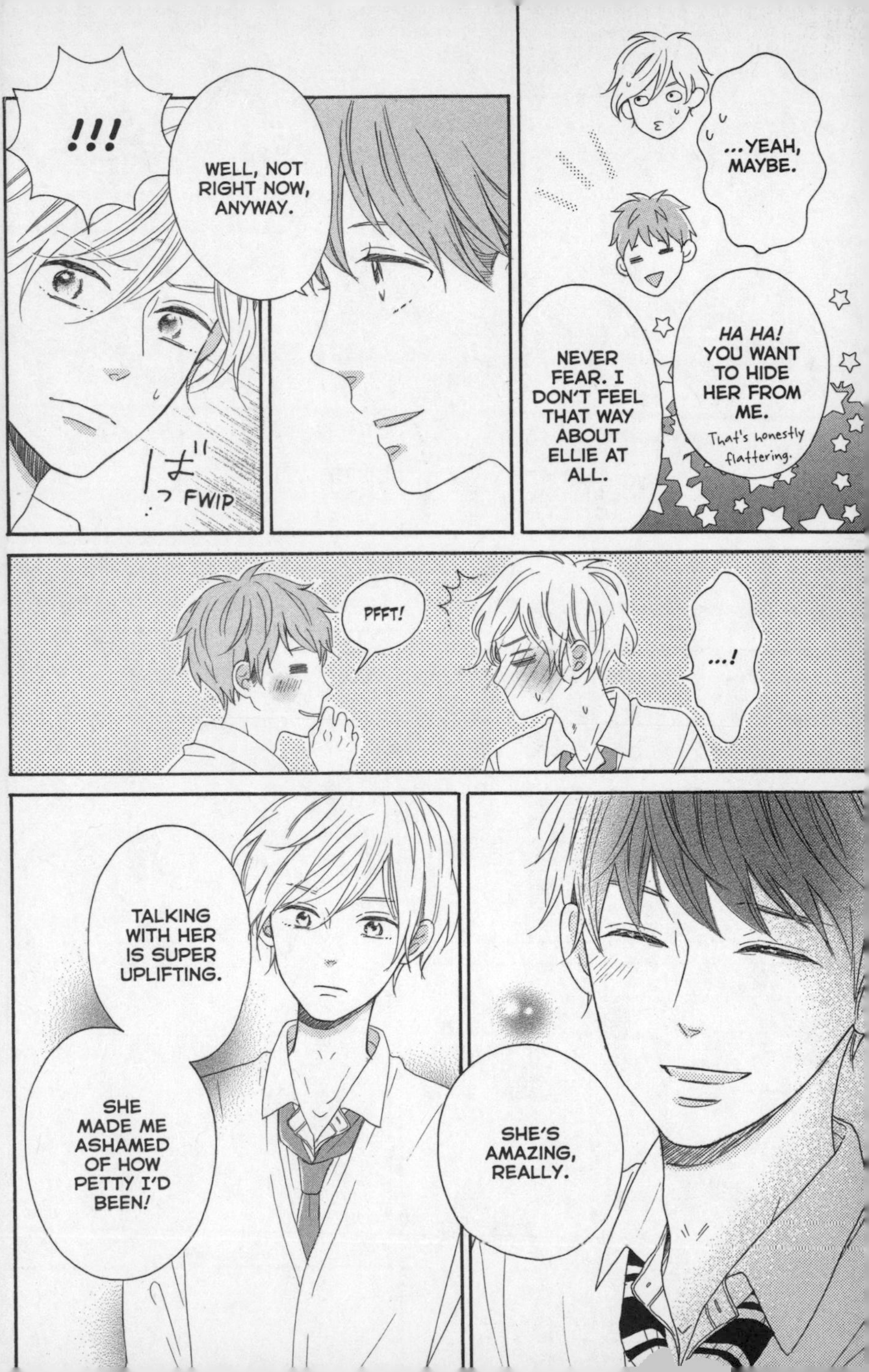
...YEAH, MAYBE.
HA HA! YOU WANT TO HIDE HER FROM ME.
That's honestly flattering.
NEVER FEAR. I DON'T FEEL THAT WAY ABOUT ELLIE AT ALL.
WELL, NOT RIGHT NOW, ANYWAY.
!!!
ばっ FWIP
...!
PFFT!
SHE'S AMAZING, REALLY.
TALKING WITH HER IS SUPER UPLIFTING.
SHE MADE ME ASHAMED OF HOW PETTY I'D BEEN!

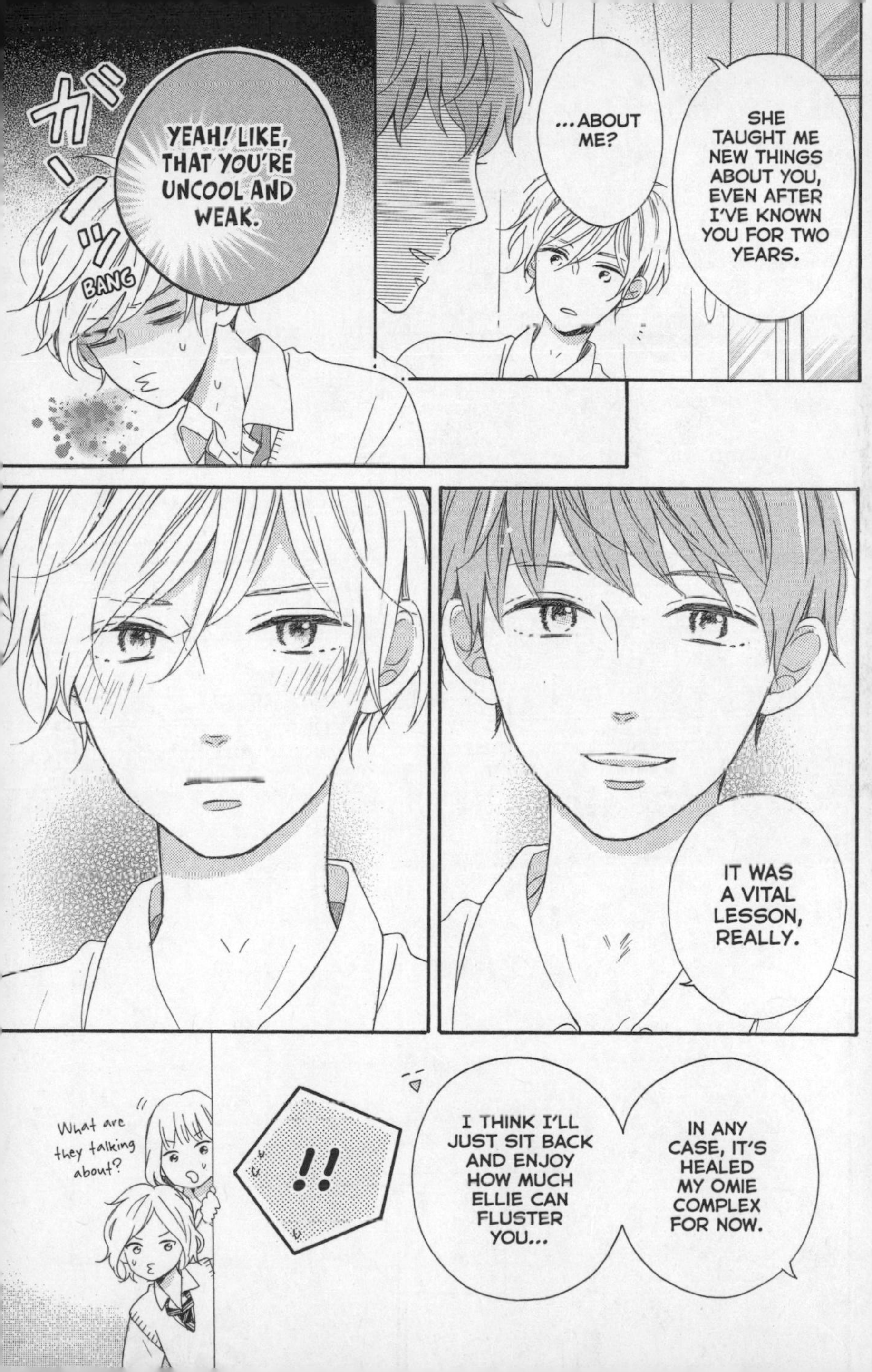
SHE TAUGHT ME NEW THINGS ABOUT YOU, EVEN AFTER I'VE KNOWN YOU FOR TWO YEARS.
...ABOUT ME?
YEAH! LIKE, THAT YOU'RE UNCOOL AND WEAK.
BANG
IT WAS A VITAL LESSON, REALLY.
IN ANY CASE, IT'S HEALED MY OMIE COMPLEX FOR NOW.
I THINK I'LL JUST SIT BACK AND ENJOY HOW MUCH ELLIE CAN FLUSTER YOU...
!!
What are they talking about?

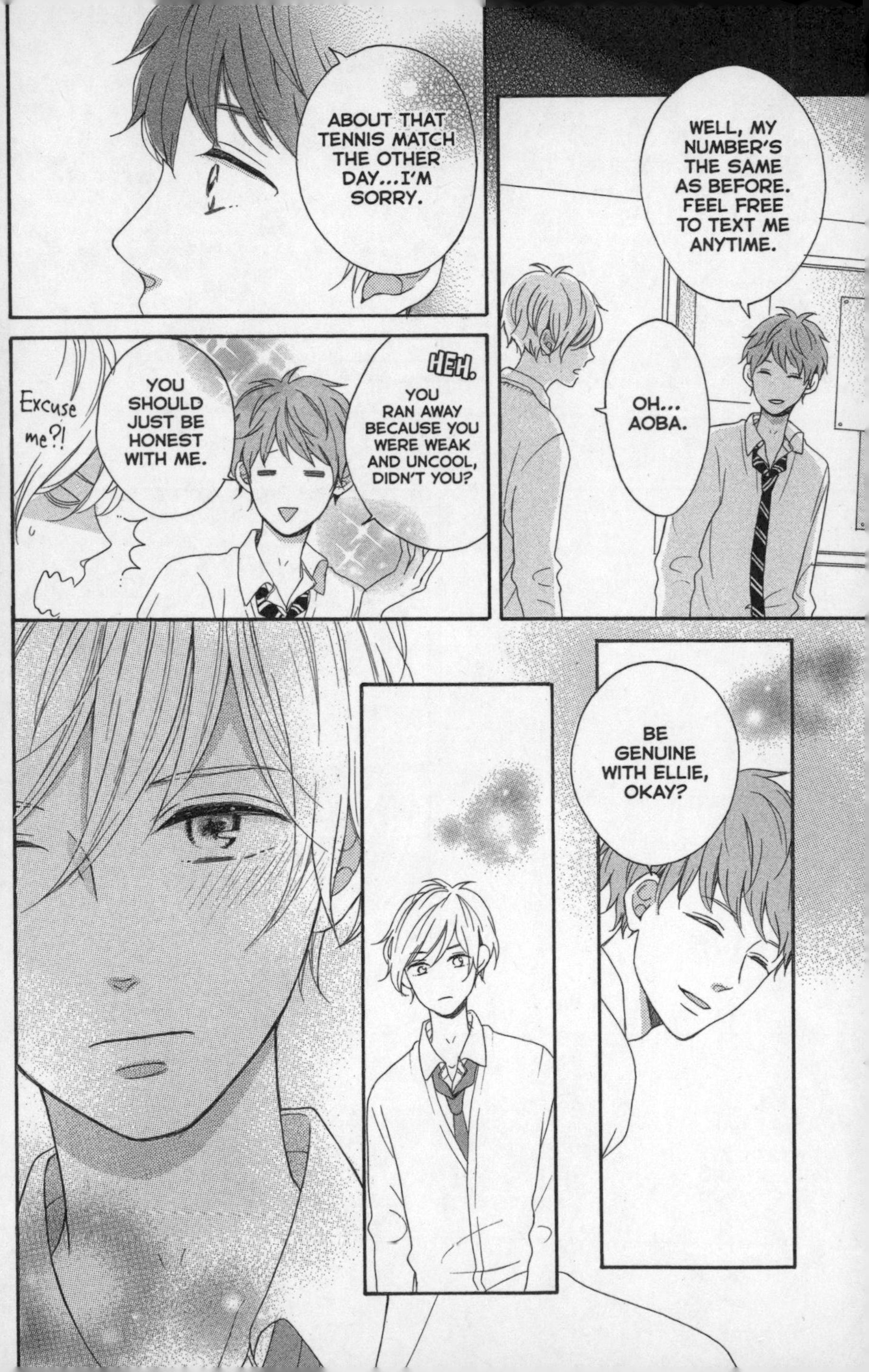
WELL, MY NUMBER'S THE SAME AS BEFORE. FEEL FREE TO TEXT ME ANYTIME.
OH... AOBA.
ABOUT THAT TENNIS MATCH THE OTHER DAY...I'M SORRY.
HEH.
YOU RAN AWAY BECAUSE YOU WERE WEAK AND UNCOOL, DIDN'T YOU?
YOU SHOULD JUST BE HONEST WITH ME.
Excuse me?!
BE GENUINE WITH ELLIE, OKAY?

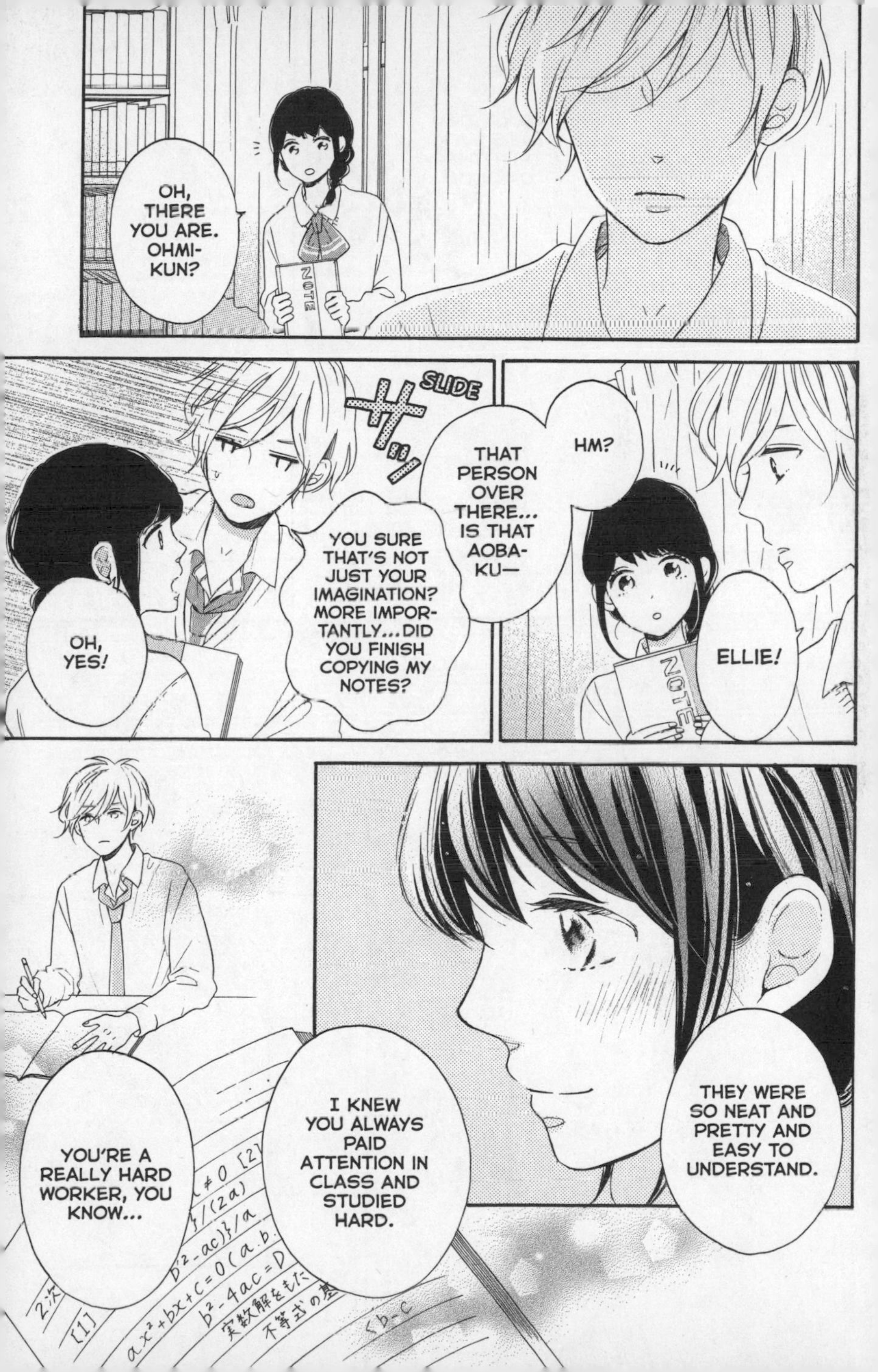
OH, THERE YOU ARE. OHMI-KUN?
HM?
THAT PERSON OVER THERE... IS THAT AOBA-KU—
ELLIE!
SLIDE
YOU SURE THAT'S NOT JUST YOUR IMAGINATION? MORE IMPORTANTLY...DID YOU FINISH COPYING MY NOTES?
OH, YES!
THEY WERE SO NEAT AND PRETTY AND EASY TO UNDERSTAND.
I KNEW YOU ALWAYS PAID ATTENTION IN CLASS AND STUDIED HARD.
YOU'RE A REALLY HARD WORKER, YOU KNOW...

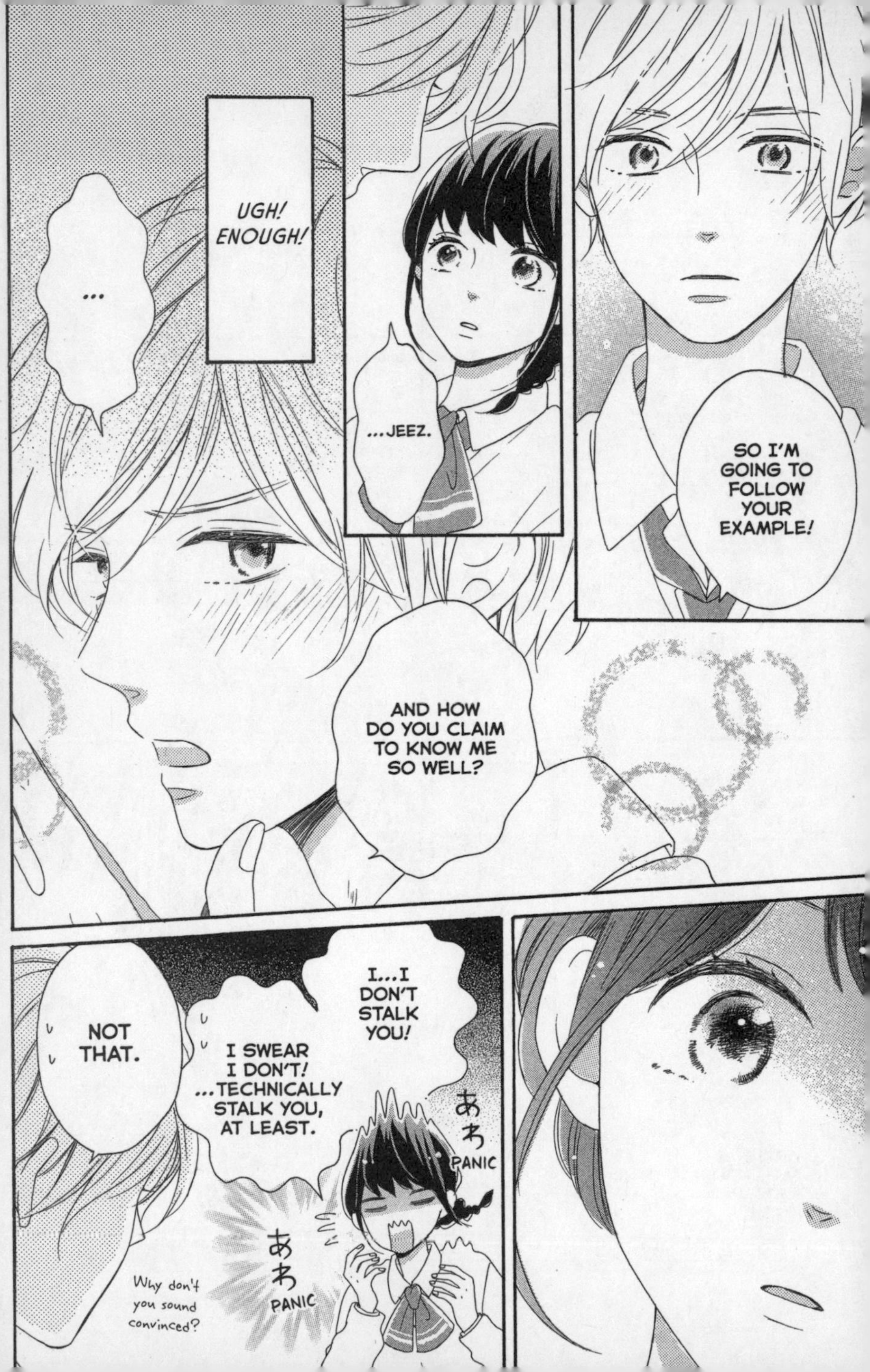
SO I'M GOING TO FOLLOW YOUR EXAMPLE!
...JEEZ.
UGH! ENOUGH!
...
AND HOW DO YOU CLAIM TO KNOW ME SO WELL?
I...I DON'T STALK YOU!
I SWEAR I DON'T! ...TECHNICALLY STALK YOU, AT LEAST.
あわ PANIC
NOT THAT.
あわ PANIC
Why don't you sound convinced?

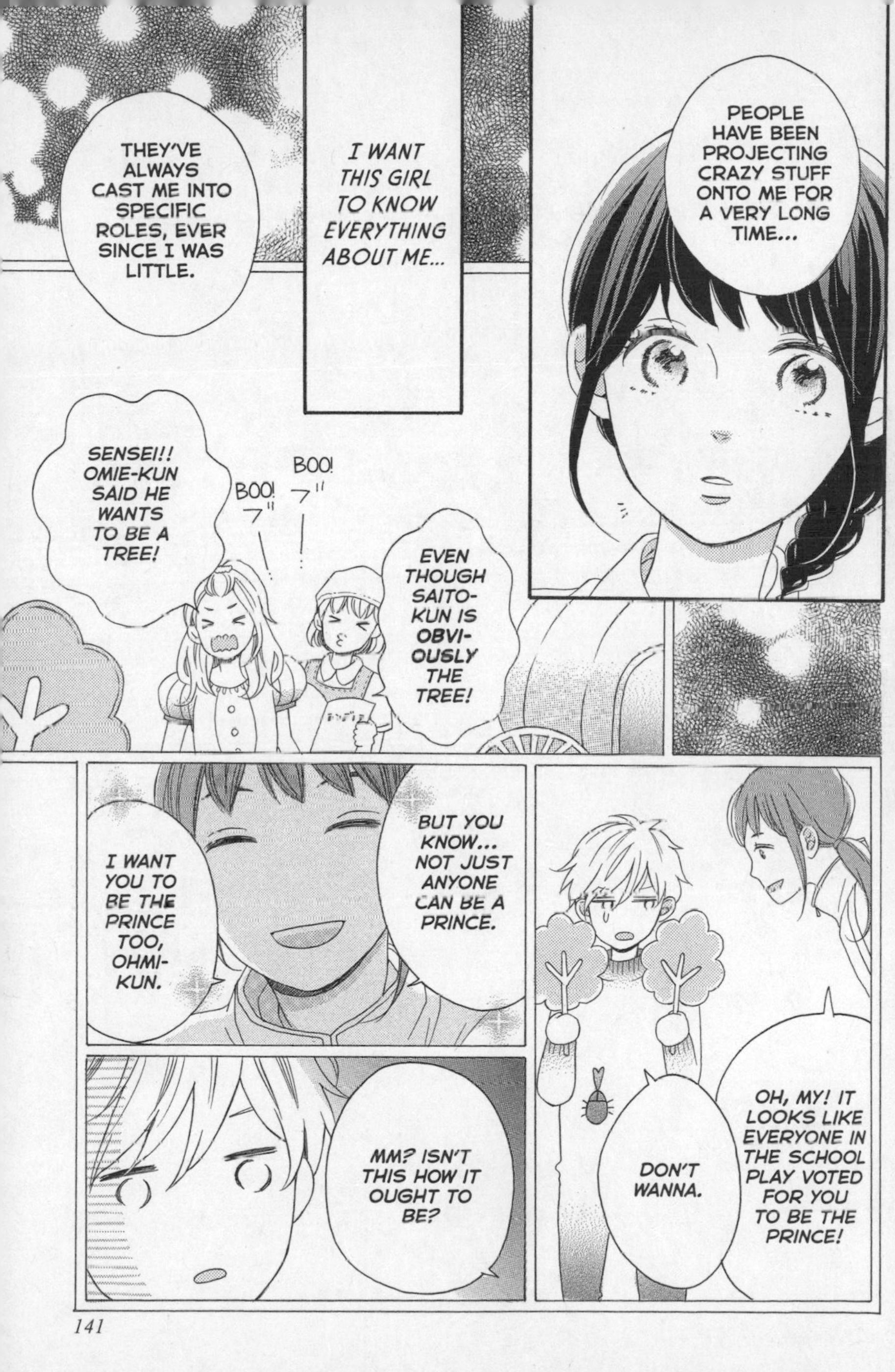
PEOPLE HAVE BEEN PROJECTING CRAZY STUFF ONTO ME FOR A VERY LONG TIME...
I WANT THIS GIRL TO KNOW EVERYTHING ABOUT ME...
THEY'VE ALWAYS CAST ME INTO SPECIFIC ROLES, EVER SINCE I WAS LITTLE.
SENSEI!! OMIE-KUN SAID HE WANTS TO BE A TREE!
BOO!
BOO!
EVEN THOUGH SAITO-KUN IS OBVIOUSLY THE TREE!
OH, MY! IT LOOKS LIKE EVERYONE IN THE SCHOOL PLAY VOTED FOR YOU TO BE THE PRINCE!
DON'T WANNA.
BUT YOU KNOW... NOT JUST ANYONE CAN BE A PRINCE.
I WANT YOU TO BE THE PRINCE TOO, OHMI-KUN.
MM? ISN'T THIS HOW IT OUGHT TO BE?

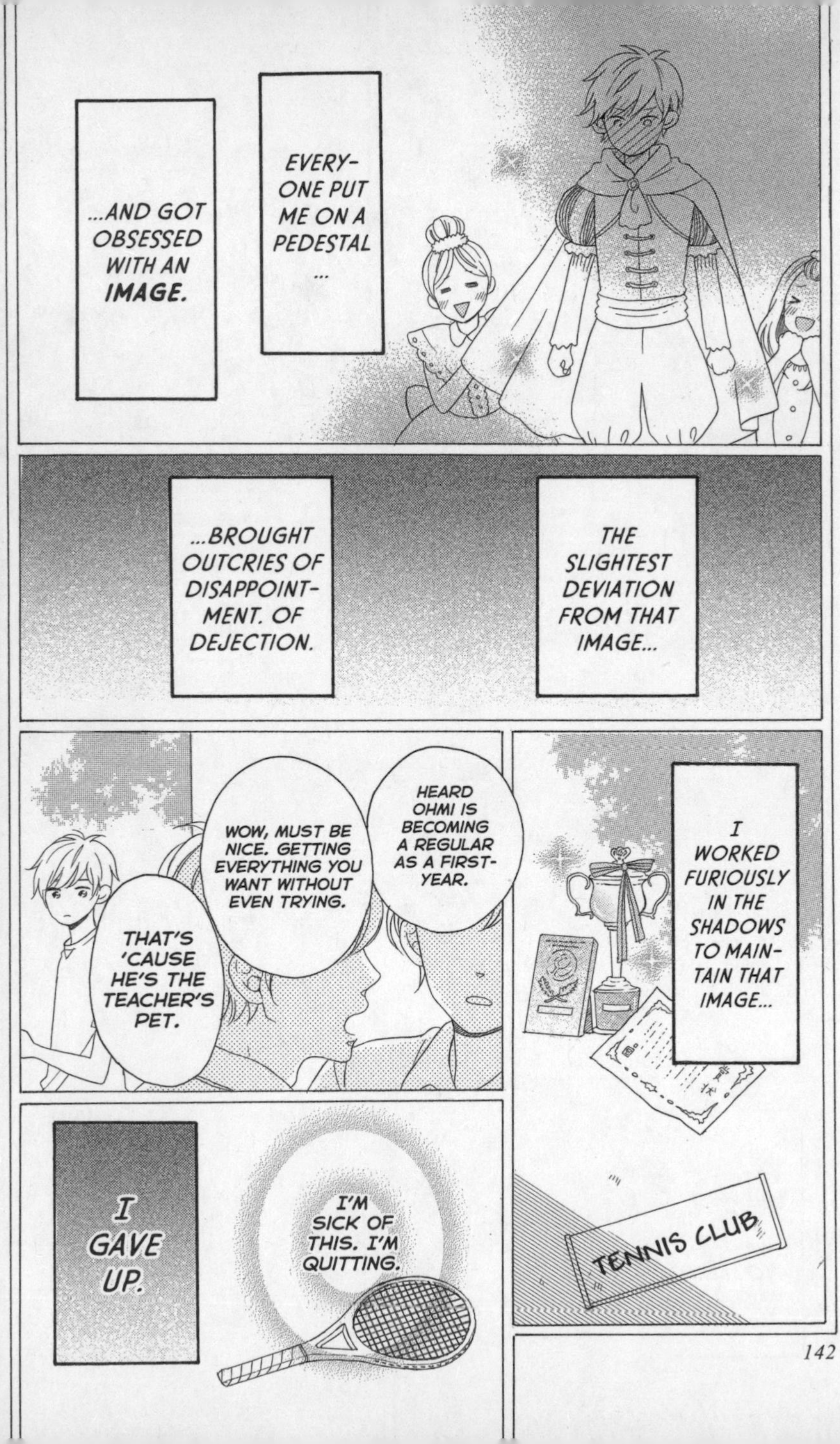
EVERY-ONE PUT ME ON A PEDESTAL...
...AND GOT OBSESSED WITH AN IMAGE.
THE SLIGHTEST DEVIATION FROM THAT IMAGE...
...BROUGHT OUTCRIES OF DISAPPOINT-MENT. OF DEJECTION.
I WORKED FURIOUSLY IN THE SHADOWS TO MAIN-TAIN THAT IMAGE...
TENNIS CLUB
HEARD OHMI IS BECOMING A REGULAR AS A FIRST-YEAR.
WOW, MUST BE NICE. GETTING EVERYTHING YOU WANT WITHOUT EVEN TRYING.
THAT'S 'CAUSE HE'S THE TEACHER'S PET.
I'M SICK OF THIS. I'M QUITTING.
I GAVE UP.

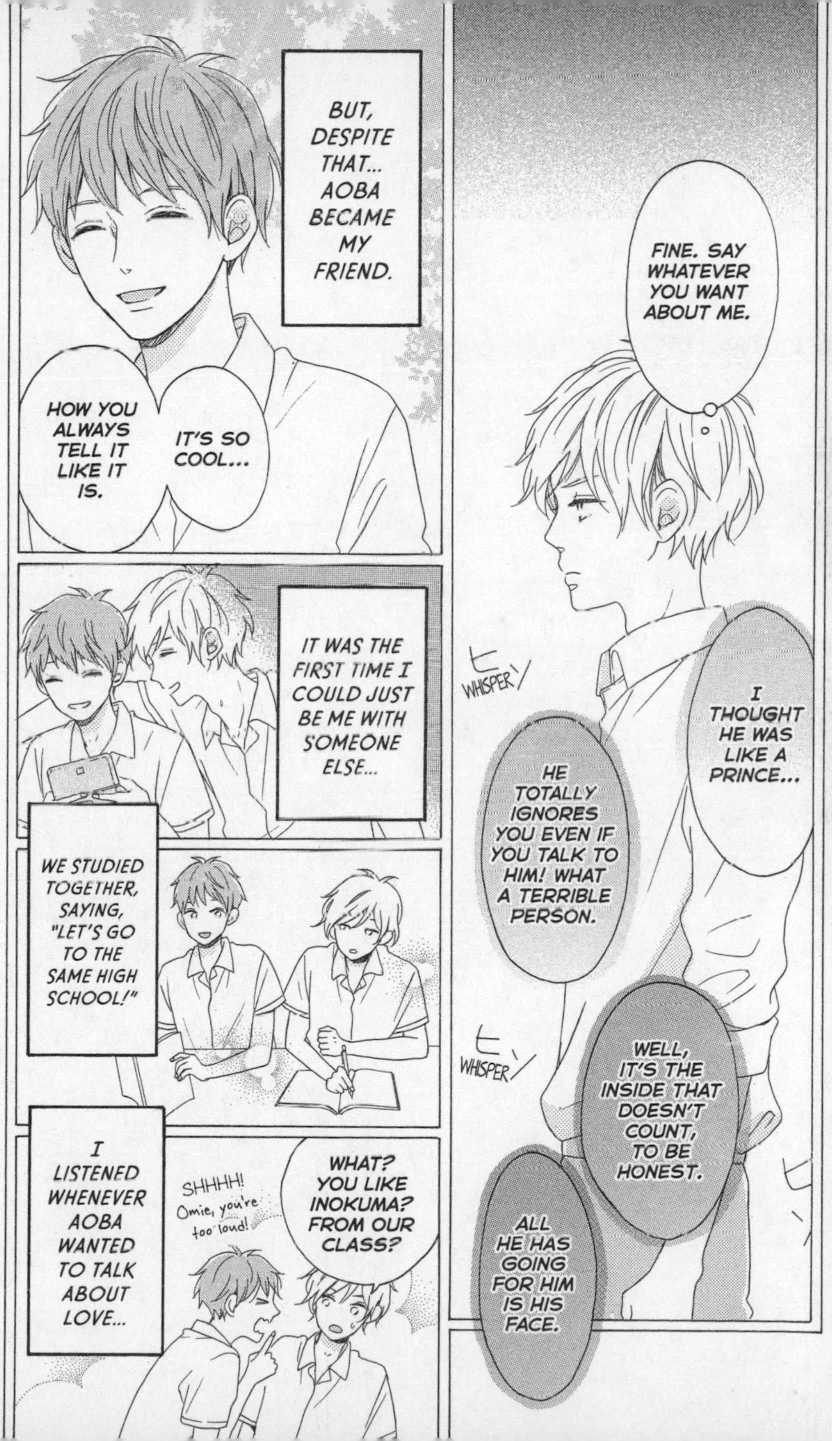
FINE. SAY WHATEVER YOU WANT ABOUT ME.
I THOUGHT HE WAS LIKE A PRINCE...
WHISPER
HE TOTALLY IGNORES YOU EVEN IF YOU TALK TO HIM! WHAT A TERRIBLE PERSON.
WELL, IT'S THE INSIDE THAT DOESN'T COUNT, TO BE HONEST.
WHISPER
ALL HE HAS GOING FOR HIM IS HIS FACE.
BUT, DESPITE THAT... AOBA BECAME MY FRIEND.
IT'S SO COOL...
HOW YOU ALWAYS TELL IT LIKE IT IS.
IT WAS THE FIRST TIME I COULD JUST BE ME WITH SOMEONE ELSE...
WE STUDIED TOGETHER, SAYING, "LET'S GO TO THE SAME HIGH SCHOOL!"
WHAT? YOU LIKE INOKUMA? FROM OUR CLASS?
SHHHH! Omie, you're too loud!
I LISTENED WHENEVER AOBA WANTED TO TALK ABOUT LOVE...

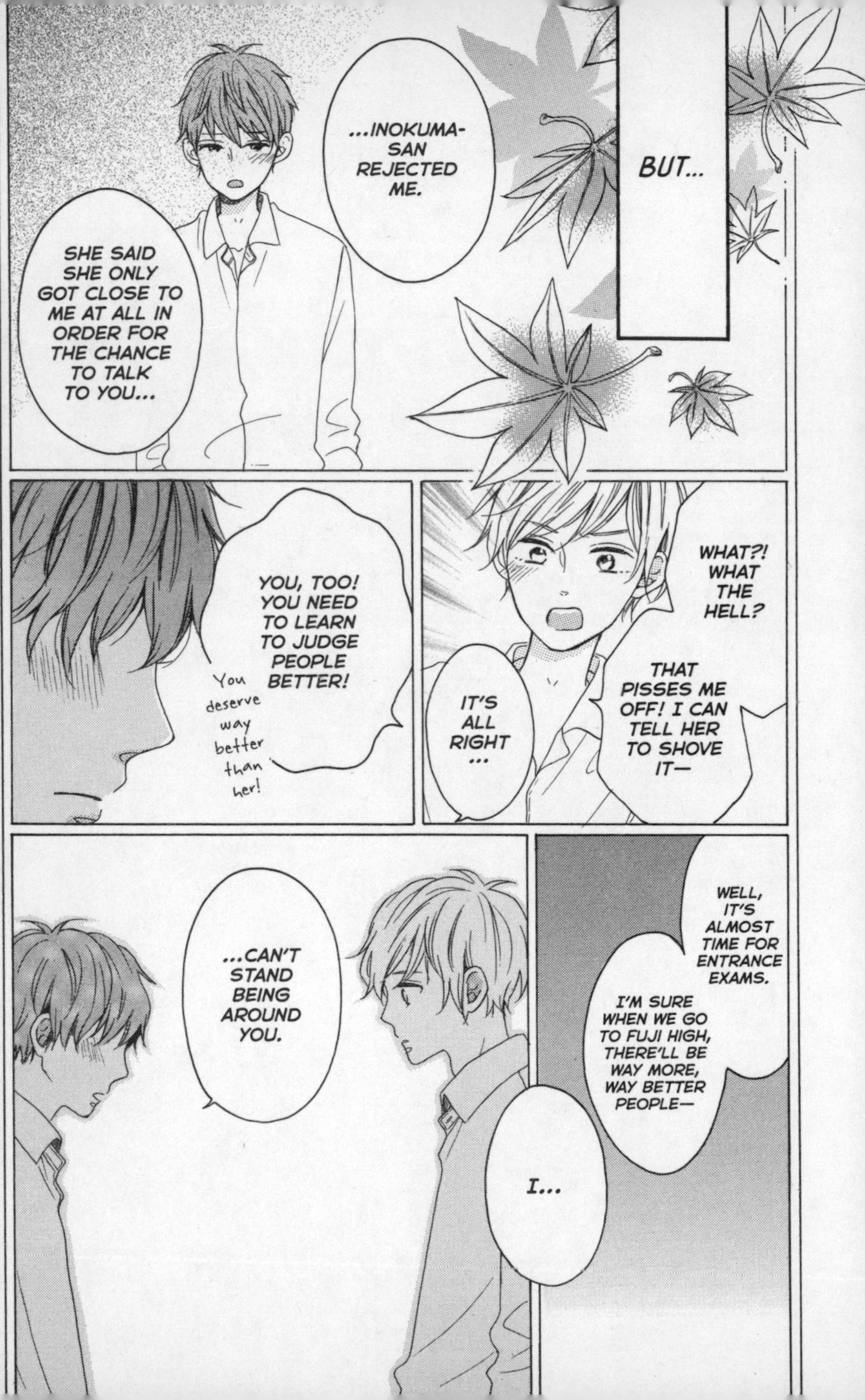
BUT...
...INOKUMA-SAN REJECTED ME.
SHE SAID SHE ONLY GOT CLOSE TO ME AT ALL IN ORDER FOR THE CHANCE TO TALK TO YOU...
WHAT?! WHAT THE HELL?
THAT PISSES ME OFF! I CAN TELL HER TO SHOVE IT—
IT'S ALL RIGHT...
YOU, TOO! YOU NEED TO LEARN TO JUDGE PEOPLE BETTER!
You deserve way better than her!
WELL, IT'S ALMOST TIME FOR ENTRANCE EXAMS.
I'M SURE WHEN WE GO TO FUJI HIGH, THERE'LL BE WAY MORE, WAY BETTER PEOPLE—
I...
...CAN'T STAND BEING AROUND YOU.

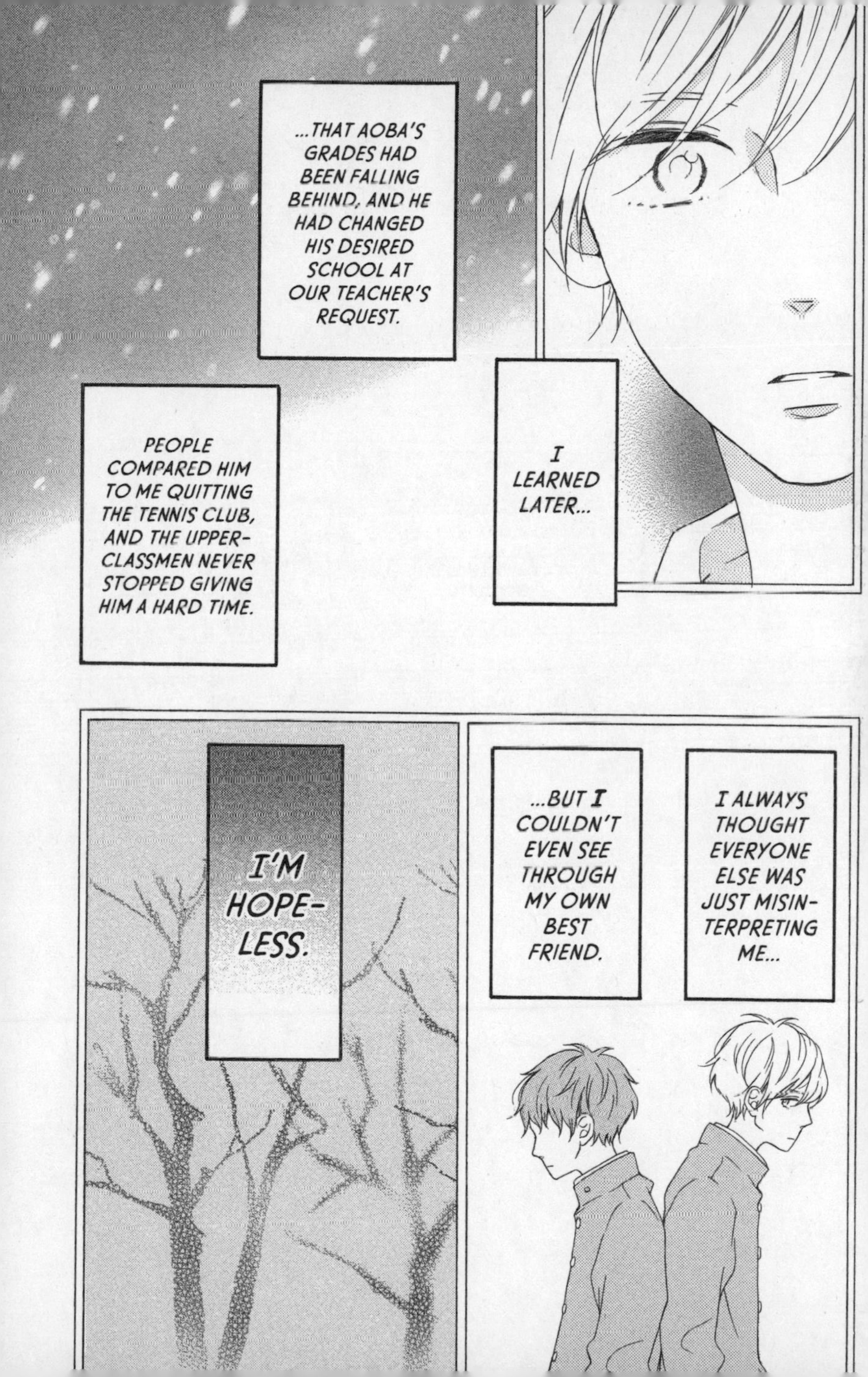
I LEARNED LATER...
...THAT AOBA'S GRADES HAD BEEN FALLING BEHIND, AND HE HAD CHANGED HIS DESIRED SCHOOL AT OUR TEACHER'S REQUEST.
PEOPLE COMPARED HIM TO ME QUITTING THE TENNIS CLUB, AND THE UPPER-CLASSMEN NEVER STOPPED GIVING HIM A HARD TIME.
I ALWAYS THOUGHT EVERYONE ELSE WAS JUST MISIN-TERPRETING ME...
...BUT I COULDN'T EVEN SEE THROUGH MY OWN BEST FRIEND.
I'M HOPE-LESS.

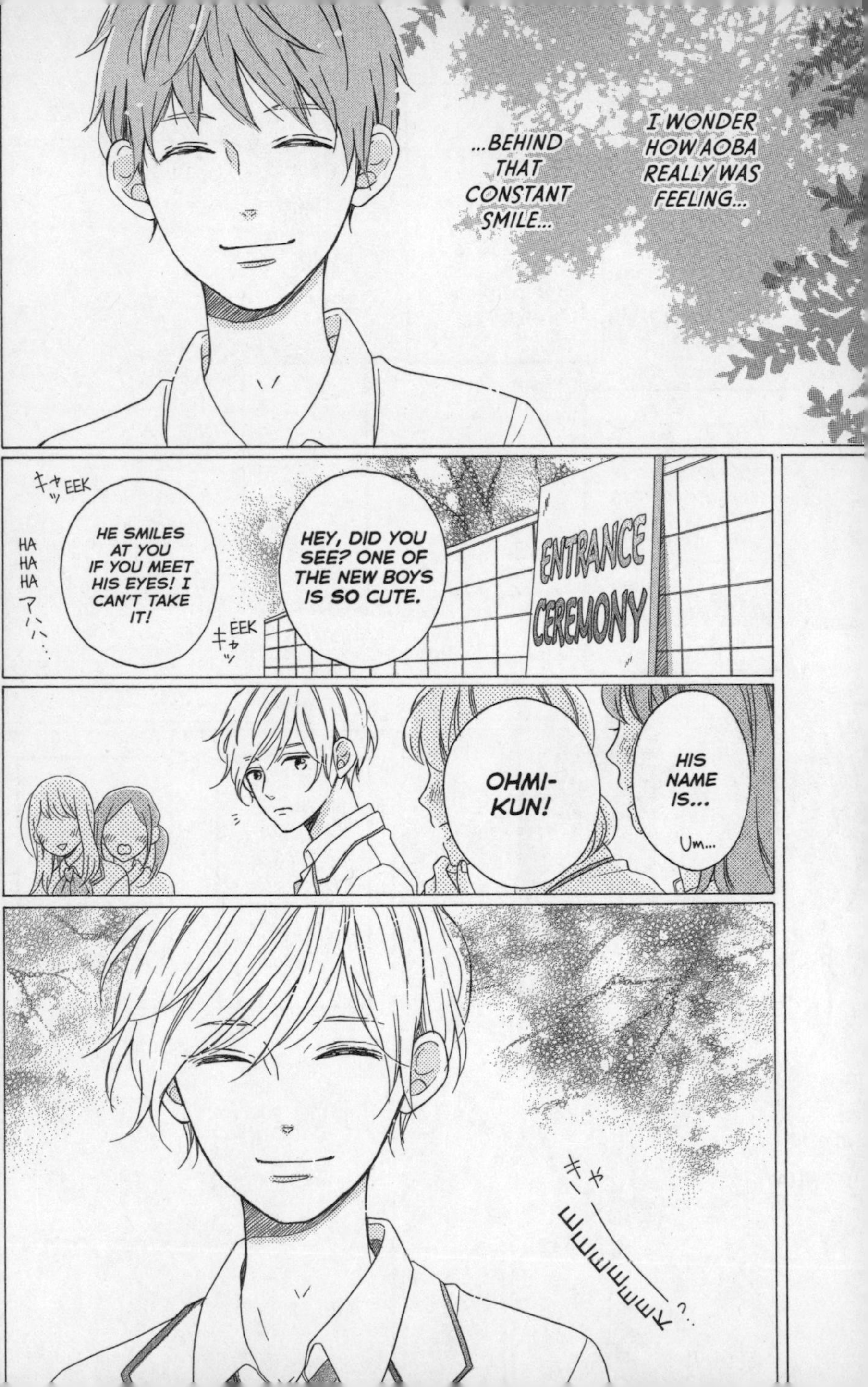
I WONDER HOW AOBA REALLY WAS FEELING...
...BEHIND THAT CONSTANT SMILE...
ENTRANCE CEREMONY
HEY, DID YOU SEE? ONE OF THE NEW BOYS IS SO CUTE.
キャッ EEK
HE SMILES AT YOU IF YOU MEET HIS EYES! I CAN'T TAKE IT!
キャッ EEK
HA HA HA アハハ...
HIS NAME IS...
Um...
OHMI-KUN!
キャー EEEEEEEK?!

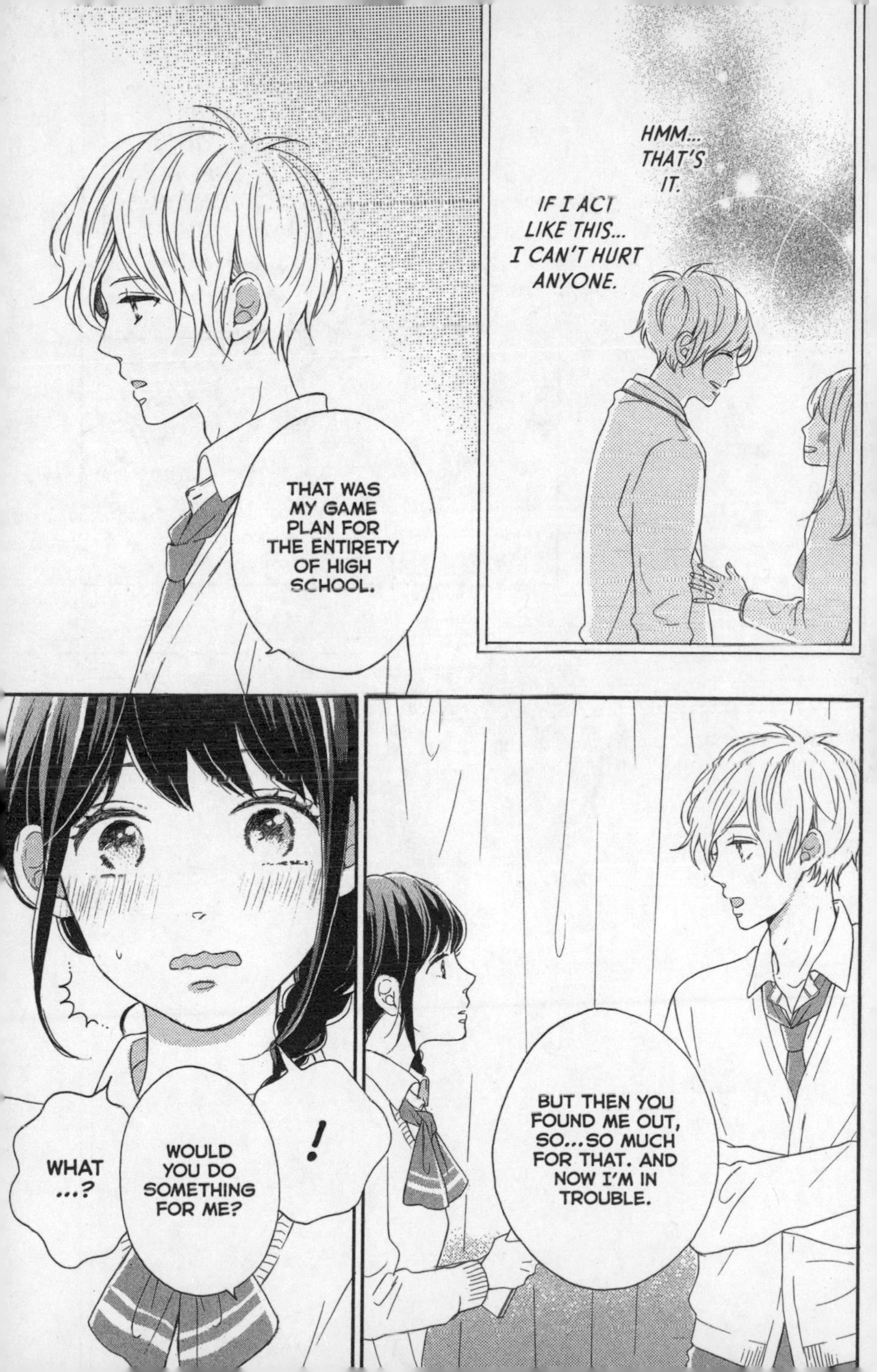
HMM... THAT'S IT.
IF I ACT LIKE THIS... I CAN'T HURT ANYONE.
THAT WAS MY GAME PLAN FOR THE ENTIRETY OF HIGH SCHOOL.
BUT THEN YOU FOUND ME OUT, SO...SO MUCH FOR THAT. AND NOW I'M IN TROUBLE.
!
WOULD YOU DO SOMETHING FOR ME?
WHAT ...?

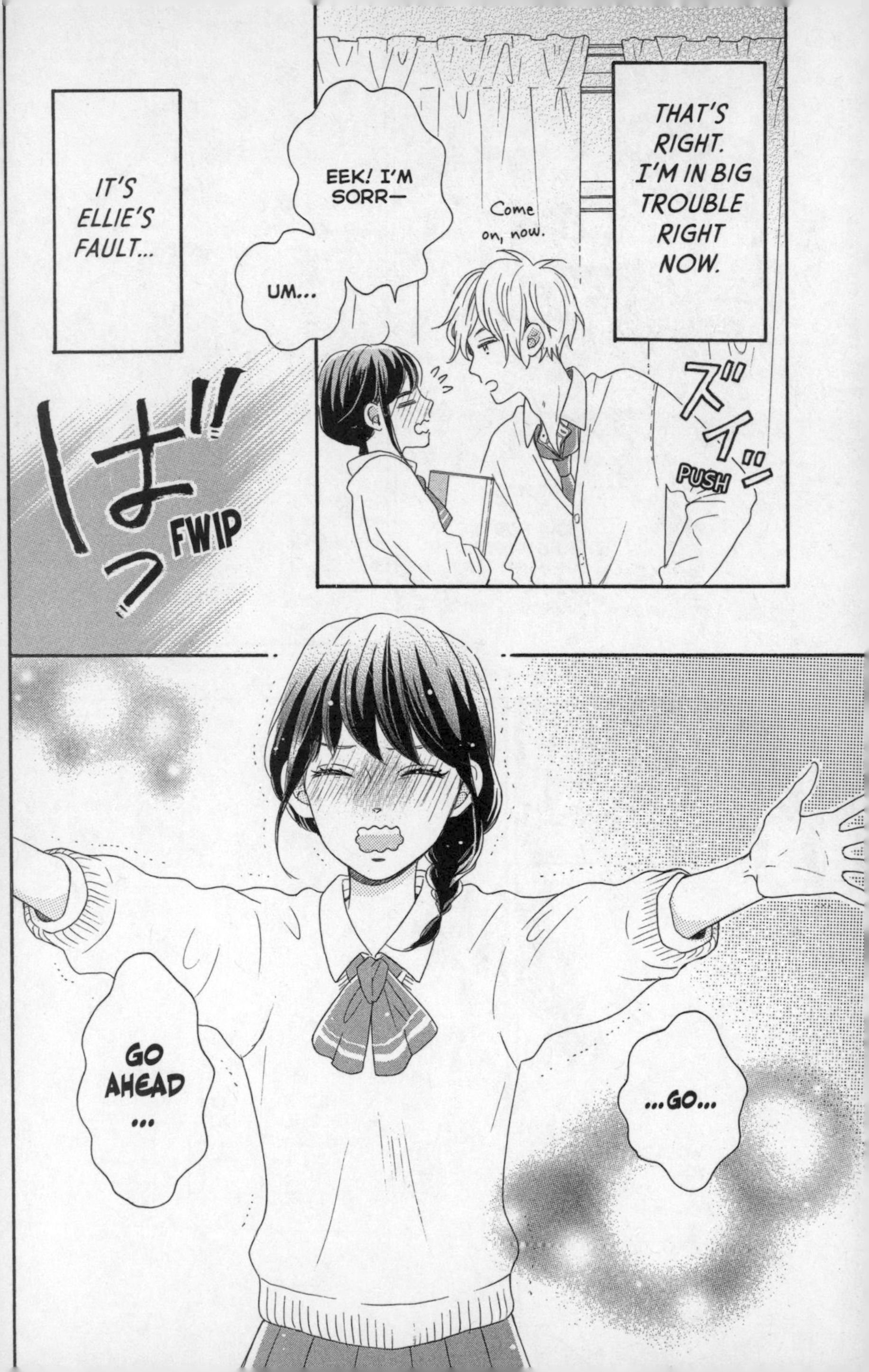
THAT'S RIGHT. I'M IN BIG TROUBLE RIGHT NOW.
Come on, now.
EEK! I'M SORR—
UM...
ズイッ
PUSH
IT'S ELLIE'S FAULT...
ばっ
FWIP
...GO...
GO AHEAD ...

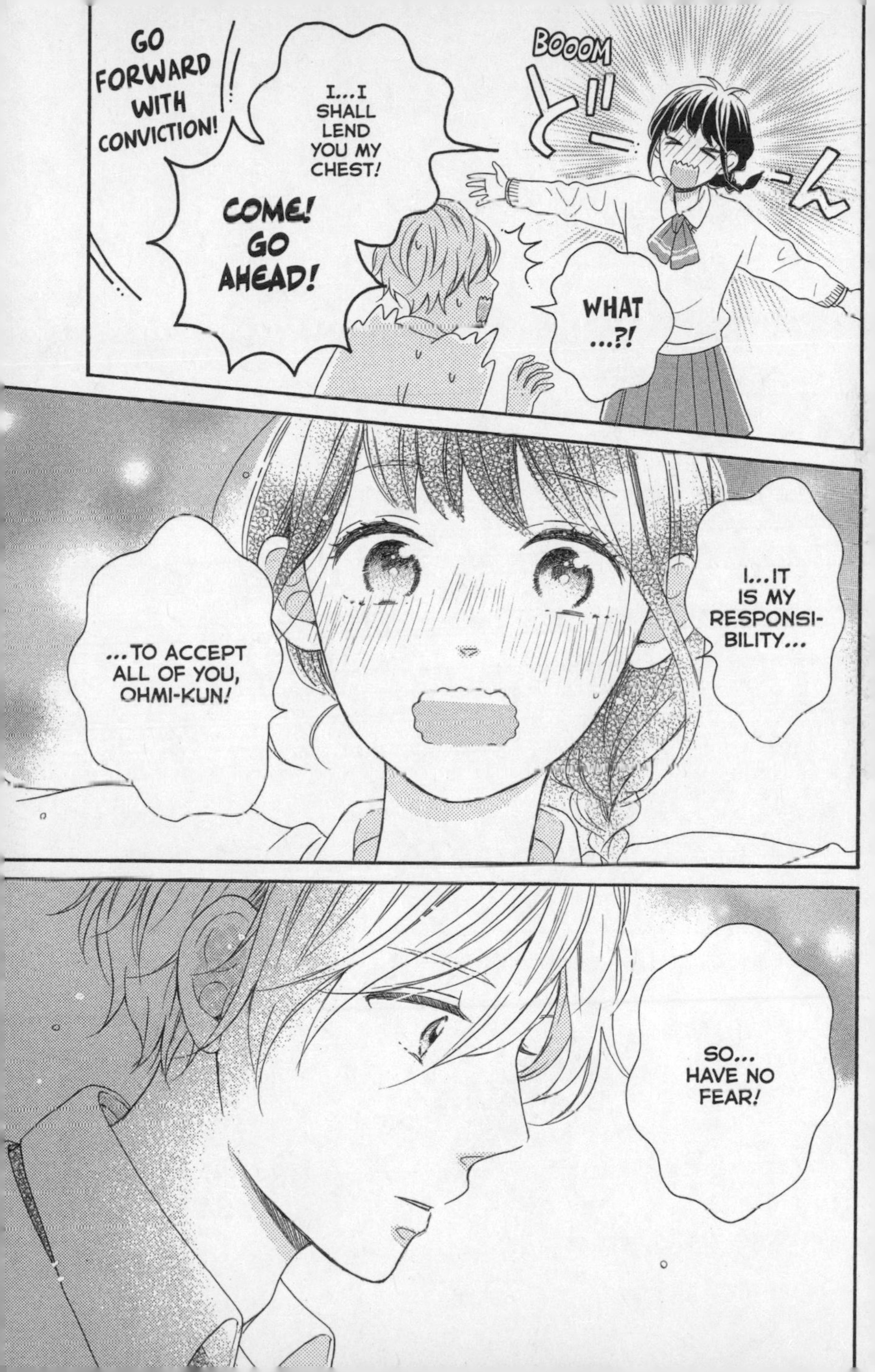
BOOOM
I...I SHALL LEND YOU MY CHEST!
COME! GO AHEAD!
WHAT ...?!
GO FORWARD WITH CONVICTION!
I...IT IS MY RESPONSI-BILITY...
...TO ACCEPT ALL OF YOU, OHMI-KUN!
SO... HAVE NO FEAR!

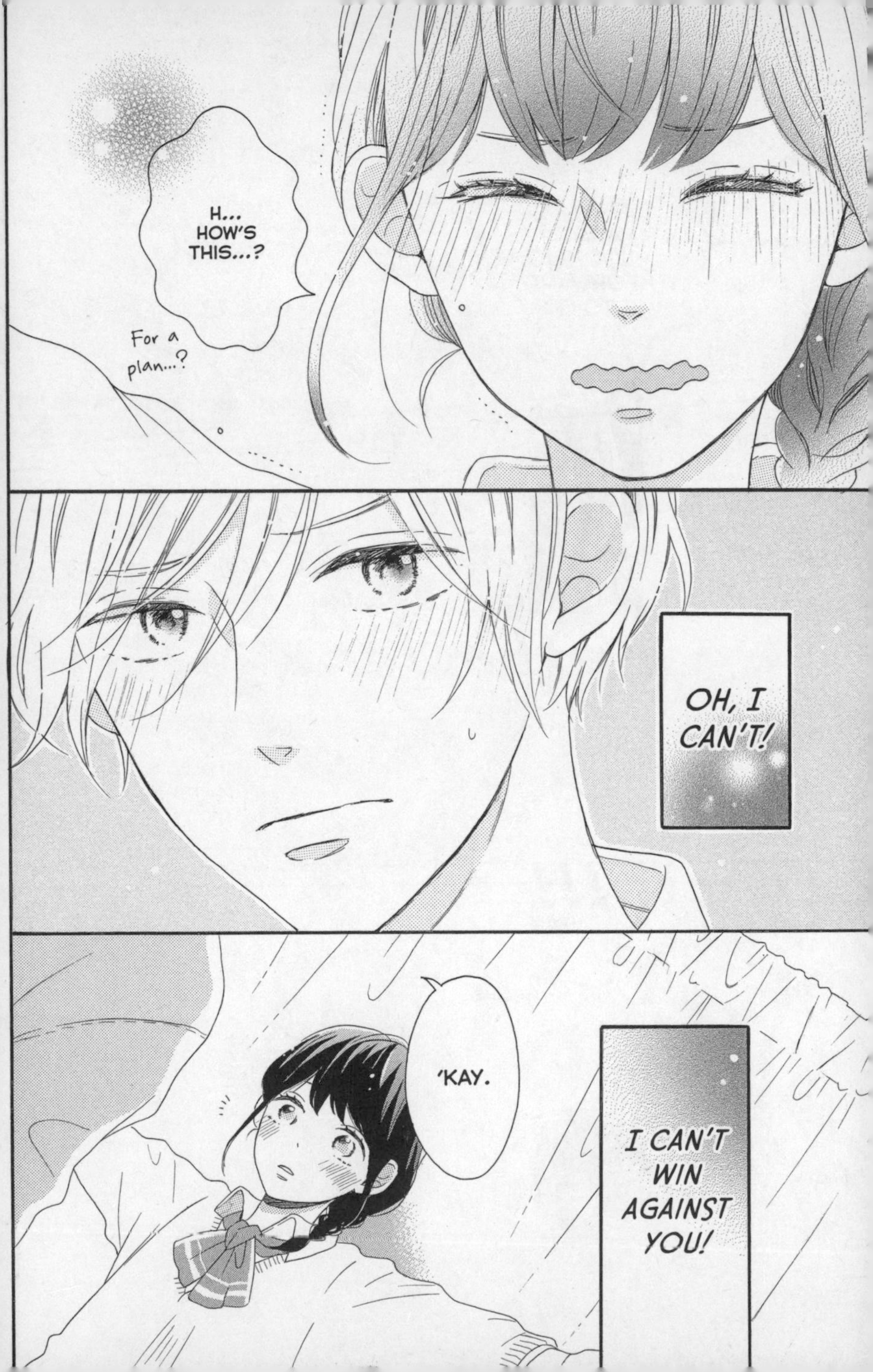
H... HOW'S THIS...?
For a plan...?
OH, I CAN'T!
I CAN'T WIN AGAINST YOU!
'KAY.

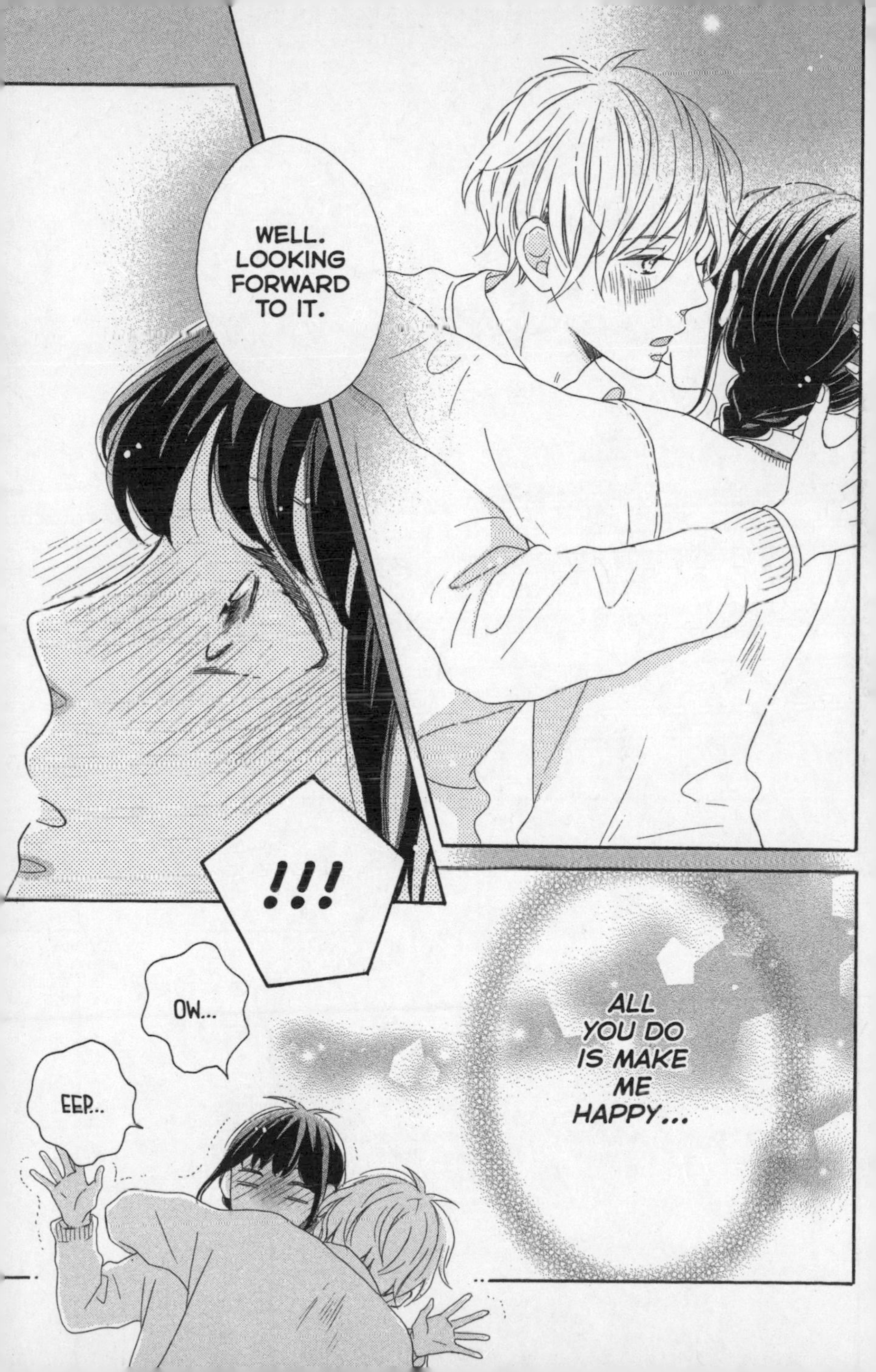
WELL. LOOKING FORWARD TO IT.
!!!
ALL YOU DO IS MAKE ME HAPPY...
OW...
EEP...

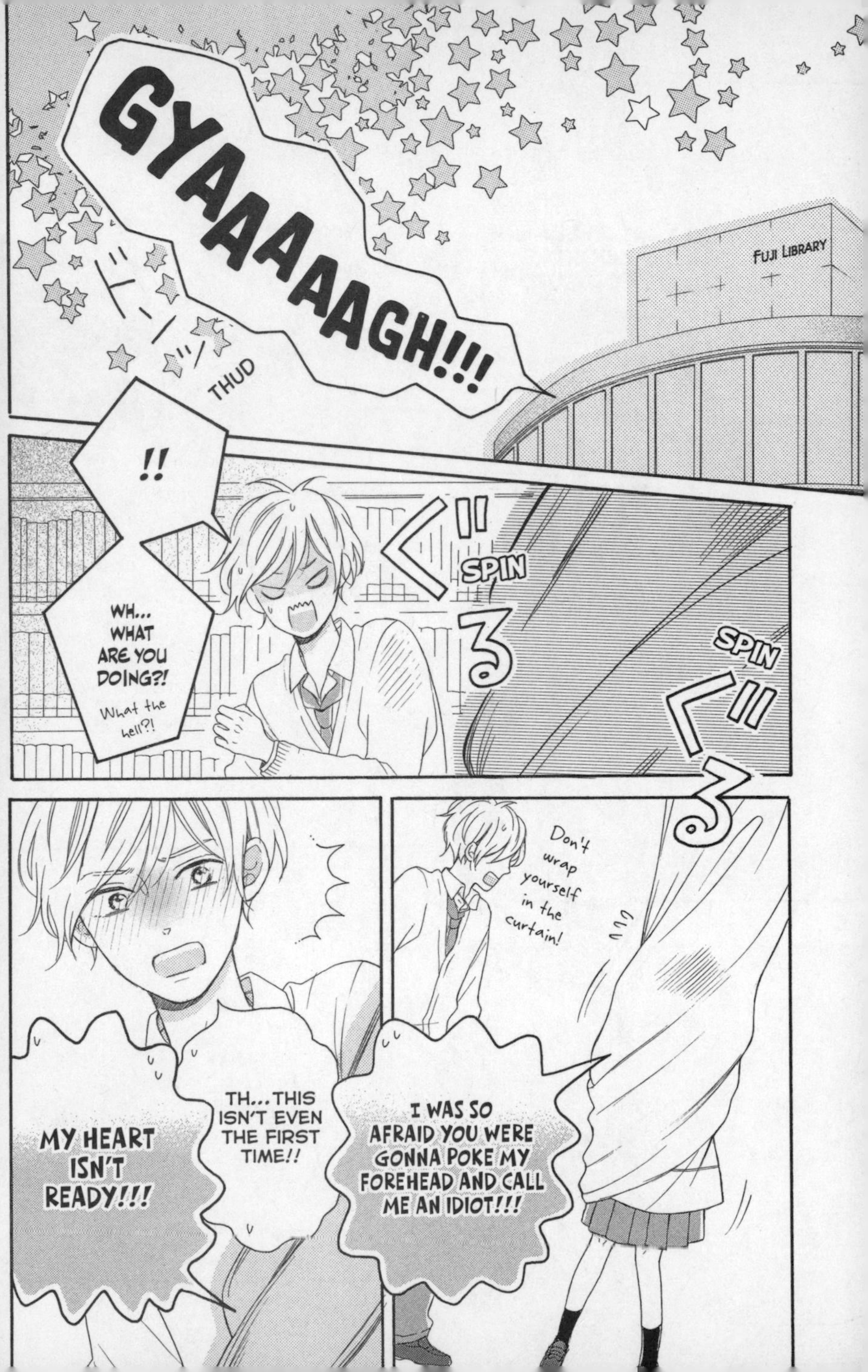
FUJI LIBRARY
GYAAAAAGH!!!
THUD
SPIN
SPIN
!!
WH... WHAT ARE YOU DOING?!
What the hell?!
Don't wrap yourself in the curtain!
I WAS SO AFRAID YOU WERE GONNA POKE MY FOREHEAD AND CALL ME AN IDIOT!!!
TH... THIS ISN'T EVEN THE FIRST TIME!!
MY HEART ISN'T READY!!!

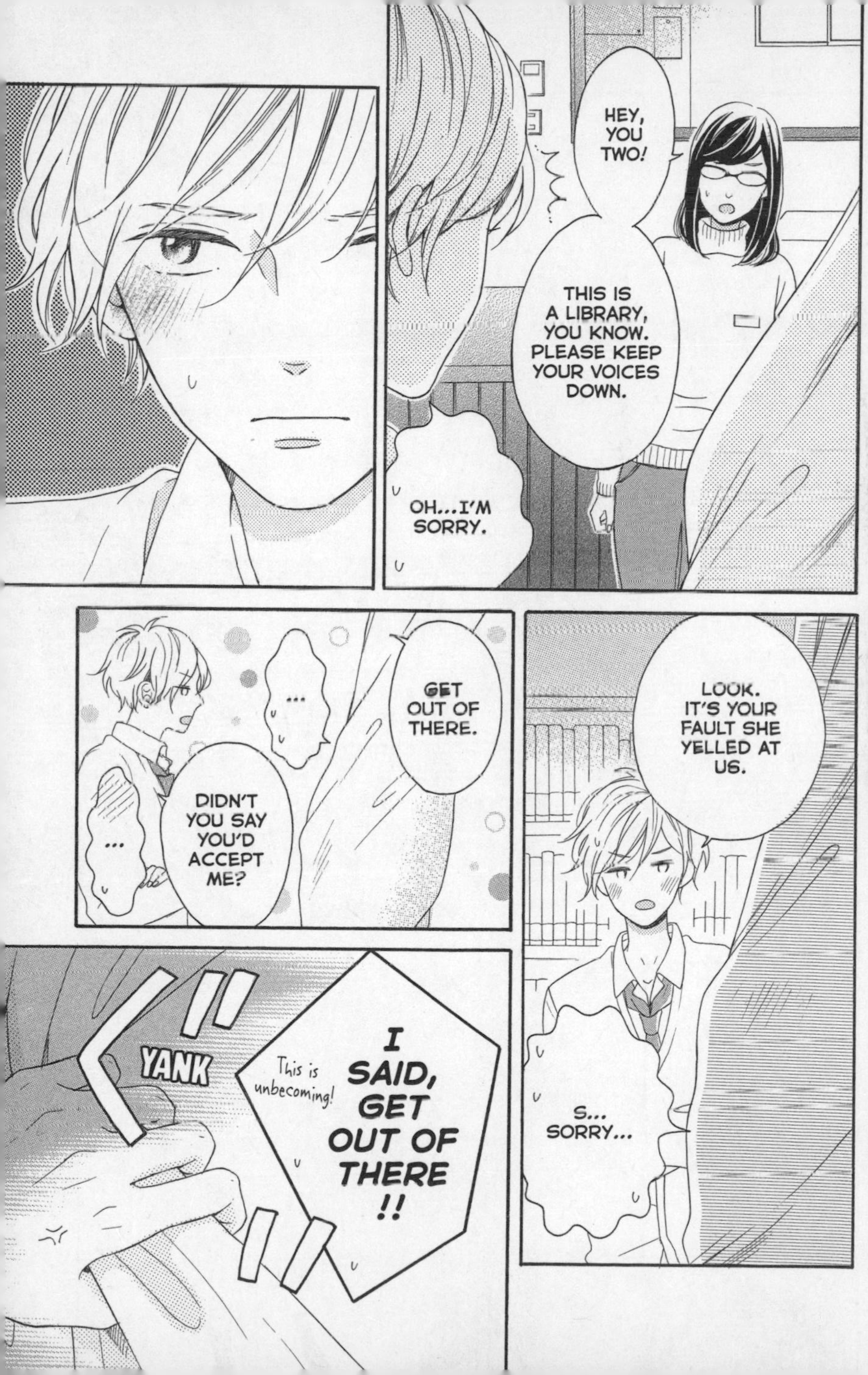
HEY, YOU TWO!
THIS IS A LIBRARY, YOU KNOW. PLEASE KEEP YOUR VOICES DOWN.
OH...I'M SORRY.
LOOK. IT'S YOUR FAULT SHE YELLED AT US.
S... SORRY...
GET OUT OF THERE.
...
DIDN'T YOU SAY YOU'D ACCEPT ME?
...
I SAID, GET OUT OF THERE!!
This is unbecoming!
YANK

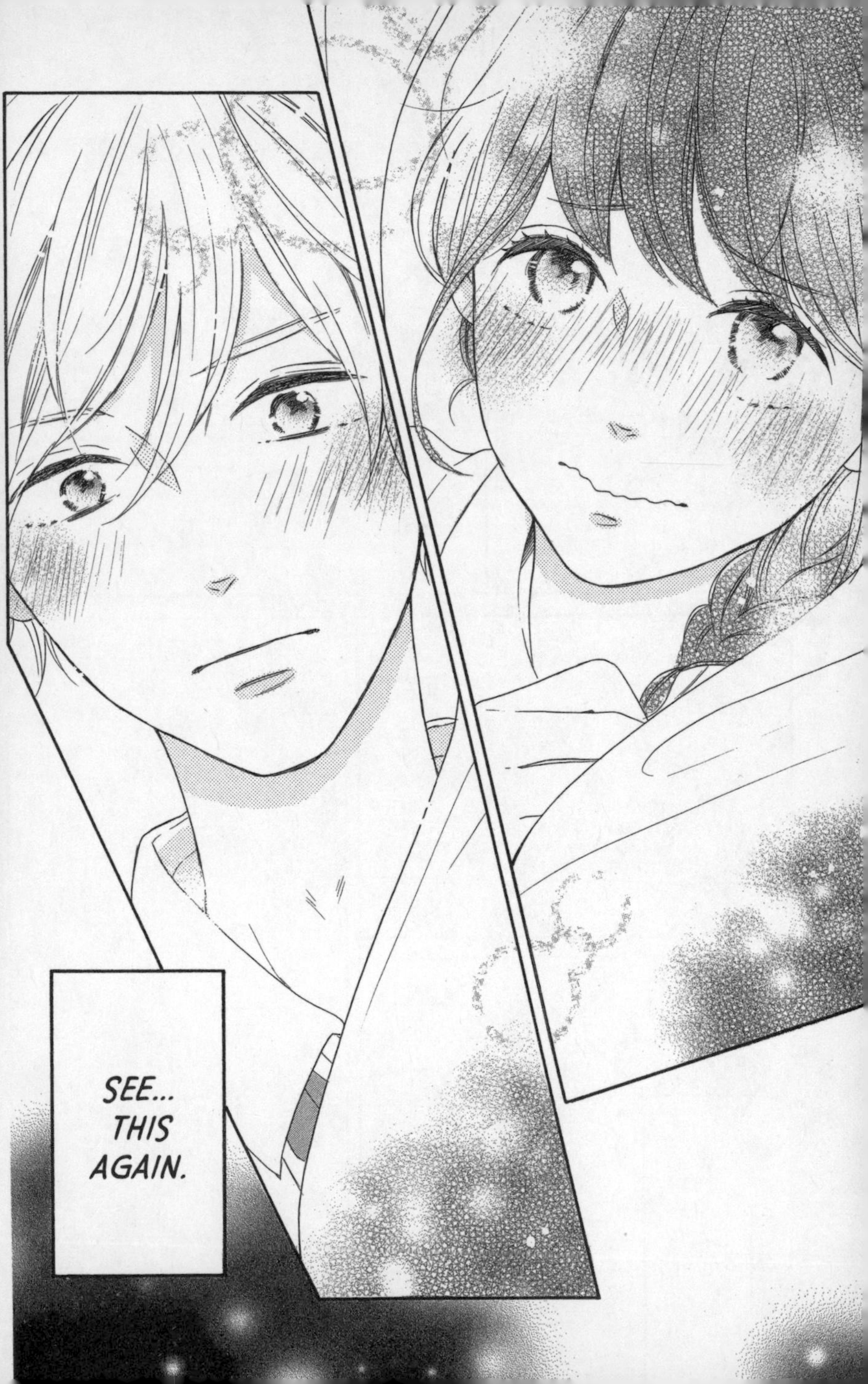
SEE... THIS AGAIN.

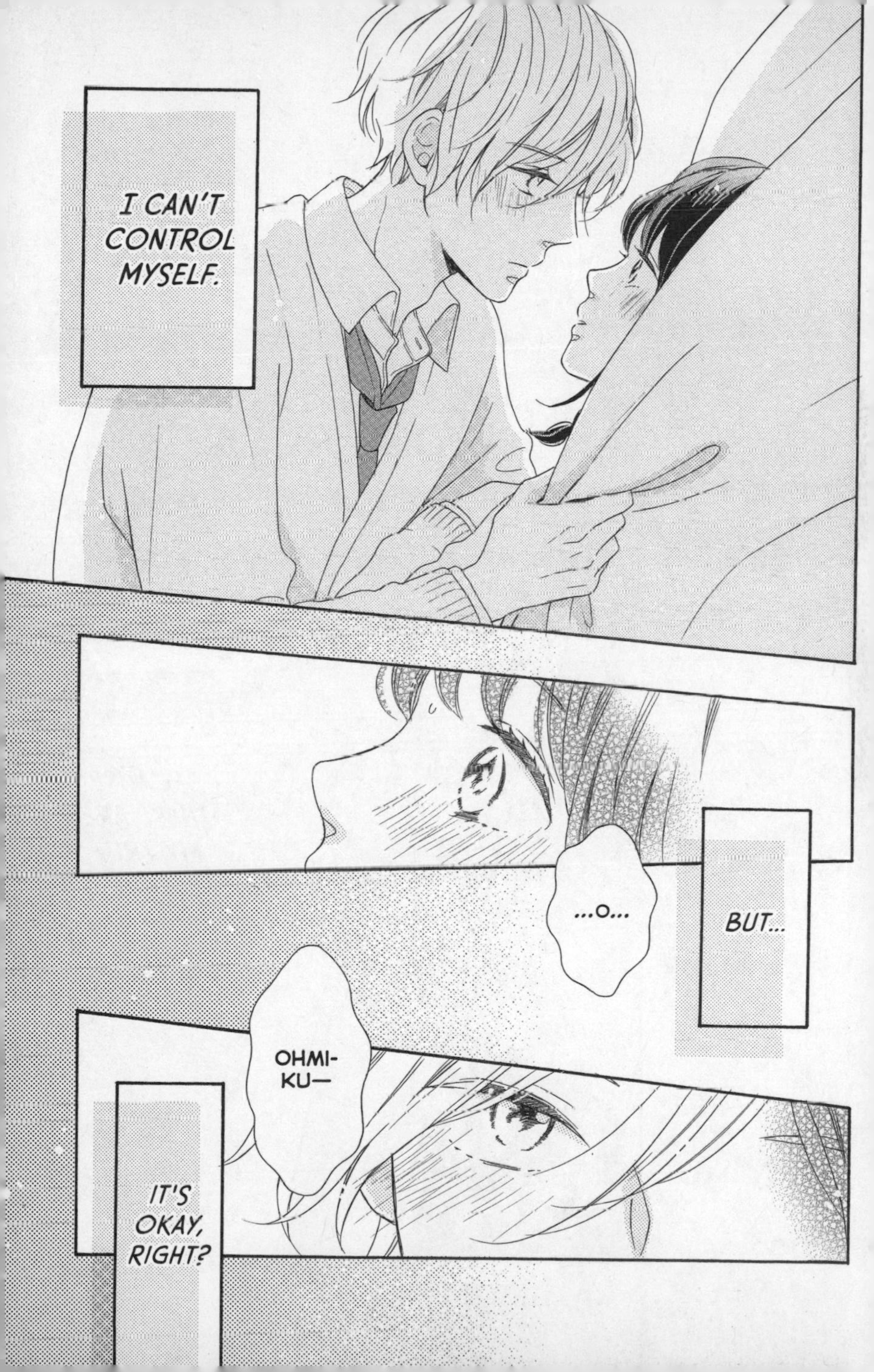
I CAN'T CONTROL MYSELF.
BUT...
...O...
OHMI-KU—
IT'S OKAY, RIGHT?

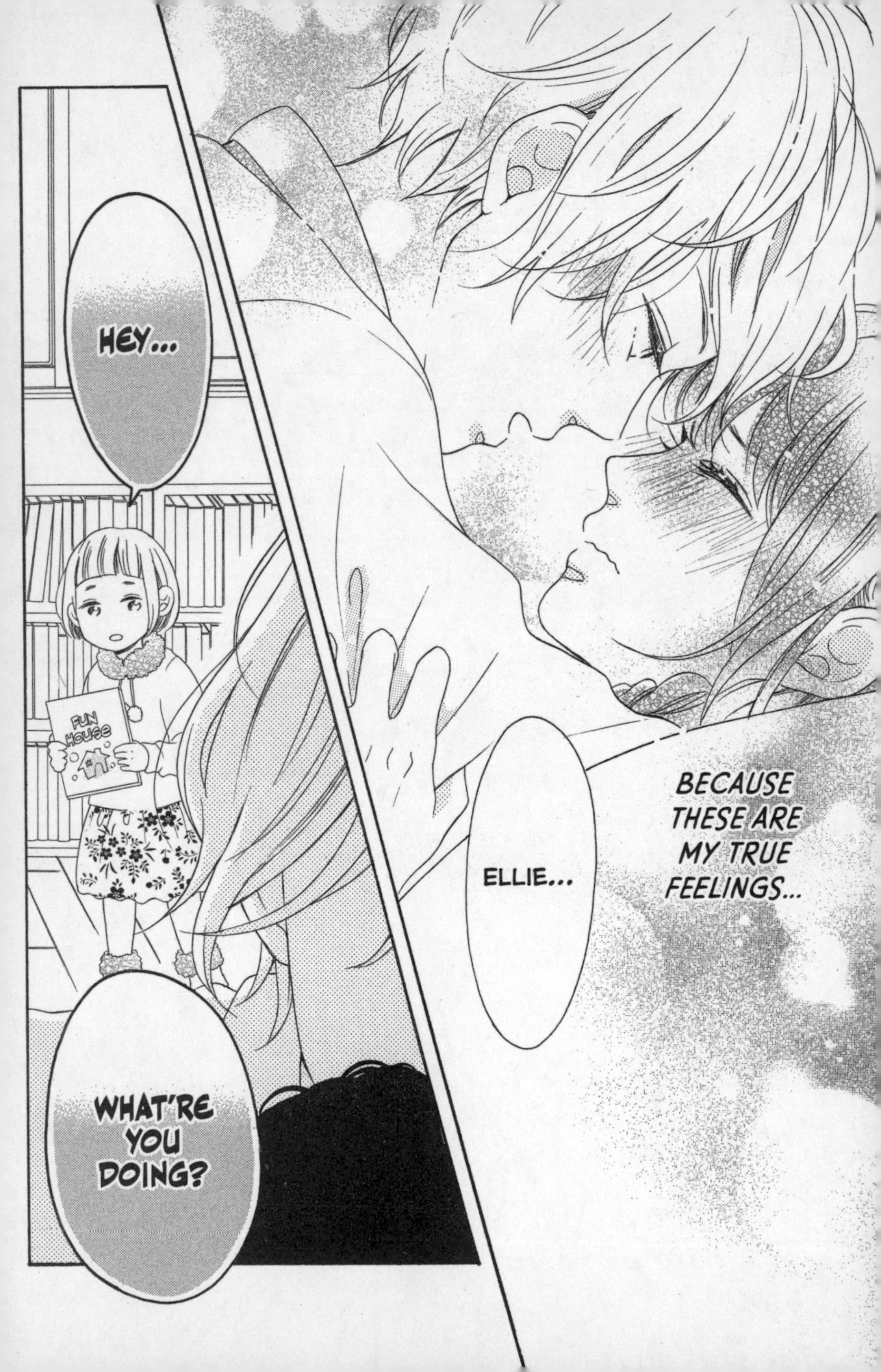
BECAUSE THESE ARE MY TRUE FEELINGS...
ELLIE...
HEY...
FUN HOUSE
WHAT'RE YOU DOING?

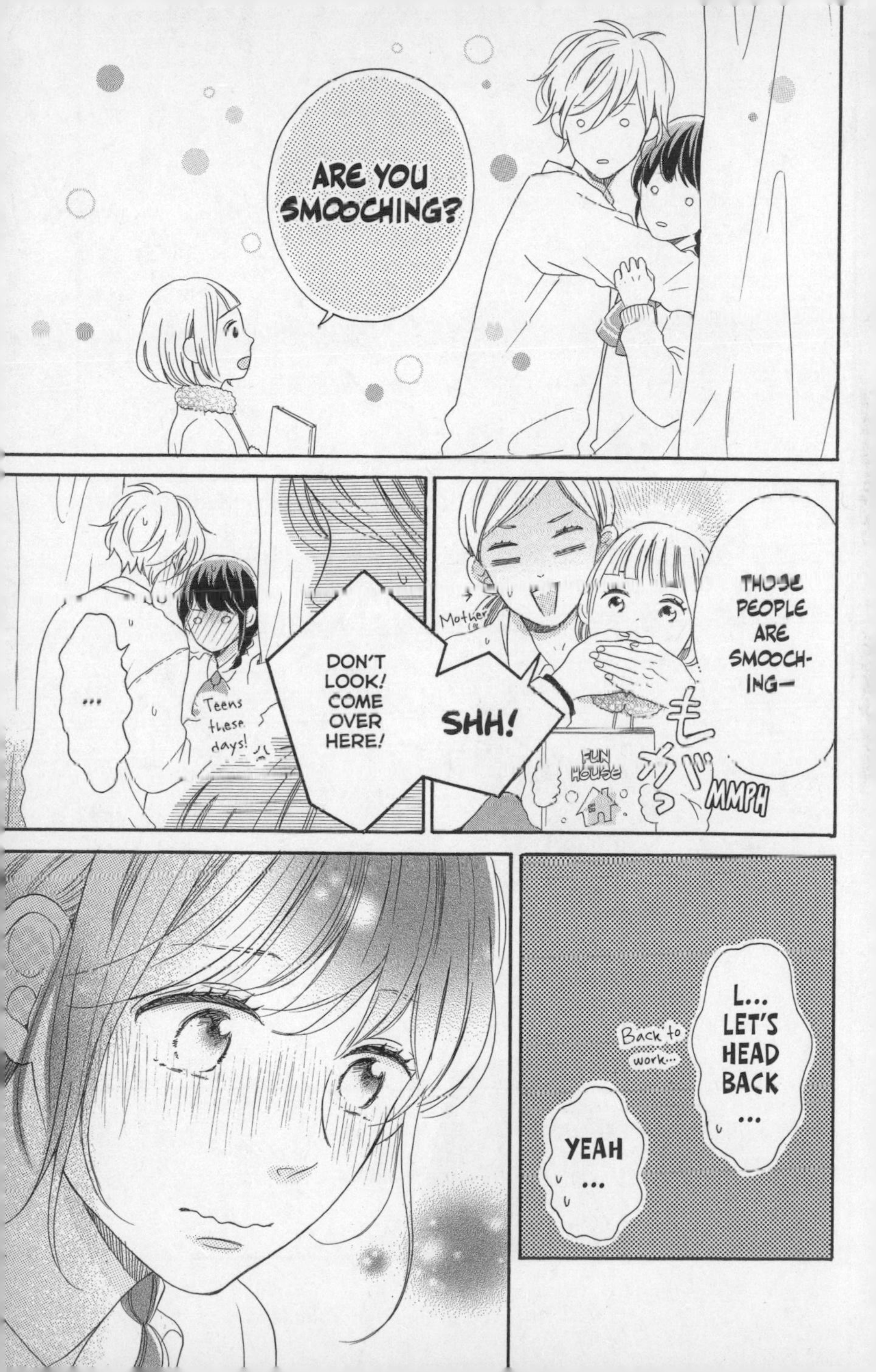
ARE YOU SMOOCHING?
THOSE PEOPLE ARE SMOOCH-ING—
SHH!
DON'T LOOK! COME OVER HERE!
Mother
FUN HOUSE
もが
MMPH
...
Teens these days!
L... LET'S HEAD BACK...
Back to work...
YEAH...

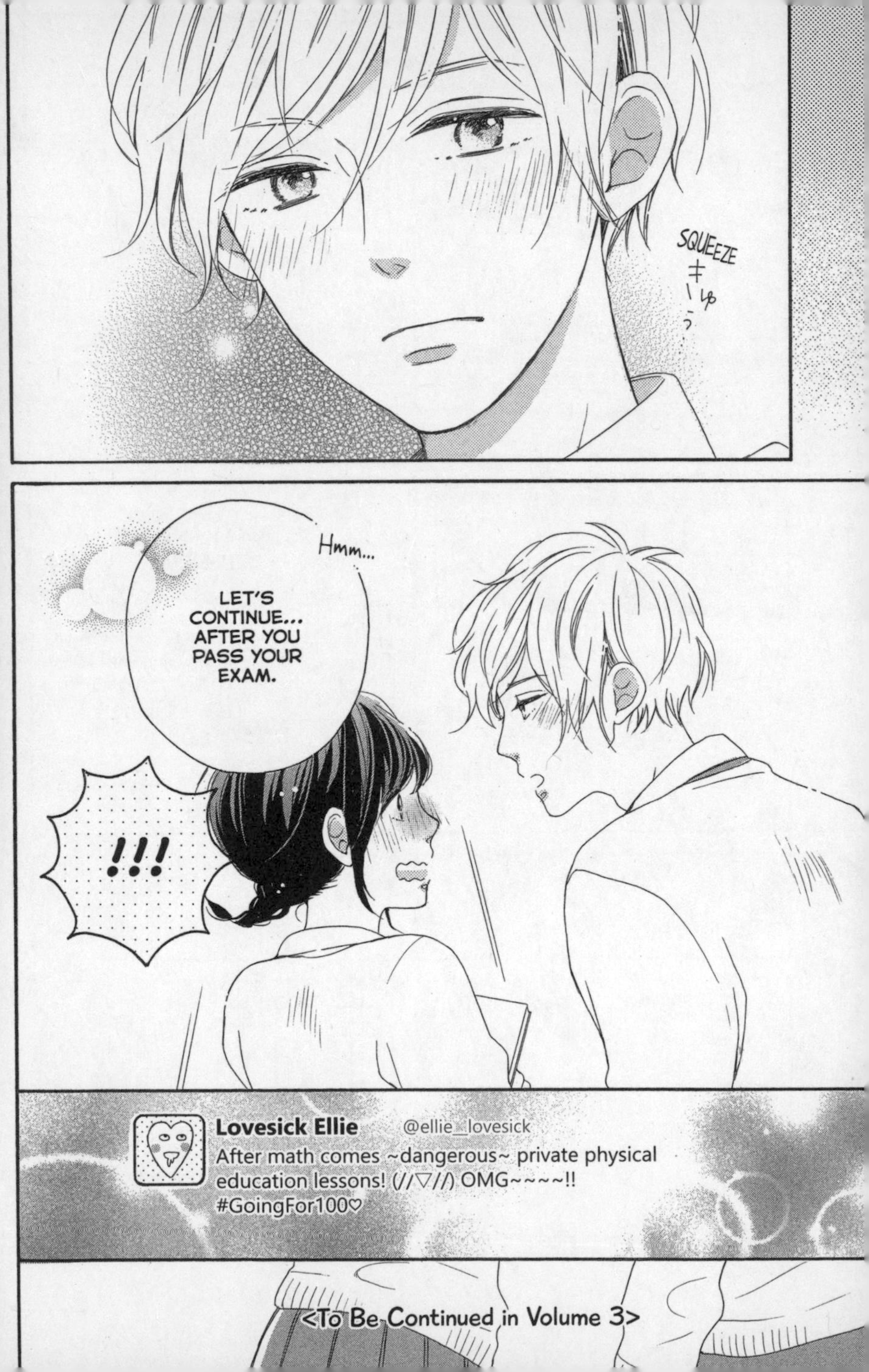
SQUEEZE
キゅぅ
Hmm...
LET'S CONTINUE... AFTER YOU PASS YOUR EXAM.
!!!
Lovesick Ellie @ellie_lovesick
After math comes ~dangerous~ private physical education lessons! (//▽//) OMG~~~~!! #GoingFor100♡
<To Be Continued in Volume 3>

★ BONUS ★

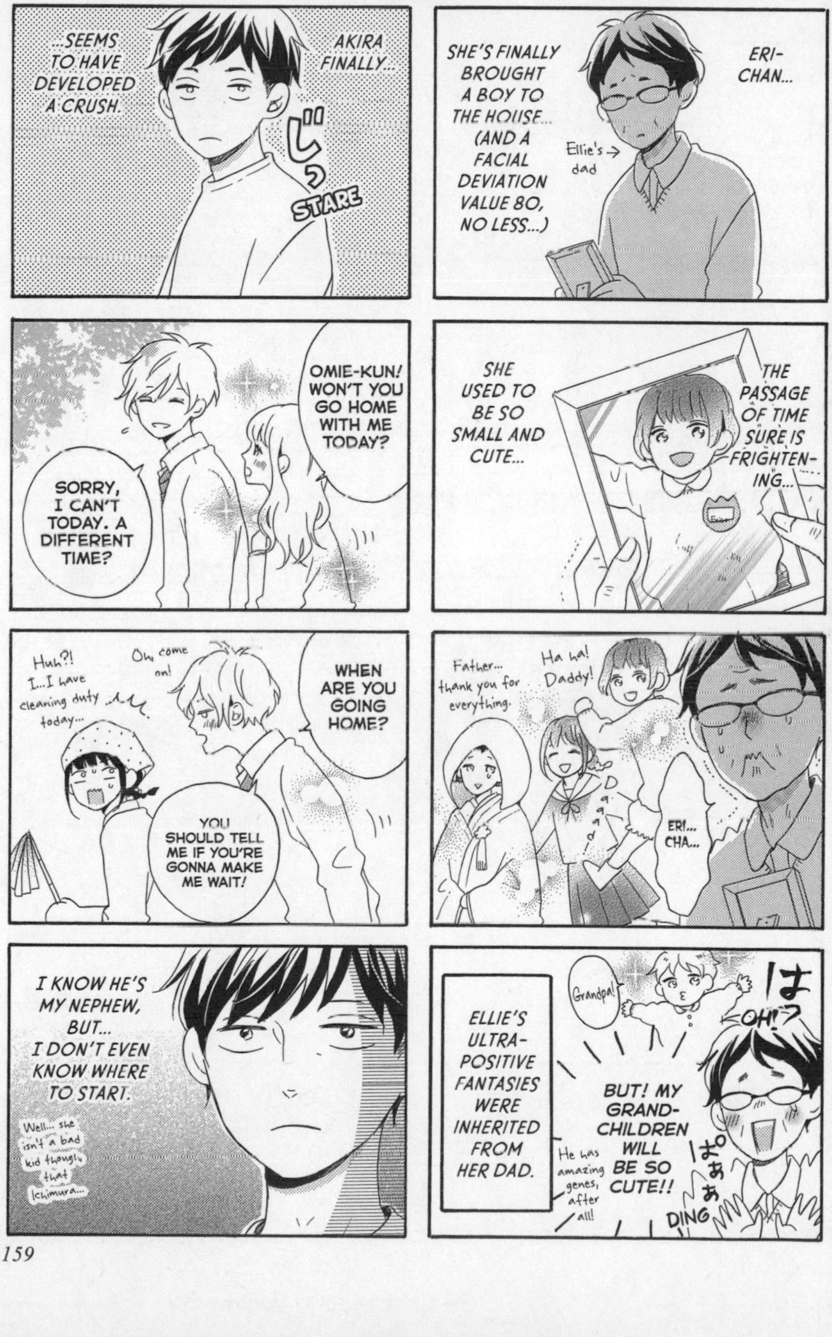
ERI-CHAN...
SHE'S FINALLY BROUGHT A BOY TO THE HOUSE... (AND A FACIAL DEVIATION VALUE 80, NO LESS...)
Ellie's dad
THE PASSAGE OF TIME SURE IS FRIGHTENING...
SHE USED TO BE SO SMALL AND CUTE...
Ha ha! Daddy!
Father... thank you for everything.
Dad!
ERI... CHA...
はっ OH!?
Grandpa!
BUT! MY GRANDCHILDREN WILL BE SO CUTE!!
ぱぁぁ DING
ELLIE'S ULTRA-POSITIVE FANTASIES WERE INHERITED FROM HER DAD.
He has amazing genes, after all!
AKIRA FINALLY...
じっ STARE
...SEEMS TO HAVE DEVELOPED A CRUSH.
OMIE-KUN! WON'T YOU GO HOME WITH ME TODAY?
SORRY, I CAN'T TODAY. A DIFFERENT TIME?
WHEN ARE YOU GOING HOME?
Oh, come on!
Huh?! I...I have cleaning duty today...
YOU SHOULD TELL ME IF YOU'RE GONNA MAKE ME WAIT!
I KNOW HE'S MY NEPHEW, BUT... I DON'T EVEN KNOW WHERE TO START.
Well... she isn't a bad kid though, that Ichimura...

★ BONUS ★

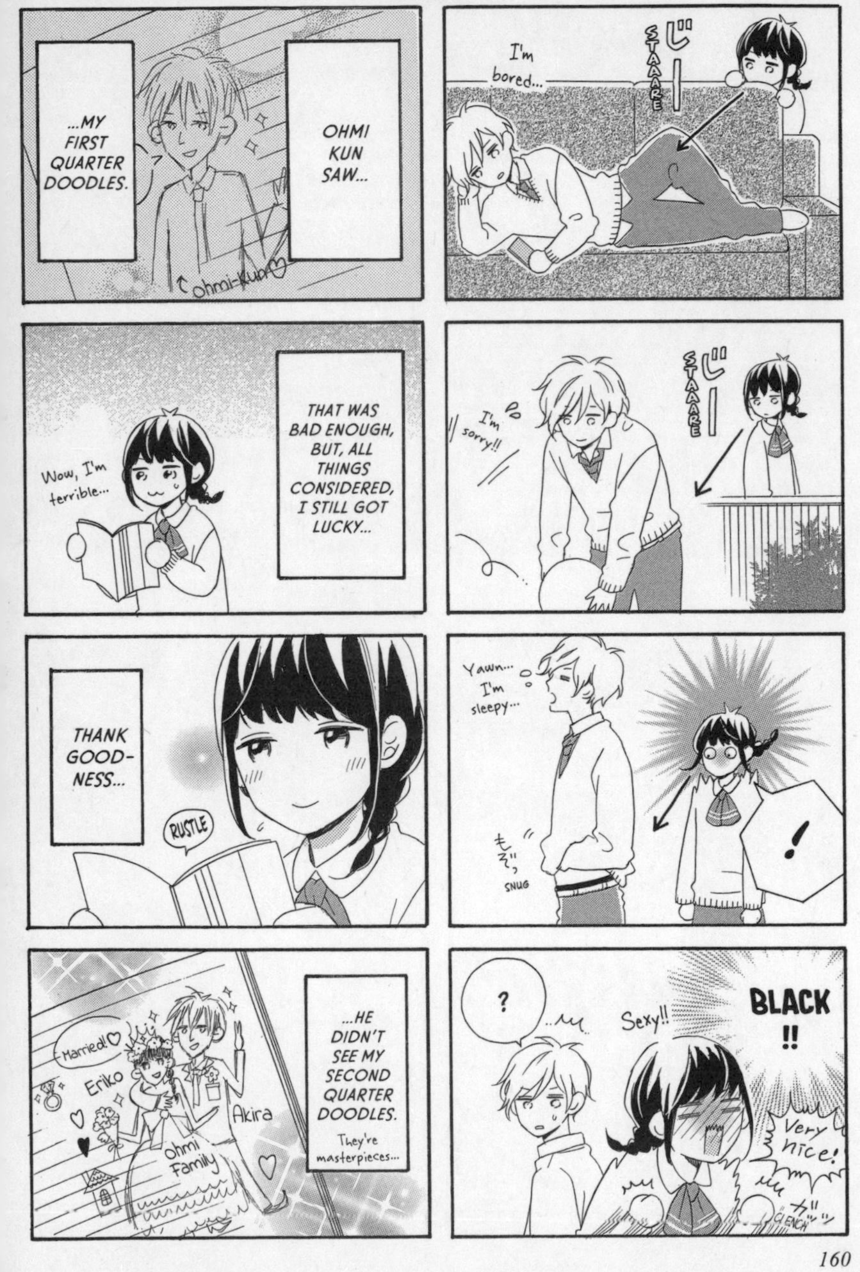

じー
STAAARE
I'm bored...
じー
STAAARE
I'm sorry!!
!
Yawn... I'm sleepy...
SNUG
BLACK!!
Very nice!
CLENCH
Sexy!!
?
OHMI KUN SAW...
...MY FIRST QUARTER DOODLES.
ohmi-kun
THAT WAS BAD ENOUGH, BUT, ALL THINGS CONSIDERED, I STILL GOT LUCKY...
Wow, I'm terrible...
THANK GOODNESS...
RUSTLE
...HE DIDN'T SEE MY SECOND QUARTER DOODLES.
They're masterpieces...
Married!
Akira
Eriko
Ohmi Family

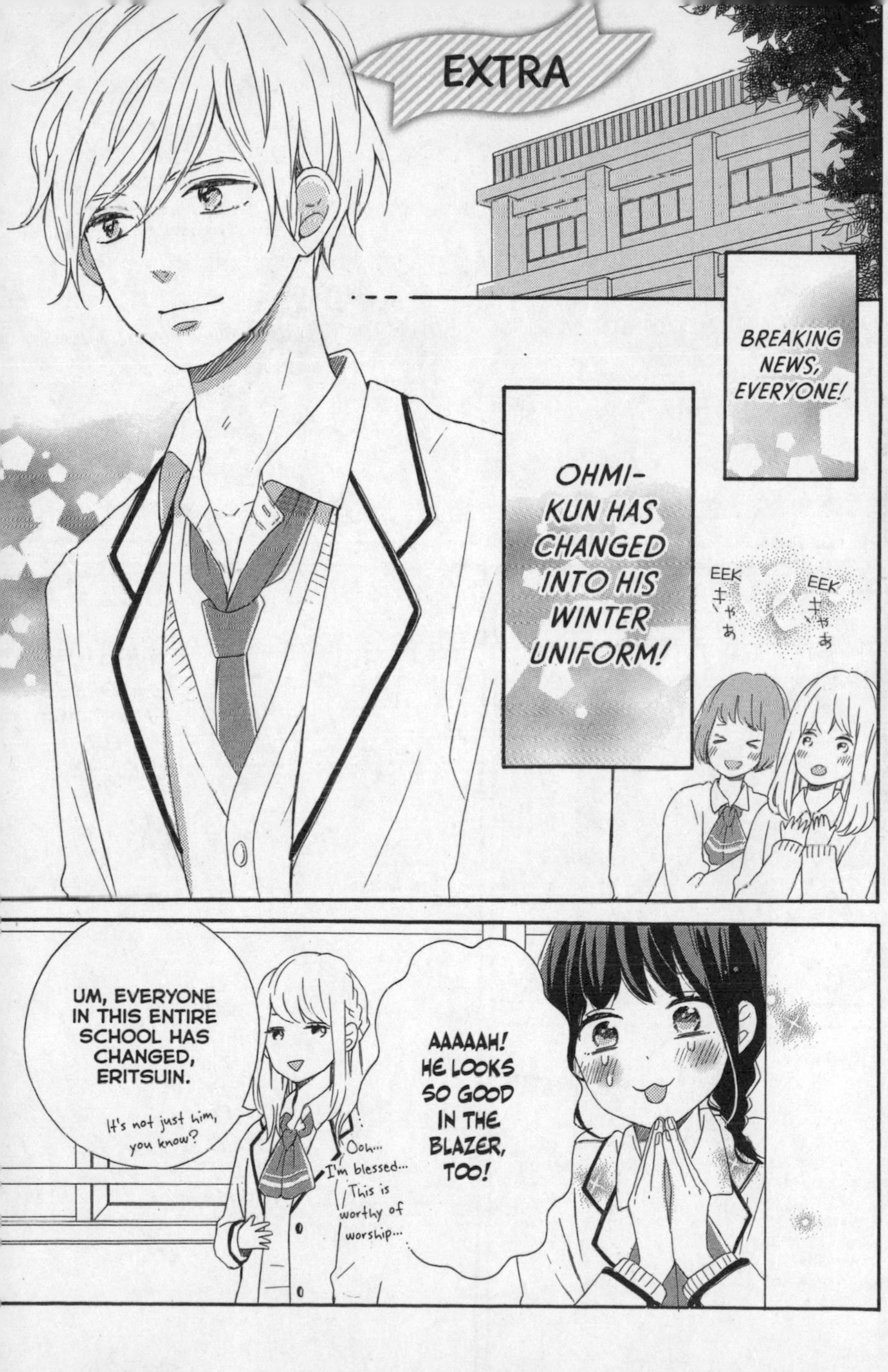
EXTRA
BREAKING NEWS, EVERYONE!
OHMI-KUN HAS CHANGED INTO HIS WINTER UNIFORM!
EEK
きゃあ
EEK
きゃあ
AAAAAH! HE LOOKS SO GOOD IN THE BLAZER, TOO!
Ooh... I'm blessed... This is worthy of worship...
UM, EVERYONE IN THIS ENTIRE SCHOOL HAS CHANGED, ERITSUIN.
It's not just him, you know?

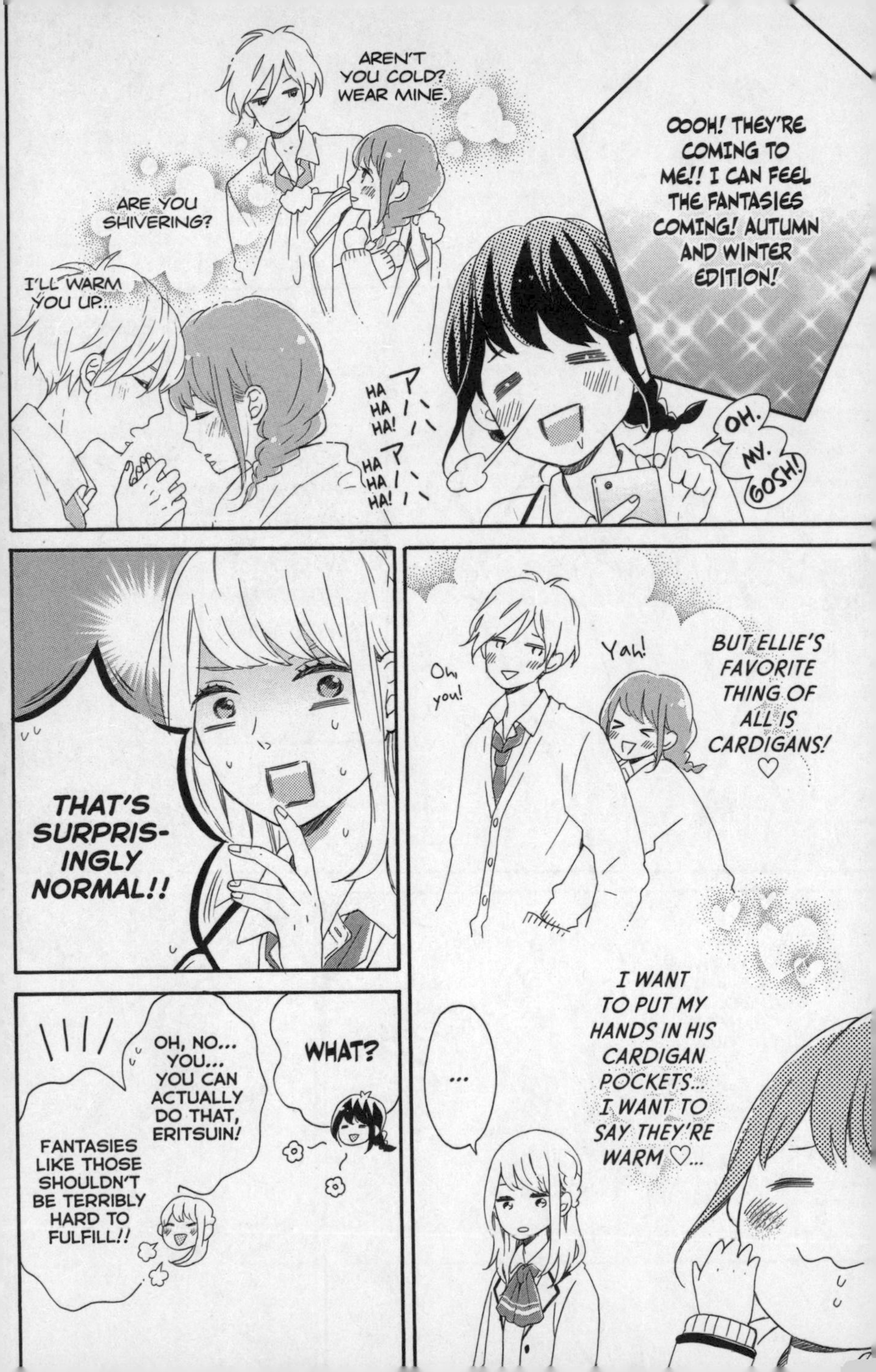
OOOH! THEY'RE COMING TO ME!! I CAN FEEL THE FANTASIES COMING! AUTUMN AND WINTER EDITION!
OH. MY. GOSH!
HA HA HA!
HA HA HA!
AREN'T YOU COLD? WEAR MINE.
ARE YOU SHIVERING?
I'LL WARM YOU UP...
BUT ELLIE'S FAVORITE THING OF ALL IS CARDIGANS! ♡
Yah!
Oh, you!
I WANT TO PUT MY HANDS IN HIS CARDIGAN POCKETS... I WANT TO SAY THEY'RE WARM ♡...
...
THAT'S SURPRIS-INGLY NORMAL!!
WHAT?
OH, NO... YOU... YOU CAN ACTUALLY DO THAT, ERITSUIN!
FANTASIES LIKE THOSE SHOULDN'T BE TERRIBLY HARD TO FULFILL!!

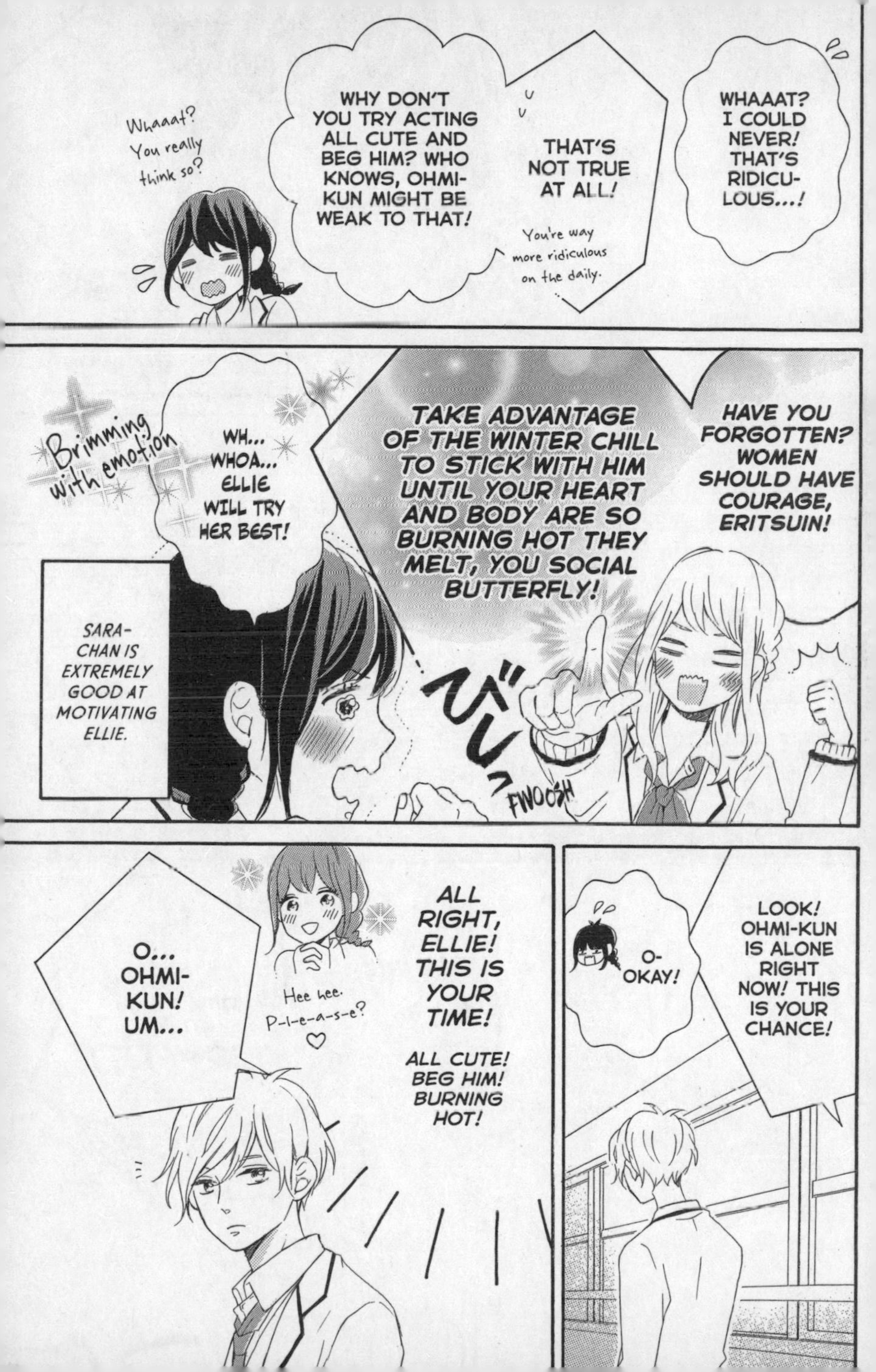
WHAAAT? I COULD NEVER! THAT'S RIDICULOUS...!
THAT'S NOT TRUE AT ALL!
You're way more ridiculous on the daily.
WHY DON'T YOU TRY ACTING ALL CUTE AND BEG HIM? WHO KNOWS, OHMI-KUN MIGHT BE WEAK TO THAT!
Whaaat? You really think so?
HAVE YOU FORGOTTEN? WOMEN SHOULD HAVE COURAGE, ERITSUIN!
TAKE ADVANTAGE OF THE WINTER CHILL TO STICK WITH HIM UNTIL YOUR HEART AND BODY ARE SO BURNING HOT THEY MELT, YOU SOCIAL BUTTERFLY!
FWOOSH
WH... WHOA... ELLIE WILL TRY HER BEST!
Brimming with emotion
SARA-CHAN IS EXTREMELY GOOD AT MOTIVATING ELLIE.
LOOK! OHMI-KUN IS ALONE RIGHT NOW! THIS IS YOUR CHANCE!
O-OKAY!
ALL RIGHT, ELLIE! THIS IS YOUR TIME!
ALL CUTE! BEG HIM! BURNING HOT!
Hee hee. P-l-e-a-s-e? ♡
O... OHMI-KUN! UM...

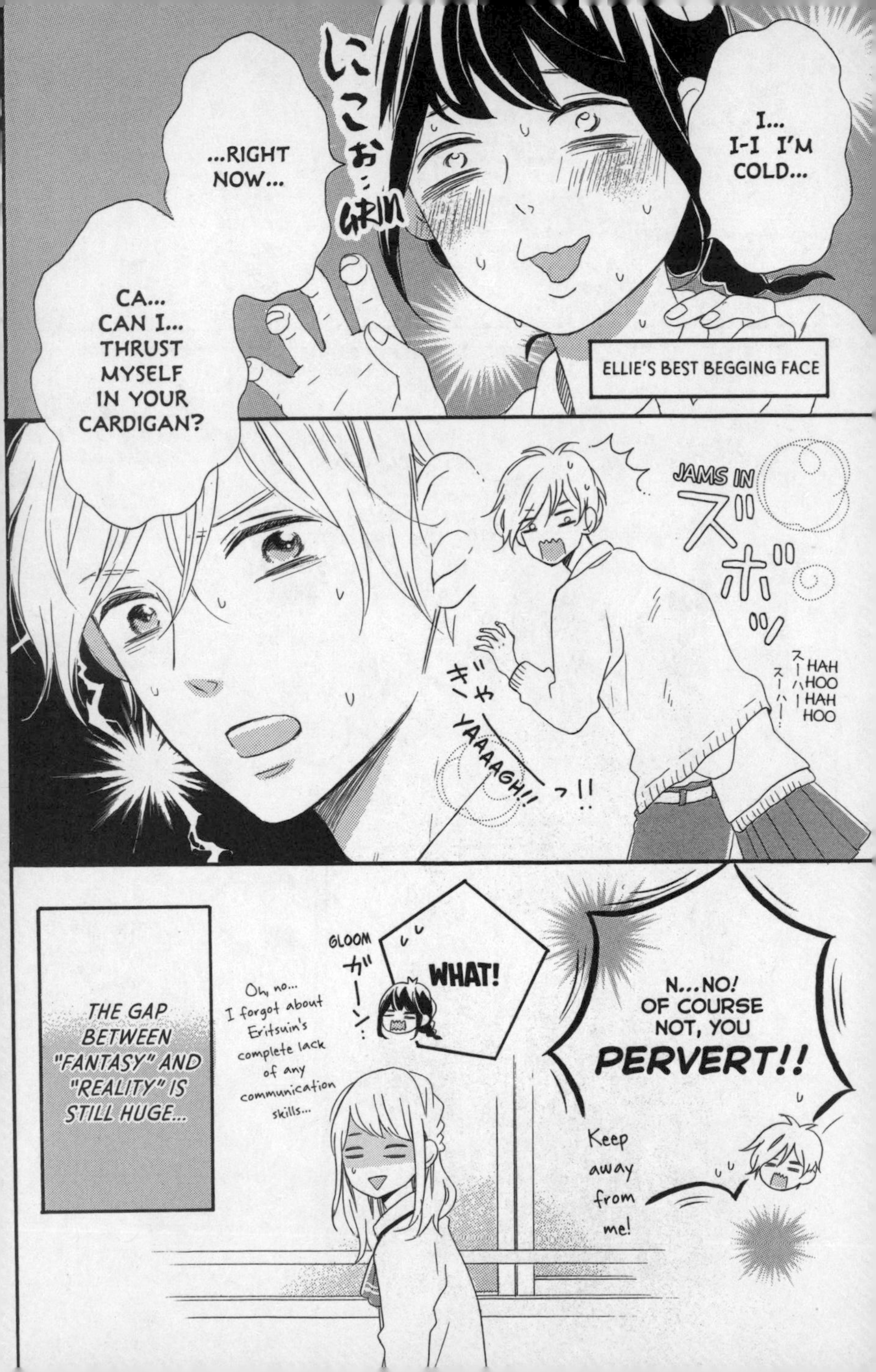
I... I-I I'M COLD...
...RIGHT NOW...
CA... CAN I... THRUST MYSELF IN YOUR CARDIGAN?
にこぉ
GRIN
ELLIE'S BEST BEGGING FACE
ズボッ
JAMS IN
スーハースーハー
HAH HOO HAH HOO
きゃーっ!!
YAAAAGH!!
N...NO! OF COURSE NOT, YOU PERVERT!!
Keep away from me!
WHAT!
ガーン
GLOOM
Oh, no... I forgot about Eritsuin's complete lack of any communication skills...
THE GAP BETWEEN "FANTASY" AND "REALITY" IS STILL HUGE...

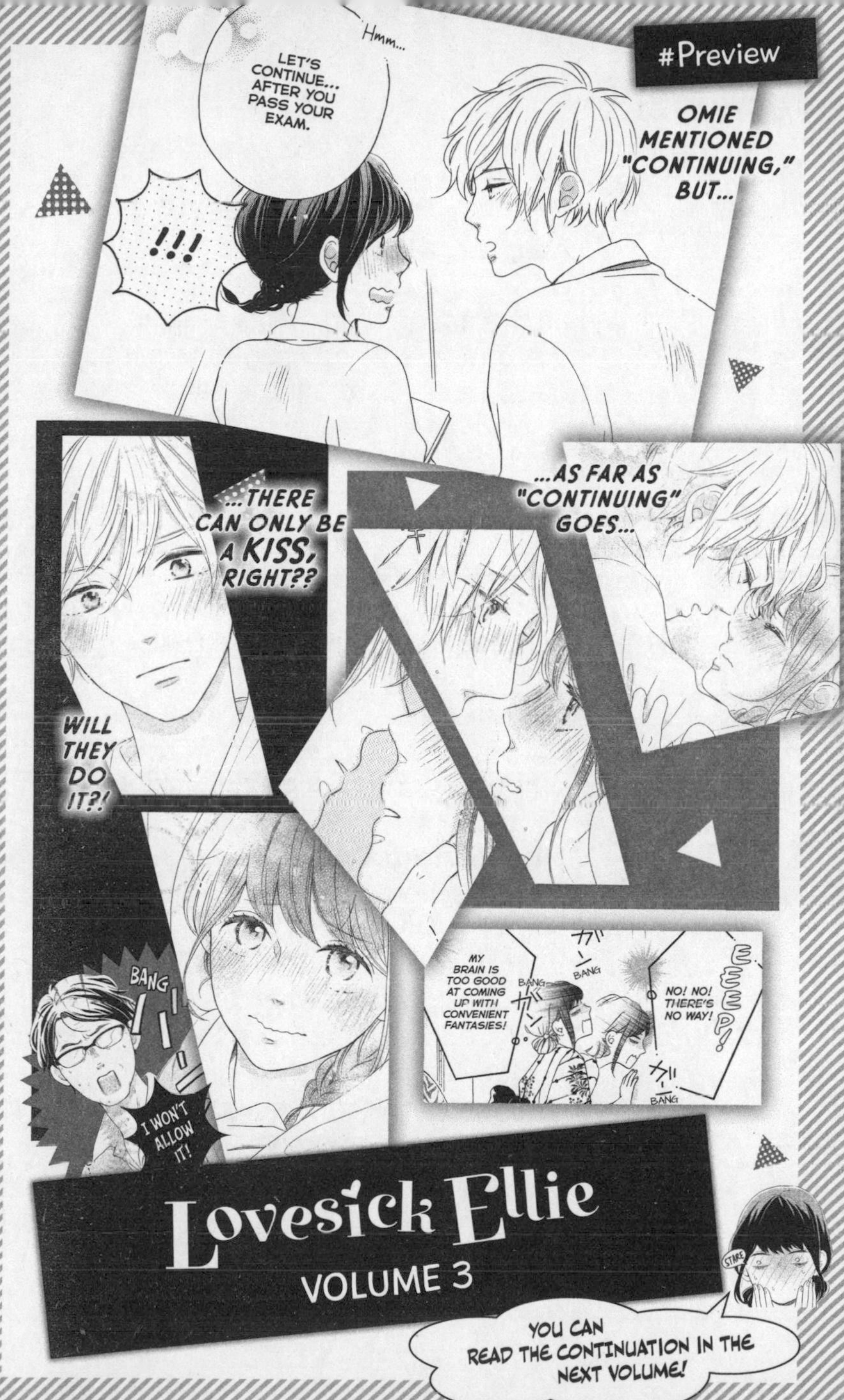
#Preview
OMIE MENTIONED "CONTINUING," BUT...
Hmm...
LET'S CONTINUE... AFTER YOU PASS YOUR EXAM.
!!!
...AS FAR AS "CONTINUING" GOES...
...THERE CAN ONLY BE A KISS, RIGHT??
WILL THEY DO IT?!
EEEP!
NO! NO! THERE'S NO WAY!
BANG
BANG
BANG
MY BRAIN IS TOO GOOD AT COMING UP WITH CONVENIENT FANTASIES!
BANG
I WON'T ALLOW IT!
Lovesick Ellie
VOLUME 3
STARE
YOU CAN READ THE CONTINUATION IN THE NEXT VOLUME!

Lovesick Ellie

@Translation_Notes

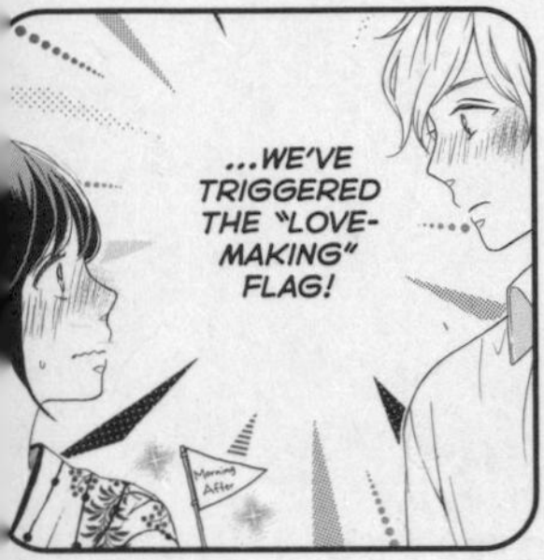
...WE'VE TRIGGERED THE "LOVE-MAKING" FLAG!
Morning After

Flag @page 6

A "flag" is a condition in game programming that affects a variable outcome. Frequently flag-determined outcomes include but are not limited to: whether a given romantic pursuit is successful, whether a given character dies, and the overall ending of the game.

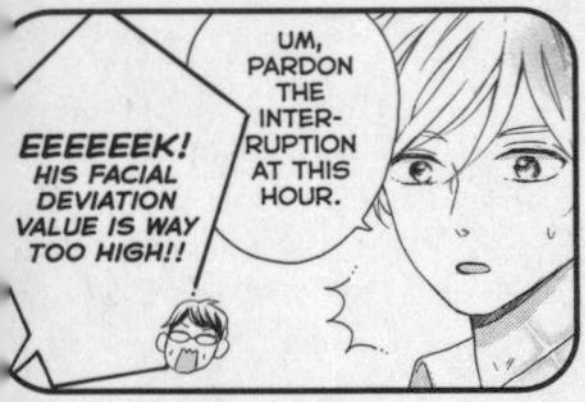
UM, PARDON THE INTER-RUPTION AT THIS HOUR.
EEEEEEK! HIS FACIAL DEVIATION VALUE IS WAY TOO HIGH!!

Facial deviation values @page 23

"Facial deviation values" are one way of colloquially rating facial beauty in Japan. The average face is a 50, with each subsequent 10 representing one standard deviation. 75 is a generally accepted cut-off point for mind-blowing beauties.

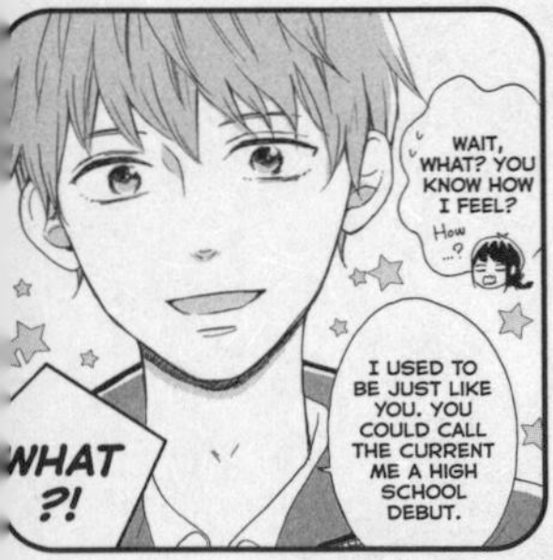
WAIT, WHAT? YOU KNOW HOW I FEEL?
How ...?
I USED TO BE JUST LIKE YOU. YOU COULD CALL THE CURRENT ME A HIGH SCHOOL DEBUT.
WHAT ?!

High School Debut @page 53

A "high school debut" is used to describe introverts who aim to change themselves dramatically and become an extroverted person at the time when they start high school. For example, they may use contact lenses instead of glasses, dye their hair, or wear makeup. In Japan, students attend elementary and junior high schools that are usually close to their home; however, in high school, students can choose where to go as it is not mandatory education. "University debut" and "work debut" also occur.

YOU... HAD A SERIOUS GLOW UP, THOUGH!
WORSHIP
HA HA... I GUESS THAT'S WHY I FEEL SO COMFORTABLE AROUND YOU. IS THAT RUDE?
QUITE THE CONTRARY, I'M SHOOK!

La'cryma Christi @page 54

In the original Japanese, La'cryma Christi was referenced. It was a Japanese visual kei rock band that was extremely popular in the 90's. Appending the band's name to the end of certain phrases is a form of wordplay used primarily by young adults.

...
OH, WHO DIED AND MADE YOU KING?
WHEN HE'S IN FRONT OF YOU, ERITSUIN, HE *REALLY* ACTS NASTY!!
Balse!

Balse @page 133

The incantation used to destroy the castle at the end of the Studio Ghibli film *Castle in the Sky*. It has since become a prominent and beloved meme on 2ch and Twitter.

Young characters and steampunk setting, like *Howl's Moving Castle* and *Battle Angel Alita*

Beyond the Clouds © 2018 Nicke / Ki-oon

A boy with a talent for machines and a mysterious girl whose wings he's fixed will take you beyond the clouds! In the tradition of the high-flying, resonant adventure stories of Studio Ghibli comes a gorgeous tale about the longing of young hearts for adventure and friendship!

A SMART, NEW ROMANTIC COMEDY FOR FANS OF *SHORTCAKE CAKE* AND *TERRACE HOUSE!*

Living-Room Matsunaga-san © Keiko Iwashita / Kodansha Ltd.

A romance manga starring high school girl Meeko, who learns to live on her own in a boarding house whose living room is home to the odd (but handsome) Matsunaga-san. She begins to adjust to her new life away from her parents, but Meeko soon learns that no matter how far away from home she is, she's still a young girl at heart — especially when she finds herself falling for Matsunaga-san.

PERFECT WORLD

Rie Aruga

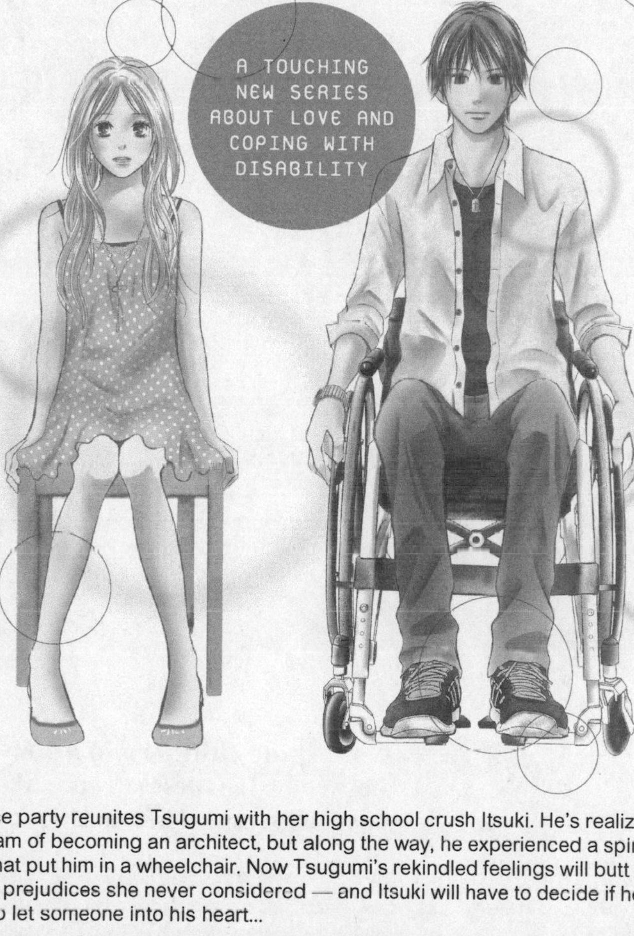

A TOUCHING NEW SERIES ABOUT LOVE AND COPING WITH DISABILITY

An office party reunites Tsugumi with her high school crush Itsuki. He's realized his dream of becoming an architect, but along the way, he experienced a spinal injury that put him in a wheelchair. Now Tsugumi's rekindled feelings will butt up against prejudices she never considered — and Itsuki will have to decide if he's ready to let someone into his heart...

"Depicts with great delicacy and courage the difficulties some with disabilities experience getting involved in romantic relationships... Rie Aruga refuses to romanticize, pushing her heroine to face the reality of disability. She invites her readers to the same tasks of empathy, knowledge and recognition."
—Slate.fr

"An important entry [in manga romance]... The emotional core of both plot and characters indicates thoughtfulness... [Aruga's] research is readily apparent in the text and artwork, making this feel like a real story."
—Anime News Network

KC
KODANSHA
COMICS

Something's Wrong With Us

NATSUMI ANDO

The dark, psychological, sexy shojo series readers have been waiting for!

A spine-chilling and steamy romance between a Japanese sweets maker and the man who framed her mother for murder!

Following in her mother's footsteps, Nao became a traditional Japanese sweets maker, and with unparalleled artistry and a bright attitude, she gets an offer to work at a world-class confectionary company. But when she meets the young, handsome owner, she recognizes his cold stare...

KC KODANSHA COMICS

THE SWEET SCENT OF LOVE IS IN THE AIR! FOR FANS OF OFFBEAT ROMANCES LIKE *WOTAKOI*

Sweat and Soap © Kintetsu Yamada / Kodansha Ltd.

In an office romance, there's a fine line between sexy and awkward... and that line is where Asako — a woman who sweats copiously — meets Koutarou — a perfume developer who can't get enough of Asako's, er, scent. Don't miss a romcom manga like no other!

The adorable new odd-couple cat comedy manga from the creator of the beloved *Chi's Sweet Home*, in full color!

Sue & Tai-chan

Konami Kanata

Sue is an aging housecat who's looking forward to living out her life in peace... but her plans change when the mischievous black tomcat Tai-chan enters the picture! Hey! Sue never signed up to be a catsitter! *Sue & Tai-chan* is the latest from the reigning meow-narch of cute kitty comics, Konami Kanata.

SAINT ☆ YOUNG MEN

A LONG AWAITED ARRIVAL IN PREMIUM 2-IN-1 HARDCOVER

After centuries of hard work, Jesus and Buddha take a break from their
heavenly duties to relax among the people of Japan, and their adventures in this
lighthearted buddy comedy are sure to bring mirth and merriment to all!

"Brilliant...the physical comedy
and facial expressions will
make you literally LOL."

—Sam Humphries
(host of *DC Daily*;
writer, *Green Lanterns,
Legendary Star-Lord*)

Saint Young Men © Hikaru Nakamura/Kodansha Ltd.

Lovesick Ellie 2 is a work of fiction. Names, characters, places, and incidents are the products of the author's imagination or are used fictitiously. Any resemblance to actual events, locales, or persons, living or dead, is entirely coincidental.

A Kodansha Trade Paperback Original

Published in the United States by
Kodansha USA Publishing, LLC, New York.

Publication rights for this English edition arranged through
Kodansha Ltd., Tokyo.

First published in Japan in 2016 by Kodansha Ltd., Tokyo
as *Koiwazurai no Ellie,* volume 2.

ISBN 978-1-64651-318-5

Printed in the United States of America.

9 8 7 6 5 4 3 2 1

Translation: Ursula Ku
Lettering: Allen Berry
Additional Lettering and Layout: Lys Blakeslee
Editing: Sarah Tilson, Maggie Le
Kodansha USA Publishing edition cover design by Matthew Akuginow

Publisher: Kiichiro Sugawara

Director of Publishing Services: Ben Applegate
Associate Director of Publishing Operations: Stephen Pakula
Publishing Services Managing Editors: Alanna Ruse, Madison Salters
Production Managers: Emi Lotto, Angela Zurlo

KODANSHA.US

KODANSHA

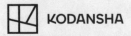